T0385374

Praise for
The Once and Future World Order

'A powerful reminder that not all world orders in history have been Western, and that we now seem headed for a new multipolar order in which non-Western states are key to the future. This timely book argues that a dominant West is not a necessary condition for a rules-based international framework'

Odd Arne Westad, coauthor of *The Great Transformation*

'In *The Once and Future World Order*, Amitav Acharya subjects the presuppositions of the quintessentially colonial discipline of international relations to rigorous scrutiny from a decolonial perspective. This book should serve as a model for many other academic disciplines that were founded on similarly colonialist assumptions'

Amitav Ghosh, author of *Smoke and Ashes*

'A refreshingly original take on a potential post-West world order. With a lucid, perceptive, and provocative critique of the current global system, Acharya's survey of the past and visualization of the future dynamic between the West and the Rest are stimulating for all who care about international relations in our globalized world!'

Shashi Tharoor, author of *Inglorious Empire*

'Fear not! The end of Western domination is not the end of human civilization. Instead, it will mark a return of many glorious civilizations which have thrived at different points of history. A rich, multicivilizational world is heading our way. Acharya brilliantly describes the old and new worlds and how they will all come together. To get a glimpse of the real future that humanity is heading toward, read this book carefully. It will dazzle and excite you and give you great hope for the future'

Kishore Mahbubani, author of *Living the Asian Century*

'Twenty-first century geopolitics will be a marketplace, not a monopoly. In this rich tapestry of a book bridging ancient civilizations and modern debates, Acharya reminds us that the unfolding multipolar, multi-civilizational world order is the historical norm—and should be celebrated as an opportunity for knowledge to spread in all compass directions. An essential guide to the post-Western world'

Parag Khanna, author of *Connectography*

'The world order is changing irreversibly, and there is no better guide to what will happen next than Acharya. This is a deeply informed vision of how nations will draw on their pasts to relate to one another in the future'

Rana Mitter, author of *Forgotten Ally*

'In *The Once and Future World Order*, Acharya weaves a new global history of world order. This is the book everyone must read not only to make sense of our past but also the twenty-first century'

Ayse Zarakol, author of *Before the West*

'A timely corrective to the blinkered arrogance about the role of the Rest which continues to infect so much Western policy analysis and history writing. *The Once and Future World Order* is prodigiously researched, lucidly written, and a compelling read'

Gareth Evans, former Australian foreign minister,
president of the International Crisis Group

The Once and Future World Order

WHY GLOBAL CIVILIZATION WILL SURVIVE THE DECLINE OF THE WEST

AMITAV ACHARYA

LONDON

First published in Great Britain in 2025 by Basic Books UK
An imprint of John Murray Press

1

Copyright © Amitav Acharya 2025

The right of Amitav Acharya to be identified as the Author of the
Work has been asserted by him in accordance with the Copyright,
Designs and Patents Act 1988.

A CIP catalogue record for this title is available from the British Library

Hardback ISBN 9781399811743
Trade Paperback ISBN 9781399811750
ebook ISBN 9781399811774

Typeset in ITC New Baskerville Std

Printed and bound in Great Britain by Clays Ltd, Elcograf S.p.A.

John Murray Press policy is to use papers that are natural, renewable
and recyclable products and made from wood grown in sustainable forests.
The logging and manufacturing processes are expected to conform
to the environmental regulations of the country of origin.

Carmelite House
50 Victoria Embankment
London EC4Y 0DZ

www.basicbooks.uk

John Murray Press, part of Hodder & Stoughton Limited
An Hachette UK company

The authorised representative in the EEA is Hachette Ireland, 8 Castlecourt
Centre, Dublin 15, D15 XTP3, Ireland (email: info@hbgi.ie)

To my family, for their loving, caring, and joyous companionship

Contents

Introduction

The Coronavirus Pandemic Will Forever Alter the
World Order.

—Henry Kissinger[1]

The End of World Order

—Robert Blackwill and Thomas Wright,
Council on Foreign Relations report[2]

The New World Disorder

—*Economist*[3]

No World Order

—Joschka Fischer, former German
foreign minister, *Project Syndicate*[4]

The headlines and laments in the West about the end of the American-led world order are louder than ever these days. They're coming from scholars, policy research institutes, journalists, and commentators, and they stem from two convictions: One is that the present world order, led by the United States and the West, has by and large been a good thing, preventing major wars and allowing for international trade, economic growth, and a remarkably stable and prosperous international system. Two is that the rise of the non-Western nations and the emergence of an alternative to the familiar American-led world order will be frightening, unpredictable, and almost surely a change for the worse. For the West at least, the Russian invasion of Ukraine in February 2022 was a stark warning about the dangers of the breakdown of the American-led world order and its replacement with a kind of Putinesque law of the jungle, a breakdown aided and abetted by an ever more powerful China.

These events and trends have, not surprisingly, created a deep sense of foreboding, especially in the United States and among its allies. Certainly the fall of the world order that we have known since the end of World War II would be a development of world-historical significance. This change would involve, among other things, not only the decline of the United States, its prestige, and its influence but also the rise of other powers, especially of an authoritarian, ambitious, power-hungry China. The Chinese leadership, so goes the conventional Western narrative, sees the world through a very different lens than rulers in the West do, and, moreover, China is allied with aggressive, resource-rich Russia and bitterly anti-American Iran. That, in the reigning conventional wisdom in the West, is a terrifying prospect.

Would the end of US and Western dominance really be so bad?

In this book, I argue, contrary to much elite opinion, that it need not be, especially over the long run. This is not because the West's fears about the rise of non-Western powers, including China and Russia, are always exaggerated, although sometimes they are, due to the loss of power and prestige. But it is because Western supremacy has itself contributed to plenty of instability, injustice, and disorder that might be eased by its decline. More importantly, centuries of dominance have led the West to a kind of arrogance and ignorance about the rest of the world, overlooking the ideas and contributions of other civilizations to stability and progress throughout history. We have forgotten that world order—the political architecture enabling cooperation and peace among nations—existed long before the rise of the West, and that many of the ideas we assume are Western inventions actually originated in other civilizations. Mechanisms and values that are central to world order—such as diplomacy, economic interdependence, freedom of seas, principles for the protection of people in war and peace, preservation of the environment, and cooperation among major powers, to name a few—emerged over millennia across the globe.

While Europe and the West might have led the way in areas of democracy, human rights, and rule of law, non-Western civilizations have also provided mechanisms for peace, cooperation, and morality, with many of these ideas emerging well before the rise of the West. And even when it comes to democracy and human rights, the West cannot claim to have an exclusive patent. These ideals have precursors in other societies—for example, in ancient republics and political councils allowing wider participation in governance and in prohibitions against cruel and unjust punishment. Moreover, many non-Western nations, after their liberation from Western colonial rule, have played an important part in developing the principles of human rights through multilateral institutions such as the United Nations (UN), while others such as India and Latin American nations have championed democratic governance, despite limitations and setbacks. Similarly, a rules-based order is not as new, as American, or as Western as Western pundits claim. There have been rules and rules-based orders in the past, and the present one in many ways is a refinement of similar institutions developed across the globe. While the West might have developed them further, it did not invent them.

Since the values and foundations of world order are not the West's exclusive property, they will endure even as Western power shrinks. The role of the West in the making of the many key elements of the present world order has been more as a pupil than as a teacher. In the future world, the West may once again look to the Rest for some of these ideas and approaches to sustain its progress and leave behind the excesses of its imperial past. The lament that the decline of the West amounts to the end of world order is misguided. This is reason enough not to fear that the decline of the West will lead to global chaos.

To some degree, Western anxieties about world disorder today are the result of its overconfidence and hubris that were evident not so long ago. Indeed, in the years immediately after the West's stunning victory in the Cold War in the late 1980s and early 1990s, the worldwide trend toward greater democracy seemed both inevitable and desirable. All of eastern Europe was freed from effective Soviet control; democracy was strengthened in Africa, Southeast Asia, and South America. Even

Communist China, now fully engaged economically and diplomatically with the rest of the world, was predicted to eventually leap onto the democratic bandwagon, so that the dominance of Western ideas and practices would grow even stronger. The most celebrated statement of this inevitability was Francis Fukuyama's thesis of the "end of history," by which he meant that Western-style liberal democracy was happily triumphant, that ideological wars were over, that the West had won, permanently.[5]

In light of that mood of triumph, it is understandably worrisome that history has not ended and that, rather suddenly, the idea that the Western system would endure forever has been replaced with the certainty that some other system will come to dominate. My essential argument is that this is not a disaster; indeed, in the long run, it might turn out to be a good thing. Why? There are several reasons. One is that the Western-dominated order was never as benign as many in the West believed, marred as it was by economic inequality, racism, and wars of choice waged usually in the global South. From the standpoint of the rest of the world, American and Western domination was less a blessing than it was a threat, not just to their well-being and independence but to their pride. To these nations, the end of Western dominance offers an opportunity to build a better world, to find more voice, power, and prosperity—in other words, a fairer, more balanced, and more equal world. As we'll see in the following chapters, other countries besides the Western ones have traditions, values, and practices that will contribute to the world order of the near future, and this will even be of benefit to the West, relieved as it will be of the anger and resentment that its domination has often caused. New balances will emerge in what will be a genuinely more diverse global community in which no single member or group of members is able to achieve hegemony.

This does not mean paradise. No world order will be, or ever has been, free of conflict and war. Simply witness the not-very-pax elements of the so-called Pax Americana in places like Vietnam, Afghanistan, and, yes, Ukraine. My aim here is not to suggest that the emerging world order will be perfect but to make the case that as the West retreats, mayhem will not erupt, and a more humane world may even emerge.

This book offers an epic history of world order itself, uncovering how it evolved and how it developed into the Western order. Going back nearly five thousand years to ancient Sumer and Egypt, I mine the past in a way that mainstream historians and analysts of the history of civilizations simply haven't done. When we think through the deep history of civilization, we open a range of possibilities that can help us reimagine what the emerging world order should look like. This book, in considering this story, advances a kind of back-to-the-future thesis. I am not saying that history will repeat itself or that it is cyclical. It isn't. But history can provide clues or possibilities for the future. I show that for most of history, China, India, and the Islamic world have been forceful actors on the world stage, that power has been dispersed among different blocs, and that cultural pluralism has been widespread. These, in other words, were the norms of centuries past. Western dominance violated these norms, and it will actually be good for everybody to restore them, bearing in mind that the core elements of the existing world order—from republican institutions to international cooperation—are not Western inventions. Rather, they were developed at multiple global locations either independently or through mutual contacts. Thus, despite the conventional wisdom on this matter, these elements won't disappear as Western dominance ends.

This should be good news for those who genuinely aspire to a world order of "the West *with* the Rest," rather than "the West *versus* the Rest," and for those who hope for a world order that no single nation or civilization, whether Western or non-Western, dominates. Instead of fearing the future, the West should learn from history and cooperate with the rest of the world to forge a more equitable order.

What Is World Order?

Before we go further, we need to clarify the key concepts used in this book.

The first is the term *civilization*. The most common associations are cultural and social advancement, urbanization, monuments, writing systems, agricultural surpluses, long-distance trade, the social division of labor, and some form of domestic political organization.[6] But this is not enough. How societies relate to each other to create peace and stability must also be counted as a crucial element of civilization. This is where civilization connects with the idea of world order.

What is world order then? The term has no precise meaning. It can simply mean the state of the world—or its main political, economic, and cultural features—during a certain era. The *Macmillan English Dictionary* defines the term as "the political, economic, or social situation in the world at a particular time."[7] But more often, world order means having peace and stability, something akin to the modern idea of "law and order" for the world at large. Combining both meanings, I see world order as the way the world, or a large chunk of it, is organized politically, economically, and culturally and how power structures, economic links, political ideas, and leadership work with the aim of ensuring the stability and peace of humankind.

But these definitions leave many questions unanswered. Who makes world order and how? What is the "world," and how far does it extend? Where and when did it all begin?

To start answering these questions, and to make better sense of this book, I urge readers to keep in mind four essential points.

First, the concept of world order that I use in this book covers both empires and a system of sovereign states. In an empire, one dominant power formally annexes and controls the internal and external relations of another state or a group of states, such as Persia and Rome did for hundreds of years. Empires get lots of attention in historical writing, and rightly so. But world order can also refer to a system of independent states bound by shared beliefs, political systems, and economic links. This was the case of the "city-states" of ancient Sumer, Greece, and Mesoamerica; the "republics" of ancient India; and the "warring states" of China, all of which I discuss in this book. Many of these city-states, states, and republics were gobbled up by empires, but before that happened, they were independent entities that had considerable lifespans as creative places for political ideas and modes of governance. They therefore must be considered to have been world orders.

But the world order as we know it today emerged in Europe at a very specific time and place: the region of Westphalia in Germany in the year 1648. It was there and then that the rulers of Europe signed an agreement ending the Thirty Years' War, which, to simplify greatly, had ravaged Europe as Protestant and Catholic states strove to impose their own beliefs and systems on each other. The Treaty of Westphalia put an end to that by asserting the absolute sovereignty of each state, thereby banning any state from interfering in the internal affairs of another, over its religion or anything else. That, nearly four hundred years later, is still the most fundamental principle of the current world order. Originally applied to states within Europe, the Westphalian model has become nearly globally accepted today.

Another form of world order—a halfway house between a formal empire and independent states—is a tributary system, where a powerful country commands obedience, receives gifts, or extracts taxes from other states without colonizing them. China offers the most important historical example of such a system. From the Han dynasty that emerged in 206 BC, China, while developing its own empire, maintained a parallel system that did not tax but exchanged gifts with its neighbors, who acknowledged China's cultural preeminence but did not surrender their independence to it.

Empires are no longer the primary building blocks of world order, but their legacy remains powerful. While the current world order bears the distinct stamp of the Westphalian system, many European and Asian states—especially Britain, France, and Russia in the former category and China, India, and Turkey in the latter—retain a good deal of their imperial makeup, controlling territories originally acquired through conquest. Another legacy of empires are the borders of many states in the global South—nations of Latin America, Asia, Africa, and the Pacific that became independent in the nineteenth and twentieth centuries— which were shaped by their former imperial masters. Similarly, after colonizing and displacing the native population, the United States built a hierarchical world order, if not an outright empire, that serves its own power and purpose. The world order that came into existence after

7

World War II has been built around this imperial primacy of the United States.

A second point is that world order does not have to encompass the entire globe. The term *world order*, as presented in this book, applies to a single civilization or region as well as to cross-national and cross-regional structures. The term "Chinese world order," developed by Harvard historian John K. Fairbank, referred mainly to the Chinese tributary system in East Asia.[8] In a similar vein, one could speak of Egyptian, Sumerian, Persian, Indian, Islamic, Mesoamerican, Andean, West African, Mongol, European, and American world orders, to name a few. Henry Kissinger was right—and this may be my only major point of agreement with him—when he wrote in 2014, "No truly global 'world order' has ever existed."[9] Although my book covers a lot more of the "world"—including Africa and the pre-Columbian Americas—than Kissinger's did, I agree that most historical world orders have been regional in scope, although some have been more expansive than others. The storied empires of Persia, Alexander, Maurya India, and Han and Tang China, as well as the Umayyads, Moghuls, and Ottomans, were in essence regional entities, albeit very large ones. Even the Mongols, who created history's largest contiguous empire, were at most Eurasian. But they can be considered world orders because their makers believed that they were central to the world known to them and that their ideas and approaches to governance were universal. And their ideas, institutions, and practices, with all the similarities and differences among them, have influenced the power relations, economic interactions, and moral principles of nations in later periods. In short, I argue that our current world order is the contribution of multiple civilizations: ancient and modern, powerful and moralistic, Western and non-Western.

In some cases, the idea of the "world" can expand as a result of new modes of communication and outside influences. For example, when the ancient Chinese developed their notion of "middle kingdom" to describe China's central place in the world and their rulers concocted the notion of *tianxia*, or "all under heaven," they did not know that, beyond the barbarians to their immediate west, there was a world of advanced civilizations, including those of Egypt, Mesopotamia, India, and Greece. With the arrival of Buddhism and the founding of the Silk Road during the Western Han dynasty (206 BC–9 AD), the Chinese conception of the world expanded to include India and Persia, which the Chinese accepted more or less as equal. Hence, *tianxia* was the world known to the Chinese at a given time, even though the Chinese imagined it to be universal.

To be sure, the "world" has become more global than ever before, thanks to the European voyages of discovery, colonization and then decolonization, and globalization, all of which have accelerated commerce, tourism, media, and the spread of political ideas and institutions. Never before in history have people in one part of the world been more aware of what is happening in other parts. But even the British Empire, on which the sun was never supposed to set, did not, and could not, conquer continental Europe. The United States, which replaced Britain as the world's preeminent power, did not control the Soviet bloc or China. A future world order could again comprise a network of regional world orders, albeit more connected than in the past.

My third point is that world orders, whether large or small, do not emerge or exist in isolation. All are influenced and shaped by outside forces and develop by learning from others. But this book is not just about connections, but also about creations, including independent and parallel origins of the core ideas and institutions of world order. In fact, too much stress on connectivity among civilizations, as seems to be fashionable these days, has its pitfalls. Olúfẹ́mi Táíwò, the Nigerian-born professor of African political thought at Cornell University, reminds us that "similar ideas found in different parts of our world do not have to be explained in terms of influences or common origins."[10] This is important to keep in mind; otherwise, one might falsely argue that everything developed by civilizations in relatively isolated parts of the world—such as in the pre-Columbian Americas or sub-Saharan Africa—was due to foreign contact, including colonization. In reality, many civilizations have developed ideas of world order that are similar to each other, but did so on their own steam. Often enough, these separately created ideas were touched by those of others, creating similarities and overlaps, if not outright convergence. Like a civilization interacting with another civilization, a world order often interacts with other world orders, including those they have conquered or mastered, and is influenced by them. It is a key argument of this book. Although Eurasian and cross-regional cultural and economic connections contributing to the rise of the West have been admirably narrated by Western writers such as John Hobson, Peter Frankopan, and Josephin Quinn, this book focuses on creations and connections on a wider global scale and pays specific attention to political ideas and institutions.[11] It shows how the West and the Rest *made each other* in laying the foundation of a global civilization and world order.

Fourth, world order is closely associated with stability. A dualism of chaos versus order has underpinned the idea of world order throughout the ages. To be sure, world order is not only about stability. There are also the goals of economic well-being, justice, and human dignity (a far more universal term than human rights). All civilizations or world orders pursue such goals, sometimes vigorously. Often, when rulers see the goals of justice and rights undermining stability, they choose stability. Indeed, from ancient Sumer to today's America, it is very rare to see justice and rights pursued for their own sake or given priority over order. But in many cases, societies and rulers have seen these goals not as mutually exclusive but as complementary, and economic development and human freedom are regarded as necessary to realize stability and order.

One notion common to individual states and world orders over the centuries is summed up in the phrase "chaos versus order." This narrative has provided the chief justification for the creation of political authority, which itself arises from the need for a strong state and ruler and from the desire of one state to conquer or otherwise control others. Narratives to this effect can be found in ancient Egypt, Sumer, Persia, Greece, and India (Hindu and Buddhist doctrines), as well as among the Mongols, the Aztecs, modern Europe, and post–World War II America.[12]

Thus, the Egyptian pharaohs legitimized their authority by representing themselves as the force of *ma'at* (order or harmony) overcoming *isfet* (chaos or violence). In ancient Sumerian stories, the gods themselves restored cosmic order by punishing "noisy" and violent earthlings by

Image 1. The Narmer Palette. King Narmer, representing order and harmony (*ma'at*), smiting an enemy, representing chaos (*isfet*). Egyptian Museum, Cairo.

sending in floods, disease, and death. The ideology of the Achaemenid Empire of Persia founded by Cyrus the Great was based on the Zoroastrian duality of *asha*, cosmic order, versus the *druj*, chaos and disorder. A central narrative of Hindu civilization pits the *Devas* (divine forces of order) against *Asuras* (demonic forces of chaos and darkness) in an eternal struggle for light and tranquility. Though it evolved separately from the Indo-European belief system, China's civilization, guided by Confucian and Daoist ideals, took the need for social harmony, balance, and stability against disorder to perhaps its greatest extreme, the impact of which persists to this day.

Though not strictly a chaos-versus-stability dualism, Islam makes a distinction between *Dar al-Islam* (house or territory of Islam), organized around Islamic principles and modes of governance, and *Dar al-Harb* (house or territory of war), whose absence of Islamic principles and safety for Muslims legitimizes it as a target of attack and absorption. Genghis Khan and his successors invoked the "eternal blue sky" (*tenggeri*), the Mongol conception of heaven, to justify their authority to rule, which meant imposing order over chaos.

In a faraway and isolated continent, rulers of the Inca Empire justified their expansion by telling their neighbors that submitting would bring them not only stability but also prosperity and justice. Further north, the Aztec rulers used the fear of chaos and need for order, provided by their own sun god Huitzilopochtli, to justify domestic rule and foreign conquests.

Across the Atlantic, in early modern Europe, the English political philosopher Thomas Hobbes (1588–1679 AD) imagined a "state of nature" where life was "nasty, poor, brutish, solitary and short" to justify a "Leviathan," a mythical all-powerful creature who would provide safety and stability. This was contested by fellow English philosopher John Locke (1632–1704 AD) and French thinker Jean-Jacques Rousseau (1712–1778 AD), neither of whom saw nature in the dark Hobbesian way but as a pristine, idyllic place—the home, for Rousseau, of the "noble savage," imagery he seems to have borrowed from Native American societies. Yet, for Locke and Rousseau, the political state was also needed. Nature alone could not create or maintain order but would degenerate into chaos as society became more complex.

Twentieth-century US leaders such as Woodrow Wilson and Franklin D. Roosevelt saw their own nation's ideals as a universal force for good, which stood in opposition to what they feared were the forces of disorder, especially communism. The United States went on to organize a world order around these beliefs, often called the liberal international order. Indeed, the image of the Leviathan has been so powerful that it has been applied to the United States with a glitteringly positive spin: America is the "liberal leviathan," whose main role in the world since it became the global superpower has been to preserve order and prevent chaos.[13] The liberal leviathan has the same political purpose in the international sphere as the Egyptian *ma'at* and *isfet* had in domestic and foreign relations. And it is the same chaos-versus-order narrative that now defines much Western fear about the end of its dominance and the rise of other nations.

Although building world order has often relied on the specter of chaos, it has not always required violence. Instead, it has rested on a variety of other means, such as moral principles and rules of diplomacy, trade, and cultural exchange among societies. Some early examples of this can be found in the rules of peacemaking and cooperation among great powers in the ancient Near East, religious tolerance and limits to violence in ancient India, cultural respect in exchange for trading privileges in Chinese history, and the vast networks built by the Islamic world, the Incas, and Indian Ocean merchants and priests to smooth the flow of goods and ideas. These principles and modes of communication became the building blocks of the contemporary world order.

Adding all this together, this book argues against the notion, widespread in the West, that the world order of today is essentially a derivative of Western history and Western political ideas, especially of freedom and democracy.

Before thinking about how to challenge this notion, let us think for a moment why such a view exists. One important factor, aside from sheer Western power, is the global dominance of the English language in the writings and debates about international affairs and world order. English has absorbed many political words from Greek and Latin, including some key terms about the modern world order. For example, the term *sovereignty* derives from the Latin *super* (above); *hegemony* from Greek *hēgemonía* (leadership, supremacy); *balance* or *balance of power* from Latin *bilancia* or *bilanx* (scale of a balance or two scaled); and *peace* from Latin *pacem* or *pax*. This linguistic heritage has led scholars and pundits across the world to assume that the ideas expressed were invented in Greece and Rome, and hence in the West. This, in turn, has led these scholars to be ignorant of terms with the same or similar meanings from the languages of other civilizations. This is a major source of the bias in favor of the West.

Moreover, we often forget that the ideas and institutions of world order that the Greeks and Romans developed were at best approximations.

The common Eurocentric belief, for example, is that democracy emerged from ancient Greece, but Greece did not in fact invent democracy as we know it today. The right to vote was restricted to male citizens only, and the Greek system did not include individual liberty. Yet, the late American political scientist Robert Dahl argued that denying ancient Greece as the source of democracy because of its flaws and limitations would be like denying the Wright brothers credit for inventing the airplane. Nor, to take another example, did the Magna Carta spell out human rights as they are defined today. It was basically a violent demand for property rights by the nobility, who had most to gain from it and who would continue to oppress the serfs. Yet, Eleanor Roosevelt, chair of the committee that drafted the Universal Declaration of Human Rights, wrote when submitting the documents to the UN General Assembly that it could "well become the international Magna Carta for all men everywhere."[14]

Using similar logic, if we accept Greece as the birthplace for democracy and the English Magna Carta as the model of human rights, why shouldn't we also accept the Sumerians as the inventors of property rights? The code of Sumerian King Urukagina forbade the rich from appropriating the house or produce of the poor unless the poor person wanted to sell for a price he deemed fair. Why should we not give similar recognition to King Ashoka's rock edicts, which prohibited cruel and unjust punishment of ordinary people, as laying the foundation of human rights? In proposing such a mode of thinking, I am guided by the explanation of human rights from Indian economist Amartya Sen, winner of the Nobel Prize. According to Sen, the "idea of human rights as an entitlement of every human being…is really a recent development." The notion of rights as "universal" never existed as an ancient idea, he argues, either in the West or elsewhere, but many civilizations across the globe maintained "limited and qualified defences of freedom and tolerance, and general arguments against censorship."[15]

Put another way, ancient Greece and the Magna Carta are best viewed as approximations of the modern concepts of democracy and human rights, which only came into their current form in the nineteenth and twentieth centuries. One should not forget that Europe's political order in the eighteenth and nineteenth centuries has been called, with not too much exaggeration, the "age of absolutism." At the same time, many mechanisms of building a stable world order—whether in their foundational or advanced forms—came from non-Western civilizations. These include the independence of states, inter-state cooperation, diplomacy, peace treaties, protection of people against cruel and unjust punishment, religious and cultural tolerance, freedom of the seas, mutually beneficial trade, and environmental protection. Add to this list the provision of security and trade benefits by a leading nation without it colonizing others. In this sense, China's tributary system is a distant cousin of the post–World War II American world order.[16]

Other examples of ideas and practices include, as we will see, peace-treaty making, diplomacy, economic interdependence, international law, and great power cooperation. Yet, the West—aided by its centuries of global dominance—has championed the narrower and most recent versions of these ideas, instead of their original, broader, and more universal roots. This has allowed the West to falsely present the contemporary world order as its unique and exclusive creation. While there can be genuine disagreement over whether modern concepts can be traced backward this way, it is hypocritical to do it for Greece, Rome, and early modern Europe but not for other civilizations. Hence, this book challenges the widespread tendency to use Greece, Rome, or western Europe as the benchmarks for assessing what constitutes progress in global civilization.

A related point is that today we think of ideas like order, peace, stability, cooperation, democracy, republicanism, human rights, and interdependence in the way Western philosophers and leaders have defined them, drawing from European or Western experience and reflecting and showcasing Western history. Similar ideas or even better pathways to peace and progress developed by other societies are ignored or dismissed. Taking a broad view of these ideas allows us to recognize their multiple points of origin, in nascent forms, and explain the contributions of diverse civilizations to the contemporary world order.

This brings us to the world order that we live in today. Conventional wisdom holds that it emerged after the Allied victory in World War II in 1945, with the creation of international institutions like the UN and, after the Cold War, the emergence of a unipolar world dominated by the United States. In fact, while there is much truth to that view, the "rise of the West"—meaning western Europe and the United States— had been occurring for centuries, as far back as the "discoveries" of America and India by Christopher Columbus and Vasco da Gama in the 1490s. The West's slow ascendance then accelerated dramatically in the mid-nineteenth century, as Western imperialism swept across the globe and crushed existing empires. Several related events were critical to this global phenomenon: the defeat of China in the two Opium Wars (1839– 1842 and 1856–1860), the crushing of the Indian revolt against British colonial rule in 1857, and the partition of Africa by European powers at the Berlin Congress in 1884. In other words, the Allied victories over Nazi Germany and imperial Japan in World War II were certainly important in consolidating the world order that we know today, but the framework was already established by European imperialism's subjuga- tion of large parts of Asia and Africa. Britain and France, the two leading colonial powers, imposed their governing bureaucracies, their schools, their police forces and courts, their languages, and, to a considerable ex- tent, their religions and values on subjugated peoples all over the world. The Germans, Belgians, and Portuguese participated in this spread of European power and practices to Africa, and the United States did much the same thing in the Philippines. China, though never directly controlled by a colonial power, was forced to cede some of its territory— Hong Kong, Macao, and portions of Shanghai, Shandong Province, and Manchuria—to foreign rule.

The current world order also emerged through multiple stages and points of origin. We may think of world order as the "situation in the world at a particular time" (the *Macmillan English Dictionary*'s definition), but the reigning order has always incorporated the elements and fea- tures of previous world orders, including those that developed in what we now consider the non-Western world: Asia, Africa, Islamic areas, and pre-Columbian America. The rise of a civilization or a world order is never purely of its own making; it is always helped by borrowing political, cultural, and technological ideas and innovations from others, especially preceding ones.

Thus, the divine kingship of Egypt, the world's first major centralized state, was itself influenced by prior Nubian political traditions, and in turn it inspired Alexander the Great's ambition to be a divine ruler. Persia rose to become the world's first big empire by borrowing from Assyrian warfare techniques. Persia's own institution of the great king was eagerly emulated by its conqueror, Alexander the Great, and might also have been the model for the Indian concept of a universal emperor (*chakravartin*), which emerged during the Maurya dynasty. Rome's world order was influenced by the Etruscans and the Greeks. In all likelihood, the emergence of the Chinese concept of *tianxia* and the Mongol concept of *tenggeri* had their roots in central Asian nomadic traditions. Indian Buddhist ideals influenced the political legitimacy of China's Tang and other dynasties, while Islamic science, technology, and philosophical debates, along with Chinese technology and Indian mathematics, helped the rise of Europe and America's world orders. A good deal of this book focuses on these prior influences and their combined legacies, showing how they lie behind our contemporary world order, which should therefore not be viewed as a unique creation of a handful of European nations and their progeny, the United States.

To be sure, civilizations never borrow others' ideas wholesale. They do so selectively, taking what they need most and leaving out what they don't. Moreover, they often modify, or "localize" foreign ideas to make them fit into their own societies. Foreign ideas never totally displace local ones but are blended into them to build more advanced and progressive societies. Creating this mixture of local and foreign ideas is fundamental to understanding the rise of civilizations and world orders.

However one sees it, the truth is that the ability to create a world order has never been the monopoly of any single civilization. Every major nation is the creator or aspiring creator of world order. World orders have existed for millennia, succeeding each other and building on each other throughout human history. What we call world order today draws on the ideas and approaches of different civilizations at different points in time. This will continue even as the Western-dominated order gives way to the new world order of the not-very-distant future.

A few words about the terms *West* and *non-West* (or *the Rest*) used in this book: The idea of the West was originally a geographic and spiritual expression, evoking the division of the Roman Empire or the Chinese pilgrim's "journey to the West" in search of Buddhist knowledge, but it became a geopolitical and racial notion in the modern era. It is a product of the self-glorifying dominance enjoyed in the modern era by western Europe and the United States, which use the division to place themselves politically and racially above the rest of the world. The terms *non-West, Third World,* and *global South* are of much more recent origin, having emerged to give collective voice to decolonized nations in the twentieth century. This broad division—West and non-West, or simply West versus the Rest—has become perhaps the defining fault line of the contemporary world order. The late Harvard political scientist Samuel Huntington, who famously coined the term "clash of civilizations" to warn that the world after the Cold War would be defined by conflicts among the world's major civilizations, was actually referring to the West-versus-the-Rest conflict, an idea he attributed to Singaporean diplomat Kishore Mahbubani.[17] While neither the West nor the Rest is a homogenous category, the idea of a West-Rest divide has had great staying power, and it will continue so long as the media, political leaders, and intellectuals identify challenges to Western dominance—such as the rise of China, to take the most frequently cited example—as existential threats, replacing world order with world disorder.

But in this book, I use *West* and *non-West* as terms of reference or convenience, rather than accepting them as fixed and homogenous categories. My aim is to subvert both, and I hope to do so by showing the long historical interdependence and mutual learning among the nations, an interdependence that refutes the West's claim of being the dominant contributor to the contemporary world order. I will challenge this pernicious and artificial division of the world, which is, in any case, rendering itself irrelevant as we enter a new stage of history. And I will argue that ending this divide, which will involve "retiring" the idea of the West first, is necessary for a fresh beginning in world order.

What Kind of Future World?

In my view, the plunge into the past does not mean the new world order will be an exact rebirth of world orders before the rise of the West, before Pax Americana, before colonialism and world wars. But non-Western nations will be more important in shaping their destinies and that of the world at large, as they were before the rise of Europe. Neither will the future world be united under a "one world" government or universal empire. It will not be dominated by any single nation or civilization. By this I mean neither the West nor the East (China) will get to shape the future world after its own interests and values.

Moreover, this future world will be shaped by cultural and political diversity. It will be a far cry from the end of history, Fukuyama's idea that Western liberalism represented the final stage of social and political development, in which ideological conflict would disappear. The future world will have competing ideas as well as a degree of convergence, similar to the world order that is passing from the scene. But it will also be a world order of new forms of connectedness and stability, where neither the Rest nor the West is dominant. In other words, it will be akin to a multiplex—and here I draw on my 2014 book, *The End of American World Order*—where there are multiple shows on offer, giving the audience a choice of producers, directors, actors, and plots.[18] This world order will be more broadly post-Western, not just post-American.

While China has played an important part in this transformation, the foundations were laid well before that country's rise was enabled by Deng Xiaoping's economic opening in 1978. The emergence of the global multiplex has been driven more generally by the return of the Rest, not just of China or India. Because of this, there will be a plurality of ideas, institutions, and approaches operating at global, regional, national, and local levels to manage common problems facing humanity:

from poverty and inequality to climate change to diseases. Political and cultural diversity will go hand in hand with economic interdependence and growing connectivity.

In contemplating this world ahead, the West needs to recognize that all civilizations that have played central roles in building world orders have been as capable of cruelty and violence as they were of compassion and stability. The West, which now claims to be the founder of the modern world order—with its tolerance, democracy, and rule of law—has been the source of a great deal of global disorder—past and present— through its violence, lawlessness, and dominance of other peoples. The Roman historian Tacitus observed that the supposed Pax Romana was "frightful in its wars" and "even in peace full of horrors."[19] The same applies to most civilizations that claim to have established peace, whether at home or abroad, including the present-day American-led world order. One should not forget that some of the most brutal ideas of the West, such as fascism (which takes off from ancient Rome's symbol of authority, fasces), have been challenged from within. There are always two sides to any civilization at a given point: German philosopher of Enlightenment Immanuel Kant's racist views were challenged by his contemporary Johann Gottfried von Herder. In ancient India, political strategist Kautilya advocated conquest and expansion at the time of the founding of the Maurya Empire. The third ruler of that same empire, Ashoka, renounced war for good and ruled with justice and compassion, although not before a bloody imperial conquest.

Similarly opposing ideas of how to deal with people, pitting Confucian benevolence against legalist oppression, emerged in ancient China. But modern leaders and intellectuals in the West have relentlessly insisted that the most profound ideas about world order have come almost entirely from the West and that only the West can provide a peaceful, prosperous, and just world order, while others would take us back to barbarism. This assertion has no foundation in history.

This argument is so at variance with the standard view on this topic— as expressed by Henry Kissinger, Niall Ferguson, Francis Fukuyama, and other popular commentators such as Fareed Zakaria, Thomas Friedman, and Richard Haass—that it may seem a radical point of view, one contradicted by the flow of current events, most recently Russia's aggression against Ukraine and the Israel-Hamas war. But a narrative history of world orders provides a deeper perspective than we can gain from day-to-day events, preoccupying as they may be. The lessons and arguments of this book ought to provide some reassurance to those worried that the decline of the West would lead to a global disaster.

There is no question that, in the long march of history, Western dominance has been but a blip and that a new world, one very different from the past few hundred years of Western modernity, is coming over the horizon, riding on the economic decline of the West, the return of major non-Western civilizations and powers, the fading global influence of the United States, and the disruptions caused by the COVID-19 pandemic, whose long-term impact is not yet clear. But this does not mean global chaos. Some elements of the old order, including good ones like multilateral bodies, will survive into the new one. No world order is a totally new beginning or a fresh start. Those who lament the chaos and violence the decline of the Western-led world order might bring must not forget that some of the old actors and ideas of the West, including the United States and Europe, will be around even as the ideas and approaches of the rising powers and non-Western nations become more visible and important for managing world order. One possibility out of this change is that the new world order will resemble what some thinkers— among them the former Czech president Václav Havel and the economist Sen—have called a "global civilization."[20]

The idea is not that there will ever be a single, seamless, homogenous culture around the globe, something like the "global village" idea popular not so long ago. Such a global civilization is neither possible nor desirable. Rather, a global civilization would mean a kind of underlying interconnectedness among civilizations, which compete but also cooperate while retaining cultural and political differences. As Havel described it, "The distinguishing features of...transitional periods are a mixing and blending of cultures, and a plurality or parallelism of intellectual and spiritual worlds. These are periods when all consistent value systems collapse, when cultures distant in time and space are discovered or rediscovered....New meaning is gradually born from the encounter, or the intersection, of many different elements."[21] We are entering such a period now, helped by the end of Western dominance.

The idea of a global civilization implies that civilizations—Western or non-Western—are seldom totally distinctive or unique unto themselves. No civilization is an island. All people of the world are connected by their shared humanity, and they tend to offer—either on their own steam or through mutual learning—similar solutions to deal with similar problems. This means there exist shared ideas and approaches to world order from multiple locations worldwide. The future world, underpinned by my idea of a global multiplex, will be built around such a confluence of civilizations, rather a clash of civilizations. To evoke the words of Ibn Khaldun, writing seven hundred years ago, there is "a world [being] brought into existence anew."[22] No past world has been a utopia, and our future world won't be one either, but the past has shown that while civilizations can clash, they can also learn from each other, cooperate, and even forge something better than what came before. History will not end but will move on and move forward.

Chapter 1

First Foundations

Two of the earliest major sites in the development of world order were Sumer in Mesopotamia and Egypt in Africa. Neither was an isolated entity. Though they were distinct civilizations that developed in different ways, they shared some features and were connected to each other and to neighboring states.[1] For our purposes, they are important because they invented some of the ideas and practices that constituted the first world orders: the diplomatic, economic, and cultural arrangements that ensured stability and peace in relations among a far-flung group of people and states.

Sumer, the earlier of the two civilizations, emerged in the fourth millennium BC. It was located in the southern part of Mesopotamia—literally "between rivers" in Greek, in this case the Tigris and Euphrates. The Mesopotamia region would see the rise of other political centers to the north: Akkad, Assyria, and Babylon among them, but these emerged after Sumer's decline in the late second millennium BC. In many ways, these subsequent civilizations carried the legacy of Sumer, helping to establish some of the first foundations of world order.

The emergence of Egypt's civilization followed Sumer's with the unification of the country by King Narmer (also known as Menes) who conquered Lower Egypt—that is, the area of the Nile delta leading to the Mediterranean—roughly around 3150 BC. The two civilizations

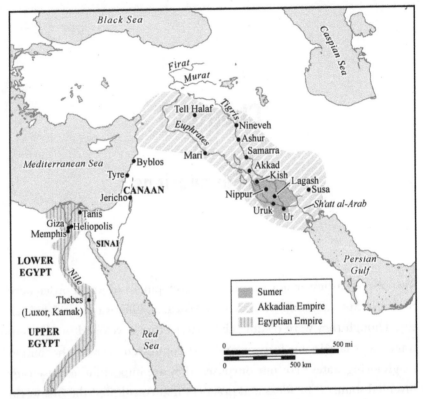

Map 1. Sumer and Egypt in the third to the second millennium BC.

coexisted for some time before Sumer collapsed, and then Egypt continued over the centuries through what historians call the Middle Kingdom
and the New Kingdom, each of them separated by periods of instability. While Egypt connected Asia and Africa and absorbed cultural and
political influences from both, African elements might have been more
foundational than Asian ones to the birth of its civilization and political
order. "It is easier to prove that ancient Egypt was 'African' than to prove
that ancient Greece was 'European,'" one historian has written.[2]

Among the southern influences on Egypt was the idea of the divine
authority of rulers, one of history's most important political belief systems. Divine kingship also emerged in Sumer, and it is possible, as historian William McNeill contends, that Sumer in its late period might have

24

gotten the idea from Egypt.[3] Egypt itself might have taken the concept of divine rule from its southern neighbors, especially Nubia. Nubian ideas of authority—such as the personal sacredness of the ruler, which goes back to the fourth millennium BC and was not yet found elsewhere in the Near East region—influenced the early political system of Egypt, whose rulers developed it further.[4] This notion also was adopted by later rulers in the neighborhood, including the Kush kingdom in Nubia that emerged around the eleventh century BC.[5] Here, as is common throughout history, the evolution of world order was fueled by the two-way flow of political ideas and institutions.

At the same time, Egypt developed significant commercial and diplomatic interactions to its north, covering the Levant (roughly the area of modern Syria, Lebanon, Palestine, and Israel) and, especially during its New Kingdom (1570–c. 1069 BC), with the region's four other "great powers": Hatti (in Anatolia in modern Turkey), Mitanni (southeast of Hatti), Assyria, and Babylon.

It is during this period—from the rise of the Sumerian city-states to Egypt's New Kingdom—that five of the most enduring elements of world order were first seen joined together: divine monarchy, the independent state system, empire, the narrative of chaos versus order, and great power cooperation. Given the contacts between Sumer and its surrounding regions and Egypt's role as a bridge between Africa and Asia, the ancient world order may be justifiably regarded as being Afro-Asian in origin.

Sumerian Anarchy

Sumer is the birthplace of the system of independent, competing states. Emerging in the southern area between the Tigris and Euphrates Rivers (in present-day Iraq), this system was most developed in the third millennium BC. Sumer is best described as an "anarchic" system. The term *anarchy* here does not imply chaos or warfare—although there was plenty of that—but to stress the fact that for most of its history, Sumer remained a system of competing states rather than an empire, at least until the conquests of Sargon of Akkad (c. 2334–2279 BC). As discussed earlier,

Image 2. Gudea, the Sumerian king of Lagash, who ruled about 2150 BC.

such systems of independent states would later emerge in other parts of the world—notably in Greece's Peloponnesian peninsula, India's Gangetic Plain, China's western region around the Yellow River, and in the Mayan civilization—during the first millennium BC. This system would then take its more developed, "modern" form in Europe after the Peace of Westphalia in the seventeenth century AD.

The Sumerian system was based on the dominance of the priestly class and the ruler's divine authority. Sumerian kings in general did not consider themselves as personally divine (as was the case in Egypt), but they derived their legitimacy from the gods they worshipped. Each city was presided over by a god and had a ruler or king representing that god. The king's duty was not only to please the gods but also to mediate between gods and humans. But the gods of the Sumerian pantheon were not equal. Enlil was the supreme god in the Sumerian pantheon, and his temple was in the city of Nippur, the holiest city in Sumer until the second millennium BC. But even this "king of gods" could not displace or interfere with the authority of other gods, and his role was mainly to adjudicate disputes among them.

The king of Kish was one of the most well-known great kings of Sumer, though his authority was far from that of an emperor. Nevertheless, he was so respected that the title of king of Kish was passed on to other rulers in Mesopotamia to signify their superior status. A Sumerian clay tablet gives an account of his role as a mediator in a boundary dispute between Lagash and Umma, two other Sumerian city-states to the south.[6] This led to the world's first recorded boundary marker, another Sumerian political innovation that would profoundly shape world orders through the ages. The Sumerians also developed land and maritime trade, and their merchant fleets could reach the Indus valley ports of India, a contemporary civilization.

As in other civilizations, the Sumerian world order revolved around a conception of good versus evil and order versus chaos. In the famed Sumerian epic named after him, Gilgamesh, the king of Uruk, defeats the forest-dwelling giant Humbaba, representing darkness and evil, while Gilgamesh is protected by Shamash, the sun god with the power of light over darkness. Gilgamesh thus secures access to the resources of the forest and cements himself as a hero to his people. But Sumerian gods could also be vengeful to the extreme in shaping order on earth. When humans became too "noisy" and violent, the gods caused the great flood to wipe out humanity, save one man who was urged by a friendly divine, Enki, to build a boat and sail to safety with his family and a specimen of all animals for future regeneration of earth.[7]

While remaining independent of each other, the Sumerian city-states did develop a myth of collective identity as well as historical continuity, which was used by the ruling class for political legitimacy. All great civilizations do this, China most extremely so. In the Sumer case, a retroactive "kings list"—supposedly written by a scribe during King Utukhegal's reign in the late twenty-second century BC—provided a record

27

of the monarchical and divine lineage in Sumer, implying a degree of Sumerian cohesion, continuity, and unity against outsiders.[8]

Another important development of the Sumerian period is the emergence of legal codes, the earliest attempt to preserve order against chaos through law. Although aimed primarily at maintaining domestic stability, these codes were viewed by their creators and subjects as universal. Their diffusion across many states of the Mesopotamia region (Sumer, Akkad, and Babylon) can be viewed as the development of a world order.

The earliest known example was the Code of Urukagina, proclaimed by Urukagina, the king of Lagash, in the twenty-fourth century BC. The actual code is lost, but references to it in later documents show that it contained measures stipulating that the rich cannot force the poor to sell land, livestock, or food against their will; giving relief to people who had been placed in indentured servitude due to debt; and limiting the power of officials to levy commissions.[9] The Code of Urukagina was followed by the Code of Ur-Nammu, issued by Sumerian King Ur-Nammu (2047–2030 BC), which also offered protections to weaker members of society—such as orphans, the poor, and widows—against the rich and the powerful. "The orphan did not fall a prey to the wealthy," it states. "The widow did not fall a prey to the powerful," and "the man of one shekel did not fall a prey to the man of one mina [sixty shekels]."[10]

These earlier law codes imposed relatively mild punishments against transgressions, but this changed with the Code of Hammurabi, who reigned in Babylon from 1792 to 1750 BC. It is the most famous law code of ancient times and was based on the principle of retributive justice, in which the punishment a lawbreaker received directly corresponded to the crime he committed: "If a man put out the eye of another man, his eye shall be put out," "If he break another man's bone, his bone shall be broken," and so on.[11] But while Hammurabi's code imposed harsh punishments, it also introduced the principle of the presumption of innocence until proven guilty and the idea that the burden of proof lay with the accuser, well before such principles could be found in the laws of ancient Rome and in modern legal codes.

In all, the Sumerian city-states were often in conflict, but order was maintained not only by seeking protection from the gods but also through such earthly innovations as marking territorial boundaries, promoting trade, developing legal codes, and settling interstate disputes through arbitration. Divine authority was supplemented by human ingenuity to solve problems of the day.

The next stage of the evolution of the early Mesopotamian world order came about when the smaller, more homogeneous city-states transformed into larger and more culturally diverse domains through the conquest of neighboring lands. Most important in this process was the rise of Sargon of Akkad, who, in expanding north and west of the classical Mesopotamia area, may be regarded as the world's first multinational empire builder, though on a smaller scale than Achaemenid Persia's empire later.[12] Another Akkadian contribution to ancient political order was the Akkadian language, which became the lingua franca of diplomacy and statecraft of the ancient Near East. But it is the institution of empire, developed in the conquests of Sargon, that would become an enduring feature of political organization into the future, through the subsequent empire of the Assyrians, and attain its most developed form under Achaemenid Persia in the sixth century BC.

Egyptian Centrality

In contrast to Sumer's system of independent states, the political organization of Egypt—the other birthplace of world order—emerged as a single centralized state. Narmer's unification of the country is symbolically portrayed in the Narmer Palette, a shield-like artifact of sedimentary rock dating back to that period and now in the Egyptian Museum in Cairo. It shows the king smiting enemies and wearing the white crown of Upper Egypt on one side and the red crown of Lower Egypt on the other. Like Sumer, Egypt developed divine monarchy, but it was based more on the idea that the king actually was a god, rather than just godlike or chosen to rule by the gods. The Egyptian king, who would be called *pharaoh* (meaning Great House because of his palace) from the eighteenth century BC, was initially regarded as the representation of the falcon god Horus. With the rise of the cult of sun worship in Heliopolis during the fifth dynasty (2465–2325 BC), the king became seen as the son of Re, the sun god.[13]

Whether the ruler was an actual god or just godlike, Egyptian order building was deeply rooted in the chaos-versus-order narrative, as presented in the Narmer Palette's imagery, which can be read as the king's subjugation of the forces of chaos to establish order. This was deeply connected to Egyptian cosmology and to myths explaining the fundamental nature of the ruler's authority. Egyptians believed that the fate of the universe was shaped by a continual struggle between two opposite forces: *ma'at* (order and harmony) and *isfet* (chaos, violence, and injustice). Order emerges when *ma'at* overcomes *isfet*. To ensure this, society needs a king who is divine, and who can navigate among the myriad gods of the Egyptian pantheon. The struggle is cyclical; new forces of *isfet* are constantly emerging, requiring a fresh response from *ma'at* to preserve the stability of the universe itself. The struggle is represented in natural forces: the sunrise and the sunset and the flooding of the Nile. If *ma'at* did not intervene, *isfet* prevailed, causing the annual flooding to cease, and thus depriving Egypt of its main source of agriculture and livelihood.[14] Chaos and destruction ensued. Like the notion of the divine ruler, this idea of constant struggle between order and chaos was adopted by subsequent civilizations as justification both for the strong ruler—the king, the emperor, the tyrant, or the dictator—and for the sets of rules that world orders have been based on.

This worldview of the Egyptians was important not just for Egypt's domestic affairs but also for its foreign relations. Egyptian rulers concocted a state ideology that held—much like the ancient Chinese view of their own country—Egypt to be at the center of the world, and foreign lands were depicted as places of chaos, while, thanks to its rulers, Egypt was a domain of order. "Without the king and his constant struggle on behalf of *ma'at*, the whole world would fall into chaos and decay."[15] Indeed, when the king appeared in public, images of ethnic "others" were placed near him, thereby emphasizing his role as the defender of *ma'at* against the foreign adversaries representing *isfet*.[16]

But Egypt, despite being highly centralized internally, almost never became a full-fledged empire, the major exception being the New Kingdom. Even at its greatest extent during the New Kingdom period, when it covered Nubia in the south and the Levant in the north, the Egyptian Empire certainly did not match the territorial reach and multicultural makeup of the Achaemenid Persian Empire. There are several reasons for this. The economic self-sufficiency afforded by the fertile Nile River, which lessened the need for conquest to acquire resources, may have played a big part. Geography—especially the natural barriers of desert on all sides—and a sense of cultural superiority fostered by a conservative priestly class contributed to an insular political culture. Not least, Egyptians had a cultural taboo against perishing abroad and having bodies being left behind in foreign lands, as would happen in imperial adventures.

But Egypt was not entirely disengaged from its neighbors. It did contribute to world order through its involvement, in both war and peace, with the other powers of the Near East, ultimately helping to establish the foundations of great power cooperation and the world's first peace treaty. Despite Egypt's differences with Sumer's independent state system prior to Sargon, the two were the progenitors of the ideology of a divine or a divinely ordained ruler, which would become one of the most enduring inventions of antiquity, adopted and exported to the wider world by none other than Alexander the Great.

A "Family" of Great Powers

In 1887, archaeologists discovered some 350 letters in Tell el-Amarna in Egypt, the site of the palace of Pharaoh Akhenaten (Amenhotep IV) of Egypt's New Kingdom. Written in Akkadian cuneiform, these letters, dated between 1352 and 1336 BC, consisted of communications among the leaders of the several major entities of the ancient world. There were five of them: Babylon, Hatti, Egypt, Mitanni, and Assyria. Their mutual dealings constituted a system of diplomacy, which some scholars have called "Amarna diplomacy," in which "the Great Powers of the entire Near East, from the Mediterranean to the Persian Gulf, interacting among themselves, engaged in regular dynasty, commercial, and strategic relations."[17] To be sure, the concept of great powers here is unlike how the term is used today, denoting international players with a capacity for projecting power and influence beyond their immediate neighborhoods. The Amarna powers did not have the geopolitical reach of modern great powers, but they still were significant players in their time over a vast geographic area.

In the Amarna diplomatic system, Egypt enjoyed a certain amount of deference from the other great powers. But all powers were able to pursue their interests and resolve their differences using terms of friendship and family politics. The rulers were addressed as brothers or fathers, and relations among them were based on social customs, such as invitations to attend festivities and arranged marriages among their families. These were the beginnings of a time-honored way to build alliances and prestige, much as rulers in Europe, Asia, and elsewhere would do in later periods. The exchanges or dialogues among the rulers reveal political relationships based on expectations of mutual support and compliance. A ruler, for example, would justify his request for gold from another ruler not because he needed it but because his "brother," the other ruler, was expected to provide it.

The language of affectionate family relations masked very real political calculations, especially the craving for equal status and reciprocity among the great kings.[18] When Assyria, a newly rising power, wanted to join the brotherhood, its king, Ashur-uballit, sent a letter to the pharaoh of Egypt, most likely Akhenaten. The letter was accompanied by gifts, as was common practice, but it also demanded a quick response and made it clear that its purpose was to gain information about Egypt and its ruler. The letter, now in New York's Metropolitan Museum of Art, reads:

> Say to the king of the land of Egypt: Thus Ashur-uballit, the king of the land of (the god) Ashur. For you, your household, for your land, may all be well. I have sent my messenger to you to visit you and to visit your land. Up to now, my predecessors have not written; today, I have written to you. I send you a splendid chariot, 2

horses, and 1 date-stone of genuine lapis lazuli as your greeting gift. Do not delay the messenger whom I have sent to you for a visit. He should visit and then leave for here. He should see what you are like and what your land is like, and then leave for here.[19]

Reciprocity was also demanded in another letter, from King Burna-Buriash of Babylon to the pharaoh of Egypt. "Now, although both you and I are friends," Burna-Buriash wrote, "three times have your messengers come here, but you did not send me one beautiful gift and therefore I did not send you one single beautiful gift."[20]

The pharaoh of Egypt, despite having a somewhat higher status in the club of powers, was also expected to treat all the other great kings equally by giving each of them gifts of similar value. Hence, when Ashur-uballit of Assyria got less gold from Egypt than did the ruler of Mitanni, the Assyrian king wrote to the pharaoh complaining that his gift was "not enough for the pay of my messengers on the journey to and back."[21] There were expectations of mutual respect and diplomatic honor, seen in protests from rulers who felt their messengers had been badly received in the Egyptian court.

The diplomatic conventions and norms of the Amarna system remarkably prefigured those of later eras. Records were kept in the Egyptian palace in Tell el-Amarna in the same way that, in later millennia, a foreign office archive in Europe would maintain records of correspondence. The Amarna system provided for continuous contact, official stamps to validate contacts, and formal ratifications of agreements by rulers, "sworn to by the parties concerned in the presence of divine witnesses."[22]

There is no evidence that the great kings ever met together as a group, as would happen in another great power club, the Concert of Europe, formed in 1815 to manage political and strategic affairs after the defeat of Napoleon. But the envoys of the Amarna rulers might have met while traveling. Envoys also might have spent time together in foreign courts, especially in the Egyptian capital. There is no suggestion in the Amarna letters that rulers of one polity got involved mediating the disputes of other polities or negotiating military alliances.

Still, through such interactions, the rulers were familiar with each other's interests and needs and the system was successful in preventing war among the major powers for two centuries. This was partly because there was no power among them that was militarily dominant. Egyptian primacy in the family of great powers was largely symbolic, a recognition—much like China's within the tributary system centuries later—of its storied and continuous civilization. The lasting peace was also because of the norms of reciprocity and equality, facilitated by communications in a common language. One key term from the Amarna letters is *ahhutu*, meaning brotherhood or collective of brothers, which implied not equality of power but equality of status.[23] The system worked because all great kings considered themselves part of an exclusive group of the "civilized," in the sense of having the art of writing and creating luxury goods. Entry into the Amarna club was selective, requiring military power, possession of vassals, and acknowledgment of equal status by other great kings.[24] More than three thousand years later, a somewhat similar notion of what it meant to be "civilized" emerged in Europe in tandem with its colonization of the world. But there is no evidence in the Amarna period of the racial bias that would be fundamental to the European notion of civilization and the idea of world order promoted by Europe and the United States during and after the Enlightenment.

In all, the Amarna system, despite its very different context, was a prototype of diplomacy and international relations. While not quite similar to the nineteenth-century Concert of Europe, it provided the earliest model of an arrangement in which great powers managed their relations without any of them creating an empire or establishing hegemony.

Ending Wars, Building Peace

Within the Amarna great power system, some bilateral relations were more developed, particularly that between the Egyptians and the Hittites in Anatolia. Following the footsteps of the Sumerian states centuries earlier—and presaging relations among the great powers of Europe millennia later—Egypt and Hatti managed their relationship in conflict and cooperation by marking borders, deciding military deployments to avoid conflict, regulating trade, and developing alliances.[25] A momentous outcome of the Egyptian-Hittite relationship was "the world's first international peace treaty," certainly the first for which documentation is available. This was the Treaty of Kadesh, concluded in 1259 BC and named after the Battle of Kadesh, fought some sixteen years earlier between Egyptian Pharaoh Ramesses II and Hittite King Hattusilis.[26] Four of the provisions of this treaty, as summarized below, are especially remarkable.[27]

1. "The Great Prince of Hatti shall not trespass against the land of Egypt forever, to take anything from it. And...the great ruler of Egypt, shall not trespass against the land of Hatti, to take from it forever."

2. "If another enemy come against the lands of...Egypt, and he send to the Great Prince of Hatti, saying: 'Come with me as reinforcement against him,' the Great Prince of Hatti shall come to him and...slay his enemy. However, if it is not the desire of the Great Prince of Hatti to go [himself], he shall send his infantry and his chariotry....If another enemy come against the Great Prince of Hatti...the great ruler of Egypt, shall come to him as reinforcement to slay his enemy. If it is [not] the desire of the great ruler of Egypt, to come, he shall send his infantry and his chariotry."

3. "If the great ruler of Egypt is enraged against servants belonging to him, and they commit another offense against him, and he go to slay them, the Great Prince of Hatti shall act with him to slay everyone against whom they shall be enraged."

4. Similarly, "if a great man flee from the land of Egypt and come to... Hatti...the Great Prince of Hatti shall not receive them [but]... cause them to be brought to...the great ruler of Egypt....If a great man flee from the land of Hatti and come to...Egypt...the great ruler of Egypt...shall not receive them [but]...shall cause them to be brought to the Prince [of Hatti]."

These provisions are striking in the way they resemble peace and security treaties in modern international affairs. The first of the above provisions may be likened to the principles of nonaggression or nonuse of force and nonintervention. Indeed, these are the core founding principles of the UN and regional bodies throughout the world. The second provision is typical of alliances through the ages, including the collective defense provisions of the North Atlantic Treaty Organization (NATO), and bilateral defense treaties such as that between the United States and Japan and the United States and South Korea. The third and fourth provisions suggest mutual support against internal revolt and a prohibition against the sheltering of domestic enemies and criminals, even calling for their extradition. All these are quite commonplace among states today, both Western and non-Western.

Not surprisingly, a copy of the Treaty of Kadesh is displayed on a wall in the UN headquarters in New York City, a modest acknowledgment that many of the things we cherish about today's Western-led order were not the result of some Western monopoly on international cooperation but were present even in the distant past.[28]

The Origins of Empire

The end of the Amarna period was followed by the rise of one of the most powerful empires of the classical period, one that far exceeded the empire of Sargon of Akkad. The origins of Assyria go back to the early second millennium BC. But it became a truly imperial power during the first millennium BC, when it became what is known as the Neo-Assyrian Empire (912–612 BC; some historians date it from 746 BC). That empire was the largest of its day, stretching from present-day Iran in the east to Egypt in the west and incorporating many smaller entities, including the Israelite Kingdom of Judah. In its various phases, from being a regional power to an empire, Assyria can be compared to Rome in terms of both longevity and military innovation, which would mark a major milestone in the evolution of the imperial organization.

First, the Assyrians were seasoned military innovators, credited with developing new military techniques, such as iron weapons, siege warfare, and the battering ram, all precursors to those used by Persia, Rome, and, later, Europe.[29] While developing an extensive trade, communication, and transport system outside of their Mesopotamian homeland, the Assyrians ruled indirectly through a system of client states (albeit with a garrison in Egypt), which contributed payments for the cost of maintaining the empire and were prohibited from having dealings with Assyrian enemies. The Assyrians distinguished themselves in knowledge preservation too: the library of King Ashurbanipal, known as the last great king of Assyria, was probably the first and largest systematic collection of knowledge in the ancient world.[30]

The Assyrians, like the Egyptians and Sumerians before them, invoked divine and supernatural forces to cement their rule and conquer other lands. Their chief deity was Ashur, the god of war, after whom their capital city was named. There are similarities between Ashur and Enlil, the supreme deity of the Sumerians, and the god Marduk, who presided in the Neo-Babylonian Empire that conquered Assyria, suggesting continuities and transfer of ideas among the ancient societies of the Mesopotamia. The Assyrian king was represented with a halo or an aura—referred to as *melammu*, meaning "supernatural and awe-inspiring"—which was designed to instill fear and respect among enemies. It is said that if the king lost the aura, as happened on occasion, he had lost divine support. The Assyrian aura is similar to that depicted in some early Christian representations of emperors.[31] And it is reminiscent of the function of the Chinese "mandate of heaven," the Confucian notion that when things go seriously awry, the emperor loses his authority to rule.

Popular modern accounts have denounced the Assyrians for their alleged aggressiveness and ruthlessness, particularly their practice of torture and relocating conquered peoples (to reduce the chance that they would rebel against the empire), which some historians have likened to the population removals carried out by the Nazis. But one has to keep in mind that such perceptions were created by the Assyrians' own reliefs and inscriptions, which—somewhat like the statements of Mongol conquerors—were aimed at instilling horror and fear among their opponents, a timeless tactic of empires from the Roman to the Mongolian.[32]

The decline of the Neo-Assyrian Empire was accompanied by much violence, as several powers competed to fill the vacuum it left behind. It is to this period that we owe the term *Armageddon*, which we now use to describe the total destruction that would be caused by nuclear war, but which comes from the battle between Josiah, the Israelite king of Judah, and the Egyptian ruler Necho II in 609 at a place called Megiddo, where Josiah was defeated.[33]

The conqueror of the Assyrians, the Neo-Babylonian Empire, has a mixed reputation in history. Its best-known king, Nebuchadnezzar II, who reigned from 605 or 604 to 562 BC, rebuilt Babylon to become the most spectacular city of the time. And, as a clay tablet map from that period now in the British Museum suggests, the city was presented as the center of the world. But he has been made notorious (including in the Bible) because of his deportation of Jews from Jerusalem to Babylon after he conquered the Kingdom of Judah and destroyed the temple in Jerusalem.[34]

Babylon made impressive advances in science, especially in astronomical observations, which were borrowed by the Greeks, and laid some of the early foundations of geometry and philosophy. Its cultural vibrancy was illustrated by such fabled architectural achievements as the Ishtar Gate and the hanging gardens (one of the seven wonders of the ancient world). But despite its view of itself as the center of the world,[35] the Neo-Babylonian Empire was conquered in 539 BC by Cyrus the Great, the founder of the Achaemenid Empire, which originated in present-day Iran and extended all the way from the Indus valley in the east to the Balkans and Egypt in the west. Given the vast extent of the territories it administered and the multiplicity of peoples under its control, the Achaemenid Empire is commonly viewed as the first truly universal empire.

Legacies

From Sumer, Egypt, and Persia emerged the three earliest prototypes of world order: The Sumerian world order was anarchical—that is, a system of independent states. The Egyptian one was hierarchical, with

Egypt being nominally equal to its brotherly great powers but enjoying greater prestige. Persia—following the footsteps of Akkad and Assyria—developed an imperial world order through outright conquest and domination of its neighbors. All three—along with divine kingship, great power diplomacy, and the narrative of chaos versus order—would become familiar features of history and continue to influence world orders through the ages.

Indeed, the institution of divine monarchy in different forms is by far the most common, durable, and widespread political system, found in every major civilization. Its main rival for that claim—the republic, where ascent to rulership does not require hereditary succession—is much further behind. And even further behind is democracy, where rulers are selected through popular voting. Athenian democracy, as I have noted in the Introduction and will discuss in the next chapter, was both limited and short-lived, until its ideals were revived much later in the modern era. By contrast, the basic idea of divinely sanctioned rule has persisted over the millennia, found in some form in every civilization of the world, surviving until today.

It is not clear whether the appearance of monarchy and divine monarchy in other parts of the world was due to diffusion from the Near East or if it developed separately. Both are likely, keeping in mind that some form of divine sanction would be a very attractive way for a ruler to enhance his authority and legitimacy before subjects and foreign friends and foes. But the Greeks and Romans took many ideas and institutions from Egypt and Asia, and there is no reason to believe divine monarchy was not one of them. As I shall discuss in the following chapter, some Greek thinkers, including Aristotle, had praised the Persian King Cyrus as a virtuous ruler. Alexander the Great, like his father Philip, wished to emulate the great king of Persia, despite the animosity between the two civilizations. Indeed, Alexander had thought of himself as having divine attributes and had promptly anointed himself both as the pharaoh of Egypt and the great king of Persia following his conquest of these two vast territories.[36] The Roman imperial eagle was an import from the

Near Eastern civilization, where it was considered a messenger of the sun god.[37] The Roman emperors, starting with Augustus, were also fascinated by the idea of personal divinity and embraced it wholeheartedly; Augustus elevated the assassinated Julius Caesar, who had adopted him as his son, to divine status, perhaps coveting the same status after his death. (He got his wish.) Elsewhere, the Indian concept of divine kingship (*devaraja*) spread to Southeast Asia to transform the loosely structured personal chiefdoms of that time into full-fledged states. Divine monarchy has since persisted through the ages, extending to King Vajiralongkorn of Thailand today. Under different circumstances, it is also reflected in the medieval and early modern European notion of the divine right of kings (such as King James I of England in the seventeenth century AD).

As with divine monarchy, the idea and institution of empire, invented by Sargon but perfected by Persia, would continue to be a major feature of world order into the late modern period, found in all major civilizations such as those of India, China, Rome, Europe, Africa, and the Americas. The decentralized independent state system would find its most developed form in the Westphalian order that emerged in Europe around the seventeenth century. The narrative of chaos versus order continues to underpin the foreign policy and national security concerns of modern nations, including great powers such as the United States and China.

Chapter 2

Greek Myths and Persian Power

In the Western mind, ancient Greece is the most storied of civilizations, believed to be the origin of the fundamental ideas and practices of contemporary liberal-democratic life. But Greece is also the most mythicized of the ancient cultures. It was indisputably brilliant, creative, and pioneering in literature, science, philosophy, and political thought. And yet, it has also attracted far too much deference from Western historians, one consequence of which is that the Western culture exaggerates ancient Greece's achievements and, even more, understates both its dark sides and its indebtedness to other civilizations, especially Egypt and Mesopotamia. And we forget that the Greek way of organizing politics and foreign affairs and its lessons for building a world order would be a prescription for conflict and disorder.

We have seen how the concept of world order began in the ancient Near East, specifically at the intersection of Egypt, Anatolia, and Mesopotamia. It is from here that some of the core institutions of world order—divine kingship, empire, great power diplomacy, and the making of peace treaties—emerged. In addition, regular interactions among Egypt, Anatolia, the Levant, and Mesopotamia created a comprehensive system of economic exchange and cultural diffusion. These laid the foundation of a world order whose elements persist to this day, despite modifications and additions over the ages.

But starting around fifth century BC, the great movement of history began to shift to two emerging cultures, Greece and Persia, and with that shift came important developments in the theory and practice of world order. Both Greek and Persian civilizations in their own ways shaped world order, but they were also very different from each other.

Briefly put, the Greek world order was a system of city-states, where there was no hegemonic power, although Athens did make a run at developing such power that ended in disaster. As most students of history learn at one time or another, the conflicts between Greece and Persia in the fifth century BC—written about so splendidly by the historian Herodotus and marked by such events as the battles of Salamis and Marathon—were among the seminal events of ancient history. After its resistance to Persian encroachments began, Athens began to collect tribute from other Greek states and to interfere in their domestic affairs. In response, these other states, including Sparta and Corinth, organized a balancing coalition that led ultimately to the downfall of Athens.

More interestingly, some Greek states maintained their anti-hegemonial posture by not siding with the victor after a war. For example, the Corinthians, fearing that supporting the victor would embolden it to seek hegemony, often sided with the loser in a conflict. This principle of opposing a state's attempt to achieve hegemony—known as the balance of power principle—is not uncommon in history; it would become a major feature of the European system in the nineteenth and early twentieth centuries. But it is not a universal tendency either: China's East Asian neighbors did not balance against it for much of history. Britian and other Western powers did not balance the United States, despite its rise as the preeminent global power after World War II. In both cases, most other states sided with the dominant power, a tendency political scientists call "bandwagoning." Therefore, the state system of ancient Greece provides only a partial window into how states have achieved stability and world order through history.

If, for Greece, world order meant a kind of balancing act, for Persia it was an extension of the twin ideas of divine kingship and of universal empire, which were adopted by many later world orders. While ancient

Greece might have given us enduring political ideas and institutions and is seen as the progenitor of western civilization, Persia was a much more important and stabilizing power shaping subsequent history.

Greco-Persian Connections

While Western intellectuals and politicians proudly invoke the term *Greco-Roman* to describe their heritage, Greco-Asian or Greco-Persian would be more accurate. In Greco-Asia, Greece was a pupil as well as a teacher, an intruder as well as a native, a victor as well as a vanquished party. Hyphenating Greece and Rome as a single civilizational complex is a modern European or Western invention, one that ignores the central role of Persia in the development of Greek identity and the survival of the independent Greek city-state system.

Ancient Greece had little strategic interaction with western and northern Europe, aside from founding settlements in the western Mediterranean islands and coastal areas. There is no question that Rome valued Greek culture and borrowed from it, but there is also no question that the origins of Greek civilization, its scientific and philosophical achievements, had more to do with the Greeks borrowing from prior civilizations in Egypt and Asia than from any civilization to its west. Indeed, to consider Greece as a European or Western civilization is one of the biggest myths of history.

On the contrary, the Greeks disparaged the Europeans' intellect as well as their ability to organize a world order, considering Asians to be superior in this area. A passage from Aristotle's *Politics* makes this clear: "Those who live in a cold climate and in Europe are full of spirit, but wanting in intelligence and skill, and therefore they retain comparative freedom, but have no political organization, and are incapable of ruling over others." Aristotle found Asians to be "intelligent and inventive" but "wanting in spirit," which kept them "always in a state of subjection and slavery." Sandwiched between the Europeans and the Asians, the Greeks were "high-spirited and also intelligent." This for Aristotle made the Hellenic race "free, and...the best governed of any nation, and, if it could be formed into one state, would be able to rule the world."[1]

Aristotle's wish remained unfulfilled and the ancient Greeks remained a divided lot for most of their history. But while they considered themselves superior to any of their neighbors, whether white Europeans and darker Africans or Asians, skin color was less important to them than cultural and linguistic pride. The Greek term *barbarian* applied to all non-Greek-speaking foreigners, including the "Europeans" to the "West" such as the Celts, Balts, Slavs, Phoenicians, Etruscans, Macedonians, Carthaginians, Vikings, Gauls, Goths, and the peoples of Africa. Their view did not follow the modern European association of dark skin with mental inferiority (or "barbarism") and white skin with superior civilization, which gives credence to the idea that racism based on skin color is a distinctively modern European invention.

In any case, ancient Greece is best described as a Mediterranean civilization with strong Asiatic foundations. The Mediterranean was a complex mosaic of different civilizations, where African, Asian, and European societies interacted closely and continuously with each other. Yet, after the Renaissance, Western scholars and leaders claimed classical Greece as their ancestor and attributed an exclusively European or Western identity to it, ignoring its Eastern connections and linkages. The extent to which this was a contrived and self-serving appropriation was well captured by the French historian Fernand Braudel. "Surely, the place that 'the Greek miracle' holds in our modern western world results from the need for every civilization or human group to choose its origins, to invent forefathers of whom it can be proud," he writes. "Belief in this ancestry has become a virtual necessity."[2] Modern Europeans, lacking a suitable ancestor that they could identify as "civilized," filled the gap with Greece and Rome.

The reality was very different from the myth arising from this need. The fact that the first blossoming of the scientific and philosophical achievements of Greece occurred in Asia, especially in Anatolia (which is now in Turkey) and the neighboring Ionian islands, is no coincidence. It had to do with the fact that Anatolia is a lot closer than the Greek mainland to the ancient civilizations of the Near East: Egypt, Sumer, and Persia. Greek settlers in the eastern Mediterranean, including those who founded such centers of science and philosophy as Miletus on the Anatolian coast, "were in the role of promising pupils rather than the bearers of a new and advanced civilization," the historian Pavel Oliva writes in his book on the birth of Greek civilization.[3] And even in their scientific understanding of how the universe worked, the Greeks borrowed from their neighbors. Thales of Miletus, regarded as the first scientist of ancient Greece, was a mathematician, astronomer, and philosopher. He considered water as a first element, positing that the world is based on water, an idea seen by many historians in the past as a pioneering illustration of the Greek scientific outlook. But Thales may have been redeploying an old Egyptian belief about the creative role of water. The "Greek miracle," writes Braudel, "was founded on a solid basis established long before," such as "pioneering chemistry in Babylon, medicine in Egypt, and astronomy in Mesopotamia."[4] The Greeks got their script from the Phoenicians, borrowed the idea of coined money from the Lydians, and were influenced in their astronomy, art, and mathematics by the earlier contributions of Egypt, Sumer, and Babylon.[5]

The Greeks are regarded as the first natural philosophers to move away from the religious idea of divine creation as the origin of the world and toward the secular idea of natural causation—of having accomplished the "demystification of the sacred."[6] But this, too, is likely not the case. While European historians present this as a sharp divide between the superstitious East and the rationalist, scientific West, the break with the beliefs of earlier Asian civilizations was not as fundamental as these historians have represented it to be.

Comparing the foundational Greek worldview with that of Egypt, one finds similarities: both were steeped in supernatural beliefs. In the Egyptians' conception, order was represented by the ruler (later known as pharaoh), who, although he was understood to be the son of a god, had to fight and defeat the mortal enemies of Egypt (the forces of chaos). In the Greek notion, order was not created by any semidivine ruler, but by four purely divine forces: Eros, Gaia, Tartarus, and Nyx/Erebus. Even after their turn to a more scientific and philosophical basis of knowledge, the Greeks did not entirely abandon the idea of divine agency. As in most ancient civilizations, the divine and the natural, rationalism and superstition, continued to cohabit among the Greeks, just as their gods continued to coexist with nature as shapers of war, peace, and other human affairs. Hence, Greeks could be recognized for "their capacity for rational thought and their adherence to...grossest superstition." They consulted oracles and based important decisions—including whether to resist the invading Persians—"on the babblings of an old woman squatting in a cave at Delphi, chewing laurel leaves."[7]

Yet the idea of Greek rationality has persisted in Western minds to the present day, reproducing itself in Western Eurocentric and Orientalist portrayals of Asia and other non-Western civilizations. This leads Western scholars to disparage non-Western historical models of world order—such as those developed by Persia, China, and India—as steeped in divinity and imperial hierarchy, in contrast to supposedly despotic, rational, secular, and above all "free" Greece. This habit of mind draws too stark a contrast between the West and the Rest.

Among these supposed contributions of ancient Greece, the most important one are the ideas of freedom and democracy. The Western imagination adores Greece as the birthplace of democracy. But Greek democracy had a very limited scope and span. Many Greek city-states were ruled by "tyrants." Democracy was mostly developed in Athens between 460 and 320 BC, although other city-states such as Corinth, Megara, Argos, Syracuse, and Rhodes were democracies for some part of their histories. There might have been over fifty Greek city-states that had democratic rule, but it was often short-lived.[8] Even these democracies were limited in the freedom they provided to the people who lived under them. Athenian democracy revolved around propertied classes, meaning that it was carried out by no more than 30 percent of the total adult population.[9] The majority of people living in Athens were not part of its citizenry and were thus excluded from the exercise of democracy, including women, children, and slaves. Another estimate, by Braudel, is that in 431 BC, out of a total population of 315,000 in Attica (the region surrounding Athens), 172,000 were citizens. Out of this, forty thousand were male citizens, the only group that had the right to vote.[10] The rest were foreigners (metics) and slaves. Going by this account, democracy was the prerogative of only 12.7 percent of the population.

The Greek idea of liberty did not mean freedom of the individual in the modern sense. To be sure, extolling Athenian virtues of democracy and tolerance, Pericles, the city-state's leader in 431 BC, celebrated—as recounted by Greek historian Thucydides—that political power in Athens was vested "in the hands not of a minority but of the whole people" and that Athenian politics was "free and open," whereby "each single one of our citizens, in all the manifold aspects of life, is able to show himself the rightful lord and owner of his own person." In the same speech, Pericles also boasted of Athenian kindness and generosity to others: "We make friends by doing good to others, not by receiving good from them. . . . When we do kindness to others, we do not do them out of any calculations of profit and loss: we do them without afterthought, relying on our free liberality."[11] Yet, Pericles was hiding some ugly truths about Athenian society. The actual record of Athenian liberty and benevolence was far less benign or inspiring, as recognized by India's Jawaharlal Nehru, one of the most prominent world leaders to have fought Western imperialism and championed democracy. Writing from British prison, Nehru noted: "Athens, lover of freedom, sacked and destroyed Melos and put to death all the grown men there and sold the women and children as slaves. Even while Thucydides was writing of the empire and freedom of Athens, that empire had crumbled away and that freedom was no more."[12]

Other writers support this view. The purpose of Greek democracy "was not to protect the liberty of the individual; it was to protect the liberty of the city and raise it to a heroic superiority over its neighbours."[13] It was at best a freedom in the collective sense; Greek democracy offered little protection to individual citizens against government encroachment, which is the essence of the modern notion of human rights. Nor did the polis protect free speech. While theoretically one had the ability to speak openly in the assembly or in public, there was no protection against punishment for disagreeing with official positions, nor was there any limit to the power of the state, provided that the state's actions were deemed valid by the established authority. Just ask poor Socrates, who was forced to commit suicide for his views on religion: refusing to accept the officially recognized gods of Athens and corrupting the minds of the youth through his philosophical doctrines.

In Athens, the birthplace of Greek democracy, "personal freedoms could be taken away at any moment by the demos when it thought its interests were at stake."[14] The worst off were the poor. Aristotle himself lamented that even the free Athenian citizens were not really free: "The Athenian constitution was in all respects oligarchical, and in fact the poor themselves and also their wives and children were actually in slavery to the rich."[15]

Due to their overriding concern with keeping the polis self-sufficient and independent—not only from outsiders but also from each other—the Greeks failed to develop a system of interstate cooperation and international order.[16] Typical of the Greek obsession with competitive power plays, rather than with developing an inclusive system of peace, is Thucydides's famous explanation of the Peloponnesian War as the result of "growth of Athenian power and the fear which this caused in Sparta." This is a punch line for students and practitioners of realpolitik all over the world today, but it ignores the economic and moral factors behind war and peace.[17] Hence, explanations and predictions about international affairs derived from Greek history, such as the claim that the United States and China are destined to fall into a "Thucydides Trap," are partial and simplistic.[18]

Moreover, Greek democracy was not an exportable model. The small size and population of the polis—plus the small number of citizens (only non-slave males) allowed to participate in decision-making—made Athenian and Greek democracy difficult to replicate in later periods of history. In modern times, only small states like Switzerland have been able to practice direct democracy on a national scale. Athenian democracy may be comparable to the village assemblies of other civilizations, but it was not suitable for larger nations. As one Indian historian writes, "Athenian democracy failed after a singularly brief span, for all the supposed wisdom of its constitution."[19]

In short, Greece is without question a major contributor to Western civilization, but this does not warrant the starry-eyed extolling of its legacy as a model for today's world order. Other civilizations of antiquity—including those in Egypt, Anatolia, Persia, China, and India—contributed more substantially and durably to core aspects of the contemporary world order, including interstate cooperation, humanitarian principles in war and governance, economic interdependence, and cultural diversity. They did so without mimicking the Greeks' unique combination of "slavery, constant warfare, institutionalized pederasty and relentless culling of surplus population."[20]

Hellenization by Sword

A major concept in the study of Greek civilization is Hellenization, meaning the diffusion of Greek culture. Hellenization occurred both before and after Alexander the Great's conquests. Between the tenth and the eighth centuries BC, Greeks trading with surrounding areas and migrating to set up colonies spread Greek ways and ideas throughout much of the Mediterranean world.

This was sometimes, if not always, marked by violence and warfare, especially in Sicily, the first major site of Greek colonization in the western Mediterranean.[21] In other cases, Greek colonization was initially peaceful, but its consolidation was accomplished by military means. Even where Greek migration was not violent, as in parts of Asia Minor, the Greeks isolated themselves culturally, disdaining local societies and customs, much as Europeans did later when they colonized indigenous societies.

Greek colonization led to the foundation of new city-states, or poleis (plural for polis). While politically separate from their mother cities, or the original Greek city-states from which the majority of the early migrants came, the new entities were nonetheless extensions of the linguistic, religious, and cultural traditions, myths, and institutions of the original poleis.[22] And they were almost exclusively Greek, with very little cultural or political mixing with the indigenous inhabitants. One estimate is that only between 10 and 20 percent of these transplanted Greek poleis—mainly in Sicily, Thrace, and Anatolia—were hybrids, with demonstrable non-Greek aspects.[23] Although some overseas poleis would lose their exclusive Greek makeup and become more multicultural over time as more and more indigenous people came into contact with the Greek settlers, this had to await the Persian conquest of Anatolia and the march of Alexander the Great to the western frontiers of India.

In the meantime, Hellenization meant very little accommodation for the preexisting local traditions and populations, which were often displaced or marginalized. The colonizing Greeks accepted some of the local deities, but for the most part, Hellenization left few traces of the cultures of the people who lived there before. One major example is the Sikel (or Sicel) tribe, a pre-Hellenic group that inhabited large parts of Sicily before the arrival of the Greeks, and from whom the name of the island is derived. Not only were they pushed to the interior, but those who stayed close to the Greek arrivals lost their native culture. "The Sikel could become a Greek yet more thoroughly than the Briton could become an Englishman," one historian writes.[24] Here one can see parallels with how the arrival of European settlers in North and South America or Australia and New Zealand extinguished the cultures of indigenous peoples.

In all, Greek colonization was far more culturally exclusionary than its Eastern counterparts: Persianization and the spread of Indian civilization, especially to Southeast Asia, in the ancient and early medieval period. In Southeast Asia, the arrival of Indian culture—what historians call the "Indianization" of Southeast Asia (discussed in Chapter 3)—invigorated preexisting people, who used Hindu-Buddhist ideas and mythology to enrich local culture and empower local rulers, as is discussed in this book's India chapter. By contrast, Greek colonization was for the most part of the Greeks, by the Greeks, and for the Greeks. It is only when it extended to southern Asia—modern Afghanistan, Pakistan, and India—that Greek civilization took on its most cosmopolitan character. There, by mingling with the local culture, Greek expansion could produce artistic marvels such as the Gandhara Buddhist imagery.

To sum up, the major elements of the Greek world order revolved around the city-state system, with its tendency to reject hegemony by any single polis. As we will later discuss, some of the core features of the modern world order—such as its decentralized nature and the balance of power—resemble the Greek system. But this was not a unique Greek contribution. Other examples of non-hegemonic systems include the Sumerian, the Mayan, and the orders established by the polities of India before the Maurya Empire. None of these, however, have fired the Western imagination as the Greek system did, in large part because of the impact ancient Greece had on the European Renaissance and Enlightenment.

At the same time, the Greek system suffered several limitations that should not be overlooked. First, for all their ingenuity, the Greeks did not on their own develop all the things they have been credited with by Western writers. They borrowed ideas about science, art, sculpture, technology, and philosophy from their surrounding cultures. Second, though it did spawn the idea of democracy, Greece followed very restricted democratic practices that coexisted with tyranny throughout its history. Third, the Greek world order was inherently unstable. The veneration of one's own polis created fierce competition with other poleis, such that unity among them was achieved only when a foreign threat loomed or when the Greeks invited an outside power to make peace among them. There was one civilization that played both roles—as a common enemy and a protector—in the Greek world order. That power was Persia, to which we turn now.

The Persian World Order

The first universal empire known to us was founded by Cyrus the Great in 550 BC, a time when Rome was still ruled by kings after having been founded as a little village on the banks of the Tiber. Cyrus's Achaemenid Persian Empire, which lasted until 330 BC, was universal in the sense that it encompassed multiple civilizations and faiths, including its native Zoroastrianism, and was the largest of its kind until Alexander the

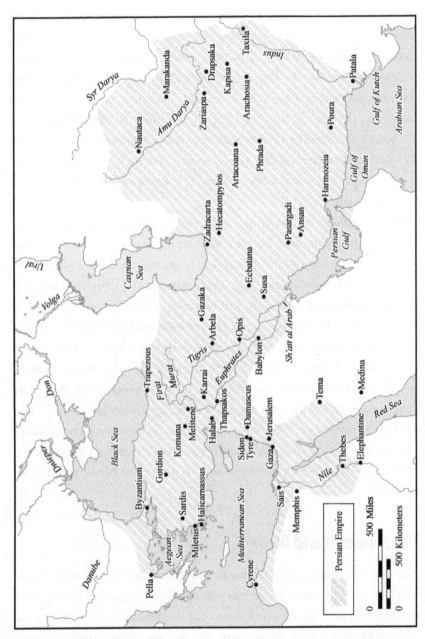

Map 2. The Persian Empire at its greatest extent.

Great's short-lived empire. Cyrus's realm extended to the Hindu-Buddhist cultures of Afghanistan, Sogdiana, and northwestern India, and it encompassed Egypt and the myriad peoples of western Asia, including Anatolians, Armenians, Mesopotamians, Greeks, and Jews. The empire had a coherent administration, maintaining an efficient communication and transport system and holding a distinctive worldview. The overriding ideology—although it was never imposed on conquered peoples—was shaped by Zoroastrianism, a central theme of which is the struggle between good and evil, as laid out sometime between 1500 and 500 BC by Zoroaster (Zarathushtra), the world's first prophet.[25] According to him, there was a single lord of the universe, Ahura Mazda, or "wise lord," who conceived contrasting positive and negative spirits, Spenta Mainyu and Angra Mainyu, which were also representations of truth and falsehood.[26]

Zoroaster died around 550 BC (although the date is disputed), but under the Achaemenids, Zoroastrianism was revived and became the state religion, with an important difference from the time of its founder. Now instead of residing in the sole creator, Ahura Mazda, the spirits of good and evil were separated into a good god, Ahura Mazda, and an evil one, Ahriman.[27] Accordingly, the Achaemenid worldview revolved around "two tenets...the claim to universal supremacy and the mandate to ensure stability in chaotic regions at the edge of the world."[28]

Contemporary Western publications usually present the rivalry between Greece and Persia as an example of the moral superiority of the West over the East. Look, for example, at the back-cover description of the Penguin Classics edition of *The Histories*, by Herodotus, which describes Greek-Persian rivalry as "the heroic and successful struggle of a small and divided Greece against the mighty empire of Persia—*with its underlying conflict between the absolutism of the East and the free institutions of the West*" (emphasis added).[29] A particularly denigrating account of Persian civilization comes from Oxford scholar Robin Lane Fox, whose book *The Classical World* denounces the Persian methods of conquest as "savage," "ghastly," and "utterly beastly."[30] He contrasts the "terrible ruthlessness" of Persians with "Greek values of restraint, modesty and justice."[31]

A good deal of this characterization of Persia comes from classical Greek writings on the conflict between the two civilizations, although one must always keep in mind that there was also substantial cooperation between Persian and Greek rulers. To cut a very long story short, beginning with the conquest of Lydia by Cyrus, in 546 BC, the Persians took control of the entire Anatolian coast, which had been settled by Greeks in their earlier waves of colonization throughout the Mediterranean. Cyrus and his son Cambyses II, who conquered Egypt, built the empire into the largest in the world of its time, maintaining a policy of respect toward diverse religious beliefs.[32]

The Persians would remain in control of the area, with brief interruptions, until the arrival of Alexander the Great in 334 BC, and during that very long stretch of time, they became deeply involved in Greek politics. But it was not long after the death of Cyrus the Great in 530 (or 529) BC and the accession to the Persian throne of Darius I (522–486 BC), the third ruler of the Achaemenid Empire, that Greeks and Persians began their epic confrontation. It is during this period, between 499 and 493 BC, that Greek cities in the Ionian region of Anatolia—which had remained relatively autonomous under previous Achaemenid rule—as well as the cities of Aeolis, Doris, Cyprus, and Caria, rebelled against the Persians.

After defeating the uprising, Darius I moved to punish the Greek states of Athens and Eretria for having supported the Ionian revolt. However, an alliance of Greek states, including Athens and Sparta, defeated the Persians at the famous Battle of Marathon in 490 BC. To avenge that defeat, Darius I started preparing an expedition to Athens but died before it could be carried out. His son Xerxes I burned down Athens and annihilated a Greek force under Sparta at a mountain pass in Thermopylae. But part of his forces were defeated by the Greeks at the Battle of Salamis in 480 BC, after which Xerxes retreated to Persia, bringing the long Greco-Persian wars to an end.

There is no question that Persians used brutal tactics in these and other wars they fought. For example, while suppressing the Ionian revolt, the Persians killed adult male survivors, castrated the boys, and sent the most beautiful women to Darius I's court. Herodotus, not known for his objectivity, wrote, "The towns themselves, temples and all, were burnt to the ground," and the surviving Ionians were reduced to slavery.[33]

But the Greeks were also savage in war and did not even spare fellow Greeks. Examples can be found during the Peloponnesian War (431–404 BC), which pitted an imperialist Athens against a coalition of Greek states led by Sparta. A famous episode of the war is the Athenian invasion of Melos, a Spartan ally, in the summer of 416 BC. Although the Melians had pleaded to stay neutral in the war, the Athenians, as Thucydides wrote, "put to death the [Melian] men of military age, made slaves of the women and children."[34] As a modern historian of genocide has argued, "By any standards the treatment of the Melians was a crime against humanity."[35] In other words, both Greeks and Persians were capable of ferocious cruelty; yet Western historians have indulged in a generalized portrayal of the Persians as universally cruel and the Greeks as moderate and restrained.

Melos gets the most attention among scholars as an example of Athenian mass slaughter, but it was not the only one. Scione in northern Greece, a former ally of Athens that had rebelled, was another. Another polis allied to Athens, Mytilene in Lesbos, almost suffered a similar fate to that of Melos. Despite Mytilene's unconditional surrender, the Athenian assembly voted to have all the males of military age there killed. Even when that decision was revoked, some one thousand Mytileneans were executed for instigating the revolt.[36] Such episodes are a useful reminder that republican or democratic states—as Athens is presented to be—are not inherently more peaceful or less inhumane, a fact we will turn to later in the book.

Just as Western historians, relying on partisan Greek accounts, have exaggerated the scope for liberty and democracy in Greek society, they have understated the openness and cultural accommodation afforded by the Persian Empire to its subjects. This dominant Western view, as noted, was heavily influenced by biased Greek writers, even though not all Greeks saw the Persians in a negative way. Plato, for example, said that the Persians under Cyrus "gave a share of freedom to their subjects and advanced them to a position of equality." He continued, "If there was any wise man amongst them able to give counsel, since the king was not jealous but allowed free speech and respected those who could help at all by their counsel—such a man had the opportunity of contributing to the common stock the fruit of his wisdom. Consequently, at that time all their efforts made progress, owing to their freedom, friendliness, and mutual interchange of reason."[37]

Plato's musings may not be taken at face value, but there is little question, based on ample historical evidence, that Achaemenid Persia was one of the most tolerant empires to have ever existed, including toward defeated populations. As the Old Testament tells us, Cyrus allowed the Jews who had been exiled in Babylon by Nebuchadnezzar to return to Jerusalem to rebuild their temple. In a text inscribed in a clay cylinder, now at the British Museum, Cyrus calls himself "king of the world" and records his conquest of Babylon in 539 BC. The text states that Cyrus stopped the slave labor of the local population, restored the temples and religious cults of the people of neighboring countries, and, as with the Jews, allowed deported people in Babylon to return to their native lands.[38]

In part because of his reputation for tolerance, Cyrus has served as a role model for world leaders through the ages, from Alexander the Great to Thomas Jefferson. Jefferson, the author of the American Declaration of Independence, read *Cyropaedia* (his copy is now at the Smithsonian in Washington, DC), the account of the Persian emperor by Greek historian and philosopher Xenophon, who looked on Cyrus as an ideal ruler. Jefferson was especially attracted to the Persian model of a state made up of diverse cultures without a dominant religion.[39]

Nevertheless, the West has typically embraced a dark portrayal of Persia, one that ignores the empire's general preference for indirect rule over its conquered territories, which allowed the extant cultures to flourish. One such example is how Persian rule over the Greek colonies on the Anatolian coast did not extinguish Greek intellectual endeavors. The region continued its scientific and philosophical achievements under the local Greek rulers installed by the Persians.[40] The origins of Greek philosophy, dated between 580 and 500 BC, straddle the onset of the Persian conquest of Anatolia. While the first Ionian heavyweight minds—Thales (624–548 BC), Anaximander (610–546 BC), and Anaximenes (585–528 BC)—were prior to Persian rule, others emerged during Persian hegemony. One such philosopher was Heraclitus of Ephesus (born 540 BC), who viewed the universe as being in a constant state of flux (rather than in stasis), and whose ideas influenced Plato.

There is little evidence that Persia or Persian-backed Greek rulers persecuted Greek intellectuals. In contrast, Greeks persecuted their own philosophers who challenged orthodoxy and sided with Persia. Anaxagoras, who provided the first scientific explanations of eclipses and meteorites, was born in Clazomenae in 500 BC, when it was under Persian control. He went to Athens to pursue his work but was banished from there for his pro-Persian views. By 500 BC, Miletus, the center of the Ionian revolt, had recovered and seemed to be "flourishing" intellectually and economically under indirect Persian rule.[41]

Politically, a fair number of Greek polities and trading settlements—including ones in central Greece such as Thebes, Argos, and Megara—preferred Persian rule or protection over that of such Greek powers as Athens and Sparta. The "mild overlordship of the Persians was a lesser evil than the destructive harshness of their Greek enemies."[42] Sometimes even the oracle of Delphi advised cities to take the Persian side. Not only was Persian rule looser and more respectful of local autonomy than Greek rule, but it also offered opportunities for the conquered state to enhance their trade, facilitated by the Persian Empire's extensive roadways and transport system.

Many Greeks also served the Persian military and administrative system. When Alexander the Great started his offensive against the Persian Empire, his opponents often included Greek soldiers and commanders serving Persia, as at the Battle of the Granicus (now Biga River in Turkey), which was Alexander's first victorious military encounter with Persia (although the Persian king, Darius III, did not take part in this battle). Persia also offered escape for Greeks from internal troubles and purges. It's a matter of some irony that Themistocles, the much celebrated hero at Salamis, himself sought refuge from Athens when the city turned against him. He fled to the Persian court and found employment there as a governor until the end of his life.

Moreover, Persia protected several Greek city-states from losing their independence to predatory Greek neighbors. In the fourth century BC, for example, some of these city-states thwarted conquests by Sparta, Athens, and Thebes only by enlisting the support of the Persian superpower.[43] Similarly, Persian intervention was decisive in the outcome of the Peloponnesian War. Here, it wasn't so much Persian military might that played a role as Persian funding, or Persian gold; the fall of Athens in 404 BC came about because of Persian financing of Spartan naval power.[44] The Greek city-states often relied on Persia to be the balancer. When it comes to world-order building, the Greek city-state system was not autonomous but was actually in many ways a Persian-Hellenic system.[45]

For students of world order, it is worth asking why Persia got involved in Greek mainland affairs after the Ionian revolt. Part of the reason, already noted, was to punish Athens for having supported the rebellion. But the Persian motive was also shaped by the Achaemenid worldview, which imposed a universal responsibility to prevent chaos and maintain stability in the empire and around its periphery.[46] There is nothing unusual about this. As we have seen, defeating chaos and establishing order have been the key motives behind world-order making in civilizations and empires throughout history. Much the same can be said about the United States after World War II, as it set about creating its own world order.

A final point about the Greek-Persian conflict: the victories meant more to the Greeks than the defeats did to the Persians. The Persians had bigger things to attend to, especially managing their vast empire, which included keeping the peace among the quarrelsome Greeks. The Greeks viewed the Persian wars as central to the development of their identity as a people, but for Persians, the Greek conflicts were mostly small, peripheral matters that caused no great distress when they went wrong.[47]

The argument here is not that the Persian world order was, by today's standards, devoid of dark and violent aspects. Rather I argue that the Western narrative of the history of world order has focused only on the unsavory aspects of the Persian Empire, as it has on the negative elements of other non-Western world orders. The overriding idea in the West has been to present Greece as the birthplace of a free and benign world order of Western liberalism. Persia and the others, by contrast, are portrayed as unrelievedly despotic and therefore unable to make positive contributions to a peaceful and progressive world order. But this exaltation of ancient Greece and denigration of non-Western civilizations is a blinkered and biased view of history, one that needs to be reexamined as the world careens toward a new, post-American world order.

Educating Alexander

The Persian Achaemenid Empire was defeated by Alexander the Great in the fourth century BC.[48] Victory made Alexander not only the greatest conqueror of the ancient world but also the greatest pupil of the East.

Alexander grew up in the court of Macedon, under the unforgiving and perhaps unloving watch of his father, Philip. Philip claimed to be a descendant of Heracles, the Greek warrior turned god. Alexander saw himself as the descendant of Achilles, the legendary hero of the Trojan War. Alexander's mother, Olympias, was convinced of his divine birth, a belief Alexander himself eventually embraced. He thought of himself as the son of Zeus—the Greek sky god, the wielder of the lightning bolt, the protector and ruler—rather than of his mortal father, Philip.

How did this transformation come about? It happened during Alexander's campaign in Egypt in 332–331 BC, especially in Memphis, the old capital, and Siwa, an oasis in the northwest. A little background will help here. When Alexander arrived in Memphis in 332 BC, he had already fought a hard campaign against the Persian King Darius III, defeating him in the Battle of Issus (in southern Turkey today) in November of the previous year. Though his mother, wife, and two daughters were taken captive by the Macedonians, Darius III himself escaped. Persia was still not conquered. But before Alexander turned to a final assault on Persia, his main goal, he decided to make a detour to Egypt.

There might be two reasons for this fateful decision. Since Egypt was part of the Persian Empire, it was logical that Alexander would conquer it, along with other Persian provinces in the area. Hence, taking Egypt would be an important step in Alexander's main political goal: the conquest of Persia.

But Egypt was the westernmost part of the empire and was only loosely administered by Persia. There was no big strategic gain to be made by capturing Egypt if the goal was to defeat Darius III, who had fled much further east to Babylon. Moreover, the detour to Egypt required more than a thousand additional miles of hazardous desert for Alexander to traverse, and, since conquering the Persian Empire was without doubt Alexander's main goal, the journey to Egypt could have but a minor strategic purpose. Alexander would have had more reason immediately to pursue Darius III after his victory at Issus before the Persian king could regroup and rebuild his forces.

This brings us to the second reason for Alexander's decision to detour to Egypt, which was less political than it was personal and psychological. Unlike Persia, Egypt was culturally attractive to the Greeks, who respected its religion and marveled at its monuments. This made it a perfect place for Alexander to realize his longing to be recognized as a god. Egypt had the pharaonic temples where Alexander could reimagine himself as a divine world conqueror.

Not surprisingly, among Alexander's first acts there was to perform a sacrifice to Hapi (Apis in Greek), the Egyptian sacred bull at Memphis. In return, he received the double crown (representing Upper and Lower Egypt) reserved only for the pharaohs. As Alexander's modern biographer Peter Green writes, this episode, and the subsequent months he spent in Egypt, "turned into a profoundly felt emotional and spiritual experience" for Alexander. When the "young Macedonian was solemnly instated as the Pharaoh...at last, [his mother] Olympias' belief in his divine birth found a wholly acceptable context."[49]

After Memphis, Alexander turned west, to visit the famous oracle temple of Siwa in the Libyan desert. This was the temple of Zeus-Amun, or Ammon, named after a hybrid Greco-Egyptian deity. The chauvinistic

Image 3. Alexander the Great as divine king of Egypt, paying homage to the god Zeus-Amun. Luxor Temple.

Greeks had absorbed some foreign deities into their own pantheon by identifying them with one of their own deities. Thus, one of Egypt's most important gods, Amun-Re, from whom the pharaohs were believed to have been descended, had been identified with ancient Greece's most powerful god, Zeus, to form Zeus-Amun.

As the Greek historian Arrian, the chronicler of Alexander's campaigns, tells the story, Alexander revered the oracle of Zeus-Amun as "truthful" and wanted to consult it to learn what the future held in store for him.[50] Once the Macedonian reached Siwa, the priest of the temple "greeted Alexander as the son of Ammon."[51] Alexander asked the oracle "whether he himself was destined for world rule."[52] The priest was believed to have replied—although Alexander would tell no one what exactly happened inside the shrine—that he indeed was.

The ancient Greeks distinguished between two types of personal divinity: being a god and being the son of a god. In Egypt, Alexander became both: "Amid the ancient splendors of Egypt—a civilization which invariably bred semi-mystical awe in the Greek mind—he learned that he was in truth a god, and the son of a god," Green writes. This was "a psychological turning-point in his life."[53]

After his religious fulfillment in Egypt, Alexander turned his attention to political fulfillment: the final defeat of Persia and the affirmation of himself as the lord of Asia. His intentions in this regard had already become clear soon after his first victorious encounter with Darius III at Issus. According to Arrian, the Persian ruler sent Alexander a letter offering him an alliance. Alexander's reply: "In the future, whenever you send word to me, address yourself to me as king of Asia."[54]

It is important to stress here that Alexander preferred Eastern-style monarchy to Greek-style republic, and he was especially inspired by the Persian monarchy. His father, Philip, had coveted the conquest of Persia to attain divine king status.[55] As Greek rhetorician Isocrates writes, when Philip "shall force the king who is now called Great [i.e., the great king of Persia] to do whatever you command...then will naught be left for [him] except to become a god."[56] Alexander was also emulating the Persian system, and in this he was likely influenced by his tutor: none other than the famed Greek philosopher Aristotle, whom Alexander had continued to revere long after his studies were completed.[57] It may surprise people today that Aristotle regarded monarchy as a superior form of government to democracy. Democracy produced "anarchic mob rule," Aristotle believed, and he left open the possibility that a monarchy could serve the common good, provided it did not serve the ruler's selfish interest (in which case it would be classified as tyranny).[58] Some historians argue that Aristotle did not see the Persian monarchy as tyranny; he had praised Cyrus the Great as a virtuous king for liberating his people from the previous rulers, the Medians.[59]

Alexander also did not establish the republican polis system of the Greeks in the territories he conquered. Instead, he emulated the great king of Persia by establishing his own rule.[60] To administer his new empire, he adopted the Persian administrative system of satraps, who would owe their allegiance to their overlord, Alexander himself.[61] In Phrygia, for example, the Greek kingdom in what is now central Turkey, he installed the general Calas as satrap, but under Alexander's overlordship. In short, Alexander did "not so much vanquish the Persian Empire as usurped its throne."[62] He was emulating and adopting the Persian world order.

While Alexander himself hailed from a monarchy, the court of Macedonia was more limited in its powers and less extravagant in its royal customs than that of Persia. Persia offered him the opportunity to display the full glamour and authority of a divine king and a universal emperor.

Alexander was also trying to create a common political order by fusing Persian and Greek civilizations to build a "world kingdom" or "brotherhood of man."[63] His actions to this end included marriages he arranged for Greek and Macedonian men with women of Persia and other conquered territories, including his own marriage to Roxana, a princess of Sogdiana, an Iranian culture in present-day Uzbekistan. He urged Macedonians and Greeks to adopt Persian customs and clothing and vice versa. From the border of India to the Mediterranean coast of Egypt, he founded a series of cities (all named Alexandria) to promote economic and cultural links among diverse peoples, which spread Greek ideas (including science and philosophy) and innovations to the east and did the reverse, spreading Eastern ideas and culture to the Greek world. Most egregiously, Alexander not only dressed up as a Persian king but also asked his Macedonian and Greek officers to prostrate themselves before approaching him. Arrian suggests that Alexander adopted this particular Persian court ritual to earn the loyalty of his new Persian subjects by demonstrating that he, too, was a divine king like the Achaemenid rulers.[64]

Alexander's policies as the ruler of Persia had paradoxical effects. On the one hand, they challenged the insular mindset of the Greeks— including Aristotle's view, which he might have conveyed to his pupil, that non-Greeks should be treated like animals and plants. Alexander's actions meant that the Greeks would now have to accept some non-Greeks as civilized, and he might have created a greater awareness of a shared *homonoia* (implying unity of mankind).

On the other hand, Alexander's ideas about shared humanity invited opposition and even ridicule from some of his fellow Greek and Macedonian officers. For example, one of Alexander's aides, Hermolaus, was so offended by his adoption of Persian customs that he told him, in the words of Roman historian Quintus Curtius Rufus:

> You delivered us to the barbarians and by a novel fashion made the victors pass under the yoke. It is the Persians' garb and habits that delight you; you have come to loathe the customs of your native land....You wished the Macedonians to bow the knee to you and to venerate you as a god, you reject Philip as a father, and if any of the gods were regarded as greater than Jupiter [as Romans called the Greek deity Zeus], you would disdain even Jupiter. Do you wonder if we, who are free men, can endure your haughtiness?[65]

The Greek philosopher Callisthenes was a vocal opponent of Alexander, arguing that by accepting such "excessive honors," Alexander was "degrading the gods unduly," because in Greek culture one prostrated oneself only to the gods.[66]

Had Alexander not died so young, his efforts to unite Greek and Persian civilizations might have borne fruit. Nevertheless, even in his death, he helped to perpetuate the institution of divine kingship, which, as previously noted, was a unique invention of the Sumerians and Egyptians of the third millennium BC. His conversion to divine pharaonic status would be emulated by the Ptolemaic kings (descended from Alexander's general Ptolemy) who ruled Egypt after Alexander's death. Today, during a visit to Luxor Temple in Egypt, one could see the reliefs of Alexander himself and the Ptolemaic rulers making offerings to the god Ammon at the "Alexander shrine," which was built by the Ptolemaic dynasty after Alexander's death. Alexander would become the role model of countless Western and Eastern rulers. The founder of the

Roman Empire, Augustus, also revered Alexander and sought to emulate him. Augustus had visited the tomb of Alexander to place flowers and a golden crown on it. When asked whether he also wanted to see the tomb of the Ptolemaic rulers, Augustus's reply was, "My wish was to see a king, not corpses."[67] In the fifteenth century AD, the founder of the Malacca Sultanate, Parameswara, claimed to be a descendant of Iskandar, a Malay name for Alexander.

The Greeks made huge contributions to Western civilization—in science, philosophy, medicine, politics, and the arts—that have been integral to the evolution of global civilization. Nevertheless, romanticizing and exaggerating the civilization of ancient Greece, which has been the bedrock of the idea of the West, is unwarranted. Moreover, this has created, in the words of the distinguished historian of ancient India Romila Thapar, an "inferiority complex" among other civilizations.[68] In contrast, Persia's role in managing Greek affairs and its contribution to world order are vilified and dismissed in Western narratives, which happen to be drawn mainly from biased Greek historians. The world needs to acknowledge the legacy of Greek civilization, but the West and the world at large can also learn from Persia's legacy, which includes religious and ethnic tolerance, an ability co-opt other cultures, and the capacity to administer vast territories.

The story of Alexander the Great provides the first of many examples—to be followed by China, India, and Islam—of Eastern ideas and institutions influencing the West and the mutual interaction among civilizations propelling world order. In 326 BC, in his quest to conquer India, Alexander fought an epic battle against King Porus at the Hydaspes River. Alexander narrowly won the battle, but his troops were so traumatized by the experience that they refused to march any further east to conquer the Indian heartland. This made the Hydaspes battle Alexander's last, and he died three years later in Babylon.

In other words, Alexander was not defeated but deterred from further conquest at the Indian frontier. He won the battle but lost the war against India. This not only saved India from potential Macedonian colonization but also allowed other Indian warriors to pursue their own territorial expansion. Among them was a youth named Chandragupta, who, if the Greek historian Plutarch is to be believed, "saw Alexander himself" during his campaigns in the area. Not long after, Chandragupta would become the founder of the Maurya Empire, India's first. After taking power, Chandragupta, Plutarch further notes, "often remarked" that Alexander had come very close to conquering India.[69] If so, this would have instilled in the Maurya leader the impulse to build a powerful empire of his own to defend against foreign intruders—such as Alexander's successor in Asia, Seleucus—something he did with success. It is to India's story that we turn in the next chapter.

Chapter 3

Conquest and Compassion

The Origins of India

The first known Indian civilization flourished in the valley of the Indus River during the third millennium BC. Known as the Indus valley civilization or Harappan civilization after one of its major archaeological sites, it declined in the early second millennium BC. But as this civilization waned, migrating Indo-European-speaking people originating from the Pontic Steppe area arrived via northwestern routes. There has been a heated political debate in India over the scale and impact of this migration, with some even questioning whether it happened at all. But recent genetic studies confirm the arrival of new people in northern India.[1] In all likelihood, this was not an invasion or displacement of the older culture by the new but a fusion between them: it is when the next phase of Indian civilization took shape, strongly influenced by the four main Vedas, or sacred texts, of Hinduism.[2] Initially centered on the plains of the Ganges River, this Hindu-Vedic culture gradually spread southward, interacting and absorbing preexisting regional civilizations and giving shape to some of the core but diverse elements of Indian religion, culture, philosophy, and way of life that exist to this date.

Politically, India remained fragmented into small polities. More than a thousand years would pass before India's first universal empire would emerge, under the Maurya dynasty in the late fourth century BC. A succession of Hindu-Buddhist empires and kingdoms would dot the Indian landscape until the arrival of Islam around the tenth century AD. Thereafter, a series of Muslim dynasties would rule northern India, some extending far to the south, the most notable among them being the Delhi Sultanate and the Moghul Empire. They would compete and coexist with Hindu states, which the British, arriving in the seventeenth century, would gradually take over as they created and ruled the crown jewel of their empire until India became independent in 1947.

India is among the oldest of the world's civilizations. Indeed, in its way, it is very likely the oldest continuing one. While Sumer, Egypt, and Peru are arguably earlier civilizations than India, the societies and countries that replaced them have retained little continuity with their earliest forms. Sumer and Egypt were culturally transformed by Islam from the seventh century AD onward, much more so than Egypt had been by the earlier Greco-Roman colonization. Peru's civilization was killed off by European colonization. This is not to say that indigenous elements did not survive or do not matter today. But India and China, despite both having been subjected to foreign invasion and rule, have maintained much more of their original cultures than these other early civilizations did, and many of their approaches to social order today evoke the ancient past. Between the two, India had an earlier start: the latest estimated date of the emergence of the Harappan civilization is about 2500 BC, and China's Xia dynasty emerged around 2000 BC. We need more research and less nationalism from both the Indian and Chinese sides to establish this. But if, as is likely, the thesis of mutual cultural assimilation between the Indus valley people and steppe migrants holds true—thereby preserving some core social features and beliefs of both groups—then India would have a fair claim to being the world's longest continuing civilization.

More important for the purpose of this book is India's role in developing some of the key features of world orders regarding politics, knowledge development, and interstate relations. These include early forms of republican government, rational and philosophical inquiry into the origins of the universe, and ways of organizing an empire. Also out of India came two contrasting ways of organizing a world order: one through ruthless warfare and imperialism, the other through morality, benevolent rule, and peaceful accommodation of adversaries. India offers the most striking example of how a civilization can export its religion and political ideas to foreign lands without conquest or coercion. Many of these foundational contributions had already emerged in the pre-Islamic period of Indian history, starting around the middle of the second millennium BC, and remained vibrant through the Islamic and British colonial periods. It is to those foundational elements that we now turn.

The social life and living conditions of the Harappan people are known from excavations (which are continuing), even though their written language has yet to be deciphered. But the available evidence, including buildings made of uniform-size fired bricks, public baths, and covered sewers, suggests that it was perhaps the most highly urbanized civilization of its time, much more so than contemporary civilizations in Sumer and Egypt. Harappan weights and measures were standardized, which points to organized commercial activity, and there is evidence of substantial trading links with contemporary Sumerian centers such as Ur. But the political system of the Harappan people remains blurry. The archaeological excavations done so far have not yet found evidence of monumental architecture—such as great temples, palaces, or rich burial places—leading some historians to view Harappan civilization as a "society of equals," unlike the highly stratified societies of Egypt and Sumer.[3]

We know more about the political systems of northern India after the second millennium BC, which gradually saw the rise of larger and more organized polities. By 600 BC, there were sixteen polities, called the Mahajanapadas, in the north: Kasi, Kosala, Anga, Magadha, Vajji, Malla, Chedi, Vatsa, Kuru, Panchala, Machcha, Surasena, Assaka, Avanti, Gandhara, and Kamboja. Some of these Mahajanapadas were ruled by hereditary aristocrats; five, known as *gana-sanghas*, literally "people assemblies," were republics.

This classical Indian state system was anarchic—the term here indicating not disorder but the absence of a higher political or spiritual authority, like an emperor or a pope. The *gana-sanghas* allowed for greater participation of people than did monarchies and empires elsewhere. The means of choosing the ruler was through elections, usually by fellow aristocrats, somewhat in the way of the ancient Greek city-states and Roman Republic, which were roughly contemporaries of the *gana-sanghas.*

One should not forget that the political system in ancient Greece was not uniform but consisted of monarchies, "democracies," and "tyrannies." The Roman Republic—which originated after the overthrow of the Roman Kingdom in 509 BC, and which is thought to have served as a model for the United States—was not a democracy, but it was a republic nevertheless. Similarly, in some of the ancient Indian republican communities, a large number of people had some say in their government.[4] Like the Greek city-states, these Indian republics were oligarchic, meaning that political participation and voting rights were limited to an economically privileged class. Viewed as such, India, too, provides some of the earliest examples of the institution of the republic in human history.

It is noteworthy that, despite the emergence of the Maurya Empire in the late fourth century BC, republican states continued to exist until at least the Gupta Empire some five hundred years later. Some historians claim that these systems existed over much of India.[5] The main political institutions in the *gana-sanghas* (although some monarchies also had them) were two: the *sabha* and the *samiti.* The *sabha* was an inner council of prominent individuals, while the *samiti* brought together heads of families.[6] While this was an elitist and clan-based system, it nonetheless allowed debate, disagreement, and decision by voting. In the *samitis,* as historian Romila Thapar describes, "the matter for discussion was placed before the assembly and debated, and if a unanimous decision could not be reached it was put to a vote."[7]

It is therefore not surprising that the *gana-sanghas* also gave the world its "earliest theory approaching that of a social contract," as Thapar has put it, outlining the likely sequence of developments that began with the notion of ownership and the family. Once property

70

rights were established, there was a need for laws and rules by which disputes could be adjudicated, and that led to the need for a single person, the Mahasammata (Great Elect), who would have the responsibility of maintaining justice through his rule.[8]

This theory of the state came to be associated with Buddhism—whose founder, Gautama, was a prince of the Shakya clan *gana-sangha*—which began as a protest against the Hindu political order, predominant until then. That order was characterized by a rigid hierarchy institutionalized by the caste system, which placed the Brahmans (priests and religious leaders) at the top and the so-called untouchables at the bottom.[9] Buddhism not only discarded the caste system but also offered a rational and practical explanation for the need for political authority, one connected to the notions of rights, justice, and order. Although Buddhism stressed *nirvana* (transcending worldly life), it also offered a secular and pragmatic view of order, somewhat similar to how Enlightenment thinker Rousseau would explain the need for political authority from an idyllic state of nature. This contrasted with orthodox Hinduism's more theological understanding, which saw order resulting from the victory of gods over demons, representing goodness and chaos respectively.

Throughout ancient Indian history, various small rival kingdoms and republics were more typical than large, dominant empires.[10] The relationships among these states were governed by war, alliance making, and diplomacy. Some accounts suggest a relationship of hostility, even "a perpetual state of warfare."[11] The eventual consolidation of these states occurred through both "conquest and encroachment." In the fifth century BC, a bipolar struggle for dominance ensued between the two most powerful states, Magadha and Kosala, as both tried to annex smaller tribal states.[12]

Competing Views of World Order

Ancient Indian political thought offers contrasting approaches to building a world order, with two concepts especially important. One is represented by the text *Arthashastra*, the title of which broadly refers to a manual about economic or material gain.[13] While the identity of the author—most widely thought to be the philosopher Kautilya—and the date of composition are debated, the authenticity of the text itself is not in doubt.[14] What is also beyond doubt is that the *Arthashastra* is the most important text from ancient India outlining a theory of statecraft, diplomacy, and warfare. It contains a highly developed system of thinking, describing how to build an empire by competing with and conquering neighboring states through such means as war, assassinations, and spying.

As such, the *Arthashastra* belongs to what modern political scientists call the realist school of politics, holding that human beings are by nature selfish and competitive. This human tendency makes the constant struggle for power and dominance a natural and inevitable facet of relations among countries, such that a country's foreign policy should take war as a necessary mechanism to advance its interests. In this respect, Kautilya is often compared with the Renaissance political thinker Niccolò Machiavelli (1469–1527 AD) and the advice he gave to his prince about acquiring and maintaining power, although Kautilya's work predates the latter by a long stretch of history. It is in the *Arthashastra* that one finds the world's first systematic framework of building alliances, practicing diplomacy, spying, and conducting foreign policy and interstate relations.

Kautilya's elaborate schema consists of a "mandala" theory, in which an aspiring conqueror (called *vijigisu*) is surrounded by four main kinds of states: friends, enemies, middle kings, and neutral states. The countries immediately bordering the *vijigisu*'s territory are his enemies, whereas those surrounding the enemies' territory are likely to be his friends.[15] Kautilya thus gave expression to the doctrine summed up in the phrase, "The enemy of my enemy is my friend." The neutral kings are expected to stay out of the conflict, while the middle kings can either support or oppose the *vijigisu*, and as such they can either be cultivated or attacked by him; they are also potential mediators in a conflict.

This is a dynamic model. The actual pattern of alliances and rivalries does not depend on a predetermined geographic location. Rather, it is the incentives and sanctions pursued by the would-be conqueror—such as compensation, conciliation, divide and rule, and force—which ultimately shape the loyalty and opposition of other states in the neighborhood and beyond. To this end, Kautilya prescribes a set of foreign policy measures to the aspiring conqueror, ranging from entering into peace treaties to remaining passive to preemptively striking the enemy to pursuing a double policy of seeking alliance with one ruler and confronting another. Moreover, Kautilya recognized popular support as key to success in empire building. He advocated attacks against strong-but-unjust kings over conquering weak-but-just rulers, perhaps the only time such a principle has been advocated anywhere in the world. Attacking countries ruled by just and benevolent kings is unwise, he believed, because this would lead people of the target country to rise up against the conqueror: "Which enemy is to be marched against—a powerful enemy of wicked character or a powerless enemy of righteous character? The strong enemy of wicked character should be marched against, for when he is attacked, his subjects will not help him, but rather put him down or go to the side of the conqueror. But when the enemy of virtuous character is attacked, his subjects will help him or die with him."[16]

The predominant element in Kautilya's realist philosophy was the necessity of force. Still, a careful reading of *Arthashastra* shows that it was not just a celebration of raw power. It also allowed some place for virtue and restraint, even if for political reasons.[17] "Power is three fold," Kautilya states. "The power of knowledge is the power of counsel, the power of the treasury and the army is the power of might, the power of valor is the power of energy."[18] To succeed, a king must not only be born into an aristocratic family and possess physical strength, courage, and energy; he must also be "pious, truthful in speech, not breaking his promise, grateful, and liberal"—in essence, moral qualities that will enhance his legitimacy before the people.[19] And he must treat his newly conquered subjects humanely. A conquering king, for example, should "cause the honouring of all deities and hermitages, and make grants of land, money and exemptions to men distinguished in learning, speech and piety, order the release of all prisoners and render help to the distressed, the helpless and the diseased."[20] Behaving this way would reduce disaffection and the possibility of future revolt. It may have been a very pragmatic reason for a humane approach, but it was humane nonetheless.

The second major political tradition from ancient India came from Ashoka, the third emperor of the Maurya Empire, who ruled between 269 and 232 BC. In contrast to Kautilya, Ashoka's concept of statecraft was based on peaceful, moral rule. Several Buddhist sources describe the young Ashoka as a cruel man who killed his siblings to seize the throne of Magadha, but after winning a bloody war against the hitherto independent eastern coastal state of Kalinga (the modern state of Odisha) around 261 BC, he became a devout Buddhist, thereby transforming himself into a virtuous ruler.[21] Ashoka's early brutality might have been exaggerated by Buddhist writers so as to make the impact of his conversion look more significant, but on one of his stone inscriptions, Ashoka did admit to the death of one hundred thousand people during the Kalinga war and many more thereafter (presumably from injuries, hunger, and disease), with another 150,000 taken as prisoners—both very large numbers in any age.[22]

What seems less doubtful is that after the Kalinga war, Ashoka never waged war again, and he forbade his descendants from doing so. To be sure, he didn't give up his empire, since that would have been impractical, but he forbade any further extension of it: "Any sons or great grandsons that I may have should not think of gaining new conquests, and in whatever victories they may gain should be satisfied with patience and light punishment."[23] Instead, Ashoka pursued a policy of dharma—the law of piety or righteousness—an early philosophy of humanitarianism based on universal affection for all people.[24] Everybody was included in a network of righteous relationships, such that monitors were appointed in the palace to ensure that nobody failed to observe the law of piety, even the emperor and empress. And it was not only a moral law governing the relations of people inside a state but applied to foreign relations as well.[25]

Ashoka's dharma has three major elements. The first concerns relations between the ruler and the subjects. This is captured in an edict of Ashoka's inscribed on a rock erected near the very site of his bloody victory against Kalinga, which reads: "All men are my children, and just

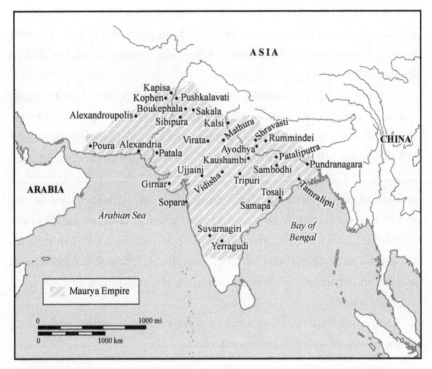

Map 3. The Maurya Empire at its greatest extent.

as I desire for my children that they should obtain welfare and happiness both in this world and the next, the same do I desire for all men."[26] Ashoka then goes on to prohibit unjust conduct, including torture and imprisonment by the state against his subjects: "While being completely law-abiding, some people are imprisoned, treated harshly and even killed without cause so that many people suffer... the judicial officers of the city may strive to do their duty and that the people under them might not suffer unjust imprisonment or harsh treatment."[27] The edict further stipulates that the principles laid out in his edicts must be "read aloud" every four months to the general public (they were frequently read at important public gatherings as well), and, more strikingly, "a single person" could demand to have them read aloud whenever he or she wished to hear them, a sort of ancient on-demand channel.[28] All this would increase awareness of the emperor's protections, especially among people who were not literate. Such readings would not only remind people of the law of dharma but also act as a check on state officials. At the very least, this rule conferred on every layperson a right to ask for and to know the law.

Hence, in his elaboration of limits on state power, Ashoka anticipated contemporary human rights norms, which also provide protection against the harsh and cruel punishment of individuals by the state.[29] What Ashoka offered, however, wasn't the same as the modern human rights notion of the legal entitlement a wronged citizen has against the actions of the government. Such protection only emerged late in the modern period, first in Europe and then more generally, and its application varies widely even among democratic societies. But Ashoka's instructions to state judicial officials prohibiting "unjust imprisonment and harsh treatment" were at the origins of the concept of human rights in ancient times.

A second element of dharma concerns relations with neighboring states, as stipulated in another rock edict:

It might occur to the frontier people outside my territory: "What are the king's wishes with respect to us?" This alone is my wish with respect to the frontier people—this, they should realize, is the king's wish, that they may not fear me, but have confidence in me that they will procure happiness alone from me, not grief; that the king will forgive what can be forgiven; that they may practice dharma on my account; and that they may secure this world and the next.[30]

A third element of dharma was religious tolerance. In another of his rock edicts, Ashoka conveys that his kingdom would honor all religious sects and their followers, whether they are ascetics or ordinary people. He urges people not to speak ill of the beliefs of others while extravagantly praising their own. As it reads, "Whoever honours his own sect or disparages that of another man, wholly out of devotion to his own... harms his own sect even more seriously."[31] He advises that people should not only

Image 4. Chakravartin, Amaravati Stupa, India, first century AD.

tolerate but also respect others' religious beliefs. Such mutual respect would advance the progress of all religions and promote cooperation in society. While religious tolerance was present in other civilizations— such as ancient Persia and Rome in practice—Ashoka's was perhaps the earliest and strongest statement of an official policy affirming religious freedom, certainly well ahead of anything the West had to offer. The relevance of Ashoka's ideas for promoting religious and political harmony in the contemporary world, including in India today, is too obvious to need elaboration.

Ashoka thus built a world order around renunciation of force (if not of empire), benevolent rule, and reassurance to independent neighbors. He implemented a policy of nonviolence that protected people as well as animals—animal sacrifice, a widespread practice in the ancient world, was forbidden under his watch. For his promotion of moral statecraft,

Ashoka would be called a *chakravartin*, which can roughly be understood as "virtuous universal emperor." The first part of the word, *chakra*, translates into wheel, while *vartin* means the one who rolls. The wheel is a major symbol of Indian culture. It is what moves a war chariot (a symbol of power) and is also the disk of the Hindu god Vishnu, whose role is to act as the maintainer of the cosmic order. One of India's major contributions to the idea of world order, the term *chakravartin* is more ambiguous than the image of a peaceful and righteous ruler. It also connotes the war-making role of the emperor to establish universal authority. The word was used by both Hindu and Buddhist rulers of ancient India—attesting to the deep connection between the two faiths—to designate a world conqueror and universal emperor. One might be reminded here that Ashoka himself, while renouncing further conquest after taking Kalinga, never gave freedom to the people there or in any of the other territories he had conquered earlier.

The idea of *chakravartin* is deeply mythologized in popular Indian lore to this day, as seen from the massive Indian TV serial of 2015–2016 *Chakravartin Ashoka Samrat* (*samrat* meaning "emperor" in Hindi). It also became, in the words of one scholar, a "paradigm" or "model" for the Buddhist rulers in Burma, Thailand, Cambodia, and Indonesia. Rulers of these countries used the idea of *chakravartin* to legitimize themselves before their subjects and neighbors, even though they never renounced their right to wage war and pillage.[32] In Tang dynasty China, as will be discussed in the next chapter, Wu Zetian, the only female emperor of China, commissioned texts and called in Indian priests to anoint herself as a *chakravartin* to fend off rivals to the throne. It is thus a prime example of Indian cultural influence over Asia.[33]

To sum up, while Ashoka and Kautilya at first glance seem to represent two radically different approaches to world order, they were not mutually exclusive. Kautilya most certainly did not advocate a purely moral conquest of the kind Ashoka practiced after his war with Kalinga. The philosopher's intention was to provide a ruler with all of the tools—espionage, assassination, alliance, and outright invasion—to subjugate other states. Ashoka called for turning swords into ploughshares.

Kautilya advised the opposite: "When one has an army, one's ally remains friendly, or (even) the enemy becomes friendly."[34] At the same time, the *Arthashastra* is not a treatise of unabashed militant realpolitik as conventionally presented, and Ashoka, while forsaking further conquest after Kalinga, did not liberate it or other territories he had already acquired through violent conquest. Nevertheless, the Ashokan paradigm of renouncing war has never been repeated, in India or abroad.

This leads to a larger point. Indian history is full of violent warfare, and Indian rulers, with the partial exception of Ashoka, have never forsaken conquest and imperial control. Even rulers who professed Buddhism and Jainism and emphasized strict nonviolence in personal life have been expansionist when they had the capability and opportunity. King Kharavela, who ruled Kalinga during the second and first century BC after it had broken away from Maurya rule, was a patron of Jainism. That religion, which much later influenced Mohandas Gandhi, is perhaps the most nonviolent one in India, or the world, as it even forbids harming insects. Nevertheless, Kharavela built one of the largest Indian empires since the Mauryas by pursuing relentless military conquest.

India is also the birthplace of some of the earliest and most powerful ideas about peace and humanitarianism in the world. Some of these principles anticipated the modern notion of just war (or war waged for a justifiable or righteous cause), as well as rules concerning the treatment of noncombatants and defeated warriors. In the words of British historian of India A. L. Basham, "In no other part of the ancient world were the relations of man and man, and of man and the state, so fair and humane.... In all her history of warfare Hindu India has few tales to tell of cities put to the sword or of the massacre of noncombatants."[35] These principles might have been the ancient Indian philosophers' solution to the constant scourge of war. If they could not prevent wars from happening, they could at least narrow their justification and limit the destruction they caused.

Thus ancient India provides the idea of *dharma-yuddha*, or war undertaken to redress an injustice and fought according to principles of restraint, including the protection of civilians and humane treatment of injured and disarmed combatants. This idea is especially found in the two major Indian epics: the *Mahabharata* and the *Ramayana*. Both illustrate the timeless struggle between the forces of good and evil, with the outcome being the victory of the good. The older of these, the *Ramayana*, is about the virtuous Prince Rama of the northern Indian state of Kosala, who is denied the throne and exiled due to a family intrigue organized by his stepmother. While the prince, helped by his brother Laxmana, is in exile, his wife, Sita, is kidnapped by the demon-like King Ravana of Lanka (approximately present-day Sri Lanka). Rama, aided by an army of monkeys led by Hanuman, successfully fights and rescues his wife, and he returns to become the king of his land, which he rules with righteousness, justice, and prosperity.

The *Mahabharata* is especially important for its insights into classical Indian politics and relations among rulers and states. It tells of the rivalry between the just and virtuous five Pandava brothers and their greedy and unscrupulous cousins, the Kauravas, who number a hundred siblings. The Pandava brothers are the rightful heirs to the throne of Hastinapura but are tricked into exile by the Kauravas when they lose a game of dice that their cousins had rigged. After completing their exile, the Pandavas return to claim the throne but are rebuffed. War ensues, ending in total defeat for the Kauravas.

In narrating the conflict, the *Mahabharata*, and especially the seventeen chapters known as the Bhagavad Gita, offers one of the clearest ancient accounts of the rules regarding the conduct of war, or what is known today as just war. This section of the book is a kind of bible of Hinduism. Arjuna, the leading warrior among the Pandava brothers, is fearful of killing his own relatives, the Kauravas, and balks at the prospect of battle. But the driver of his chariot, Krishna, disagrees and tells Arjuna that war is sometimes justified, especially when the cause is just, when one's honor is at stake, and when one's enemies are at the door. Arjuna's cause was just, because his brothers had been cheated of their kingdom by the Kauravas. At the same time, fighting and winning the war would bring him not only honor but also territorial gain, while withdrawing from battle would convey weakness and cowardice and encourage aggression by his enemies. We can all relate to these motivations as rational and self-interested. They can be found in any contemporary discussion of war and peace. But Krishna the charioteer—who has divine attributes—adds another powerful reason Arjuna should fight instead of being overcome with guilt and remorse. To put it starkly, Krishna argues that worrying about killing one's relatives is pointless because the soul is immortal. This reasoning may seem metaphysical or spiritual, but ancient Indians more or less believed that the soul is real and its existence can be proven, something the Greeks possibly learned from them.[36] In any case, the *Mahabharata* illustrates the ways in which Indian civilization was eclectic in nature, combining spiritual, mystical, and rational elements.

Accompanying these ideas about why one should fight are principles of how to fight. The clearest exposition of humanitarian conduct in warfare comes from *Manusmriti* (Code of Manu), a classical and influential legal text dating to the first century BC. This text has close parallels with the modern principles of the Geneva Conventions concerning humanitarian treatment in war. Compare the relevant texts of the two:

Geneva Conventions

Persons taking no active part in the hostilities, including members of armed forces who have laid down their arms and those placed *hors de combat* by sickness, wounds, detention, or any other cause, shall in all circumstances be treated humanely.[37]

Manusmriti

When [the ruler] fights with his foes in battle, let him not strike:
who joins the palms of his hands (in supplication), who [flees]
who sits down, who says "I am thine"
who sleeps
who is disarmed, who looks on without taking part in the fight
whose weapons are broken
who is afflicted [with sorrow]

who has been grievously wounded, who is in fear, nor one who has turned to flight.[38]

Another idea of this period stresses inclusiveness, encapsulated in the Sanskrit phrase *vasudhaiva kutumbakam*, meaning the whole world is one family. This term, which comes from the *Maha Upanishad*, an Indian classic text, is inscribed on the walls of the Indian Parliament and has been part of the lexicon of India's leaders from Jawaharlal Nehru to Narendra Modi. It was uttered by US president Barack Obama in his address to the Indian Parliament in 2010.[39] Like the concept of *tianxia* (all under heaven) in China, *vasudhaiva kutumbakam* serves as a point of reference for the Indian worldview.

Emergence of Philosophy

India produced perhaps the earliest flowerings of philosophy, understood, first and foremost, as a debate over the universe's origin. This goes back to Vedic literature, emerging in the fifteenth century BC, long predating Greek philosophy, whose foundations in sixth century BC Ionia had several parallels with the earlier Indian concepts. A passage of the *Rig Veda*, known as the Song of Creation, reads:

> *Who really knows?...*
> *Whence is this creation?*
> *The gods came afterwards, with the creation of this universe*
> *Who then knows whence it has arisen?*[40]

The very suggestion that gods came after creation, not before, left room for inquiry and debate, rather than accepting a received wisdom about how the world was created by a god. In other texts of ancient India, the creation of society and life is attributed to natural elements such as fire (Agni), air (Vayu), and water (Varuna), even if these are worshipped as gods. The idea of Thales of Miletus—that water was the original single material cause of nature—for example, is strikingly similar to the Vedic notion of "primeval waters as the origin of the Universe."[41]

The rejection of the theory of the divine origins of the universe, a rejection that scholars regard as a hallmark of the secular modern world order, can also be found in other strands of ancient Indian philosophy. One relevant example here is the Samkhya school of thought, which originated in the Vedic period but became a distinct philosophy perhaps around the ninth and eighth centuries BC.[42] The two key concepts in Samkhya are *purusha*, a Sanskrit term understood as consciousness, and *prakriti*, literally "nature" in Sanskrit but understood as primeval matter, which can take endless forms. Unlike earlier Hindu schools of thought, which see both as the gods' creation, Samkhya philosophy views the *prakriti*, or the natural and the material, as independent of God or the soul. It is not the *purusha* but the *prakriti* that is the source of causation and evolution.[43] By stressing causation of the universe from nature and matter, rather than god, the Samkhya system is "essentially rational, anti-theistic, and intellectual." A key aim of Samkhya "is to explain the workings of nature through perceptual knowledge," and it "contradicts divine origins of the universe and the tenets of supernatural religion by substituting evolution for creation."[44] Instead, it holds that the primary constituents of the world, such as earth, water, fire, and air, were "eternal" and "the direction of the world was caused by the world itself."[45]

This has distinct echoes of the doctrine of the "eternity of the world," which is credited to Aristotle. That doctrine rejected divine creation and held that the universe was eternal, meaning that it was born out of cosmic and natural forces and therefore preexisted God. In Vedic India, which predated Greek civilization, one finds elements of both natural and divine creation, although the natural and rational elements of Indian civilization are often ignored in the West. Yet, "it was in Samkhya doctrine that complete independence and freedom of the human mind was exhibited for the first time in history."[46]

Indian philosophy did not completely rise above theological explanations. Rather, to the extent that the natural and the divine are deeply intertwined, India was similar to Greece, although in India, natural philosophy, scientific inquiry, and religion were more closely integrated. As S. Radhakrishnan, the Oxford University professor who became the second president of independent India, has written, "Religion, science, and humanism were sisters in ancient India; they were allies in Greece."[47]

There are other parallels between Indian and Greek philosophy, which might have been either coincidental or brought about by mutual contact. One example, already mentioned, is the immortality of the soul, which was a very influential idea in ancient India and Chaldea (in Babylon) before the Greeks, including Plato, made extensive use of it.[48] The Greek mathematician Pythagoras and his followers believed that beans and meat contained the souls of people and therefore shouldn't be eaten. Pythagoras himself claimed to remember four of his past lives. Moreover, both the Greeks and the Indians accepted the transmigration of the soul, but a key difference was that the Greek soul could choose its next life with the help of a guardian spirit after journeying to the river Lethe. For the Hindus, karma determines what kind of next life one might have.

Hinduism also has concepts of the recurring struggle of good versus evil and order versus chaos. One of the most important beliefs of Hindus, contained in the Bhagavad Gita, is that in every age, whenever there is a severe threat to dharma (righteousness) and a corresponding increase in unrighteousness, the god Vishnu will appear in an avatar, who will defeat the force of evil and reestablish virtue.[49] One of these avatar stories provides clues to the origins of Indian civilization: the story of the great flood, contained in the Vishnu and Matsya Puranas (meaning "lore" or "scripture"). Thapar calls this story the narrative of the "beginnings of India," which also begins the political history of India:

> The first rulers of the earth were called Manu, and the very first of them was called Manu Svayambhu. Svayambhu means self-born, but here it means he was directly born from Brahma. During the reign of his seventh descendant, a great flood occurred. The god Vishnu had warned of the Flood and asked Manu to prepare for it by building a boat. When the Flood came, Vishnu emerges as a large fish, ties the boat carrying Manu and seven sages to its horn, and takes them to a mountain peak until the flood eased.[50]

Although this is an account of the origins of India, it has striking parallels with the great flood of Mesopotamian legend and the Jewish story of Noah's ark, which might have been borrowed from the people of the Indus valley civilization.[51] The remarkable similarity of these myths shows the cultural diffusion that took place between the Indus valley people and the Mesopotamian and other civilizations. For the most part, as we've seen going as far back as Egypt and Sumer, civilizations have never been disconnected but have always been informed by exchanges of culture, technology, and materials, as well as by the violent exchange of warfare, and this rule applies as much to concepts of world order as it does to myths of origin.

The Indian Cosmopolis

Indian trading activities extended beyond Mesopotamia to Africa and to central Asia, Southeast Asia, and East Asia through the Eurasian and maritime Silk Road. The maritime dimension was important, consistent with India's location at the northern midpoint of the Indian Ocean trading network, which linked East Africa, the Red Sea, the Arabian Peninsula, and Persia to Southeast Asia and the China-centered East Asian region.[52]

India would continue to play a major role in long-distance trade, both through the Eurasian heartland and in the Indian Ocean. The Kushan Empire, built in the first to third centuries AD by the Yuezhi tribe—after they were pushed out of the western frontier areas of China by their Xiongnu rival during the Western Han dynasty, migrated from the lands west of China, and ruled northwestern India—was instrumental in developing Eurasian trade. The empire linked the Indian subcontinent, Afghanistan, and central Asia and became an important part of the Silk Road, which ran from China to the Mediterranean and was founded in the second century BC during China's Western Han dynasty. The Kushan domain was a hub of cultural fusion and transmission among Hindu, Persian, Chinese, steppe, and Mediterranean societies.

It was most likely the Kushans who brought Buddhism into China via the Silk Road.[53] A popular Chinese legend has it that in 65 AD, the

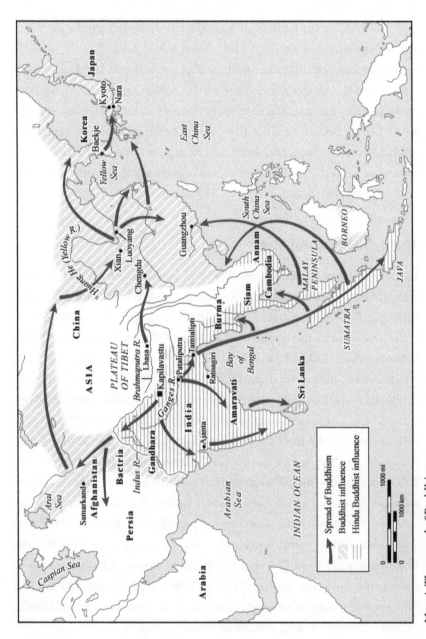

Map 4. The spread of Buddhism.

Eastern Han Emperor Mingdi had a dream about a shining image hovering above his palace. Searching for its meaning, he dispatched his officials to get more information about a magical figure then being worshipped in the lands to the west of China. These officials returned with two Indian monks and some images of the Buddha carried on a white horse, which were then placed at a newly constructed temple in Loyang, the White Horse Temple, China's first Buddhist shrine.[54]

A stream of cultural exchanges between India and China followed. The Chinese monk Faxian (337–422 AD) came from China across the desert to India and returned by the sea. The celebrated monk Xuanzang reached India in 629 AD and spent the next sixteen years studying Buddhism and collecting Buddhist scriptures for translation. Indian monks also traveled to China to preach, teach, translate, and advise. During the fifth and sixth centuries, a parade of them spread out in China, founding monasteries and temples and translating Buddhist sutras. Some of these Indian monks were even fluent enough to write books in the Chinese language. One prominent monk was Paramartha (Zhendi in Chinese), who arrived in China in 546 AD and played a key role in the introduction of Buddhism there.

Buddhism found its way from China to Korea in the fourth century AD and then from Korea to Japan in the sixth century. Japan's first and second capitals of Nara and Kyoto were built around Buddhist temples. Buddhism in Japan did not displace native religion but intermingled with the traditional Japanese animistic belief, Shinto. Japanese society came to see the Buddhist pantheon, including bodhisattvas (spiritual beings on the path to full Buddhahood), as Shinto deities, or kami. This combination of Buddhist nirvana and Shinto magical power gave Japanese emperors much of their legitimacy. Japanese Buddhism also absorbed a huge number of Hindu deities, including Brahma and Saraswati, in one of the most interesting fusions of the two religions outside of India.

A remarkable aspect of this spread of Indian ideas to North and Southeast Asia was that it was accomplished without coercion or conquest. One might compare this Indianization—as some historians refer to this phenomenon—with Hellenization, the spread of Greek ideas and institutions to the western Mediterranean and western Asia.[55]

Hellenization was backed by either military conquest (as with Alexander the Great) or the displacement of native people (as with Greek city-states in Sicily). Indianization was peacefully accomplished without either conquest or displacement. Hellenization was carried out by the Greeks and benefited the Greek settlers; it was of, by, and for the Greeks. Indianization was of, by, and for local societies. While Hellenization often meant the imposition of Greek culture, ideas, and institutions, Indianization often meant the selective adaptation of Indian culture, ideas, and institutions by local societies in accordance with their prior beliefs, practices, and needs.

Indianization, moreover, had a more lasting impact on the receiving societies than Hellenization did. The Greek temples and polities in the Mediterranean were built for the Greeks. Not so the Indian temples and polities in Southeast Asia. Like their rulers, these institutions were Indianized but not Indian. The spread of Indian ideas to other parts of Asia was voluntary, and mostly through the initiative of its recipients. In the case of Indonesia, for example, historians have argued that Indian civilization arrived at the behest of Indonesian ruling groups, who invited Brahman priests to learn about Hindu ideas of political organization and legitimation so as to consolidate their authority. It is important to keep in mind that before the arrival of Hinduism and Buddhism, states in Southeast Asia were generally small, weak, and fragmented. Newly arriving Indian ideas, including "magical, sacral legitimation of dynastic interests and the domestication of subjects," empowered local rulers to expand their political authority.[56] They built not only larger states and even empires, notably Angkor in modern Cambodia and Majapahit in Java, but also such monumental architecture as Angkor Wat in Cambodia, the world's largest Hindu temple complex, and Borobudur in Java, the world's largest Buddhist monument.

The End of Classical India

The Maurya Empire came to an end in the early fourth century AD, to be followed, after a period of fragmentation, by the Gupta Empire, which lasted from the early fourth to late sixth century AD. The Guptas, like the Mauryas, observed the principle of retaining defeated rulers rather than taking away their territory. But in contrast to the rather centralized Maurya Empire, the Guptas developed a looser administrative structure; even villages in the Gupta Empire had a great deal of autonomy.[57] This was a practical necessity, given the vastness of the empire and the rapidity with which the Gupta conquests were made. To manage their empire, the Guptas created a tributary system, somewhat like that of China, which is often mistakenly given the sole credit for inventing a world order based around a suzerain. In this system, secondary states acknowledge the primacy of a leading state, often to avoid outright colonization, by making some form of financial offering or gifts without surrendering their sovereignty. Through such methods, Gupta rule not only provided India with stability but also fostered the outstanding artistic and literary achievements of the period, known as India's "golden age."

The Guptas were the last major universal Hindu empire of India. They were followed by the empire of Harsha in the seventh century, which, although powerful and highly culturally accomplished, faced political competition for India-wide sovereignty from King Shashanka and the Pulakeshins in north India, the Pala Empire of east India, and the Chalukya and Pallava dynasties in south India. India thus returned to a competitive system of states, until, in the seventh century AD and onward, Arab invasions in northwest India put an end to the classical Indian world.

The extent and period of Muslim rule in India is debatable. For much of their history, the Islamic states and the Moghul Empire covered only part of India, mostly in the north and central areas. They had to coexist or compete with regional non-Muslim states, including some powerful ones, such as the Vijayanagar, Maratha, and Sikh empires. The Delhi Sultanate, which lasted for 320 years (1206–1526 AD), was, despite its name, not a single entity but a succession of five different Muslim dynasties with no blood link among them, several of which controlled only territories in northern India. Similarly, its successor, the Moghul Empire (1526–1857 AD) did not control south India until the last stage of

Aurangzeb's rule (1658–1707 AD). After Aurangzeb, the Moghuls faced serious competition from the Hindu Marathas and the Sikhs, and the Moghuls were gradually reduced to being their puppets until the formation of the British Raj in 1858. These regional centers would ensure that elements of the classical Indian world order, based on Hindu philosophy and statecraft, would continue. They would also attest to and preserve India's more pluralistic structure and ensure the continuity of Hindu political orders after foreign (Muslim and British) conquest.

As the classical Indian world order evolved through the Vedic age, the sixteen Mahajanapadas, and the Maurya Empire, its neighboring civilization was developing its own world order, with striking parallels as well as differences. China, too, started with a system of competing states that were conquered by the strongest among them, a hundred years after the Mauryas established India's first empire. Like India, China faced a constant threat of foreign invasion but was able to accommodate foreign influences through cultural assimilation. Like India's, China's civilization has maintained continuity to this day. But the Chinese story is different in many respects, with a greater degree of centralization of bureaucracy and politics than the Indians had ever developed.

Chapter 4

Heaven's Way

China has been a changing and adaptive civilization, much more so than the once-fashionable Western view of China as a stagnant nation impervious to progressive outside influences held. At the same time, the claim made by China's contemporary leaders of their country being a nation with a "peace gene" that "does not carry aggressive or hegemonic traits," as its current leader Xi Jinping once put it, is a bit of mythmaking, although such claims are hardly unique to China.[1] So is the claim that China expanded and strengthened itself more by its cultural and commercial attraction than by the sword.

The reality is that China has conquered other states and has been conquered by others. Its majority Han population has been influenced by foreign cultures as much as it has influenced them. After the establishment of its first unified empire, the Qin dynasty, in the third century BC, China expanded, incorporating neighbors through the migration of the Han people southward across the Yangtze River and through military conquest as well.[2] But in subsequent centuries, like India, China suffered through long periods of disunion and rule by foreigners, as during the Mongol Yuan dynasty and the Qing dynasty, created by the Manchu people who invaded China from the northeast. While many of the conquering "barbarians" were "Sinicized" by living alongside the Han people—adopting their language and their imperial, bureaucratic form

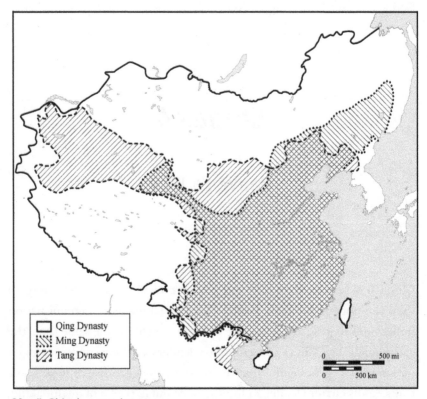

Map 5. China's expansion.

of government—China itself might have borrowed some beliefs from the barbarians to the west, including the veneration of heaven, which is a shared trait among central Asian nomadic cultures, including the Mongols. In any case, the alternating expansion and retraction of the Han Chinese introduced a good deal of diversity into the Chinese civilization and nation, which belies the image of continuity and homogeneity stressed by Chinese governments in the modern era. This should be kept in mind when considering the history of the Chinese world order.

Yet, China gave the world one of its enduring models of world order. As a key foundation of that order, somewhat like in ancient Egypt, was China's self-image to be at the center of the world: the quintessential middle kingdom, demanding and often receiving at least notional deference from the countries on its borders and beyond. This was, for intermittent centuries, the actual situation of China's relations with the rest of the world, even if dynastic records of China tended to exaggerate the country's unity, continuity, strength, and integrity, as well as the degree of submission and assimilation of foreigners.

What is beyond doubt is that this Chinese model of world order is different from that of Rome (which was simultaneous with a major period of Chinese power) or that of the British Empire centuries later. The Chinese world order was based on a cultural and commercial reciprocity, by which many other countries acknowledged China's preeminence without surrendering their sovereignty, usually by giving gifts in elaborate ceremonies, in return for trading privileges. While this system did not preclude China from embarking on colonizing missions, especially in contiguous areas, it generally did allow China, for much of its history, to keep its place at the top of a hierarchy of nations in East and Southeast Asia without actually sending troops and colonial bureaucrats to occupy and directly administer subordinate territories in farther areas. This was a far cry from the world order Europe and the West built over much of the world.

From Heaven to Earth

The first conclusively proven Chinese dynasty was the Shang, founded around 1600 BC in the Yellow River valley in the Henan province, with centers in Zhengzhou and Anyang and covering neighboring areas. It might have had a predecessor in the Xia "dynasty," which emerged about four centuries earlier, in an area between Luoyang and Zhengzhou. However, the place of the Xia as a preceding "dynasty" remains to be proven beyond doubt.[3] The textual references to the Xia came much later from the Zhou dynasty, which took power in the eleventh century BC. The founder of the Xia, Yu, was believed to have protected people from the "great flood" by channeling its waters into the rivers of China, including the Yellow River.

By the time of the Shang, China had already developed cultural sophistication and a system of writing consisting of thousands of ideograms on oracle bones. Later dynasties developed some of the most identifiable elements of China's culture—for example, its system of ideographic writing—but accounts of the Xia and the Shang and archaeological discoveries show the beginnings of centralized authority, the importance of rituals, and the concept of the ruler's personal virtue in the Chinese political order, which was developed and refined in subsequent Chinese traditions, especially Confucianism.[4]

A civilization does not automatically produce a world order by organizing the "world" known to it. India's first worldview emerged with the *Rig Veda*, the earliest dating of which is about the fifteenth century BC, more than a thousand years after the first Indian civilization took shape in the Indus valley. Similarly, organizing the "world" in Chinese civilization came about a thousand years after the Xia. Having conquered the Shang, the Zhou developed two of the most enduring Chinese ideas about political authority: the mandate of heaven and *tianxia* (all under heaven).[5] China thus became the quintessential celestial kingdom, where heaven's way ruled the earth.

The main idea is that the ruler receives the right to rule from heaven (*tian*). As a verse in the *Book of Odes* goes:

Heaven, looking down upon the House of Zhou
Sees that its light reaches the people below
And to protect the Son of Heaven.[6]

Another verse reads:

The Mandate of Heaven,
How beautiful and unceasing!
Oh, how glorious
Was the purity of King Wen's virtue.[7]

If the ruler was not wise and ignored the welfare of the people, heaven would send warnings in the form of natural disasters, eclipses, or peasant rebellions. If the ruler did not change his ways, heaven would withdraw its mandate and with it the ruler's right to rule. The mandate of heaven was used by the Zhou dynasty founder Wu to justify the overthrow of the preceding Shang dynasty. But the mandate was a double-edged sword: Rulers could use it to suppress any rebellion as an act against the will of heaven. But it could also be used to justify rebellion against the ruler on the pretext that he was cruel and unjust. If the rebellion succeeded, it could be presented as evidence that the ruler had lost the mandate.

The other Zhou concept, *tianxia*, is an inclusive notion originally intended to ensure the loyalty of competing Chinese states to the Zhou as the dynasty became weaker and others aspired to hegemony. The concept has been revived and applied by Chinese scholars to the contemporary world order, who argue that *tianxia* rejects the European model created in 1648 by the Treaty of Westphalia, which led to the adoption of the principle that each country was sovereign and had the authority to determine its way of life without interference from other powers. That system of individual state primacy, in this Chinese view, produces competition and war. The ideal of *tianxia* instead holds that the highest unit should be the world, not the state.[8] *Tianxia* envisages the political system of the world as a family—a harmonious and cooperative one but also one in which no single power exercises hegemony.[9]

This of course does not describe the present reality of China's approach to world order. China continues to pursue and uphold a Westphalian system, especially the principle of noninterference. What we are talking about here is how the classical Zhou notion of *tianxia* has been interpreted by Chinese scholars. For the most part, today *tianxia* is a rather theoretical and rhetorical concept, an ideal type of world order that can be derived from classical Chinese philosophy, though it has been criticized as envisioning Chinese cultural and political hegemony and legitimizing the official discourse on China's "peaceful rise."[10]

Whatever its merit, the Zhou solution to the problem of governance proved neither effective nor long-lasting. The dynasty degenerated into a group of rival states, with the Zhou king acting as a figurehead, even though some other local rulers were more powerful than him. The *tianxia* system's aspired harmony and inclusiveness gave way to a radically different worldview and philosophy: legalism.

As the Zhou weakened, China descended into chaos during what is known as the Spring and Autumn period and the Warring States period, when seven competing states—Qin, Chu, Zhao, Wei, Han, Yan, and Qi— challenged the Zhou dynasty's symbolic supremacy while competing with each other. In 221 BC, the Qin prevailed, establishing China's first truly unified empire under Shihuangdi, the first emperor.[11]

The Qin (pronounced "chin," from which "China" might have derived) dynasty has been heralded by recent Chinese leaders for its measures of national unity, such as standardized weights and measures and even axle lengths so all carts could travel all roads. But the Qin's rise involved the suppression not only of the Zhou philosophy of inclusiveness but also of the more pacifist political ideas in Chinese philosophy, especially that of Confucianism. Confucianism is a philosophical and political doctrine that stresses the essential goodness of human nature and the importance of tradition. It also emphasizes the mutual respect and obligations between ruler and ruled, similar to those between parent and child, teacher and pupil, master and disciple, and between friends. It is based on the mandate of heaven idea: the ruler is responsible for his people's welfare and the maintenance of peace and order in exchange for their loyalty and obedience. For the Qin rulers, whose own philosophy of legalism called for absolute and harsh political control of subjects, this idea was a direct threat.

To elaborate, like the mandate of heaven, Confucianism was both legitimizing and delegitimizing. The ruler's legitimacy was conditional upon just and wise exercise of authority that served the people's welfare and happiness. While elitist and not democratic, Confucianism did not provide an absolute justification for harsh authoritarian rule either. Instead, it sanctioned rebellion against unjust or repressive rulers. Confucian thinkers, including those who held political office, notably Xunzi in the third century BC, promoted the ideals of the "kingly way" (*wang dao*) and "humane authority": a sort of official moral code for the state that called for policies of restraint, justice, benevolence, reduced punishment, and lower taxes.[12] At the same time, the Confucian tradition provided elements of an ethics of just war. One test of whether a war is just or unjust lies in the welcome that a conquering army gets from the liberated people. A just ruler that defeats tyrants and liberates oppressed people, and is therefore welcomed by the liberated, must not abuse the welcome by committing offenses. On this point, there are some similarities with India's Kautilya, who also advised a conqueror on the benefits of attacking states with unjust rulers and recommended treating the new subjects humanely. To quote the Confucian sage Mencius, "If you killed the old, bind the young, destroy the ancestral temples, and appropriate the ancestral vessels, how can you expect the people's approval?"[13]

Some aspects of Confucianism blended with another major Chinese philosophy, Daoism, developed by Laozi, a philosopher in the sixth century BC. Both philosophies emphasized "simplicity, balance, restraint... as a way to achieve harmony," although Confucianism was less preoccupied with the metaphysical world and more with present social and political life.[14] But Confucianism was diametrically opposite to legalism, the philosophy of the Qin. First formulated by the philosopher-politician Shang Yang in the fourth century BC and expanded by Han Feizi (also a philosopher-politician) a century later, legalism stressed the need for power and order. It rejected Confucianism's emphasis on tradition and humanity, on ruling by virtue, and on the idea of a ruler's obligation to his people. While Confucianism saw human nature as essentially good, legalism, perhaps reacting to the constant warfare and instability of the period, saw it as inherently wicked, needing to be kept under control by a code of law strictly enforced by harsh punishment.

Although legalism was focused on domestic rule, it had clear implications for interstate relations and world order. It held that, in order to conquer enemies and govern territory, a ruler needed to control his own people first. "In the past, those who were able to regulate All under Heaven first had to regulate their own people," the *Book of Lord Shang* said.[15] This was because "when the people are weak, the state is strong; hence the state that possesses the Way devotes itself to weakening the people."[16] "Weakening the people" required strong rulers. To quote

Han Feizi, "No country is permanently strong, nor is any country permanently weak. If those who impose The Law are strong, the country will be strong; if they are weak, the country will be weak."[17]

Legalism was the ideology of the first emperor, Shihuangdi, who famously executed Confucian scholars and banned and burned books. But the Qin dynasty was short-lived, and Confucian and Daoist thinking were revived during the next major Chinese dynasty, the Han. But the legalist initiatives and reforms undertaken by the Qin, including a centralized bureaucracy and rule by law—that is, the law as a set of rules enhancing state power over individuals rather than rules protecting individuals against the power of the state—would leave a long-term legacy in China.[18]

Before moving on, it is important to keep in mind that—just as in ancient India, where Kautilya and Ashoka espoused opposing views—Chinese ideas about world order were not uniform, especially when it came to morality, in the sense of restraint in the use of force. As Chinese scholar Yan Xuetong puts it, while Confucius and his followers—such as Xunzi and Mencius—stressed morality as "a necessary condition" for maintaining stability and interstate order, except when the cause was just, Han Feizi believed that "normally violent force is the sole factor in play." On the pacifist end of the spectrum was Mozi, another major ancient Chinese philosopher, who held that "morality alone is sufficient to maintain interstate order."[19]

To this mosaic of ancient Chinese political thought, a new tile was added with the spread of Buddhism, introduced from India. The new religion did not replace Confucianism and Daoism but comingled with them, despite periodic tensions that flared into religious conflict. The arrival of Buddhism influenced the Chinese worldview. While the ancient Chinese thought of their emperors as "rulers of the world," they had little or no understanding of geography in the modern sense, especially about the existence of advanced civilizations in other parts of the world.[20] The Silk Road, along which Buddhist monks traveled between India and China, introduced to China the idea of a world with multiple centers, not just one. In contrast to a singular all-under-heaven image, with China at its center, Buddhist cosmology holds that the world is composed of four continents with their own rulers, rather than one "son of Heaven."[21]

Buddhism was adopted by the Chinese not only as a spiritual means for seeking happiness in the afterlife. It also influenced Chinese political thinking and practice, becoming, for example, an element in the legitimization of rulers. One of the most important examples is Wu Zetian, China's only female emperor, who started as a concubine of Tang Emperor Taizong. By 690 AD, over stiff opposition from Confucian officials who objected to a woman of low birth assuming political power, Wu had usurped the Tang throne. Instrumental to her effort was help from the Buddhist clergy, who identified her as a female Maitreya (a future Buddha), descending from heaven into Loyang, the capital city. When this seemed too far-fetched, Wu got Bodhiruci—an Indian monk she had earlier invited to China, along with scores of other Indians including Brahman alchemists and astrologers popular in the Tang era—to write an entirely new Buddhist text, the *Ratnamegha Sutra*, that anointed her as the female Bodhisattva Vimalaprabha, a semidivine, compassionate figure on the verge of enlightenment.[22]

To sum up, China's various traditions of political philosophy were much too complicated to reduce to a single concept, either Confucianism, legalism, Daoism, Buddhism, or any of their varieties or offshoots. But what remained almost entirely constant through the long epochs of Chinese history was the notion of a powerful, almost godlike ruler at the center, who employed a combination of the country's competing philosophies to justify his (or, in one instance, her) power and to maintain order over the country's vast territory. China's conception of itself as the highest form of civilization was modified by such major developments as the arrival of Buddhism from India and losses to conquering armies from central and Northeast Asia. Nonetheless, the ideal remained that the emperor as the "son of heaven" at the top of a hierarchical system should use his wisdom, example, and influence to assure order not only inside the country but in the rest of the world as well.

Trading Prestige for Profit

The Chinese world order's core element was a notion of hierarchical political relationships, which has come to be known as the tributary system. In essence, the system offered trade privileges and diplomatic recognition to countries that acknowledged China's cultural and political primacy. However, its geographic extent and benefits changed, sometimes considerably, depending on who was in power in China and in the neighboring states.

The origins of this system can be traced to the Han dynasty, and it lasted for more than two millennia, until the final dynasty, the Qing, was overthrown in 1911. Tributary systems are not uncommon in the history of civilizations, mainly as a way for a powerful state to exercise control over weaker ones, collecting revenues and gaining their military support without directly colonizing or governing them. The Chinese tributary system, too, had economic and political-military objectives, but its greater reliance on cultural prestige than on military power made it distinctive. The Chinese believed in the inherent superiority of their civilization, and they sought to use that superiority to manage their relations with others, especially the violent Asian tribes that posed the most direct military threat to China. As the late Harvard Sinologist John Fairbank explained it, through rituals such as kowtowing, foreigners acknowledged the superiority of the Chinese emperor and recognized, at least implicitly, the benefits of being "transformed by civilization."[23] The acceptance by foreigners of the emperor's superiority as a ruler had the additional benefit of enhancing his legitimacy before his own subjects.[24]

There was an important economic aspect to this: an exchange of gifts signified the permission to trade with China, granted by the emperor to tributary states. Indeed, trade might have been the most important reason why so many of China's neighbors participated in the system and why it persisted for such a long time. For much of the system's long duration, China was a leading economy of the world and provided a large market to foreigners (just as it does today). The tributary states would send missions, on a periodic basis, to China, where, in elaborately choreographed ceremonies, they received the right to trade. For China's neighbors, access to the Chinese market through the tributary system was far more desirable than trading illegally, which would invite harsh punishment or death, although such unofficial trade continued side by side with tributary trade.[25]

Image 5. Foreign envoys bringing tribute to the Qing emperor. Portion of an eighteenth-century painting.

The tributary system also operated as a way of conducting diplomatic relations in East Asia, especially as some of the tributary states sought Chinese protection against their enemies.[26] One element of this was to provide legitimization to rulers or would-be rulers seeking to gain recognition in domestic succession squabbles. Parties to dynastic-succession conflicts would send a mission to the Chinese emperor to get his approval, given in an official letter stamped with the imperial seal. This recognition was commonly used by Southeast Asian rulers to enhance their prestige, even when they had assumed power by legitimate succession. In the fifteenth century, for example, the rulers of one tributary state, Malacca, received Chinese recognition as a way to deter rival Siam (modern Thailand), another tributary state, which was threatening to attack.[27] In urging Siam to refrain from threatening Malacca, Ming

Emperor Yongle wrote to King Borommarachathirat, "Those who are fond of employing troops, do not have virtuous hearts.... If you develop good relations with neighboring countries and do not engage in mutual aggression, the prosperity which will result will be limitless. You king, should bear this in mind."[28] This shows how the the tributary system gave China influence to mediate in disputes among its neighboring states by calling for restraint.

At the same time, while the tributary system did not constitute a formal empire, it enshrined an inequality among states. The tributary states may have been deemed as equal to each other by the Chinese, but they were not equal to China. Chinese court officials and dynastic histories often exaggerated the show of deference by foreigners, especially when they met the emperor with tribute; the word "trembling" is often used in Chinese dynastic sources to suggest the fear and deference shown by a foreign mission bedazzled and intimidated by Chinese splendor. However, the system was not always based on voluntary participation. To enhance the legitimacy of the emperor and the status of China, the Chinese often imposed tributary status unilaterally. This sometimes got rebuffed, a particular striking example being Japan's Shogun Ashikaga Yoshimitsu, who gave this reply to a demand for tributary submission by Emperor Hongwu, the founder of the Ming dynasty: "Heaven and Earth are vast; they are not monopolized by one ruler.... The world is the world's world, it does not belong to a single person."[29]

The Chinese were pragmatic enough to recognize such power realities and adjust their behavior accordingly. For example, during Emperor Yongle's rule in the fifteenth century, China treated the ruler of the Timurid Empire (which stretched from present-day Turkey to Afghanistan) as an equal.[30] Sending a tribute mission or embassy to China did not necessarily mean submitting to China or accepting inferior status. The tributary system's claim to being a relatively benign, noncoercive international order has been subject of debate and controversy. At one extreme, it has been hailed for providing long-term stability and economic benefit. Or, as one Chinese scholar has put it—echoing the claims often made on behalf of the US-led world order—"China, as the most powerful state and the most advanced civilization in the region, played an overwhelming role in maintaining peace and trade, providing public goods, and governing the system."[31] In its ideal form, another scholar has claimed, the system fits the notion of "perfect peace," in which "rival states submit without having first to be subjugated."[32]

But there are many huge exceptions to this: the long colonization of Vietnam during the first to the tenth centuries; the conquests and absorption of the Nanzhao and Dali kingdoms in Yunnan, despite their tributary relations with China; and the colonization of Xinjiang during the Qing dynasty. The tributary system was also a prelude to Tibet's annexation by communist China. Although China did not undertake large-scale colonization of distant lands like the Europeans did after the fifteenth century AD, when it did choose to conquer, its warfare could be brutal, even genocidal. The Qing dynasty's campaign in Xinjiang in the eighteenth century AD killed over four hundred thousand Zunghars, a Mongolian tribe, more than half of their total population. The rest either fled or were pressed into servitude.[33]

Although tributary relations were maintained through cultural and economic exchange, they had to be backed up by force or the threat of force. During their invasion of Yunnan in 1381–1382 AD, Ming generals Lan Yu and Fu Youde castrated more than three hundred Mongolian and Muslim captives, in order to make them eunuchs in the Ming court. Among them was a Muslim boy with the name of Ma Sanbao, whose ancestor had served under the Mongol court. At the imperial court, Ma Sanbao took on the name of Ma He and later would become known as Admiral Zheng He, who could lay claim to being Asia's most famous naval commander. Zheng He led a series of seven naval expeditions to the Indian Ocean between 1405 to 1433 at the behest of Emperor Yongle.[34]

The reasons behind these expeditions were political and strategic as well as economic. The historian Warren Cohen argues that the Zheng He voyages were meant to showcase Ming power and prestige and to bring tributary envoys to China, reflecting a grand strategic Chinese imperial objective.[35] Australian historian Geoff Wade contends that they were "intended to create legitimacy for the usurping emperor [Yongle], display the might of the Ming, bring the known polities to demonstrated submission to the Ming and thereby achieve a pax Ming throughout the known world and collect treasures for the Court."[36] As such, these expeditions were vaster in scale than what would be required for even the most ambitious diplomatic or economic missions. Zheng He's voyages were a kind of "gunboat diplomacy," because his "ships were indeed gunboats," and some twenty-six thousand out of twenty-eight thousand men, in Wade's estimate, were soldiers. These missions used coercion to gain the Ming "control of ports and shipping lanes...nodal points and networks." The Chinese also resorted to violence on the shore, such as capturing the king of Ceylon (for allegedly attacking the Chinese fleet) and bringing a Sumatran prince who had usurped his throne to the imperial court in Nanjing, where he was executed. The Zheng He missions, Wade writes, were an "early form of maritime colonialism by which a dominant maritime power took control (either through force or the threat thereof) of the main port polities along the major East-West maritime trade network, as well as the seas between, thereby gaining economic and political benefits."[37] When Emperor Yongle dispatched Zheng He on his voyages to "all the known world under the Heaven," his purpose was to announce China's hegemony in Asia.[38]

The above view can be disputed, although the Zheng He voyages, along with the Chinese conquest and colonization of Yunnan and Vietnam, challenge the idea of a non-imperial, noncoercive Chinese world order. But the Chinese Empire was not always powerful enough to conquer and assimilate its neighbors. Vietnam's fierce resistance to Chinese invasions, throwing off Chinese rule in the tenth century, would have discouraged further attempts. Attempted invasions of Java and Burma failed. In the late thirteenth century, the Yuan dynasty under Kublai Khan invaded the Javanese Hindu kingdom of Singhasari in order to punish its ruler for refusing to send tribute to China. But that invasion failed, thanks to a combination of political intrigue (a local prince who had surrendered to the invaders and agreed to pay tribute turned against them), the monsoons, and patient harassment by the Javanese opposition, leading to a final counteroffensive that might have destroyed a large part of the invading fleet.[39] Burma was attacked by successive Chinese empires from the thirteenth to the eighteenth centuries, but the last such attack was a terrible defeat for China, one that ensured Burma's independence until the advent of British imperialism.[40]

Overall, while cultural and symbolic factors mattered, the Chinese based their decision to resort to force or not on their assessment of the nature of likely resistance. They could be ruthlessly aggressive when facing what they regarded as lesser powers and cautiously self-protective in the face of stronger ones.[41] Hence, the nature and instruments of the tributary system changed from dynasty to dynasty, depending on China's relative power, security threats facing it, and its domestic situation.[42] It was never the unified, consistent system that it is often assumed to be. The Han, Sui, and Tang dynasties maintained "'brotherly' or equal relations" with nomadic neighbors in the north and west: the Han with the Xiongnu and the Sui, and the Tang with the Turkic, Uighur, and Tibetan states, though eventually these were defeated.[43] The accommodating nature of the tributary relationship changed to competitive and adversarial when the power of neighboring states grew. The Tang dynasty, for example, did not insist that Japan—which was setting up its own political system by borrowing heavily from the Chinese political and administrative model—declare itself as a vassal state.[44] And at times when China was weak, the tribute system was more theoretical than real. Weaker Chinese dynasties were forced to pay tribute to foreign rulers who vanquished them. For example, in 1127, the Jin, a Manchurian tribe, captured the Song dynasty capital of Kaifeng and pushed its rulers to the south, where the dynasty's remnant, the Southern Song, had to pay tribute to the conquerors.[45] In cases like these, the Chinese world order ceased to exist.[46]

By extinguishing the Song altogether in 1279 AD, the Mongol Yuan dynasty expanded China's imperial frontiers and the tributary system. The Ming, which expelled the Yuan in 1368 AD, pursued an even more militaristic and imperialist agenda, which demanded tributary status from states in East and Southeast Asia and, as seen above, sent a powerful fleet to assert that demand. The Ming went beyond persuasion and the attraction of Chinese culture, which is supposed to be a key driver of the traditional tributary system, to resort to "blackmail" and war.[47] The Ming successor, the Qing dynasty, became more isolationist and inward looking in its later stages, especially after the arrival of Europeans. But it adopted different attitudes to different foreign powers, becoming more accommodating toward the British than others, especially the weaker European powers.[48]

The tributary relationship between China and Korea was shaped more by political and strategic factors than by economic ones, and it involved military coercion. Korea's three early kingdoms extensively adopted China's culture, customs, arts, writing system, coinage, and ceramic production, as well as its political ideas and institutions. Korea also participated in the tributary system, starting with the largest of the three kingdoms, Koguryo, which sent a tribute mission to the Han court as early as 32 AD and adopted the title of king (after Chinese *wang*). But all three kingdoms rebuffed Chinese efforts at direct colonial rule, and, even as tributary states, there were limits to their political subservience to China.[49] While Korea accepted China's view of itself as the middle kingdom and the highest civilization, Korean adherence to the tributary state was "usually ceremonial, and...did not imply a loss of autonomy."[50] This autonomy was evident in Koguryo's raid on China during the Sui dynasty in 598 AD, prompting China to revoke the imperial titles it had bestowed on the kingdom. Later, the Silla Kingdom used its alliance with the Tang to defeat Paekche in 660 AD and then Koguryo in 668, thereby creating for the first time a unified Korean state. But it, too, soon turned against the Tang.[51] In general, over the centuries, China regarded an independent Korea as a counter to Japan, while Korea's deference to China was its way of satisfying China's need for cultural prestige while avoiding conquest.

Built around economics and geopolitics, the Chinese world order depended on the country being a major hub of international commerce and a crossroads of cultural and political ideas. The most famous Chinese contribution in this area was the Silk Road, which emerged during the Han dynasty—although the term itself was developed in the late nineteenth century by German geographers Carl Ritter and Ferdinand von Richthofen, who called it *Seidenstraße* (silk road) or *Seidenstraßen* (silk routes). It was the ancient and medieval world's most famous land trading route, connecting the eastern and western ends of Eurasia. It helped to connect China with other major civilizations: India, Persia, Rome, Constantinople, the Islamic centers in the Middle East, and beyond, thereby ending China's relative isolation and challenging its insular worldview. As China became a leading innovator and economic power, the Silk Road facilitated the diffusion of Chinese goods, ideas, and inventions, which were important for trade but also for security, warfare, and the spread of knowledge. These included printing, which goes beyond the mere invention of paper; gunpowder, which revolutionized warfare; and the compass, which revolutionized navigation.

China's Cultural Imprint

Like ancient Greece and India, China often spread its culture, political ideas, and institutions to other regions. Its impact was most heavily felt in Korea, Japan, and Vietnam. In this sense, China was to Northeast Asia what India was to Southeast Asia. The major borrowings were Confucianism, the imperial examination system of the Tang dynasty, and Buddhism, for which China was an intermediary between India and Northeast Asia. But neither the Japanese nor the Koreans borrowed Chinese culture and institutions wholesale. Rather, they adapted them to suit their own needs while preserving their prior beliefs, such as shamanism in Korea and Shinto in Japan. At the same time, Korea and Japan voluntarily adopted the Chinese character as an integral part of their writing systems. In these countries, as well as in Vietnam, Chinese culture was considered refined and elegant.

Korea played an especially important role in the spread of Buddhism, which arrived in the Korean kingdom of Koguryo in 372 AD, brought there by a Chinese monk, Sundo. Soon thereafter, Buddhism was brought to the kingdom of Paekche by an Indian monk, Marananta.[52] For Korean rulers, adopting Buddhism was a way of maintaining good relations with China; it gave both leaders a sense of commonality as they resisted the threat posed by Manchurian tribes. Buddhism also helped to enhance the status of the Korean aristocracy, from which monks mainly came. Many of these monks became royal advisers in addition to their religious duties. (This role of Buddhism as a source of social privilege was the inverse of the situation in India, where Buddhism had first emerged as a protest against the socially privileged Brahman class.) Buddhism also became the inspiration for one of Korea's greatest innovations: movable metal printing. In 1011 AD, the Goryeo Kingdom had printed the entire corpus of the most sacred Buddhist text, the Tripitaka, apparently inspired by the belief that this would protect the kingdom against invasion from the increasingly threatening proto-Mongol Khitan tribe. The text was printed again in 1234 AD with movable metal type, a technique that might have been invented in Korea.

The first Buddhist images in Japan came not from China or India but from Korea. This occurred in 552 AD, with the gift of a Buddhist statue from the king of Paekche to the Japanese ruler Kimmei Tenno. At first, Buddhism was opposed by some sections of the Japanese feudal elite, who thought it would undercut the local Shinto belief. This set off a struggle between the two most powerful families of Japan: the pro-Buddhist Soga, who thought Japan should not be left behind in embracing a belief that had been adopted in Korea and China, and the Mononobe, who feared worshipping a foreign deity might anger the kami, the holy powers venerated in Shinto. But such conflicts were resolved by marrying the new Buddhist beliefs with long-established Shinto customs. For example, the very first Buddhist image built in Japan was made from a log of camphor wood, which in Shinto tradition is imbued with kami spirits. The first ordained Buddhist in Japan was an eleven-year-old girl, Shima; this was consistent with the Shinto practice of having daughters of noble families serve the kami. And the Japanese term for Buddhist relics, *shari*, also came to mean "rice," the all-important Japanese staple and cultural symbol.

Buddhism, along with Confucianism, also shaped Japan's political system. In 604 AD, Prince Shotoku—the regent to Empress Suiko of the Soga family, which had prevailed in the rivalry with the Mononobe— established Japan's governance practices for next few centuries.[53] He blended Buddhist ideals such as devotion to the Buddha, the monastic community (sangha), and Buddhist laws with Confucian political ideals, including obedience to the emperor and respect for "Heaven."[54]

More borrowing from China came soon afterward. In 645 AD, under the initiative of Prince Nakano Ōe (who later became Emperor Tenji), the Japanese adopted Chinese ideas and institutions from the Sui and Tang dynasty periods to develop the *ritsuryō* system, whose main features included a centralized administrative state under an emperor (*tenno*, "heavenly sovereign") and a bureaucracy based on the Chinese model.[55] However, the position of the emperor in Japan was significantly constrained by the feudal system. The feudal lords controlled landholding and the bureaucracy and thus wielded effective power for much of Japan's history. Moreover, Japan only made a brief attempt to adopt the Chinese imperial examination system and granted exceptions to children of nobility.[56]

The Chinese influence on Japanese cultural and political life reached its peak during the eighth century AD, during which Japan adopted the Chinese writing system, its architectural styles (such as the curved roofs of temples), its painting, its sculpture, and its principles of urban planning. The layout of Japan's first two capital cities, Nara and Kyoto, mimicked that of Chang'an, the Tang dynasty capital. China would remain an important intermediary in the transmission of Buddhist ideas to Japan. Chan Buddhism, the Chinese practice based on *dhyana* ("meditation" in Sanskrit), came to China from India. Transmitted to Japan, it developed into Zen.[57]

China's cultural imprint in Southeast Asia was also extensive and long-lasting, although—with the exception of North Vietnam, which was colonized by China for much of the first millennium AD—its reach was not comparable to that of India. China played a more assertive geopolitical role in Southeast Asia under the tributary system; aside from colonizing Vietnam, it mounted invasions of Java and Burma, among others. India's role was primarily cultural and religious, which proved less threatening and more amenable to Southeast Asians. Compared to China's military conquests and occupations, India's cultural penetrations seemed relatively peaceful and benign. Southeast Asian countries were able to develop their own societies within the transplanted Indian frameworks.[58]

There were, of course, other reasons for India's greater cultural influence on Southeast Asia. Above all, it was India, not China, that provided Southeast Asia's two most important classical religions: Hinduism and Buddhism. India was also closer to the major maritime trading centers of Southeast Asia, and maritime trade has always been a major conduit for the transmission of ideas. Nonetheless, Southeast Asia borrowed heavily from Chinese art, cuisine, and architecture, which were brought to the region by the migration of southern Chinese tribes. This included the non-Han tribes of southern China who settled in mainland Southeast Asia, especially Thailand and Laos, some of them after fleeing the Yuan dynasty's thirteenth-century conquest of the Dali Kingdom of Yunnan province. Beginning in the Song dynasty, Han Chinese traders and laborers also settled in maritime regions of Southeast Asia. Some Chinese scholar-officials, fleeing the Mongol conquest of the Song, went to Vietnam. And then, after the Ming reconquest of China from the Mongols, Chinese Muslims fled to Java. Zheng He's naval expeditions stimulated further emigration from China; from the sixteenth to eighteenth centuries, Chinese merchants gained a significant presence in European colonies such as the Philippines and Java.[59]

These migrations brought with them ethnic tensions that have continued to erupt over time, sometimes violently, and including recently in places like Malaysia and Indonesia. But the Chinese were by and large able to settle and even flourish in "Nanyang"—or South Seas region, their name for Southeast Asia—by providing labor and becoming successful traders. These migrations and exchanges have furthered the diffusion of Chinese food, education, language, and Confucian political philosophy well beyond the borders of China itself, such that most Southeast Asian countries today remain amalgams of native cultures and the powerful influences that came from both China and India over many centuries.

The West's Learning from China

The sixteenth-century English philosopher and statesman Francis Bacon famously noted that printing, the compass, and gunpowder were the three inventions that were crucial to the rise of Europe, especially in its early stages. All three came from China, but they weren't the only things. Britain especially used many Chinese technologies—the moldboard plow, the rotary winnowing machine, the seed drill, the blast furnace, and cotton manufacturing (some of these also coming from India)—as it forged the industrial revolution. The idea of the steam engine, a key to British and Western industrialization, was essentially first conceived in Song dynasty China. It is well-known that Europeans adopted both Chinese habits and products, from tea and porcelain to landscape gardening. But it is less known that the Chinese influence on Europe also came in the form of ideas about economics, politics, and philosophy.

This was especially the case from the early seventeenth to the mid-eighteenth century, during what we now call the European Enlightenment. During this period, many Chinese texts, including those of Confucius, were translated into European languages, with Jesuit missionaries playing a key role, as they were especially successful among the Christian missions in finding acceptance in China. Similarly, Enlightenment thinkers such as Gottfried Wilhelm Leibniz, Voltaire, François Quesnay, Christian Wolff, David Hume, and Adam Smith also admired China and its ideas about philosophy and the economy.

At a time when Europe's progressive thinkers were searching for ideas to free society from the feudal aristocracy, the dogmas of the church, and the doctrine of divine right of kings, China offered a progressive example. It had a political system in which the emperor ruled through a bureaucracy that was selected through open and competitive civil service examinations, instead of relying on hereditary feudal aristocrats, as in Europe. The Chinese political order, which had emerged earlier and independently from Europe's, had in Confucianism its own well-developed system of morals but without a powerful and politically manipulative priesthood. These elements of the Chinese political order were thus viewed as more governed by human reason compared to the political order of Europe.

Chinese ideas and institutions helped stoke the revolutionary ferment against Europe's ancien régime. As William McNeill writes in his magisterial *The Rise of the West,* "The picture of Chinese sages, whose morality did not depend upon revealed religion...and such aspects of Chinese society as its civility...the absence of a hereditary aristocracy and the principle of appointment to government office on the basis of public examination all chimed in with radical movements of thought that gathered way, especially in France, during the eighteenth century. China became for Voltaire and some other *philosophes*, a model to be held up to Europe."[60]

The association of China with human reason was exemplified in an influential 1687 translation of Confucius's work, titled *Confucius Sinarum Philosophus*, which noted, "Never has Reason, deprived of divine Revelation, appeared so well developed nor with so much power" as in China.[61] The German philosopher Gottfried Wilhelm Leibniz (1646–1716) found in China a rational civilization from which Europeans could learn. In a book published in 1697, *Novissima Sinica*, or "latest news from China," he wrote: "I almost think it necessary that Chinese missionaries should be sent to us to teach the aims and practice of natural theology, as we send missionaries to them to instruct them in revealed religion."[62] Christian Wolff (1679–1754), also a German Enlightenment thinker, found in the Chinese system a way for reconciling individual happiness with the welfare of the state. He was persecuted by the church for being an atheist.

The most influential European thinker who drew on Chinese ideas was Voltaire (1694–1778), the French Enlightenment philosopher who inspired the French Revolution. He wrote that the Chinese imperial political system was "the best that the world has ever seen." He staged a play, *The Chinese Orphan*, in 1755 aimed at showing that the Chinese system was more down-to-earth, practical, and workable than Europe's.

François Quesnay (1694–1774), the influential French Physiocrat, admired Chinese agriculture, which to him provided the key to Europe's economic prosperity. Under his influence, a Chinese agriculture ceremony was performed in the French court in 1768 by the son of Louis XV, using a model of the Chinese plow. Austrian Emperor Joseph II would perform the same ceremony the following year. While Europe would not follow the agrarian path to economic success, Quesnay's Chinese learning did leave a legacy. He borrowed from the Chinese idea of *wu wei*, meaning "everything should be allowed to do what it naturally does," to challenge the prevailing mercantilist approach emphasizing government regulation to achieve economic self-reliance. Quesnay advocated an alternative approach, known to us through the French term laissez-faire, from which the idea of the free market is derived. This was also the philosophy of Quesnay's more influential contemporary, the Scottish economist Adam Smith. While one cannot credit the emergence of European capitalism to *wu wei* alone, it did have an impact on some key European thinkers at a time when capitalism was emerging in Europe. It also shows how different civilizations develop similar ideas about progress, thereby making the building of world order a shared enterprise.

The Chinese public service system based on meritocracy and competitive examinations—transmitted to Europe by missionaries along with other Chinese ideas—would inspire new ways of civil service recruitment in the West. The Chinese system was more democratic, and it helped reformists who wanted to replace Europe's old political order, held in place by officials selected from scions of the nobility. In France, where the value of the Chinese system was recognized by intellectuals such as Voltaire, Montesquieu, and Rousseau, a civil service examination was established in 1791, in the chaotic aftermath of the revolution. Although interrupted by corruption allegations, it was reestablished fully in 1875, being seen as essential to the development of a more open and democratic way of choosing government officials. The Chinese examination system influenced the British, first through the East India Company, which started to use an examination to train its colonial administrators first at the Fort William College in Calcutta (established in 1801) and later in its training college facility in the United Kingdom in Haileybury. The British government would follow after a report prepared by two senior officials (the Northcote-Trevelyan Report) in 1854. One of them, Charles Trevelyan, who was the permanent secretary to the Treasury, had lamented that the existing British system of recruiting civil servants produced types that "really could neither read nor write...almost an idiot."[63] This report led to the creation of its first civil service commission in 1855 and the emergence of a uniform civil service system in Britain.[64]

The Chinese examination system was also a model for the United States, where it was supported by Ralph Waldo Emerson. In a move to "reform of the civil service of the United States," an 1874 report by the US Civil Service Commission noted that China, as "the most enlightened and enduring government of the Eastern world had required an examination system as to the merits of the candidates for office." The British, it further noted, had "profited by those methods," and there was no reason "to deprive the American people of that advantage." The report went on to add that while the commission had no "intention of commending either the religion or the imperialism of China," it was a country where "Confucius had taught political morality, and the people of China had read books, used the compass, gunpowder, and the multiplication table, during centuries when this continent was a wilderness."[65]

Some of the European views of China turned out to have been too rosy, and perceptions turned more negative after the second half of the eighteenth century, as China experienced instability and decline. Contemporary China under Communist rule may not be seen as a role model for the West, although some of its approaches to climate change and technological innovations are being adopted around the world. Moreover, the Chinese state-led economic development model, adapted from Japan, has now found resonance in the developing world. But while China may not be a political model to the world, its past contributions should not be dismissed as irrelevant to the making of the modern world order or to the possibilities of a new, post-Western world order. There is little question that, at a crucial moment in its transition toward modernity, Europe found in China political ideas and institutions more "progressive" than its own.

China, throughout its history, was not a peaceful nation; there is hardly evidence of the peaceful rise of its empires or dynasties of the sort that the country's leaders are promising today. There is no Ashoka-like figure in China's history, promising not to expand his empire. At the same time, the Chinese were pragmatic, allowing due recognition of the power and culture of other civilizations. Despite seeing itself at the center of the known world, China was also a borrower of ideas, such as Buddhism from India, to help maintain stability and to reinforce the legitimacy of its rulers.

There is little question that a rising West borrowed not only Chinese technology but also the Chinese examination system to reform its bureaucracy, which is one of the most important instruments of governance and stability in any civilization. Combining both realpolitik and moral statecraft, China provides the most developed example of a world order straddling a system of independent states and outright empire. The Chinese tributary system, which relied more on rituals than coercion, gave significant economic and diplomatic benefits to other nations without colonization. The fact that it lasted nearly two thousand years and was supported by China's neighbors attests to its effectiveness and legitimacy.

Chapter 5

The Wrath of Rome

Rome, founded in the mid-eighth century BC, was a relative latecomer to the imperial world orders of the classical period, following the empires of Persia, India, and China. It evolved from being a monarchy, to a republic from 509 BC, and finally to an empire under Augustus in 27 BC. The original Roman Empire would last until 476 AD, but Emperor Constantine (the Great), pressured by barbarian attacks from the north, moved the capital east to Byzantium in 330 AD, renaming it Constantinople. This city became the center of the Eastern Roman Empire, popularly known as the Byzantine Empire, until it was finally conquered by the Ottomans in 1453 AD. While there is some conceptual continuity between the Western and Eastern Roman Empires, thus giving Rome an exaggerated longevity as a civilization and world order, in reality, the two were strikingly different in size, power, and religious orientation. In contrast to classical Rome's pagan beliefs, the Eastern Roman Empire was Christian from the beginning, with its founder Constantine the Great having converted to Christianity in 312 AD, before he moved to Constantinople. While Byzantine Emperor Justinian managed to recapture some of the lost Roman territory in North Africa, Italy, and the western Mediterranean in the sixth century AD, the Byzantine Empire would remain a far weaker entity than the undivided Roman Empire. Hence, the idea of a Roman world order—with its parallels with the contemporary American

Map 6. The Roman Empire, 44 BC–117 AD.

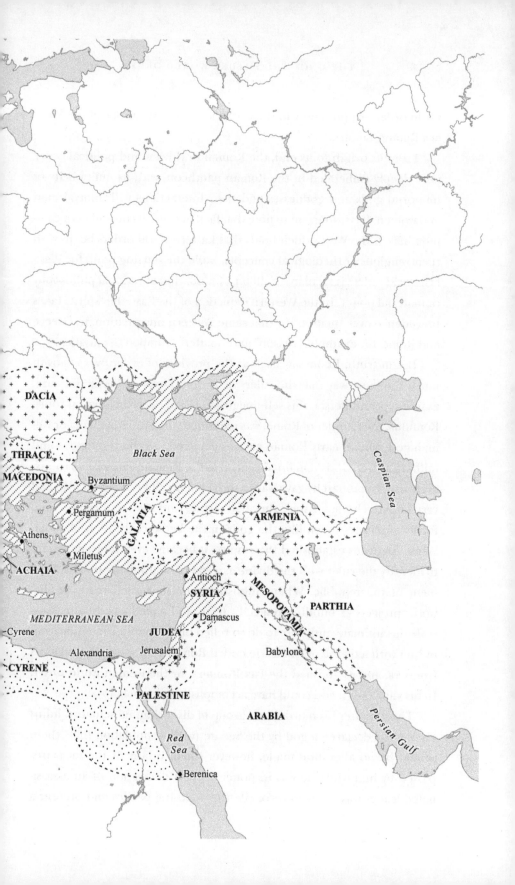

DACIA

THRACE

MACEDONIA

Byzantium

Black Sea

Caspian Sea

Pergamum

GALATIA

ARMENIA

Athens

Miletus

ACHAIA

Antioch

SYRIA

MESOPOTAMIA

PARTHIA

MEDITERRANEAN SEA

Damascus

Cyrene

Alexandria

Jerusalem

JUDEA

Babylone

CYRENE

PALESTINE

ARABIA

Red
Sea

Persian Gulf

Berenica

world order—applies only to the worldview and institutions of the Western Roman Empire.

From its origin to its end, the Roman worldview and political order were deeply embedded in the Roman pantheon, with its multiplicity of immortal gods and goddesses and their interactions with mortal men and women. It is important to note that fact, because it contradicts a common bias in the West, which holds that Eastern world orders begin with their religious or theological concepts, while the starting point for Western world orders is secular—built on a foundation of rational philosophy or material power. In the Western depiction of the East, the "spirit" takes precedence over "matter." In that same Western imagination, in Greece and Rome, for example, "reason" and "matter" trumped the mystical.

But in truth, Rome saw itself as the provider of order over chaos in much the same way that the rulers of ancient Egypt or Persia did, and, as in Egypt and Persia, this self-imagination had deep theological roots. Romulus, the founder of Rome, was identified with Quirinus, a major Roman god, who in early Roman art was depicted with both religious and military attire.[1] Gods remained central to the Roman state and its rulers, even after its monarchy gave way to the republic. But these gods also had very human characteristics; they had virtues and vices and represented forces of nature, much like the gods in the Vedic civilization of India. When Augustus established the empire, it became even more necessary to identify the ruler with the divine as a way of legitimizing the displacement of the republic. When Augustus undertook such costly public-works projects as building roads, bridges, and aqueducts on a massive scale, his ultimate authority to do so relied on the public's identification of him with a divine persona. He ended Rome's civil wars, expanded its frontiers, and established the Pax Romana, or the Roman world order. In his view, only a god could have accomplished so much.

The day after his murder by a group of disenchanted senators, Julius Caesar was declared a god by the Senate (with a stipulation that "there should be no alteration made, however small, in any of the measures passed by him while he was in power").[2] This deification of an assassinated leader was a way to reconcile the opposing parties and prevent a civil war. While both Caesar and his anointed son and successor, Augustus, were deified after their deaths, some of their successors claimed the status of gods during their lifetimes. These included such debauched emperors as Caligula and Nero, though both were so unpopular that the Senate declined to deify them.[3] Still, deification soon became a standard practice sanctioned by the Senate, giving rise to an imperial cult that considered emperors and their families to be divine and led to the dedication of temples wherein people could worship their emperor.[4] All of this evoked the precedent set by Alexander the Great, who, as we saw in Chapter 2, considered himself divine and anointed himself as both pharaoh in Egypt and great king in Persia. Whether Roman emperors were conscious of their emulation of Alexander or not, copying the Alexandrian model would hardly have been surprising, since Roman society imitated all things Greek—from arts and culture to ideas—and the Roman elite was deeply enamored of Alexander. The deified Roman emperors were worshipped for at least a generation after they died.[5]

The Roman Republic replaced the monarchy in 509 BC and lasted until 27 BC. The main republican principle that Rome adopted was not selecting rulers strictly on the basis of heredity, as was common to monarchies. But old tribal and family connections remained critical to political success. Ancient India also had a system of republics, called *gana-sanghas*, where tribal and family connections mattered much. The Roman Republic nevertheless had many relatively unique features, including the election of two coequal consuls as the highest-ranking officials to a one-year term; and the appointment of a dictator for a six-month term when there was a major crisis. The republic also featured two assemblies: The centuriate was a military group with the authority to vote for war and peace and elect magistrates with jurisdiction over military matters. The other, the tribal assembly, was tasked with general legislation and adjudicating public offenses.[6] After Augustus established the Roman Empire, the two assemblies were abolished and their roles transferred to the Roman Senate.

It is important to keep in mind that many institutions of ancient Rome now associated with democracy were actually feudal, clan-based, and oligarchic. The Roman Republic, like the ancient Indian republics, was an oligarchy, in which only wealthy male citizens could vote and become members of the Senate, which in turn elected the consuls. Additionally, the two main classes of Roman society—the wealthy, politically privileged patricians and the general citizenry—could not, before the system was abolished in 445 BC, intermarry.[7] The Senate had first emerged during the monarchical period, as a tribal assembly representing powerful families, whose descendants became Rome's ruling class or the patricians.

In its rise to Mediterranean hegemony, republican Rome gradually but steadily overwhelmed a number of other states that were culturally and economically more advanced, notably the Etruscans and the Carthaginians. Rome's immediate neighbors to the north were the Etruscans. Their origins are uncertain; historians view them either as migrants from Lydia in Asia minor or from the Aegean, or as the indigenous population of their area. Etruscan civilization emerged around the ninth century BC, and they maintained trade and other relations with the Greeks and Phoenicians. Organized initially in a system of city-states, the Etruscans in the seventh century formed a loose league, and for more than a century Rome was ruled by an Etruscan king, until that monarchy was overthrown in 509 BC. The conflict between the Etruscans and a rising Roman Republic continued until the leading Etruscan city of Veii was defeated in 396 BC, and the last site of Etruscan resistance to Rome, Volsinii, was crushed in 264 BC, after which the Etruscans adopted the Latin language and culture.[8] While the Etruscans were absorbed by Rome, the Romans also borrowed a good deal from the Etruscans, such as engineering, architecture, religious practices, clothing (including the famed toga), and urban planning. They also benefited from the Etruscans' draining of the marshes around Rome. It was simultaneous with this that the Romans had their first exposure to Greek literature and philosophy.

But Rome's principal strategic rival was Carthage, founded in what is now Tunisia centuries earlier by Phoenicians from Tyre, in modern Lebanon. These Phoenicians had settled throughout the western

Mediterranean, including in the western part of Sicily, where they dominated Mediterranean trade for centuries.

Rome and Carthage were strikingly different societies in three respects. First, the Roman system was dominated by the military. Romans venerated their army and its generals. Roman consuls, as noted above, were the leaders of both the army and the civilian administration. By contrast, in Carthage there was a strict separation between the Senate and the armed forces, which were mostly made up of mercenaries. Second, Roman society had an extremely rigid hierarchy based on the difference between patricians and plebians, such that even a person of newfound wealth could not become a patrician. Carthaginian society allowed a much higher degree of social mobility; a person who acquired wealth through trade or other activities could become a member of its powerful Senate. Which system was superior may be debated, but it's noteworthy that Aristotle recognized Carthage as a "democracy," a judgment that seems validated by the fact that the common people of Carthage never lived under the rule of a tyrant and never mounted any rebellion worth speaking of.[9]

These two differences led to a third. Overall, the Carthaginians, inheriting the maritime orientation of the Phoenicians, were more preoccupied with trade. The Romans, more engaged with their immediate overland northern neighbors, were focused on security. Carthage acquired its prominence through commerce, Rome through military organization and power. The contrasting worldviews of the two great powers of the Mediterranean contributed to their strategic competition, which ended only with the Third Punic War in 146 BC. The first two such wars, in 264–241 BC and 218–201 BC, had already stripped Carthage of its political power, although it remained a vibrant economic entity, but it was completely annihilated in the third war, its population killed or enslaved. The decisive defeat of Carthage eliminated Rome's main strategic rival. Rome's conquest of Greece, culminating in the defeat and destruction of Corinth in the same year as the sack of Carthage, resulted in the Latin cultural takeover of the Mediterranean, even though Rome borrowed a great deal of Greek culture and especially art.

The Roman Republic has been much admired by Western intellectuals and leaders (including the founding fathers of the United States) for its institutions and practices. To them, the secret of the Roman Republic's success was the system whereby the consuls, the Senate, and the public kept each other in check, preempting the emergence of a dictatorship. But this model society was beset by endless competition for power and wealth that spawned many a civil war as well as ceaseless external expansionism. Before it fell, the Roman Republic was probably more brutal and violent than the Roman Empire.

The republic's victory over Carthage provides a striking illustration of this. Roman legions moved from house to house to kill Carthage's inhabitants, who are estimated to have been between one hundred thousand and two hundred thousand people.[10] Those who survived the massacre were taken as slaves. The city was systematically demolished after days of burning, its destruction, as Roman historian Polybius put it, "immediate and total."[11] William D. Rubinstein, a historian of genocide, estimates Carthage's population at 200,000 people and concludes that 150,000 were slaughtered and the other 50,000 taken as slaves.[12] Similarly, Julius Caesar's invasion of Gaul cost a million lives and the enslavement of a million people.[13]

When the Roman Republic collapsed, to be replaced by the Roman Empire, all semblance of democratic rule ended. This was reflected in the changing meaning of the word *imperium*. During the republican period, imperium meant granting a limited command or authority to carry out some official function. The term combined military and judicial authority and was accorded to a wide range of officials: magistrates, consuls, proconsuls, dictators, praetors, military tribunes with consular power, and masters of the cavalry, as well as private citizens entrusted with a special command and members of certain commissions. To be sure, the privilege of imperium had some limits, with checks and balances imposed on magistrates. One such check was the principle of collegiality, which "provided that each of the magistrates of the same level (e.g., the two consuls) who held it [imperium] should hold it to the same degree" and for a limited period of time, often just one year.[14] Another check on governmental power was the law that Roman citizens accused of capital crimes must have trials and the right of appeal.

But in the Augustan era, the imperium idea became more powerful, absolute, and hereditary, in the sense that emperors could pass it to their own chosen successors. While the title of imperator (commander) under the Roman Republic could be enjoyed by victorious generals, it was now reserved exclusively for the emperor. The imperium became synonymous with empire.[15]

Pax Romana

The downfall of the Roman Republic and the advent of the Roman Empire in 27 BC also marks the beginning of Pax Romana, the Roman peace, the principal point of reference for the Roman world order. The term is deeply enshrined in the Western mind as an ideal system of hegemony, which brought peace and prosperity all around the Mediterranean through its suppression of piracy and its expansion of trade and communications. It has been associated with two major contributions to world order: the provision of the common or collective good and the system of indirect rule.

Despite this positive image, Rome after the collapse of the republic turned out to be a highly predatory and oppressive empire and world order. Mindful of the fate that befell Julius Caesar when he attempted to acquire too much power, Augustus kept the institution of the Senate and maintained the pretense of sharing power with it.[16] In reality, he was an absolutist and expansionist emperor. While this brought stability to the empire and facilitated trade, the Pax Romana was based on Rome's very direct and coercive rule over the entire Mediterranean coast and beyond. Pax Romana describes the condition of peace that lasted for about two centuries, from the start of the reign of Augustus in 27 BC to the end of the reign of Marcus Aurelius in 180 AD.[17] During that time, the Mediterranean was a Roman lake, or as the Romans called it, Mare Nostrum ("our sea"). No single part of its littoral was outside of direct Roman rule, and this was essential, since an ability to maintain peace on the seas—that is, to abolish piracy and ensure the safety of transportation and trade—was critical to the effectiveness and legitimacy of the empire. As one historian has written, "Pax Romana went hand in hand with Mare Nostrum."[18]

It bears stressing here that the benefits of security and trade that came to the ancient Mediterranean under Rome's rule were directly related to its military hegemony. Pax was underwritten by conquest, colonization, and repression. A strikingly different situation prevailed in the Indian Ocean before the European colonizers came, where, as Chapter 7 will discuss, trade flourished without the watch of any empire.

The Mediterranean became the main route for commerce, because many of the resources and commodities Rome depended on for its survival lay across the water in Africa and Asia, and also because the Roman roads, designed for feet or hooves rather than for wheels, were not optimal for the long-distance transport of goods. Rome's suppression of piracy allowed smaller settlements to exist in economically advantageous locations without the threat of disruption. According to the historian Suetonius, when the passengers and crew of a ship met with the dying Augustus near Campania, they "lavished upon him good wishes and the highest praise, saying that it was through him that they lived, through him that they sailed the seas, and through him that they enjoyed their liberty and their fortunes."[19]

But although trade flourished under Pax Romana, it was not a system of free trade as we know today. The Mediterranean remained a Roman lake, and the right to freely engage in commerce in its waters was not enjoyed equally by all. For the most part, freedom of seas, the key principle behind free trade, was limited to Roman vessels or ones officially sanctioned by Rome.

Pax Romana has also been praised for allowing considerable autonomy to its provinces and tributary states and for being accommodating to its subject people from diverse cultures. Roman rule, in this view, was similar to the system of rule used by the Persians before.

Rome's loose empire, with its benefits of increased trade, has generally been well regarded by Western historians and political scientists, some of whom have compared the Pax Romana with the nineteenth-century British Empire or the American-led international order that followed World War II. Both presented themselves as the providers of peace, stability, and prosperity, leading to a view that stability and prosperity in the world, key elements of a well-functioning world order, require a dominant power that will ensure the collective good.[20]

It is noteworthy that although other ancient empires—including the Chinese, the Indian, and the Islamic—fostered an extensive degree of collective good and used indirect rule in their extended domains, only the Roman Empire, the British Empire, and the American world order have been so closely associated in the Western mind with the notion of pax.

The idea of Pax Romana, to some extent, was a product of the Romans' own self-glorifying narrative. Much like the celebrations of the British Empire during the Victorian age, or of the American world order after World War II, the Roman Empire made pax central to its official ideology. It maintained the idea through propaganda—going as far as issuing coins with the word "pax" printed on them, for example, or fostering the publication of popular literary works extolling it—and ceremonies, like the closing of the gate of Janus in the Roman Forum to mark periods of peace.[21]

But this leads to the question: Was Pax Romana really a pax? For whom? These are also questions for the British Empire and the American world order. Neither the British nor American world order was peaceful, stable, or very orderly for much of the non-Western world. In this respect, they were following Rome's example. The historical reality is far harsher in all three cases than the concept of pax would suggest.

In Rome's case, one can start by looking at the draconian measures taken to ensure that its loose empire was held under tight control by the Roman center. Roman governors wielded total power over non-Roman citizens, backed by Roman soldiers willing to coerce and kill dissidents and rebels.

Rome did allow some neighbors to remain nominally independent, at least for a time, or to serve as vassals and client kings, who would thus be spared harsh submission. Such clients included Commagene, Emesa, Armenia, and Judea (the notorious King Herod).[22] Such client or tributary relations are not uncommon in history. But compared to China, which had the most well-known of such systems, Rome had a much smaller circle of client states. Rome preferred direct submission to indirect rule. It ruled over all the states in the Mediterranean littoral, and hence it had more direct control over its immediate neighbors.

In the Roman world order, client status was sometimes a temporary phase before full-scale annexation, and full-scale exploitation. For example, Egypt could have remained a client state, rather than a province, but its economic importance as the main supplier of grain to Rome prevented that. While Roman culture did have its attractions for the people it colonized, cooperation between the provinces and the imperial administration was mostly due to the opportunities it gave the local elite to gain wealth and status or was based on their fear of violent retribution from Rome.[23]

In addition, while it marked the end of the civil wars that had plagued and brought down the Roman Republic, Pax Romana did not mean the absence of war. Pax meant but the total subjugation of enemies and the suppression of internal resistance to Roman hegemony. This entailed significant violence, including three brutal wars against the Jews: the First Jewish-Roman War (66–70 AD), the Kitos War (115 AD–117 AD), and the suppression of the Bar Kokhba revolt (132–135 or 136 AD). There was also the suppression of the revolt led by Queen Boudica in Britain (c. 60 AD). Several times the Romans waged war against the Parthians, their mightiest opponent since Carthaginian general Hannibal. Rome first fought the Parthian Empire (today's Iran) in 58–63 AD, then under Trajan in 113 AD, and under Septimius Severus in 198 AD. To these conflicts must be added Trajan's Dacian conquest and Rome's continuous confrontations with Germanic tribes, such as in Teutoburg in 9 AD.

The brutality of Roman conquests was captured vividly by Tacitus in the *Agricola*. Here Calgacus, a Caledonian commander, denounces the Romans while exhorting his troops to fight a Roman army led by General Gnaeus Julius Agricola.

The plunderers of the world they have laid waste the land till there is no more left, and now they scour the sea. If a people are rich they are worth robbing, if poor they are worth enslaving; and not the East and not the West can content their greedy maw. They are the only men in all the world whose lust of conquest makes them find in wealth and in poverty equally tempting baits. To robbery, murder, and outrage they give the lying name of government, and where they make a desert they call it peace.[24]

The persistence of war under the Pax Romana came from the vastness of an empire whose subject peoples were often restive and rebellious, and from the militaristic culture of Roman society, which insisted on complete obedience to its dictates. Even Hadrian—who is sometimes referred to as the "peaceful" emperor because of his decision to give up territories in Mesopotamia, Assyria, and Armenia conquered by his predecessor, Trajan—resorted to military means to keep the pax, and those means were brutal by any standard. Hadrian's "expeditio Judaica" to suppress the Jewish revolt (132–136 AD) led by Simon bar Kokhba, resulted in horrific massacres involving the destruction of fifty rebel garrisons and nearly a thousand villages, with total casualties of 585,000.[25] Hadrian's decisions to give up the eastern territories and build a wall in Britain (the famous Hadrian's Wall) to keep out barbarian tribes might have seemed pragmatic and defensive, reflecting his realization that the Roman Empire was overstretched. But in other provinces his approach was unyielding and aggressive. "The nations conquered by Trajan were in revolt," wrote Roman historian Aelius Spartianus. "The moors were on a rampage; the Britons could not be kept under Roman sovereignty; Egypt was ravaged by uprisings; finally Libya and Palestine displayed their spirit of rebellion."[26] Even Hadrian's defensive gestures, especially giving up the eastern territories, were criticized by the Roman elite for undermining Trajan's legacy (some felt this was precisely Hadrian's intent). They certainly did not imply any change in the Roman strategic culture, which continued to glorify military success.

Not only did wars and massacres occur during the Roman peace but there seems to have been no remorse on the part of the emperor about the death and destruction. This is in stark contrast to the expressions of regret made by King Ashoka of India after his war against Kalinga, for example.[27] "Roman peace," historian Neville Morley writes, "for the vast majority of the population...was the peace enjoyed by the domesticated animal."[28] It was military might and a brutal readiness to use it that kept the fifty to sixty million Roman subjects under the rule of a single emperor.[29]

The Roman imperial system featured an almost continuous stream of assassinations. Of the overall rate of Roman regicide, estimates vary; according to one study, of the seventy-seven emperors that ruled Rome between 27 BC and 476 AD, a total of 503 years, thirty-three were murdered, thirty of them by sword or knife, the rest by strangulation, hanging, and stoning. During the early period, which is the period of Pax Romana, only 56 percent of the emperors died of natural causes; 44 percent were murdered.[30] These royal murders were variously carried out: by the Praetorian Guard, which became a major arbiter of power; by regular troops, sometimes at the behest of other aspirants to the throne, sometimes on the orders of the Senate; or in some combination. And the assassinations claimed the lives of all types of emperors, including the sadistic and maniacal, like Caligula, and simply those deemed incompetent and inefficient. Royal assassinations by relatives, usurpers, and soldiers happened in all civilizations and empires—including the Chinese, Indian, and Islamic—but only Rome draped itself so completely in the mantle of pax.

Slavery was also especially widespread during the period of Pax Romana and beyond. Perhaps as many as every fifth person in the Roman Empire was a slave, some ten million slaves in all.[31] Walter Scheidel estimates that the capital city of Rome had somewhere between 240,000 and 440,000 slaves, or one slave for every three people living there.[32] Wars were often the major source of slaves. Crito, an adviser to Trajan, reported that the emperor's Dacia campaign netted five hundred thousand slaves.[33] Notably, however, the Romans took slaves from people of all races. There is little evidence that slavery reflected or created racial prejudice, as it would in early modern Europe.[34] The association of slavery with skin color would come much later, in the period of the West's rise, with the United States being a prime theater of this link, as will be discussed later. Rome also occasionally gave slaves Roman citizenship, perhaps from seventh century BC onward, whereas the United States did so in 1886, more than 250 years after slavery began there.

But one should not make too much of this. Slave or not, Roman citizenship brought limited privileges to newcomers. Rome is remembered and admired in the West for having introduced the idea of "universal citizenship." However, this only came relatively late in the course of the empire, with Caracalla's edict in 212 AD that granted full citizenship to all free men in the Roman Empire and accorded free non-Roman women the same status as Roman women. Prior to the edict, the rights associated with citizenship were only accessible through a few channels, such as military service, grants from the emperor, or as a bargaining chip in Roman foreign policy. Political pressure was also a critical factor: the majority of people living on the Italian peninsula only became citizens after the revolt known as the Social War (91–88 or 90–89 BC). Though citizenship was steadily becoming more accessible to non-Romans in the lead-up to Caracalla's edict, perhaps as many as 60 to 80 percent of non-Romans in the empire were not citizens at the time of the edict.[35]

Roman citizenship came with certain rights—such as the right to appeal to the Roman judicial system against punishment, and the recognition of marriage and contracts—in exchange for taxes.[36] In fact, revenue might have been the major motive behind Caracalla's decision to expand citizenship. But this did not create a true Roman identity or a sense of genuine loyalty to the idea of Rome—certainly not to the extent that pan-Hellenic identity emerged in ancient Greece after the Persian wars, or even as far as the more limited Athenian identity that Pericles called for in his famous funereal speech. Rome held itself together mainly through force, not shared identity. The extended grant of citizenship might have been a strategy to preempt and manage internal revolts, but it was controlled by the state. There was no voluntary assimilation or Romanization except that "imposed by the state rather than an organic will."[37] Roman law, another widely acclaimed legacy, did give its citizens the ability to appeal against the arbitrary exercise of authority. It is seen today as a system of clear, established, written and unwritten codes that, at least in theory, guided and constrained the behavior of individuals and the government. This is not an unjustified claim, and it is precursor to the modern rule of law. But it is not the only one. Principles and rules—formal and informal—to guide and constrain official policy also existed in Sumer, India, Africa, and Islam. In these places, as much as in Rome, such laws had limits. Ultimately, Rome was an empire that brooked no dissent, revolt, or attempt at secession.

One should not forget that there would be no Roman law without outright Roman imperialism. Before the Roman Empire, Rome had pursued a two-track policy: democracy in Rome, autocracy in conquered places. Much like in later-day European colonies in Asia, Africa, the Americas, and elsewhere, there was little justice for the Roman colonies. While some Roman emperors were regarded as "fathers" of conquered peoples, there was no recourse when colonial subjects faced injustice, tyranny, and violence, whether from imperial governors or from local officials. The subjects' petitions seldom reached Rome, and when they did elicit a response, Rome's rulings were mostly ignored by local officials.

Social life in ancient Rome also embraced violence and brutality with little sense of remorse. Comparing Rome's gladiatorial combats with ancient India, the Indian historian D. P. Singhal notes, "In the third century B.C., whilst [Maurya King] Asoka had renounced war and was preaching non-violence and compassion for all other beings [including animals], the Romans were indulging in human sacrifice."[38] While the Aztecs used human sacrifice to please the gods, the Roman practice was to please the people. Gladiatorial combats featured slaves and convicts who were forced to fight and be killed for the pleasure of the audience. One particular Roman innovation was *damnatio ad bestias* (Latin for "condemnation to beasts"), in which "a human being faced a snarling pack of starved beasts, and every laughing spectator in the crowd chanted for the big cats to win, the point at which the republic's obligation to make a man's death a fair or honorable one began to be outweighed by the *entertainment value* of watching him die."[39] Rome's punishments for crime would be considered extreme even by the standards of the ancient period, such as decimation (ten soldiers drew lots, and whoever had the shortest straw was beaten to death by the nine others), burying alive (for vestal virgins who took oaths of chastity), and *poena cullei* ("penalty of the sack," whereby a person was sewn up in a leather sack along with live dogs, snakes, monkeys, chickens, or roosters and then thrown into water).[40]

Why Rome expanded so relentlessly and maintained such a large empire is a question that should be of interest to all students of world order today. After all, as Greek historian Polybius posed more than two thousand years ago, "Can anyone be so indifferent or idle as not to care to know by what means, and under what kind of polity, almost the whole inhabited world was conquered and brought under the domination of a single city of Rome, and that too within a period of not quite fifty-three years?"[41] The answer to this begins with a major and familiar motive, which is the desire for personal power and wealth. Rome's frequent and bloody struggles for both have been well captured by Tacitus, who noted, "That old passion for power which has been ever innate in man increased and broke out as the Empire grew in greatness.... When the world had been subdued, when all rival kings and cities had been destroyed, and men had leisure to covet wealth which they might enjoy in security, the early conflicts between the patricians and the people were kindled into flame.... Henceforth men's sole object was supreme power."[42]

But profit and predation were also important factors, including the plundering of conquered territories—for both their gold and their art—and the collection of heavy taxes. "Under the protection of Rome, swarms of usurers spread over the provinces like hungry leeches, to suck the blood of the innocent," one historian has written.[43] Also important was the intense internal competition among the Roman generals, who often served as consuls, for wealth and power.[44] Foreign expeditions provided the only real opportunity for them to secure the necessary personal wealth to keep or boost their power. Another motive was to pay off debt—both the private debt of generals and that of the state—which had to be incurred to pay for troops and campaigns. Debt and military campaigns formed a vicious cycle. The wealth from Egypt "wiped out all of Octavian's debts in one fell swoop."[45]

Foreign wars were also needed for domestic political purposes, something that one could see in other civilizations, including the American world order. In Rome, foreign adventures were useful in gaining popular support and asserting or consolidating claims to power. An example is Nero's dispatch of Vespasian to destroy the new Jewish state in Judea in 66 AD. At first, Vespasian delayed the final assault on Jerusalem, but when Nero's suicide prompted a vicious power struggle, Vespasian, needing the prestige of a foreign conquest to validate his claim to the throne, moved quickly to finish the task.[46]

Rome's sheer dependence on foreign resources, including food, also contributed to the expansionist impulse. After conquering Egypt and using its immense wealth to stave off a looming bankruptcy in Rome caused by the prolonged civil war, the empire became heavily dependent on Egyptian resources. Egypt was to the Roman Empire what India was to become to the British: the jewel in the crown. Egypt was also Rome's breadbasket, much in the way Ukraine would be to the Soviet Union. So precious was Egypt to the survival of the Roman Empire that it was counted as the personal province of the emperor, rather than as a senatorial province. Hence, even a Roman senator could not enter Egypt without the emperor's personal permission.[47]

A comparison with China is instructive here, because it provides clues to why Rome absorbed the nations it defeated, while China maintained a trade-oriented tributary system. As noted, like China, Rome had some tributary states where local rulers were allowed to govern for a while, but that status was short-lived as they were quickly annexed and absorbed into the empire as provinces. Why? Rome was dependent on imports for its very survival, while China, which was both the main producer and the main market, was not. China could afford the tributary states to profit more from trade, especially given that what it mostly needed to import, aside from horses, were luxuries, religious goods, and spices. Whereas China's prosperity did not depend on an overseas empire, Rome needed an empire for its political and economic stability.

The vital trade for Rome was in such essential products as grain and oil, which came from nearby Egypt and Carthage. Because this trade was essential and could not be conducted on equal terms, it fueled Rome's annexation of its trading partners.

All this accounts for the differences between China's concept of world order and Rome's. In contrast to Rome's use of direct military force to protect trade, China continued to rely primarily on the tributary system, which offered security to its neighbors but didn't require that they be absorbed directly into its empire. To a much greater extent than the Mediterranean under Roman rule, the East Asian, Southeast Asian, and Indian Ocean maritime spaces remained open and noncoercive, despite China's political and strategic reach.

Another of Rome's major legacies is the spread of its culture and identity. Rome's innovations, such as concrete, aqueducts, the Julian calendar, law, literature, philosophy, and architecture, have a worldwide impact to this day. But this is different from Romanization, or "becoming Roman" by adopting its culture and values. It may be compared to the spread of Indian and Greek ideas. As previously discussed, the spread of Indian ideas was largely peaceful and voluntary on the part of the recipient societies. This contrasted with Hellenization, which was not without violence and coercion. Hellenization involved the displacement of native populations (in the western Mediterranean), and it was backed by conquest and imperialism in the eastern Mediterranean (Anatolia, Persia, Mesopotamia, Afghanistan, and Egypt). But that still left room for considerable voluntary adoption by the local societies of Hellenic ideas, culture, and institutions, thanks to their prestige and brilliance.

To be sure, Romanization did appeal to elites from the colonies who were attracted to Roman culture, including food and dress, and the benefits of Roman citizenship. It spread because non-Romans wanted to gain status and acceptance into Roman society—for many of the same reasons why people from the colonies picked up European customs and habits in the modern era. But as with European imperialism, Romanization was ultimately a product of outright imperialism, and for the most part it followed, rather than preceded, coercion and conquest. This was a far cry from the way Indian, Chinese, and to some degree Hellenic (after Alexander's conquests) civilizations spread. It was only after the fall of the Western Roman Empire that Romanization became a voluntary process, mostly in Europe and the West, where, as will be discussed next, the memory of Rome served as a potent symbol for European rulers seeking legitimacy by claiming to be Rome's successors.

Rome's Enduring Legacy

Perhaps the most powerful legacy of Rome is its contribution to the idea of the West, led today by the United States and western Europe. To be sure, it was not the only or most decisive reason why the West emerged as a modern idea—credit for that belongs to the European civilizational chauvinism from the eighteenth century onward—but it did play a role. While ancient Greece holds a similar place as a foundation of the West, it is mainly for its creativity in art, democracy, science, and philosophy. The Roman Empire, by contrast, not only evokes power and dominance but is more directly and physically associated with the creation of the West. After the political seat of the empire moved east to Constantinople, the division between its Orthodox Christian religion and the Catholic Church in Rome became foundational to both the idea of the West and modern European identity. The political association of Rome and the West was crystallized when the pope backed Charlemagne, the Frankish king, over the Byzantine emperor and crowned him the Holy Roman emperor in 800 AD. After Charlemagne, the idea of a Holy Roman Empire would survive into the Napoleonic Wars, allowing various European rulers to claim legitimacy as imagined heirs of classical Rome, although often without its actual power—so much so that the Holy Roman Empire has been derided as being neither holy, nor Roman, nor an empire. But other European rulers have also claimed Rome's legacy; after the fall of Constantinople to Ottomans, Ivan III of Russia assumed the title of czar (Caesar), as orthodox clerics promoted the idea that Russia was a "third Rome." The Seljuk Turks, who preceded the Ottoman Empire, did call their newly established state in Anatolia the "Sultanate of Rum," but this was because it was located in the territory taken from the Eastern Roman Empire, rather than due to any desire to emulate Roman civilization. Instead, the Sultanate of Rum was a thoroughly Persianized state, adopting Persian administrative structure, art, and architecture, and combining it with Turkish and Arabic elements.

But the Roman Empire's impact was more far-reaching even than this, and in a sense its influence has been more sweeping and long-lasting after its downfall than during its lifetime. As historian Walter Scheidel argues, the fall of Rome was at the origin of both Europe's political disintegration and the birth of its competitive political culture. It triggered a long-lasting struggle for political and economic power among kings, their vassals, feudal aristocrats and lords, clergymen, and traders and precluded the rise of another European empire of Rome's relative power and scale. After long periods of warfare, this fiercely competitive political climate produced management frameworks such as the Treaty of Westphalia and the Concert of Europe. At the same time, the competition that raged among the European countries prompted them to acquire land and establish trading posts in the Americas, Asia, and Africa, often to prevent their rivals from doing the same thing. It was merchants and traders who set up outposts on other continents, enriching governments as they did so, which induced states to then send armies of soldiers and bureaucrats to protect the traders from local leaders and foreign competitors alike. In such a way, the collapse of Rome might have contributed over the long term to the impulse for European expansion and colonization over much of the world.[48]

Rome has exerted a powerful and enduring influence in the West. One of the darkest imprints of Rome was Benito Mussolini's creation of a fascist state in Italy before World War II. In a statement on April 21, 1922, the traditional anniversary of the founding day of Rome, Mussolini evoked the concept of *Romanità* or "Roman-ness," linking it explicitly with fascism. "Rome is our point of departure and of reference; it is our symbol, or if you like, it is our Myth. We dream of a Roman Italy, that is to say wise and strong, disciplined and imperial. Much of that which was the immortal spirit of Rome resurges in Fascism."[49]

Mussolini's efforts to invoke Rome were consequential not just for Italian domestic politics but also for foreign relations, as he would soon join Adolf Hitler in seeking to establish an alternative order for Europe and the world. Even though this effort failed, at huge costs to humanity, ancient Rome remains an inspiration for contemporary far-right movements, both in Europe and in the United States.[50]

Rome would also fire the imagination of modern Western leaders, and it did so in many ways, including inducing them to follow the Roman model and to seek empire. One such example can be found in nineteenth- and early twentieth-century British novels written by schoolmasters. These were aimed at encouraging young Britons to be inspired by the glory of the empire and to venture abroad to help govern what was called the "second Rome." Rudyard Kipling, for example, often equated the British and Roman empires.[51]

The United States did not build a world empire comparable to Britain's, but Rome's enduring legacy has been salient in many ways in American history, political institutions, and even architecture, where the styles of both Rome and classical Greece have been reincarnated in the buildings of Washington, DC. The Roman Republic's political institutions, especially the Senate, were influential in writing the US Constitution. The empire's idea of the Pax Romana then became the model for the basic structure of American world order—namely, democracy at home, expansion and intervention abroad. The very term Pax Americana is clearly an echo of the Pax Romana of two millennia ago, as the United States too claims to have forged a world order by providing the benefits of trade and stability to the world by its superior military and economic power.[52] Rome also shapes American society's glorification of violence and masculinity; as a TikTok trend goes, "Men Think About the Roman Empire All the Time."[53]

Rome's major contribution to world order was to offer two competing ideas: republic and empire. The republic was not a democracy but an oligarchy, where the voice of ordinary people mattered only a little. It was also an aggressive expansionist state, a fact ignored by the founders of the United States, who sought to emulate the republic in their domestic politics. Then, under imperial rule, Rome spawned the modern idea that stable peace requires the presence of a dominant power. This is known as "hegemonic stability" in today's political science jargon, and the idea can be traced from Rome to Britain in the late nineteenth century to the United States after World War II. But the pax of Pax Romana was limited at best, dependent as it was on Rome's readiness to use its military power to ruthlessly slaughter its enemies. The Roman Empire also thrived on slavery, and its much-vaunted Roman law did not constrain political absolutism or imperialism. Yet, ancient Rome, whether republic or empire, remains a role model for the West, and it is, with ancient Greece, imagined to be at the core of Western civilization. This both romanticizes and idealizes Rome while ignoring the alternatives to its style of rule offered by less-dominating systems of world order, such as Persia, India, and China.

In the Western imagination, the end of the Western Roman Empire in the fifth century ushered in the Dark Ages of Europe. While the truth of this view has been questioned, there is little doubt that, during the same period, civilizations and empires in the East became more vibrant, prosperous, innovative, and powerful than any in the West. These included not only the classical civilizations of Gupta-age India and Tang and Song China but also that of a newcomer: the world order of Islam.

Chapter 6

Rejuvenating the World

Islam, founded in the early seventh century by the Prophet Muhammad (570–632 AD) in Arabia, is the youngest among the major world religions, but it was the fastest to evolve into a global system of belief. Less than a century after Muhammad's death, Islam spanned West Asia, North Africa, and Spain. This expansion occurred both through force—the sword, as it was put—and through attraction, with the mix of the two changing from period to period, empire to empire, and ruler to ruler. A notable development for world order was the Arab conquest of Spain from 711 AD onward; parts of Spain remained under their rule until 1492. Islam also moved east, gaining a foothold in Sind (in today's Pakistan) in the eighth century and becoming a much stronger political force in north India in the eleventh century, before moving to Southeast Asia not long thereafter.

During this period, Islam conquered not only lands but also minds. Europe's Dark Ages, to use popular if tired expressions, were Islam's golden age. In this, Islam drew upon the ideas of other civilizations—chiefly Persia, Greece, India, and China—while adding much that was its own. It was this collective pool of knowledge that would prove indispensable to the rise of Europe and the West.

Through its expansion, Islam developed a fundamentally distinct idea of world order. While all world orders—Egyptian, Indian, Chinese, and European—have their foundation in religious beliefs, in Islam the gap between religious belief and political order is the blurriest and the distinction between believers and nonbelievers the strongest. In Islam, the world is divided into two spheres, Dar al-Harb, territory of war, and Dar al-Islam, territory of Islam. This division profoundly shaped the medieval world order and beyond. Dar al-Harb refers to "territory that does not have a treaty of nonaggression or peace with Muslims," while Dar al-Islam, denotes a "region of Muslim sovereignty where Islamic law prevails."[1] This suggests an adversarial vision of world order, one that was predisposed to conflict or war between believers and nonbelievers, since it makes Dar al-Harb subject to Muslim conquest and absorption rather than peaceful coexistence.

While many associate the distinction between the two realms with the origins of Islam, in fact it was not explicitly stated in the Koran or Hadith, the sayings of the prophet, but was proposed by later theologians as a justification for the newly rising Islamic powers in expanding their empires. Much has been made of this distinction as testimony to Islam's aggressiveness, but using religious concepts to launch wars or build empires was neither new nor unique to Islam. Aspiring conquerors of all religions have done much the same: The European powers used Christianity to justify their colonial wars throughout the Americas, Africa, and Asia. The Hindu-Buddhist concept of *chakravartin*, as previously discussed, offers another prominent example.

More importantly, Dar al-Harb and Dar al-Islam were often terms of convenience, used to simplify the domains of actual control by Islamic rulers. They did not imply zero-sum relationships. Islamic rulers found it more pragmatic to pursue policies of accommodation and coexistence between Muslims and non-Muslims. Still, even if these concepts were not always rigidly applied the same way, they remained important distinguishing features of the Islamic notion of world order. In the early modern period, the political importance of Christianity in Europe was diluted by the rise of the Westphalian system, which included the separation of church and state. Islam, on the other hand, would continue to fuse them.

While dividing the world in theology and politics, Islam unified it in philosophy, science, and technology. Early Islamic empires acted as commercial and intellectual bridges between the East and the West, the ancient world and the modern era. Consolidating advances in science, philosophy, and technology from classical civilizations of the Near East, Greece, India, and China and adding its own considerable innovations, Islam provided a vast pool of knowledge that would eventually be eagerly borrowed by a rising Europe. Islam is thus the most consequential catalyst of what came to be known as globalization. Although the Roman Empire covered West Asia and North Africa, the Islamic world order spread far more extensively and covered large chunks of the three different cultures and continents: Asia, Europe, and Africa.

The rise of Islam also brought another new concept to the notion of world order. Unlike India, China, and Rome, whose political centers were confined within or close to their original places, the Islamic world order was spread across many political centers in different countries, such that rulers in different Islamic capitals—Baghdad, Cairo, Cordoba, and Ottoman Constantinople—claimed to be caliph, a successor descendant of the Prophet Muhammad and the leader of the entire Islamic world.[2] Given the emergence of these several centers of religious authority and secular power, it would have been impossible for any one of them to politically and administratively control the far-flung domains of Islam.

Despite this, the Islamic world in general functioned with a set of shared concepts that would underpin the Islamic world order. These centered on the ideas in Islamic theology about social and political orders based on *asabiyyah* and *ummah*. *Asabiyyah* is the bond among people based on the natural solidarity of a community, which is found in pre-Islamic societies. *Ummah* is the basis of solidarity in Islamic society; it is defined by "a moral link, a common obedience to law, and acceptance of the reciprocal rights and duties laid down in it."[3] *Asabiyyah* does not disappear as society makes the transition from pre-Islamic to Islamic, but in Islamic political theology, *ummah* prevails, and political power is seen as "a delegation by God (wilaya), controlled by His will."[4] *Ummah* is the expression of "the essential unity and theoretical equality of Muslims from diverse cultural and geographical settings."[5]

Given the intense and vicious conflicts in the world today, some of them between Muslim countries—the Iran-Iraq conflict of the 1980s, for example—and many between Muslim state and non-state actors and non-Muslim countries—most conspicuously, as these words are being written, between Israel and Iran-supported proxy forces in Gaza, Lebanon, Syria, and Yemen—it is easy see Islam itself as prone to violence. Adding to this conception, of course, is international terrorism—including such events as the al-Qaeda attack on the United States in 2001—and its association with Islamic extremists.

But in the long sweep of history, there is little to justify this association with violence. Nothing has occurred under Islam that has not, and does not, occur under other religions, whether it's the Buddhist persecution of the Rohingya people in today's Myanmar or the Chrisian crusades and inquisition of medieval times. Nor is Islam in any sense a monolithic faith; like other systems of belief, it has given birth to many varieties. For centuries, the world's most progressive scientific, artistic, and literary cultures were centered in the Islamic world, which, in general, was far more tolerant and open to diverse influences than the Christian world was.

All world orders—past and present—have had an association with some kind of religious belief. The difference is that, today, the Islamic world is more attached to religion than competing world orders are, and this attachment is bound to be an element in the world order of the future.

The Expanding Frontier: Political and Cultural

Islam expanded rapidly after the death of the Prophet Muhammad in 632 AD. First, his companion and father-in-law, Abu Bakr, became caliph, ruling for two years until his death in 634. In that short time, Abu Bakr unified the Arabian Peninsula. The major early expansion of Islam then occurred under the second caliph, Umar ibn al-Khattab, who ruled from 634 to 644 and conquered neighboring states, including Persia, Iraq, Syria, Palestine, and Egypt. While military conquest was the primary mode of expansion, the common view has been that the spread of Islam was motivated by religious conviction, the messianic urge to share the Prophet's word. In fact, there were other factors that contributed to the rapid expansion of Islamic power, including the need to acquire resources and to forge the unity of the community or *ummah*. Islam's rise was also made easier by the weakness of the Persian Empire, riven as it was by factional struggles. The constant military confrontations taking place between the Sassanian Persians and the Byzantine, or Eastern Roman, Empire also left both regimes weakened, their populations suffering and receptive to a new order. Some Roman Christians found Islamic rule more tolerable than their Greek Orthodox rulers in the Eastern Roman Empire. Far from forcing the conversion of conquered peoples to Islam, the Arabs left them to practice their own faith; indeed, conversion to Islam was even discouraged until the middle of the eighth century AD. Financial considerations played a part: For the Arab conquerors, converting their new subjects meant loss of revenue from the poll tax, or *jizya*, that non-Muslims paid to their Islamic rulers. For the conquered peoples, converting to Islam offered privileges, including exemption from the tax.

But by the end of the seventh century, the Arab forces were stretched thin and their conquests slowed down. They were then forced to consider how to manage their relationships with non-Muslims while developing a common political identity among their Islamic subjects. At this stage, the concepts of Dar al-Harb and Dar al-Islam were developed, but this was at first mainly a religious concept: a division of the world into Muslim believers and nonbelievers. In practice, relations between the two worlds were largely peaceful.[6]

Keeping this in mind, it is not surprising that Muslim scholars have fiercely debated the legal and political connotations of these two fundamental concepts, even as they added new ideas about how the world should be ordered. These scholars envisioned different places, or abodes, where a particular principle or condition, negative or positive, dominated. In the negative category, there was Dar al-Maslubah, or the Abode of Pillaged Land; Dar al-Bid'ah, the Abode of Heresy; and Dar al-Baghy, the Abode of Usurpation. In the positive category, there was Dar al-'Adl, the Abode of Justice, and Dar al-'Ahd, the Abode of Treaties. None of these concepts were foundational to Islamic faith. The understanding and use of them was never clear-cut and varied among Islamic centers of power through the ages.

Such extensions and reinterpretations of founding beliefs is commonplace in other religions, including Hinduism, Buddhism, and Christianity. But these abodes are especially important for understanding Islam, because they challenge a common misperception of it as an overly homogeneous or united religion—a perception has led to Islam being seen as posing a threat to the pluralistic and inclusive world order allegedly spearheaded by the West. At the very least, some of these Islamic concepts—especially Dar al-'Ahd, the Abode of Treaties—clearly held out the possibility of peace and coexistence with the non-Muslim world.

Overall, Islam retained a universal worldview, the idea that its beliefs and practices could and should apply to everyone across the globe. But because of its vast spread, it developed localized features, ensuring differing interpretations and applications of its political doctrines. Major Islamic powers—such as the Abbasid Caliphate, the Fatimid dynasty, the Mamluks of Egypt, the Caliphate of Cordoba, the Moghul Empire in India, and the Ottoman Empire—developed distinctive cultural and administrative approaches. Thus, Islamic Spain, Al-Andalus, developed Spanish features. The Abbasid Caliphate was very Persianized: its language was Persian written in Arabic script. The Moghuls acquired considerable Indian features: their Indo-Islamic art hearkened back to the development of Indo-Greek art after the campaigns of Alexander the Great. Moreover, different Islamic centers competed and were intolerant of each other. The Safavids, an orthodox Shia empire that ruled northern Iran from 1501 to 1736 AD, persecuted Sunnis. The Fatimids in North Africa, based in Cairo, were mortal enemies of the Sunni caliphate in Baghdad. While intra-religious competition is hardly unique to Islam, because of its nearly global scope, the Islamic world order for many centuries was more differentiated within itself than any other major civilization—though Christian Europe would later become even more globally spread out and diverse.

Starting in the fourteenth century and lasting until the twentieth, the Ottoman—or Turkish—Empire encompassed most of the major

Islamic centers and embodied the Islamic worldview as well as its practical application. Founded in northeast Anatolia by Osman I at the very end of the thirteenth century, the Ottoman Empire eventually extended from the Balkan states to the Caspian Sea, a vast, multicultural, and multireligious entity straddling Europe, Asia, and Africa and lasting for six hundred years. It developed a governing bureaucracy and a military that included a large number of non-Turks and Christians who hadn't converted to Islam. The Ottomans also had substantial interactions with Europe, some of their rulers marrying into eastern European families (as long as they converted to Islam). This practice probably emerged from the fact that, unlike Arab families, eastern Europeans would be less of a threat to the throne and less prone to reclaim important positions.

The Ottoman Empire played a key role in organizing the modern Middle East's frontiers. While as an empire it was theoretically Dar al-Islam, its internal territorial divisions or provinces—such as Egypt, Yemen, Habesha (Abyssinia, present-day Ethiopia), Basra (southern Iraq), Baghdad (northern Iraq), Lahsa (al-Hasa, present-day Kuwait)—each had their own political and governance needs. Western historians usually credit the emergence of the modern state in the Middle East to Western powers and arrangements negotiated by them, such as the Sykes-Picot Agreement (the British-French arrangement of 1916) and the San Remo conference of 1920 among the Entente powers of World War I (Britain, France, Russia, Italy, Japan, and the United States).[7] But this view ignores the important role played by the Ottoman Empire in creating centralized bureaucratic structures, legal systems, and civil rights, especially during the Tanzimat reforms undertaken from 1839 onward. These reforms established a secular school system, protected the lives and property of Muslims and non-Muslims, and granted more autonomy to the provinces, such as Iraq and Syria. Hence, although nation-states supplanting the Islamic notion of caliphate is considered a legacy of European influence and decolonization, the Ottoman Empire had already shown the way, which would orient the Muslim provinces of the empire to accept a more secular view of sovereignty.[8]

Moreover, Islamic rulers provided space for non-Muslims in their states. "There is no compulsion in religion," says a Koranic verse (2:256).[9]

These words have been interpreted as "enjoining tolerance and forbidding the use of force, except in certain well-defined circumstances."[10] Islamic rulers devised the system of *dhimmi* to designate non-Muslims living under Muslim rule. *Dhimmi* status was a "pact between the Muslim state and a non-Muslim community, by which the state conceded certain privileges and the [non-Muslim] community accepted certain duties and constraints," which included clothes they could wear, weapons they could use, and animals they could ride.[11] In addition, they were required to pay *jizya*. Except in Arabia, Muslims "allowed non-Muslims to live under their rule and share their countries, though not their identity."[12] In Muslim Spain, Jews and Christians lived together, mostly peacefully, but after the Christian conquest of 1492, Jews and Muslims were expelled.[13]

Given this tradition of treaty making and tolerance, what about the Islamic notion of jihad, which has received much attention in the West as a byword for Islam's belligerent and intolerant nature? Although often associated in the West with "holy war," jihad means "struggle" and "primarily refers to the human struggle to promote what is right and to prevent what is wrong."[14] It can be fulfilled in different ways, "by the heart, the tongue, the hand (physical action short of armed combat), and the sword." The idea of jihad as holy war was regarded as a misinterpretation of Islamic theology by Arab scholars such as Ibn Rushd, and it is now being challenged by non-traditionalist Islamic intellectuals. Modern interpretations of jihad stress "the Qur'ān's restriction of military activity to self-defense in response to external aggression."[15] Hence it is worth noting that jihad, along with Dar al-Islam, was frequently invoked by anti-colonial struggles in the Middle East and Asia in their fight against Western colonial powers.[16]

In this context, Islam offers, like India and China, a notion of just war. In a striking parallel with Indian ideas from the Code of Manu, the first caliph, Abu Bakr, gave his soldiers ten rules as they went into battle with the Byzantine Empire over control of Syria, telling them how they should conduct themselves in the battlefield.

Stop, O people, that I may give you ten rules for your guidance
in the battlefield. Do not commit treachery or deviate from the

right path. You must not mutilate dead bodies. Neither kill a child, nor a woman, nor an aged man. Bring no harm to the trees, nor burn them with fire, especially those which are fruitful. Slay not any of the enemy's flock, save for your food. You are likely to pass by people who have devoted their lives to monastic services; leave them alone.[17]

Sufism was another tolerant strand of Islam that emerged, and it would have a lingering influence in the eastern frontiers of Islam, such as India. Sufism is sometimes viewed as a distinctive sect of Islam, although its supporters claim that it cuts across or "transcends" sectarian divides, such as that between the Sunni and Shia.[18] There is little doubt that Sufism emerged as a moderate and inclusive stream of Islam by adapting to preexisting local cultural beliefs and practices. A good example is the Nizamuddin Dargah Sufi shrine in Delhi, founded in the thirteenth century under the rule of the Delhi Sultanate of Alauddin Khalji. The shrine accepts visits and prayers from persons of all faiths—Hindu, Sikh, and Christian—who are allowed to touch the tomb of Sufi saint Nizamuddin Auliya, Alauddin's contemporary. It is thus not surprising that Sufis are denounced by orthodox Muslims and extremist groups as mystics, heretics, or apostates.

In other times and other parts of the world, Islamic conquerors have been extraordinarily cruel and intolerant, to both non-Muslims and Muslims. The conquests of Timur, or Tamerlane, who claimed descent from Genghis Khan, were especially brutal. Timur spared neither non-Muslims nor Muslims, and he especially targeted Muslim rulers whose love of pomp and luxury he considered decadent and corrupt. Timur conquered Anatolia, the Mongol khanates of Chagatai and the Golden Horde, and Persia. His sacking of Delhi, which was under Islamic rule, saw the massacre of some one hundred thousand prisoners "so as to free his army from the trouble of guarding them."[19] Timur was fond of erecting towers or "pyramids" of the severed heads of people killed in cities he had taken; one account gives estimates of towers of seventy thousand heads in Isfahan (1387 AD) and ninety thousand in Baghdad (1401 AD).[20]

Some contemporary and later sources, perhaps with some exaggeration, suggest that Timur's conquests claimed the lives of seventeen million people, or 5 percent of the world's population.[21]

Other Muslim conquerors also committed massive atrocities. The Persian invader Nadir Shah in his sacking of Moghul-ruled Delhi in March 1739 massacred between twenty thousand and thirty thousand people.[22] He also seized the Koh-i-noor diamond, now part of the British crown jewels. The Islamic conquest of India, leading to the establishment of the Delhi Sultanate in 1206, was accompanied by sustained and horrific displays of cruelty and intolerance. "The Muslims, who were few in number, and based solely in larger towns, could not rule the country except by systematic terror," the French historian Fernand Braudel has written. The savagery was extraordinary even by the brutal standards of world history and included torture, executions, and crucifixions. Mosques were constructed on the ruins of Hindu temples, and non-Muslims were sometimes forced to convert. Where uprisings took place, they were met by the burning of houses, the slaughter of men, and the enslavement of women.[23]

Moghul Emperor Akbar was known for his tolerance of Hindus and had devised a syncretic faith called Din-i Ilahi ("Godism"), combining Hinduism, Islam, and Christianity. Nevertheless, he ordered the massacre of tens of thousands of people when subduing the Rajput kingdom of Mewar in 1567–1568. And his great-grandson, Aurangzeb, was excessively intolerant. Aside from his severe discrimination against non-Muslims, he organized the execution of his elder brother Dara Shukoh, not only to secure the throne for himself but also to punish Dara's promotion of mutual learning between Hinduism and Islam. Dara's specific crimes were the translating of Hindu scriptures into the official Moghul language (Persian) and writing a text, *Majma 'Ul-Bahrain* ("The Confluence of the Two Seas"), in which he found common ground between Islamic and Hindu philosophy.[24]

There is no avoiding these terrible facts of Islamic conquest, even if people belonging to other religions, from the Romans to the Nazis, carried out similar or perhaps even worse atrocities. Yet there was another side to the Islamic world. For centuries, it was the main repository of civilization and learning, without which it is difficult to imagine later developments—notably the Renaissance and the flourishing of European civilization—taking place.

A Bazaar of Ideas

In the vast area they reached and ruled, the Arabs and other Muslims soon emerged as preeminent transmitters and creators of ideas and innovation. Braudel called Islam a "successor civilization," which is somewhat ironic but not unjustified.[25] While Islam contributed to the fall of the classical civilizations of Greece, Rome, Persia, and India, it also did much to relay the wisdom of those civilizations to modernity.

The Arabs adopted from China the technique of papermaking around in the eighth century, and the Islamic world played a crucial role in spreading it to Europe over the next several centuries. This facilitated the diffusion of knowledge not just from the East to Europe but within Europe as well. The Arabs acquired the Indian numeral system, including the all-important zero, and transmitted it to Europe, where it displaced the inefficient Roman numeral system and made an indispensable contribution to the advancement of Western science. While the Abbasid Caliphate had seen the translation of Greek and other texts into Arabic, Islamic Spain became the center of translations of Arabic texts into Latin and French, which in turn directly influenced the Renaissance in Europe.

During a period of intellectual stagnation or even decay in Europe, the Islamic world was, along with China and India, the world's major center of learning; in a sense, it took the baton from Greece and Rome and then, centuries later, passed it on to Europe, enabling the slow rise of the West to world hegemony. Like the civilizations of India, China, and Greece, Islamic civilization blended theology with rational philosophy. Islamic philosophers such as Ibn Sina and Ibn Rushd did not see any contradiction between religion and philosophy and sought to reconcile the two. One aspect of this rationalist theology is the idea of *ijtihād* (meaning "effort") in Islamic law, which implies "independent reasoning" as opposed to "imitation."[26] This method of acquiring knowledge is different from learning directly from the Koran, Hadith, and *ijmā'* (scholarly consensus); it represents another way of learning that emphasizes "unaided and individualistic human reason." The work of some Islamic philosophers stressed "the centrality of the individual" and countered the belief prevalent in the West of "the authority of the divine."[27] Braudel argues that Islamic literature from the medieval period also presaged ideas about nationalism, capitalism, revolution, and secularism—ideas that would become critical ingredients for European and global political thinking and action, a core element of modernity.[28]

Literacy rates in the Islamic domain during the medieval period were far greater than those in Europe, allowing it to become both a creator and a circulator of knowledge and techniques that have been critical to human progress. Some of these were borrowed and improved upon from earlier advances made by other civilizations, such as the Greek, Hindu, and Chinese. Others were Islam's own distinctive creation, from algebra to windmills to optics. At the same time, Islam contributed to existing knowledge in areas such as trigonometry, mechanics, chemistry, and metallurgy, as well as agriculture and irrigation.

After the destruction of the library in Alexandria and other centers of classical knowledge, the House of Wisdom (Bayt al-Hikmah), founded in the eighth century AD under the Abbasid Caliphate, collected a wealth of texts on philosophy, mathematics, astronomy, medicine, chemistry, zoology, and geography.[29] The House of Wisdom was considered "the greatest collection of knowledge in the world" of its time.[30] Here the translation of Persian, Indian, and Greek texts—such as those by Aristotle, Plato, Hippocrates, Euclid, and Pythagoras—was undertaken on a vast scale. Many classical books by these authors and others would have been lost had it not been for their Arabic translations.[31] (See Table 6.1.)

Why did Arab people translate Greek texts in such large numbers? Partly for practical, scientific reasons. The Greeks' knowledge of medicine and their understanding of natural forces and the technology for controlling them were helpful in building a new empire. But intellectual

Table 6.1 How Islam Circulated Classical Knowledge: Translations from Arabic to Latin and French

---

The House of Wisdom (Bayt al-Hikmah) was founded in the eighth century AD under the Abbasid Caliphate and gathered knowledge from Persian, Indian, and Greek texts. It contributed to the European Renaissance by not only preserving Greek knowledge but improving upon it. Later, these Arabic texts were translated into Latin in Cordoba and other places in Islamic Spain. Here are some examples:

- Euclid's *Elements* was translated by Adelard of Bath c. 1126 AD.
- Muslim scholars' contributions were essential to the birth and development of astronomy in the West (two-thirds of the stars have Arabic names).
- Ptolemy's *Optics* was translated in 1154 AD by Eugenius of Palermo.
- Ibn al-Haytham's *Book of Optics* was translated by Gerard of Cremona to Latin in the twelfth century. This book served as the basis of the Renaissance's use of perspective in art. A copy annotated by Lorenzo Ghiberti, who made the famous bronze doors of the Baptistry in Florence, was found in the Vatican Library.
- The Hindu-Arabic numeral system was described by Leonardo of Pisa (later known as Fibonacci) in his *Liber Abaci* (*Book of Calculation*), 1202 AD.
- Al-Khwarizmi's *Algebra* and astronomical tables (also containing trigono-metric tables) were translated into Latin by Robert of Chester in 1145 AD.
- Al-Khwarizmi's *Zij al-Sindhind* was translated by Adelard of Bath and Petrus Alfonsi in the twelfth century. It was based on Muhammad al-Fazari's book *Sindhind*, written in Bagdad, which drew from Sanskrit works like *Surya Siddhanta* (Greek-influenced Indian astronomy and trigonometry) and *Brahma-sphuta-siddhanta* (mathematics, including the zero).
- Ibn Rushd's commentaries on Aristotle's *Physics* and *Metaphysics* were trans-lated around 1220–1235 AD by Michael Scot. Until the thirteenth century, the world's knowledge of *Metaphysics* was based on Ibn Rushd's commentary.
- Aristotle's *Meteorologica* (books 1–3), *Physica*, *De Cælo et Mundo*, and *De Gener-atione et Corruptione* were translated by Gerard of Cremona in Toledo during the twelfth century.
- Ibn Sina's *Qānun dar Teb* (*Canon of Medicine*) was translated to Latin by Ge-rard of Cremona in the twelfth century. The *Canon* remained the standard medical textbook in European universities until the eighteenth century.

---

curiosity also played a major role. Al-Kindi, a ninth-century Arab scholar who was a founding figure in Islamic philosophy, argued, "We should not be ashamed to acknowledge truth from whatever source it comes to us, even if it is brought to us by former generations of foreign peoples. For him who seeks the truth there is nothing of higher value than truth itself."[32]

In this, Islamic thinkers such as Ibn Sina (Avicenna) were combining independent reasoning, or inquiry into causes of phenomena, stressing natural, rather than of divine causation.[33] Aside from their deep engagement with Greek philosophy, the Arabs also translated and incorporated Persian and Indian texts. Persia had fallen to them, and its dominant religion, Zoroastrianism, had given way to Islam. Sanskrit texts were also translated, their ideas borrowed and transmitted first to the Islamic world and then to Christian Europe. This could count as the first true internationalization of science.

Some of the original Greek texts were later found in the Byzantine Empire. These were translated directly to Latin, along with some texts that had most likely not been translated by Arabs, such as Aristotle's *Politics*. But the fact remains that, to a large degree, Arabic translations gave Europe its first major taste of the core Greek ideas in science and philosophy. Even after the direct translations from Greek were made, the Arabic translations, interpretations, and additions remained influential in developing the European mind, especially Ibn Rushd's commentaries on Aristotle relating to the "eternity of the world." At the same time, lest we forget, a good deal of the knowledge the Europeans took from Islam had nothing to do with Greece but consisted of ideas developed originally by Islamic intellectuals.

Hence, Islamic scientists and philosophers did not just preserve classical knowledge but advanced it through interpretation, refutation, and reformulation. They also made new inventions and discoveries.[34] For example, Islamic scientists embraced the use of instruments, methods, and experimentation to an extent Greek science never did. Ibn Sina's *Canon of Medicine* became the "founding text for European schools of medicine." Al-Razi, founder of clinical pharmacology, introduced quarantine.

Ibn al-Shatir of the Maragha school developed mathematical models that would influence Nicolaus Copernicus's heliocentric theory 150 years later. Al-Khwarizmi improved upon Ptolemy's *Geography* and produced new maps showing the positions of stars. He also for the first time calculated the circumference of the Earth to within a margin of error of less than 0.04 percent.[35] And it was an eleventh-century Arab named Ibn al-Haytham, born in Basra and educated in Baghdad, to whom one can credit the science behind perspective in art, from which the art and architecture of the Renaissance—of Filippo Brunelleschi, Michelangelo, Raphael, Sandro Botticelli, and so on—took inspiration.[36]

Muslim Spain (Al-Andalus), especially under the "Western Caliphate" centered in Cordoba (929–1031 AD), became a flourishing center for the exchange of knowledge, with a library that had four hundred thousand volumes, "more books than all the libraries of the rest of Europe put together."[37] Western political leaders today make little mention of their debt to Islamic civilization. A rare exception is a statement by King Charles III of Britain: "Many of the traits on which modern Europe prides itself came to it from Muslim Spain. Diplomacy, free trade, open borders, the techniques of academic research, of anthropology, etiquette, fashion, various types of medicine, hospitals, all came from this great city of cities."[38]

Ibn Rushd, whose full name was Abu al-Walid Muhammad ibn Ahmad ibn Rushd, ranks among the most brilliant thinkers of medieval Cordoba and of world history. A qadi (judge) who was born and raised in the city, Ibn Rushd significantly developed the "doctrine of the eternity of the world." This idea, originally proposed by Greek philosophers led by Aristotle, challenged the orthodoxy both of Islam and of the Catholic Christian doctrine of creationism. Derived from the opening words of Genesis ("In the beginning God created the heaven and the earth"), and still adhered to by twenty-first-century evangelicals, creationism holds that "the universe had a distinct starting point" and was created by God in a single act out of nothing.[39] By contrast, the "eternity of the world" holds that time and matter are eternal, rather than God's creation. The origin of the universe is due to prior and continuing natural forces.

This theory was intensely debated among Christian, Islamic, and Jewish philosophers in the medieval period. However, Aristotle's work would have been lost or ignored to the world after the fall of Rome but for Arabic translations, which happened at a time when Greek philosophy and science were being suppressed by the Catholic Church in Rome and by the Orthodox Christian Byzantine rulers of Constantinople. Ibn Rushd's commentaries on Aristotle—collectively known as in the West as Averroism—translated into Latin and French, inspired progressive European philosophers and theologists, especially Thomas Aquinas, to develop the rationalist worldview in Europe. Ibn Rushd's critique of creationism not only was more powerful than Aristotle's but it also reconciled creationist (pagan, Christian, Jewish, and Islamic) beliefs and rationalist ones by arguing that the idea of creation did not preclude prior events and processes. While the West today has largely forgotten this Muslim philosopher, a minor recognition can be found in *The School of Athens*, Raphael's famous sixteenth-century fresco in the Vatican, which has Ibn Rushd sitting on the stairs while the standing Socrates, Plato, and Aristotle take center stage at the podium.

Without Ibn Rushd's philosophy, argues British writer Nicolas Pelham, "the Enlightenment might never have happened."[40] Neither would have the Renaissance occurred—it is fair to say—without borrowing a wide range of ideas and technology from Islam.

Cordoba also provides one of the most striking examples of the accommodation between different religious communities and their respective philosophical traditions in the medieval world order. For four hundred years, a governing principle of the city was the Andalusian *convivencia*, the word meaning a kind of coexistence among different groups, specifically Cordoban Muslims, Christians, and Jews. A Cordoban native who deserves recognition here is Jewish philosopher and physician Moses ben Maimon (1138–1204) or Maimonides. A contemporary of Ibn Rushd, Maimonides wrote in Arabic and for a time lived in Cairo to serve as the personal physician of the sultan. Among his major works is *The Guide for the Perplexed*, where he expounds on the origins of the universe. Unlike Ibn Rushd, Maimonides rejected Aristotle's view that the world was eternal. Nor did he accept the traditional Jewish and Christian belief that God created the universe out of nothing at a single point in time. While recognizing the importance of God in maintaining social harmony, Maimonides seemed to share the neo-Platonic position of many contemporary Arab scholars that the universe might have emerged from some preexisting or primeval matter.[41]

Eclecticism, or the mingling of Greek, Islamic, and Judaic ideas, was not rare for the period. It informed the work of philosophers such as al-Ghazali, Ibn Rushd, Ibn Arabi, and Thomas Aquinas.[42] But not surprisingly, it also angered orthodox scholars and officials in these faiths. Ibn Rushd's unorthodox Islamic beliefs led to the burning of his books and his expulsion from Cordoba by the ultraconservative Almohad sultan in 1195 (although he was allowed to return a year later). Maimonides was also criticized by traditionalist Jewish and Christian authorities: the Dominicans of Montpellier would burn his books in 1232. Nevertheless, Maimonides influenced later Christian rationalism and is remembered today as the most prominent Jewish thinker of the medieval age.

In 1236, Cordoba fell under the control of a Christian coalition that would gradually succeed in taking over Al-Andalus, bringing about a far more intolerant regime—both in religion and ideas—that expelled Jews and Muslims alike. While Muslim intellectual creativity would survive Cordoba's fall, it would lose its earlier vigor. Of all the later Arab intellectuals, Ibn Khaldun (1332–1406 AD), deserves our particular attention, since his work directly concerns the rise and fall of civilizations. Ibn Khaldun was born in Tunisia, where his family had settled after fleeing Al-Andalus. His classic *Muqaddimah*, published in 1377, was an enormously ambitious effort to trace the entire historical evolution of humankind using what he called "a new science," empirical research that is seen as a precursor to modern sociology. The book was praised by English historian Arnold Toynbee as "a philosophy of history which is undoubtedly the greatest work of its kind that has ever yet been created by any mind in any time or place."[43]

Ibn Khaldun was especially interested in the history of nomadic tribes, some of whom had led to the downfall of Islamic dynasties in

North Africa. To research the history of the Tatars and Mongols—other nomadic peoples who had conquered settled peoples—he ventured to meet with Timur in Damascus in January 1400 and personally witnessed the siege and destruction of one of the greatest seats of Islamic civilization. Ibn Khaldun would try to make sense of the causes of such tectonic historical changes as he elaborated a broad-reaching theory about the rise and fall of political dynasties, which he came to see as the result of the endless, cyclical conflicts between sedentary and nomadic peoples. The nomadic barbarians, attracted by the wealth and culture of sedentary societies, embark on their conquest. After victory, they settle into a life of comfort and relative prosperity, losing their competitive edge in the process. This makes them ripe to be conquered by a new group of barbarians, until they, too, become complacent and decadent. "When the natural tendencies of royal authority to claim all glory for itself and to acquire luxury and tranquility have been firmly established, the dynasty approaches senility," Ibn Khaldun writes.[44] This invites another wave of barbarian intrusion, and the cycle goes on.

That Ibn Khaldun's thesis explains, at least partly, the rise and fall of many world orders in China, India, central Asia, and North Africa is beyond doubt. The context may differ and the causes may be wider, but his thesis is confirmed by many historical examples, including the conquest of the classical Hindu empires by the Kushans and the Huns, as well as the repeated defeats of ethnic Han empires in China by the Northern Wei, the Khitans, the Jurchens, the Mongols, and, later, the Manchu. To a lesser degree, it might also explain the Turkic invasion of India that founded the Delhi Sultanate or the conqueror Babur's invasion of India that founded the Moghul Empire, both of which were acts by nomadic warriors against sedentary societies.

Ibn Khaldun's theory of history doesn't seem to apply to the rise of the West, or to Europe's colonization of much of the rest of the world. These involved in many cases clashes between two sets of already civilized societies, even if the Europeans, thanks to their combination of ignorance and racism, thought of their conquests as the victory of civilization over barbarism. But, applying Ibn Khaldun's logic, an argument can be made that when Europe embarked on its predatory "voyages of discovery" and colonization of the world, it was relatively uncivilized and economically more deprived. When Europe was still underdeveloped and stagnant, the Hindu, Chinese, and Muslim civilizations were flourishing, and the wealth and resources of these oriental civilizations were a prime motivation behind Europe's global expansion.

It is no exaggeration to say that the giant figures of the Islamic world—Ibn Khaldun, Ibn Rushd, and the scientists, mathematicians, philosophers, and translators who lived in the great arc of territory from Baghdad to Cordoba—kept alive the flame of civilization during the long centuries when Europe was the slow mover. At this critical stage, the Islamic world not only took the lead in the development of scientific and philosophical ideas, but it also stimulated Europe's and the world's economic prospects through the circulation of technology, goods, and money.

Globalization and Modernity

From the outset, the followers of the new religion had a keen sense for rational economic activity and trade; the Prophet himself was a trader. Muslim traders created commercial networks that linked civilizations from Europe and North Africa to Asia. Islamic societies came up with many essential innovations and inventions, including the lateen sail for long-distance voyages, the astrolabe for navigation, and proto-capitalist institutions, such as partnerships, contract law, banking, and credit, all critical foundations of economic globalization. It was in this way that the Islamic world joined hands with the civilizations of China, India, Africa, and others to lay the foundation of what we today call globalization.

Islamic long-distance trade was first controlled by the Arabs and later by Egypt and the Ottomans, and eventually Italian city-states like Venice and Genoa profited.[45] "In the middle-ages," writes Jared Diamond, "the flow of technology was overwhelmingly from Islam to Europe rather from Europe to Islam. Only after the 1500s did the net direction of flow begin to reverse."[46] But globalization itself long preceded this reversal, marking the onset of the rise of the West; it goes back a thousand years to 500 AD or so, when economic relations among many peoples—Persians, Arabs, Africans, Chinese, Indians—created an intercontinental economy.[47] Although the true global economy had to await European imperial expansion across the Atlantic and the Pacific, the Islamic world did establish a vast network of civilizations, empires, and economies, especially connecting Asia, Africa, and western Europe, with the Indian Ocean taking the center stage. Islamic commerce intensified and extended the Eurasian-African trading economy that had existed since at least 200 BC, when the Silk Road, linking China with the countries to the west, was first formed.

The Islamic world extended as far as Southeast Asia, arriving in the region via the Indian Ocean. Muslim traders joined hands with other communities, including Hindu merchants, in maintaining and developing vibrant commercial and cultural links between the western and eastern parts of the Indian Ocean, which also linked China and Japan. In one prominent case, Malacca's Hindu ruler embraced Islam partly to better connect with the Muslim trading networks in the Indian Ocean.

Much has been made in recent times of the revival of "traditional" Islam and the challenge it poses to the Western-dominated world order. But what constitutes traditional Islam is not agreed upon among Muslims. This is not surprising, since Islam has never been a singular or internally homogeneous culture. Throughout history, Islam has represented one of the globe's most dynamic civilizations, acting as the world's hub for the transmission of commerce, culture, and knowledge. As we have seen, Islam—like the civilizations of India, China, and the West—incorporated ideas from other civilizations and transmitted its own ideas to others.

Still, Islamic concepts such as *ummah* and *asabiyyah* are different from the ideas of the nation-state and Westphalian sovereignty. During the heyday of pan-Islamic ideology before World War II, and even today in some parts of the Middle East and Asia, some Islamic authorities have seen the division of the Islamic world into separate nation-states as temporary, a dispensable legacy of Western colonialism. These leaders have

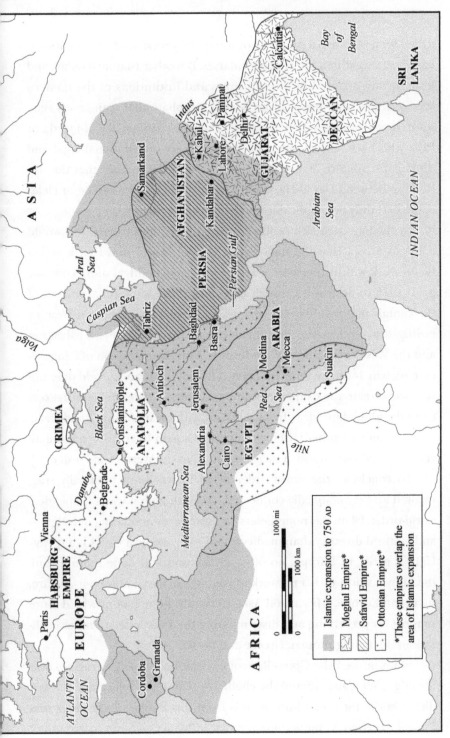

Map 7. Ottoman, Safavid, and Moghul Empires.

called for a return to a caliphate or some other version of a transnational Islamic state without internal boundaries. But other Islamic scholars and leaders have adapted to the principles and institutions of the modern state.[48] Today, the dream of an Islamic caliphate that transcends state sovereignty is being pursued only by extremist groups like al-Qaeda or ISIS, who have no legitimacy in contemporary international legal and diplomatic practice. Nontraditionalist views of Islam hold that the distinction between Dar al-Harb and Dar al-Islam, never absolute or clear-cut, is certainly not applicable to contemporary times.

In the late twentieth century, most Muslims and their rulers would come to accept that the nation-state is here to stay and that it is better to work within that system to achieve their political and economic goals than to destroy it through holy war. At the same time, citizens of the Islamic nations—like the peoples and leaders of other non-Western civilizations—reject the presumed superiority of Western civilization and the Western standard of modernity. With the exception of fringe elements, which can be found in every religion, the Islamic world does not seek to recreate the caliphate. Rather, Islamic societies believe that one can take and adapt ideas from the West without imitating it and weakening Islamic identity. This melding offers a path to creating a more diverse and inclusive world, a successor world to the Western-led order.

To conclude, the world order of Islam was both politically fragmented and economically connected, and although it was a theological world order, Islam was nonetheless far more accommodating of religious and cultural diversity than medieval and early modern Christianity was. Until the rise of Europe, no other civilization had done more to link the known world with a network of commerce, ideas, and even warfare, spanning Europe, Africa, and Asia. Certainly, none had provided more support for preserving and disseminating the knowledge of other civilizations, including those of Greece and Persia.

Islam pushed the Greco-Roman civilization, already decaying, over the edge, but it also offered the challenge that would rejuvenate the medieval world, including Europe. It is from this Islamic world order that Europe received its most consequential influences—more so even than from China—in science, technology, and connectivity, all of which powered the rise of the West.

There were, in addition, two other elements in the picture: the Mongol Empire and the Indian Ocean trading network, both of which played a vital role in connecting the world. When the Mongol horsemen under Genghis Khan established the largest land empire in world history in the early thirteenth century, they built trading networks that long outlasted their own relatively brief period on the world stage. Similarly, the trade that took place in the Indian Ocean—which incorporated Africa, Arabia, India, Southeast Asia, and China in a vast network of ports that was ruled by no single country—did for the maritime world what the Mongols did for the interior regions of Eurasia. Both, as we are about to see, had a profound effect on the emergence of the modern world order.

Chapter 7

The World Connectors

The Mongol Empire in thirteenth and the first half of the fourteenth century AD, and the Indian Ocean region before the arrival of the European powers in the fifteenth century AD, were contrasting theaters for world-order building. The Mongols not only created the largest contiguous empire in history, but they also gave what is known today as the Silk Road—a nineteenth-century term—its most stable period. The Mongol world order imposed no religious or cultural dogma but fostered extensive trade and exchange of ideas in the areas under its influence.

The Indian Ocean did the same, but in a vastly different manner. No single empire or centralizing authority controlled it. To be sure, militarism by empires did take place in the Indian Ocean from time to time, such as the southern Indian Chola Kingdom's attacks on Southeast Asian port cities in the eleventh century and the Chinese admiral Zheng He's imperial voyages in the fifteenth. But the Indian Ocean was for the most part managed with rules and methods developed by small port cities, such as Malindi, Mombasa, Mogadishu, Zanzibar, Aden, Hormuz, Calicut, Malacca, and Palembang (in the Srivijaya Empire). The Indian Ocean network is a powerful challenge to the contemporary Western myth that creating and managing a world order, and fostering free trade, requires a power like Britain or the United States.

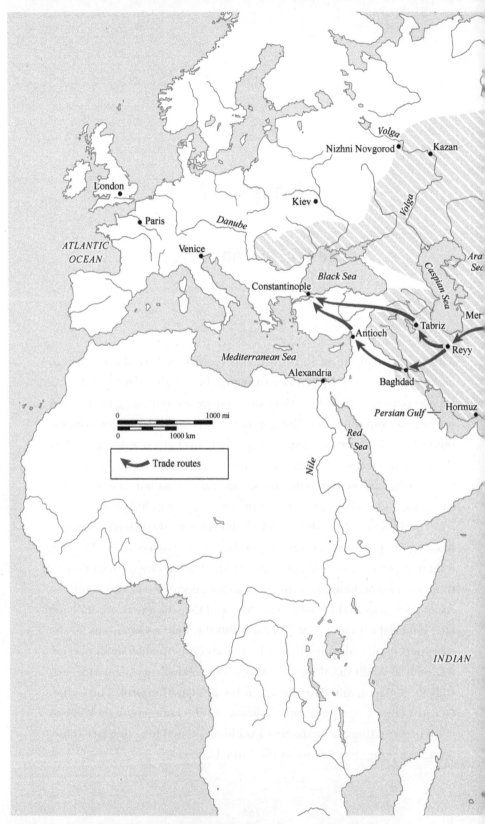

Map 8. The Mongol Empire in the late thirteenth century.

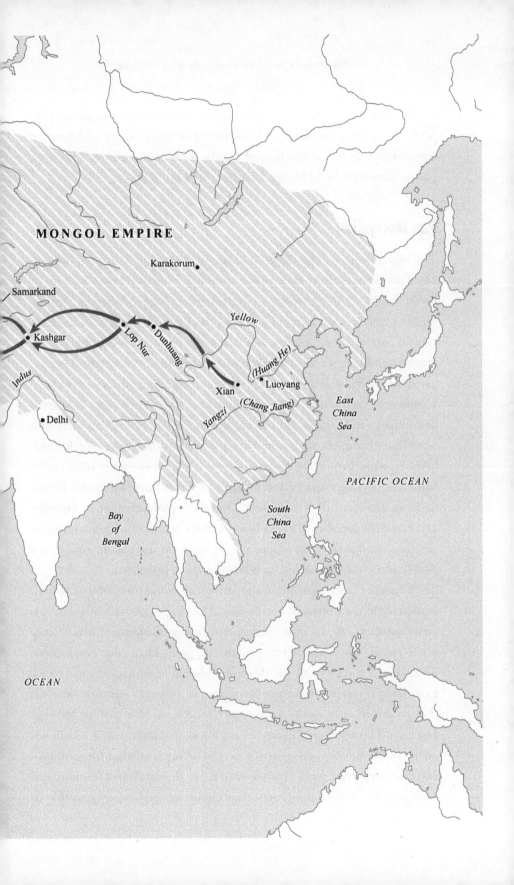

MONGOL EMPIRE

Samarkand

Kashgar

Lop Nur

Dunhuang

Karakorum

Yellow

(Huang He)

Xian

Luoyang

(Chang Jiang)

Indus

Delhi

Yangzi

East
China
Sea

PACIFIC OCEAN

Bay
of
Bengal

South
China
Sea

OCEAN

Despite these differences, the two networks served a common purpose; they linked vast areas of humankind as never before and became transmission belts for the flow of goods, ideas, and culture. And both played a crucial role in facilitating the rise of the West.

Pax Mongolica

The Mongols have gone down in history as particularly brutal conquerors. This is not entirely undeserved, although estimating mass killings in battle is difficult due to the scarcity and unreliability of sources. One estimate puts the total number killed in the five-year Mongol invasion of central Asia at fifteen million. But that estimate would mean that, on average, each Mongol soldier would have to have killed one hundred people per day over five years—surely an exaggeration.[1] The Mongols gave forewarnings of their attack, and those who surrendered were usually spared; in combat, the Mongols did not engage in torture or mutilation. There would have been reasons for the Mongols to cultivate a reputation for brutality. As with the ancient Assyrians, having a fearsome reputation would instill fear among enemies and in that way secure their surrender before fighting. This, in turn, would have reduced the number of future enemies and eased the logistics of long-distance campaigns—which was especially the case for the Mongols—since cooperation on the part of conquered people was less burdensome than keeping them prisoner.

Whatever their reputation, the Mongols earned themselves a prominent place in the history of world order. The origins of the Mongol worldview had much to do with climate and forces of nature. Unlike many other rulers, the Mongol khagan, or the great khan, did not present himself as a god or of divine descent. Political legitimacy instead came from *tenggeri* (derived from the Mongolian word *tenger*, meaning "sky," although the term is also translated as the "eternal blue sky" or "eternal heaven"). The worship of heaven or sky is a shared feature of nomadic societies in the steppes and central Asia, where harsh weather conditions—extreme cold, drought, or storms—can make the survival of humans and their precious animal herds extremely challenging. Hence, veneration of the sky reflected their interdependence with, and fear of, natural forces. There are some similarities between such nomadic beliefs about sky and heaven and China's mandate of heaven idea, which originated in the Zhou dynasty, prompting speculation that the Chinese might have borrowed this crucial political idea from the steppe cultures, along with technologies such as bronze casting, chariots, and iron metallurgy. At the very least, both concepts saw heaven as the force behind natural calamities—floods, droughts, and earthquakes—that forewarned rulers of dangers to their political authority and decided their eventual survival. The Mongols saw heaven as their ruler's protector and enabler, giving him the ability to create order and dispel chaos.[2] As the *Secret History of the Mongols*, the thirteenth-century Mongol chronicle, says, "Appointed by mighty Heaven and escorted by Mother Earth," the great khan claimed his right not only to rule but also to conquer the world.[3] Again, one can draw parallels with the Chinese concepts of all under heaven (*tianxia*) and mandate of heaven.

In creating their world order, the Mongols were avid centralizers and connectors. Their imperial system grew out of the traditional steppe nomadic tradition but was then combined with the need to have authority concentrated in one central place as the territory under their control expanded. The political, administrative, and military system the Mongol Empire created grew to be much vaster and more centralized than the previous nomadic steppe polities of the Xiongnu, the Uighurs, or the Khitans. One powerful tool of this centralization was an imperial guard, some ten thousand strong during Genghis Khan's rule, which both protected him and provided bureaucrats to run the empire.

At the same time, the Mongols kept the flexibility of their nomadic heritage, which gave local rulers considerable autonomy without threatening the authority of the great khan. The empire relied on a network of aristocrats, each with their own spheres of influence. Their size and degree of autonomy varied, but all were nonetheless firmly under the khagan's supreme authority. This is similar to medieval European rulers, who also relied on the subordinate aristocracy and vassals for support.[4]

The Mongol Empire lasted for just over a century and half, from 1206 to 1368 (when the Yuan dynasty in China collapsed). But at its height the empire pacified many previously independent and disparate domains under a single authority. This produced a kind of Pax Mongolica: a vast territory where the roads were safe, armed uprisings were quelled, and prosperity spread. As the thirteenth-century Persian historian Ata-Malik Juvaini noted, Genghis Khan "brought about complete peace and quiet, and security and tranquility, and had achieved the extreme of prosperity and well-being; the roads were secure and disturbances allayed."[5]

An important feature of the Mongols' ideology was a respect for cultural differences, which enabled them to maintain a stable world order based on coexistence.[6] Once in charge, they practiced religious tolerance. "The Mongols," as one historian puts it, "believed in taking as much celestial insurance as possible."[7] This might mean that, if another peoples' religion helped to justify Mongol rule, they were happy to incorporate those beliefs.

The conventional view that the Mongols were brutal conquerors obscures the fact that their empire was also built and maintained with trade and diplomacy. After creating what would become the largest land empire in the history of world order, the Mongols developed trade on a vast scale, linking East Asia, the Middle East, and Europe into an enormous economic network. Although the Chinese take credit for founding the Silk Road, they were unable to maintain order along it beyond their imperial borders. It remained a hazardous route, offering little protection to monks, merchants, and other travelers against bandits, tribal violence, and natural calamities. It was the Mongols who controlled and pacified the entire Silk Road for the first time in history. They prized international trade—reversing the Confucian principle that valued farmers over merchants—and they increased the volume of commerce without necessarily controlling the territories they captured. They standardized money and weights, and they built roads, bridges, and a system of relay stations consisting of caravansaries placed about twenty miles apart, allowing travelers to rest, eat, and exchange goods and information in conditions of security. These way stations were also used by officials and military commanders for security and administration.

At one end of the system was China, the hub of Mongol manufacturing and other economic activity and the world's largest economy. At the other end was western Europe, which was in the early stages of developing its modern capitalist economy. To ease the management of their vast empire, the Mongols divided it into four interlocking segments, known as the *khubi* (meaning "share" or "sharing") system, which divided the spoils of war and the wealth of the empire among the members of the ruling family. It consisted of four segments: the Chinese Yuan dynasty in the east, with its capital in Beijing; the Chagatai Khanate in the center; the Ilkhanate in central Asia and Iran; and the Golden Horde on Russia's border in the northwest.[8] Ideally, each segment would have control over the resources and wealth within its jurisdiction, but would also facilitate the trade and diplomatic exchanges of others through its territory. The Mongol communication network—encompassing China, central Asia, Iran, and Iraq—enabled a messenger to travel a hundred miles per day.[9]

By maintaining this network, the Mongols served as a conduit for the diffusion of knowledge and skills to both the East and the West. Partly to serve the health of their forces in long-distance missions, the Mongols created hospitals and training centers, such as the "house of healing" near Tabriz in present-day Iran, which promoted exchanges of medical knowledge and practices, especially those developed in the Islamic world. One area where the Chinese benefited was surgery, which was underdeveloped in the Confucian cultures because of their injunction against the mutilation of the human body. In Europe, the expansion of the Mongol Empire contributed to the beginning of medical training.[10]

The implications of all of this for global power relations cannot be underestimated. Indeed, while trade and travel across Eurasia go back to the Western Han period in China, it was really the Mongols who created the first fully developed and pacified link across Eurasia, something that would never be done again to the same extent, even by Timur. This connection also played its part in the rise of Europe. Among other things, the unification of Eurasia by the Mongols meant there would be fewer local rulers competing for gifts and tribute from the traders. This, in turn, benefited not only Muslim and Jewish merchants but also Europeans seeking to profit from trade with the Mongols.[11] The Mongols also allowed an early version of currency convertibility; on a route between Beijing and Italy, one could exchange silver or gold coins for silk or paper currency and vice versa. In essence, the Mongols revived the Silk Road, reestablishing connections between Europe and China after a thousand-year hiatus. Somewhat like the Roman Empire but over a much larger territory, Pax Mongolica provided security not only for traders but also for travelers, missionaries, diplomats, and scientists transmitting ideas and innovations across a large number of societies. More generally, the Mongols created conditions of stability and exchange across a vast area that was an essential ingredient of later European expansion. The Mongol communication system greatly facilitated the spread of Chinese inventions to Europe. As historian Peter Frankopan writes, "Fundamental to European expansion was the stability that the Mongols provided across the whole of Asia."[12]

Everyone's Sea

The Indian Ocean did in the maritime arena what the Mongols did overland, connecting Asia, the Middle East, and Europe in a way that facilitated Europe's eventual rise. But the Indian Ocean trading and cultural network went much further in supporting European ascendancy: it handed the European newcomers a ready-made road map for empire and dominance over Asia. It was through the Indian Ocean's preexisting and well-developed port cities that the early European colonizers conducted their trade, starting with the Portuguese. But in that process, the Europeans, ironically, also destroyed one of the most precious rules of encounter among civilizations: the idea of the sea as the common heritage of humankind. Long before the European "discovery" of America, and the subsequent creation of a commercial route across the whole Pacific, the Indian Ocean trading network—linking the Middle East and Africa with China and Japan via India and Southeast Asia—was the world's largest and busiest oceanic trade route. As such, when the Europeans arrived, it quickly became the principal artery of European dominance of Asia.

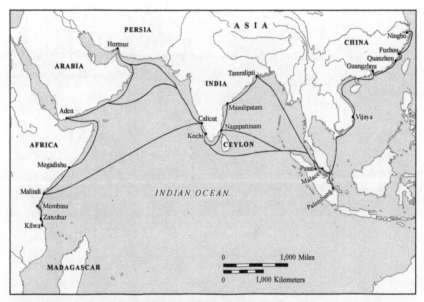

Map 9. Selected ports on the Indian Ocean trading network.

The body of water now known as the Indian Ocean is a modern construct. Different parts of it were known by different names throughout history.[13] The ancient Greeks called the water from the Red Sea to India the Erythraean Sea. The Arabs called it Baḥr al-Hind or Baḥr al-Zandj.[14] Early modern European maps used the term Eastern Ocean, as opposed to the Western Ocean (used for the Atlantic). The term associating it specifically with India was Oceanus Orientalis Indicus, a modern Latin expression that came into vogue in the early sixteenth century.[15]

The Indian Ocean trade before the Europeans' arrival was not simply peddler trade, as some Eurocentric accounts claim. Aside from luxury goods, it involved essential commodities required for sustaining the port city-states of the Indian Ocean, such as Aden, Hormuz, and Malacca. The trade also involved foodstuffs traveling from the East African coast to Aden and Hormuz and then to the Malabar Coast of India.[16]

Indian Ocean trade was open, in the sense that it was not regulated by a notion of maritime sovereignty. This is in contrast with the Western model, in which states vied fiercely for exclusive control of maritime

173

Image 6. Relief of a Javanese outrigger ship in the Buddhist monument of Borobudur, Indonesia. Coastal vessels played a major role in the Indian Ocean trading network, which was managed by port cities.

territory. Instead, multiple port cities—from East Africa through the Arabian Peninsula and India to Southeast Asia—shared the management of trade.

This absence of exclusive maritime sovereignty in the India Ocean stemmed from the difficulty that any empire faced in conquering and controlling its vast extent. The Mediterranean was tiny by comparison; it could be turned into a "Roman lake." While the Romans called the Mediterranean "our sea" (Mare Nostrum), the Indian Ocean was for much of history a *mare commune*, a communal sea.

But another, more important reason might well have been the long-standing regional tradition of leaving the sea alone, declining to regard it as part of the territory of any nation. To be sure, there were conflicts, pirates, customs duties, and gifts to be paid to local sultans. The Indian

Ocean wasn't a paradise of tranquil cooperation, but neither merchants nor local rulers ever seem to have tried to establish a monopoly over any aspect of trade or to put all of maritime commerce under their control.[17] A vivid example of this tradition can be found in an early seventeenth-century argument made by Sultan Alauddin of Gowa, a state in South Sulawesi in what is now Indonesia. The Dutch, striving to enforce a monopoly on the spice trade, were barring merchants from the sultan's capital, Makassar, from trading with the Maluku Islands, which produced cloves, nutmeg, and mace. "God made the land and the sea," Sultan Alauddin told the Dutch. "The land he divided among men, and the sea he gave in common. It has never been heard that anyone should be forbidden to sail the seas."[18] The Dutch response was to destroy Makassar's defenses and rename it Fort Rotterdam. In 1622, the faujdar, or military commander, of Balasore, a major Indian port in the Bay of Bengal, was approached by the king of the Maldives. The king asked him to petition the Moghul emperor to ban Dutch and English shipping from the Maldives. The faujdar refused, on the grounds that the emperor was "master only of land and not the sea."[19]

The overall principle was what historian K. N. Chaudhuri calls the Indian Ocean's "ancient and honored law of reciprocity," which meant not "interfering in the commercial affairs of merchants from abroad" in return for their "good behaviour."[20] The great port city of Malacca, on the western side of the Malay Peninsula, was a key node of Indian Ocean trade, open to merchants of all nationalities, who were subject only to a low, standardized customs duty. Malacca had a population of about one hundred thousand, mostly foreign traders; eighty-four languages were spoken. As the Portuguese visitor to Malacca Tomé Pires wrote, "There is no doubt that Malacca is of such importance and profit that it seems to me it has no equal in the world." Not only was Malacca "a city...made for merchandise, fitter than any other in the world," but it was also key to controlling trade with Europe, so much so that "whoever is Lord in Malacca has his hand on the throat of Venice."[21]

Malacca's trade was open, but "well-regulated" and rule based.[22] The city allowed foreign trading missions to appoint their own officials, known as shabunders, to regulate and look after the interests of their merchants. To determine the amount of tariff to be levied, the ruler of Malacca appointed a panel of ten merchants—five from Kalinga (an area now straddling the eastern Indian states of Odisha and Andhra Pradesh) and five from other trading communities—to jointly determine the value of cargoes and allocate their distribution. This helped to reduce corruption and cleared the cargo of visiting trading ships quickly and efficiently, enabling ships to follow precise sailing times in accordance with monsoon winds. With this system in place, the range of prices foreign goods could fetch in Malacca was predictable. Malacca's overall trading system not only gave merchants autonomy from interference by the local ruler but also was deemed fair to all parties.

The Indian Ocean trading system was supported by both tradition and written laws, as illustrated in the Maritime Laws of Malacca (Undang-Undang Laut Melaka), a legal code of the fifteenth-century Malacca Sultanate drafted by a group of sea captains, drawing on long-established principles and conventions in the region. The code specified the authority of a trading ship's captain and the responsibilities of the crew, as well as rules of profit sharing, compensation for collision damage, penalties for cheating on port duties, and guidelines for settling contractual obligations and debts. These principles, fair and transparent, governed the movement of vessels at sea. For example, the captain had to consult all the crew members before deciding which port to visit for trading purposes. When throwing cargo overboard to stabilize a ship, all those who had a share of the cargo had to be consulted, and if some cargo was left, it would be allocated to the merchants on board in proportion to their respective share in the total cargo of the ship. In a collision between two ships, the owner of the damaged vessel could, on filing a claim before a local judge, be compensated up to two-thirds of the loss.

What is remarkable is that the open and rules-based trading system of the Indian Ocean functioned on its own steam; supported by local rulers but without requiring the authority of any major power, such as India and China. This is in marked contrast to the Western idea that free trade requires the hegemony of a great power, whether Rome in ancient times or Britain and the United States in the modern era.[23] India had a strong cultural and economic role in Southeast Asia but never became dominant there, despite some aggressive forays by south India's Chola dynasty in the eleventh century AD. Neither did the Indian Ocean become a Chinese sphere of influence. Although many Southeast Asian states—including Srivijaya, Malacca, and Siam—had tributary relations with China, that system, as discussed, was primarily symbolic and loosely enforced. The early fifteenth-century Zheng He voyages sought to establish commercial and strategic influence in a way that might have been emulated by the European colonial powers, but the results were short-lived.[24] The Indian Ocean did not become a Chinese lake, China was not the center of Indian Ocean trade. One of the main trading items in the Indian Ocean was cotton, and India was the world's leading cotton fabric and clothing supplier. Also prominent were Buddhist religious products: incense, ivory, sandalwood, stupas, statues, and glass vessels for temple rituals. The other frequently traded goods were spices, dyes, and medicinal substances.[25] The eastern Indian Ocean was less the "maritime Silk Road," as contemporary Chinese authorities like to present it, than it was the Spice Road and the Nirvana Route, as I would call it. By and large, it remained an open sea. While India and China and their products were a major part of the Indian Ocean trade, neither civilization controlled it, and they went along or supported the ocean in emerging as an open, cross-cultural site of major global importance.

It was into this vibrant, open, and diverse world of the Indian Ocean that the European colonial powers stepped, starting with the Portuguese and followed by the Dutch, the British, and the French. The arrival of Vasco da Gama in Calicut, India, on May 20, 1498—followed by the Portuguese capture of Goa in 1510 and that of Malacca a year later—ushered in the era of European imperialism in Asia.

The motivations behind the European intrusions were both religious and commercial, as was made clear by the Portuguese governor of Goa, Afonso de Albuquerque, as he exhorted his captains before their final assault on Malacca in 1511:

This town is the greatest source of spices, medicines and wealth in all the world. It is populated with the richest traders, and it exists on the benefits of trade. The people are mostly Muslims [by this time the ruler of Malacca had converted to Islam from Hinduism], who live in all the known lands in the Indies as well as in other lands. Through Malacca they are able to trade in numerous places, and without Malacca they cannot supply Cairo, Alexandria and Venice with so great a quantity of spices, medicines and the resulting wealth....By throwing the Muslims out of Malacca the fire of the sect of Mohammed will be extinguished and the creed will not extend itself any further. It may also cause the Muslims to leave the Indies....You will realize that the eight Muslim ships which we have captured can hold more cargo than twenty of our galleons. How much more can be carried in all Malacca ships that daily leave the port, besides those belonging to the foreigners!...With only half a turn of the key this route will be closed, and the [Portuguese] King, our sovereign, will be the Lord of all this trade.[26]

Albuquerque's speech, while placing profit and faith (Christianity) at the center of the motivations for the conquest of Malacca, also prefigured Europe's intention to disrupt the traditionally free pattern of Indian Ocean trade and to replace it with monopolies and other forms of control backed by force, including outright piracy. The Portuguese started this by turning the island of Madagascar, which they already controlled, into a major center for piracy, involving French, Dutch, and Danish pirates who were often commanded by English adventurers.[27] In such a way did the Europeans introduce forms of large-scale and systematic violence that were not previously part of the traditional Indian Ocean trade; its history of piracy does not negate this fact. Until then, the trade network—linking port cities such as Aden and Hormuz in the west to Calicut and Masulipatam in India to Malacca and Palembang in the east—functioned not on the basis of military power but "on the strength of their trading institutions."[28] By contrast, the Portuguese "introduced a novel form of state violence to seaborne trade," while the Dutch "decimated the indigenous population of Banda Islands [in today's Indonesia] to achieve their monopoly in the spice trade."[29]

The Europeans also practiced slavery, and they made it an even harsher institution than it had been before. To be sure, the Indian Ocean had its history of slave trading, but it differed significantly from the Atlantic slave trade that would come later. Before European intrusion, the Indian Ocean's slaves came not just from Africa but from different parts of the region, and the types of labor they performed varied widely, including military service, agriculture, and household work. The Indian Ocean slave trade was also subject to Islamic norms, which generally offered more protection from mistreatment and opportunities for freedom and integration into local societies than the later Atlantic slave trade did. But the Dutch reintroduced slavery to their colonial possessions, such that Cape Town, Ceylon, and Indonesia had seventy thousand slaves according to a 1688 census.[30]

The consequences of European actions were enormous for Indian Ocean trade. The Portuguese turned open trade into what was known as the Cartaz system, a word derived from the Arabic word *qirtas*, meaning "paper" or "document."[31] The new system can be likened to a protection racket, whereby ships of other countries had to buy a pass to be allowed to trade. Ships without a pass were at risk of being seized or even destroyed.[32] The system was not always effective; it could be bypassed by ships that avoided the Indian Malabar Coast and nearby areas and sailed directly to non-Portuguese ports like Aden and Aceh. Eventually, the cruel Portuguese methods helped to unite local Muslim rulers against them, such that when the Dutch arrived in the region, these rulers welcomed them, evidently hoping that they would turn out to be better than the Portuguese, though they would soon prove to be "even more brutal."[33]

The advent of the European powers and the competition among them led to the fragmentation of trade in the Indian Ocean. The European system of trade monopolies, in which single national companies were given exclusive access to specified regions, increased conflict while barring access to other countries' trade monopolies. The expansion of European commercial and political power into the region and the seizure of trading posts by countries such as Portugal, the Netherlands, and Great Britain ensured that trade moved more and more between Europe and Asia, rather than, as before, among the Asian states.[34] The Dutch established links between Batavia, Colombo, and Cape Town, from which they tried to control the spice trade, especially in cloves, nutmeg, and mace from Indonesia. The English had their first major footholds in the coastal areas of India: Madras, Bombay, Calcutta, and Surat. Whereas the Portuguese had occupied strategic points, the Dutch introduced outright and extended colonization. The English approach was similar to the Dutch one; they created trade and tax monopolies, which were then followed by colonization. All this would have a lasting effect on Asia and the Indian Ocean region well after European imperialism ended, hampering the development of regional economic integration after decolonization.

There is an almost painful irony in Europe's undercutting of the openness of Indian Ocean trade and its division of the vast maritime region into zones of influence. It has to do with the notion of freedom of the seas, which assisted in European expansion in Asia and became a key foundation of globalization, even as the European practice was to deny free access to maritime trade to competitor countries.[35]

Western scholars trace the origin of the concept of mare liberum, or freedom of the seas, to the Byzantine Emperor Justinian in the sixth century AD and to the writings of the Dutch legal scholar Hugo Grotius (1583–1645).[36] Grotius is widely regarded as the father of the doctrine in its modern, contemporary sense, even though freedom of the seas was a shared maritime convention in the Indian Ocean. In fact, Grotius's acclaimed role in developing this concept has a dark side to it. He was hired in 1604 by the Dutch East India Company (Vereenigde Oostindische Compagnie, or VOC), founded two years before, to write a legal brief defending the seizure of a Portuguese merchant ship, the *Santa Catarina*, near Singapore by a Dutch vessel, whose captain happened to be Grotius's cousin. Since their conquest of Malacca, the Portuguese had been the dominant players in the eastern Indian Ocean, practicing a monopoly that had barred or obstructed other European companies, including the VOC, from trading in the region. In defending the VOC, Grotius expounded his theory that the seas were open to all, and the Portuguese therefore should not be allowed to monopolize trade in the Indian Ocean. In preparing his brief, Grotius received from the VOC documents on historical Indian Ocean maritime affairs, which provided a precedent for the absence of trade monopolies. The legal brief he produced to defend the seizure of the *Santa Catarina* was then turned into the book *Mare Liberum* published in 1608–1609, giving Grotius exaggerated credit for inventing the modern principle of freedom of the seas.[37]

Hugo Grotius is celebrated today as a founding philosopher of modern international law and Western liberalism. But his defense of the VOC, which quickly became another European monopoly, and his subsequent role in helping the company negotiate unequal treaties with independent Asian states make him one of the "intellectual fathers of Dutch [and European] colonial rule in Asia."[38]

The European colonization of the Americas and Asia represented a new phase in globalization, one that was built on the preexisting Eurasian and Islamic foundation. Europe further expanded existing connections and created new ones thanks to its imperial advances. Crucially, Europe established trade networks not only between Europe and the Americas, with the help of African resources and slaves, but also between Latin America and East Asia, via the Pacific Ocean, intended for the export of silver from the former Inca Empire to China, then the largest economy in the world. The abundance of silver eventually led to a fall in its value, creating massive inflation and ruining China's economy as well as Spain's, whose rise to great power status had depended on its control of silver from the New World. This allowed other Atlantic powers—which were trading in sugar, gold, and tobacco with the help of a thriving slave trade from Africa and indentured labor plantations in the Pacific, Caribbean, and elsewhere—to drive globalization and gain the upper hand in the world power balance.

Chapter 8

The Rise of the West

After the prominence of India, China, and Islam in world-order building came Europe's—especially western Europe's—turn. From the European Enlightenment in the seventeenth century onward, the very idea of world order has become indistinguishable from the fact of Western global dominance. Before we turn to the nature of the Western-led world order, we need to address a basic question: How and why did Europe rise to global ascendancy in the first place?

There is endless debate and discord surrounding this question, which no one can claim to have settled. But the debate is central to understanding how the contemporary world order came about. Particularly important is the question of whether the rise of western Europe was entirely due to its own scientific, economic, and political ingenuity. Or, did it owe its paramountcy to influences and resources from other parts of the world, acquired through imperialism and colonization?

Europe and the "West": What's in a Name?

But first, what and where is Europe? In truth, like *Asia* or *Africa*, the term *Europe* is a changing and controversial construct. The Greeks divided the world into Asia, Europe, and Libya (Africa) and, as discussed, did not see themselves as European; Greece and Rome were Mediterranean

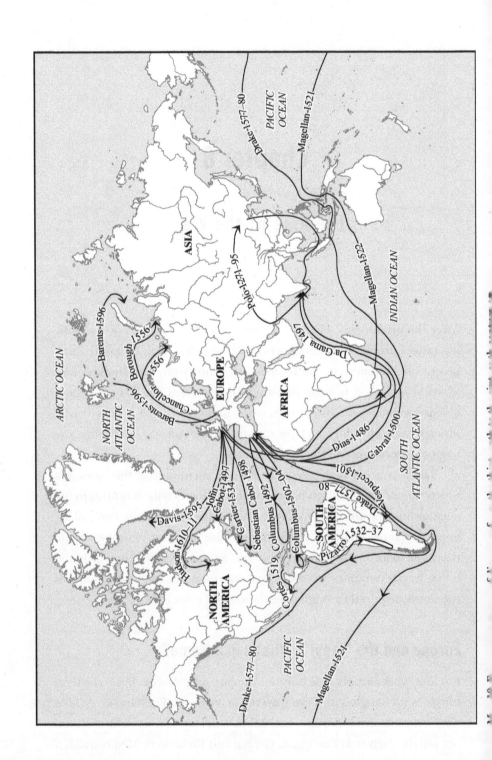

civilizations, not European ones. In fact, the idea of Europe as a distinctive entity (not to mention as a rising actor in international relations) came only many centuries later, during the Renaissance and the Enlightenment, when Greece and Rome would be appropriated retroactively as the foundation of European and Western civilization.

The origin of the West—an offshoot of Europe—is even more contested; it is an artificial, invented, modern concept. The Chinese conception of the West included central Asia and India. Hence the popular Chinese novel about seventh-century Buddhist monk Xuanzang's pilgrimage to India, *Journey to the West*. Over the ages, the West has been a Christian notion, a white racial notion, and an imperial notion. It also served as a Cold War construct: shorthand for the nations of the NATO alliance facing the Warsaw Pact nations led by the USSR. Today, the term West serves not only to underscore difference and hostility vis-à-vis its presumed adversaries like China, Russia, and Iran, but also to highlight its sense of cultural and racial superiority against the nations of the global South. The West continues to organize and act like an exclusive political and racial club of a handful of nations against the vast majority of nations and people in the globe.

The notion of the West might have started with the division of the Roman Empire into western and eastern domains, cemented by the division of Christianity into Catholic and Orthodox systems of belief. Europe's eastern part, including Russia and Greece, would thus be part of the East, not the West. More importantly, this East of the Orthodox world was disparaged, considered inferior by its Western neighbors, an ironic twist given the importance the West attributes to ancient Greece. The Latin pope, head of the Roman Catholic Church, refused to anoint the Byzantine emperor as the Holy Roman emperor, giving that honor to Charlemagne instead. But the considerable mutual animosity between the East and the West extended beyond religious doctrine. Later, the West would regard its East, the Orthodox realm, as having been untouched by the Renaissance and Enlightenment, even as it saw these periods as reviving the wisdom of ancient Greece.

This is a critical concept in the West's view of itself and of the East. The Renaissance was followed by the rise of European imperialism, and it was accompanied by the downgrading and othering not only of the civilizations of India, China, and Islam, but also to some degree of the Orthodox Christian nations of Europe, including Russia. This process was furthered globally by the political and legal doctrine called the "standard of civilization." This notion justified in the collective Western mind Europe's move away from the Rest and its transformation into a distinctive, dominant, and supposedly superior cultural entity. It was the measure by which Europeans justified their dominance by decreeing other civilizations uncivilized, their inhabitants, as the common identifiers had it, "savages," "barbarians," or "heathens."

Centuries after the Renaissance, the idea of the West got a powerful dose of vitality from Cold War geopolitics, otherwise known as the East-West conflict, in which the West was identified with the United States and its European NATO allies, plus Japan and a few former European colonies such as Australia, New Zealand, and Canada. These Western nations collectively tried to prevent the takeover of the world by the East, meaning the Soviet Union and its socialist allies, joined together in the Warsaw Pact. Decolonization added another basis to the idea of the West, this time by othering the newly independent countries who collectively came to be regarded as the Third World, neither Eastern nor Western.[1]

Whatever the origins of its name, it is clear that Europe, and in particular western Europe, was a latecomer in the story of civilization. The question then arises: Why and how, after lagging behind the great Eastern empires of China, India, and the Islamic world, did Europe forge ahead?

Europe's Magic Potion

There have been several leading explanations addressing what is sometimes called the "Great Divergence," when western Europe began to grow with historically unprecedented speed and outstripped Asia and eastern Europe in wealth.[2] In addressing this question, some scholars have stressed "indigenous" European factors such as scientific inquiry, political and economic competition, and liberal governments.[3] The historian Philip T. Hoffman argues that the intense competition among the European states (or political entities) between 1300 and 1500—what he calls "the tournament"—improved the military technology that was key to Europe's ascendance.[4] For Ian Morris, Europe, and the West more broadly, rose because of its superior urbanization, ability to capture energy, war-making capacity, and information technology.[5] The historian Mark Elvin has focused on China's stagnation, theorizing that its efficiency in the preindustrial period resulted in a "high-level equilibrium trap," in which there was little perceived need for economic and technological advancement, whereas Europe's highly competitive preindustrial condition incentivized innovation.[6]

The answer from Jared Diamond boils down to the key role played by geography and environment, especially Eurasia's east-west continental spread versus the north-south orientation of the Americas and Africa.[7] An east-west position, he argues, makes it far easier for the plants, animals, agricultural techniques, technological innovations, and ideas that are key to development to spread. This is because, in Diamond's accounting, an east-west axis lies along similar lines of climate, while the north-south orientation doesn't. Being part of Eurasia, western Europe could benefit from the ideas and innovations of the Eastern civilizations of Mesopotamia, China, and India. By contrast, such diffusion was blocked in continents with a north-south orientation, for example between the urban centers of the North American East Coast, Mesoamerica, the Andes, and Amazonia. Moreover, through the centuries, Eurasians developed a strong immunity to diseases such as smallpox, measles, and influenza, partly due to a greater abundance of livestock and relative density of population in many areas. This explains why the New World populations were so easily subjugated by western Europeans.

If geography and environmental factors help explain the rise of Europe, why did other great civilizations of Asia—which were also part of or connected to the Eurasian landmass and had for most of history far surpassed Europe in wealth, culture, and technology—fall behind?

Diamond's answer once again focuses on geography. For China in particular, the culprit is the differences in river geography. Historically, China developed only two core areas around the Yangtze and Yellow Rivers, which over time came to be well-connected with each other through canals. By contrast, western Europe's two major rivers, the Danube and the Rhine, smaller and less well-connected, led to the emergence of multiple core areas, "none big enough to dominate the others for long, and each the center of chronically independent states."[8] The result: China's geography allowed easier unification, while western Europe's created perennial division and competition. Such competition produced more innovation and strengthened European economies and states, while China's geography produced large empires that stifled innovation and ultimately led it to fall behind Europe.[9]

Diamond's thesis is especially useful in pointing to the key role of the diffusion of knowledge and culture, since western Europe, being part of Eurasia, enjoyed easy access to Eastern resources, ideas, and technology before becoming dominant. The thesis, though hardly the first one to do so, also helps explain why the New World populations were so easily subjugated by western Europeans. But Diamond's sweeping explanation is incomplete and simplistic. If geography—the size of states and the nature of their rivers—was so central, why did China, with its river-united imperial rule, remain far more innovative and advanced than western Europe for so long? Diamond offers no explanation for this. His thesis relies on the flawed, incomplete logic of geographic and environmental determinism. Worse, it diverts attention from, and even excuses, the role of European imperialism and colonialism in pushing the West ahead of the Rest.

The role of imperialism and colonialism has figured in some Western explanations of the Great Divergence but certainly not to the degree it deserves. One prominent theory holds that Europe's leap forward, as compared to Asia, did not occur until after 1800, when the European countries' access to overseas resources in the colonies spurred its industrialization.[10] Others acknowledge that Europe's miracle was made possible by colonialism.[11] But if there are anti-imperialist voices among Western scholars in explaining the Great Divergence here and there, they are rare.

On the other hand, the biggest denier of imperialism, with a far greater hold on Western readership, is the historian Niall Ferguson.[12] He argues that Asia, especially China, had an overall economic edge over Europe, specifically England, as late as 1750. England, he allows, was ahead of China in terms of per capita income, but it still had higher mortality. Despite being behind, Europe's race past China or other eastern civilizations in practically every economic and technological category had nothing to do with culture, geography, good luck, or weather. Nor was imperialism the reason why the West came to dominate the Rest, insists Ferguson.[13] "Empire," he points out, "was the least original thing the West did after 1500. Everybody did empire."[14] Empires existed both in the West and the East, yet the former was able to leave the latter way behind in the march to modernity and power. Why? Ferguson credits Europe's rise to what he calls six "killer apps": competition, science, property rights, medicine, consumer society, and the work ethic.

Ferguson's killer apps thesis requires close scrutiny, given his prominence in the world of public intellectuals today, and because he exemplifies the mainstream, Eurocentric view of the rise of the West. My argument with Ferguson is in the form of two key questions. First, who made these killer apps possible? Or, put another way, what role did the knowledge and ingenuity of other civilizations—Chinese, Muslim, and Indian—play in the making of these killer apps? Second, what role did imperialism play? In short, without drawing on Asia's knowledge pool, and without the colonization of much of the rest of the world, would the killer apps that Ferguson claims to have powered the Great Divergence have come about?

My answer to these questions takes me back to the evening of March 17, 2017, when I had a public debate with Ferguson about his killer apps thesis at Beijing's Tsinghua University, where we both happened to be visiting professors. We taught the same group of students but offered them dramatically different explanations about the rise of the West. Our students decided to make our differences public by setting up a debate. My argument against Ferguson, whom I found very amicable even as we clashed, was blunt: his killer apps would not have "scored," meaning they would not have become as powerful or effective as they did, without Europe's borrowing of Eastern ideas and without its imperialism. While Ferguson's thesis has attracted criticism before, my response deployed the information contained, surprisingly enough, in his own book *Civilization*.[15]

Science and medicine are the two killer apps whose development in Europe depended critically on foundations laid in Asia. Ferguson uses the term "scientific revolution" narrowly to refer to developments in Europe from the eighteenth century onward. These include a range of inventions, from Newtonian physics to the machinery of mass production. But there were other, wider scientific advances achieved by Eastern civilizations that brought not just Europe but the world to the edge of modernity. These include Indian numerals (transmitted by the Arabs); Chinese inventions like the compass, gunpowder, the printing press, paper, and paper money; and the Islamic world's medical knowledge, long-distance navigation instruments and techniques, iron and steel production, windmills and water mills, and commercial innovations such as partnerships, contract law, banking, and credit. Many of these were transmitted to Europe, both before and after the Renaissance, with the Arabs and the Mongols playing crucial intermediaries. Even as Europe began to make its more dramatic scientific advances—including Newtonian physics, the Copernican idea of astronomy, and a whole set of advances in chemistry, biology, and botany—it borrowed ideas from Asia and the Islamic world.[16]

When it comes to the idea of work ethic, Europe might not have learned anything from Asia, but the concept certainly wasn't unique to the West. Asia had its own versions of the work ethic: the Confucian work ethic in China, for example, had remarkable parallels with the Protestant work ethic in such habits as exercising discipline and saving money. So, if this is a killer app, why didn't it propel China ahead of Europe?

I now turn to the second question: What role did imperialism play in powering Europe's killer apps? It did so in specific relation to four of them: competition, property, medicine, and consumer society, as summarized in Table 8.1.

190

Table 8.1 Imperialism and Four of the Killer Apps

- Competition: While economic and political competition occurred in Europe and elsewhere through the ages, intra-European competition from the fifteenth century onward intensified over the search for overseas colonies. The "spice race" for Asia and the "scramble for Africa" are good examples of how imperialism honed and sustained the European killer app of competition.
- Property: Colonization is all about land and property. Property rights got considerably strengthened with the establishment of colonies, especially in North America. Here, European settlers advanced property rights by replacing the idea that land was part of the God-given, natural commons with a new and self-serving principle. This idea—which was invoked from the writings of European philosophers such as John Locke, himself a colonial administrator and a participant in the African slave trade—was that if a person had appropriated land using his labor, then the land was removed from the commons and became private. In such a way did the European settlers justify seizing land from Native Americans, who had always held property to be communal.
- Medicine: Colonies became crucial sources of discovering resources for medicines, such as quinine, and testing grounds for new medicines, which further helped advance European imperialism.
- Consumer society: Indian cotton helped to create British consumer society. British import restrictions on Indian cotton textiles helped to create the British "economic miracle."

Out of these four, two—medicine and consumer society—provide the clearest example of how the rise of Europe piggybacked on imperialism. Medicine was, in Ferguson's own words, the "West's most remarkable killer application."[17] Remarkable because it reduced mortality, extended lifespans, and invigorated society, allowing Europeans to compete with and dominate the rest of the world. But what made some of the most important advances in medicine possible? Ironically for a staunch denier of imperialism's impact on the rise of the West, Ferguson suggests that some of the crucial advances in medicine would not have been possible without European adventures into Asia and Africa. As he himself puts it, "Africa and Asia became giant laboratories for Western medicine. And the more successful the research—the more remedies (like quinine, the anti-malarial properties of which were discovered in Peru) could be found—the further the Western empires could spread and, with them, the supreme benefit of longer human life."[18] For what purpose and benefit were these medical advances undertaken? To preserve the lives of European settlers and maintain and advance European colonialism. They were not so much meant to benefit Africans, who were viewed through the prism of "social Darwinism," which saw them as "biologically inferior, an inconvenient obstacle to the development of Africa by more advanced white 'Aryans.'"[19]

In discussing the rise of the West, Ferguson mentions disease, but ever so passingly, even though after the arrival of Spanish conquistadores in Hispaniola in 1518, diseases brought by Europeans killed millions of indigenous people, including in the Aztec and Inca empires. The years following European colonization might have seen the deaths of some twenty million people, or up to 95 percent of the population of the Americas.[20] Here is a sort of seventh killer app brought by Europeans, which actually killed millions and helped to subjugate the survivors and deserves far more emphasis in Ferguson's grand explanation of why Europe forged ahead.

The case of consumption provides an even more striking example of how imperialism created the killer apps. Consumer society, defined as a materialistic society in which people's lives revolve around mass-produced and relatively cheap consumer goods, is the bedrock of a capitalist economy. And no other item played a more central role in the emergence of British consumer society and the British Industrial Revolution than Indian-made cotton clothing. British colonization played a crucial role in this.

To quote Ferguson, "The Industrial Revolution would not have begun in Britain and spread to the rest of the West without the simultaneous development of a dynamic consumer society, characterized by an almost infinitely elastic demand for cheap clothes."[21] But where did these cheap clothes come from? The answer is India. Britain's Industrial Revolution, admits Ferguson, was stimulated by the "large-scale import of Indian cloth" by the British East India Company.[22]

But that "import" was strongly conditioned by British colonial practice. And the story of this transaction is not a pretty one. In the seventeenth century, when cotton garment exports from India to Britain started, Indian cotton fabrics were "both superior in quality and cheaper" than those of English, French, Dutch, and other European producers.[23] Moreover, while other fabrics were available, none could beat cotton's simplicity and versatility. Wool, though popular, is more useful in cold weather and more suitable for outerwear, rather than for direct contact with the skin. And wool could not be laundered and dried under the sun. Europeans knew, since Herodotus's time, of cotton as "a wool exceeding in beauty and goodness that of sheep."[24] Silk, by comparison, was not nearly as cheap or available in medieval or early modern Europe, which meant that the poor had to settle for clothes made of flax linen. But harvesting flax stems, which had to be done before the seeds ripened and involved soaking them in a large body of water, took time and effort, and the process polluted the water, making it unfit to drink.[25]

When Indian cotton was introduced to the British market, it was a godsend not only for the poor but also for high society. As Daniel Defoe, author of the novel *Robinson Crusoe*, complained, Indian chintz (cotton textiles printed on woodblocks) "crept into our houses, closets, and bedchambers; curtains, cushions, chairs, and at last beds themselves.... In short, almost everything that used to be made of wool or silk, relating either to the dress of the women or the furniture of our houses, was supplied by the Indian trade."[26]

Initially, the British East India Company, the vanguard of colonial rule in India, exported cotton garments from India to Britain. But to procure these Indian goods, the British used violence against independent Indian merchants who were not controlled by the East India Company or its local agents. Such merchants were flogged, their faces were painted black, and they were marched through the streets with their hands tied behind their backs.[27] Moreover, back home, British domestic manufacturers got the idea

Image 7. Dress made by the Mochi community in India and sold in Britain around the late seventeenth century.

that more money was to be made manufacturing Indian textiles than importing them.[28] This led to a historic shift. To protect manufacturers of cotton garments from competition, the British government first imposed high tariffs and then banned the import of most Indian cotton textiles. These restrictions were then adopted by other European countries, including France, Prussia, Spain, Flanders, Venice, and even the Ottoman Empire. It was sometimes extended, as in Prussia, to a ban on wearing Indian-made clothing.[29] However, African slaves could only be procured in exchange for Indian cotton fabrics and clothing, and so an exception to this ban was made for so-called Guinea textiles.[30] These indigo-dyed cotton fabrics were produced in India and acquired by European slave traders to be reexported to West Africa and the Caribbean, where they were hugely popular.

This protectionist policy powered the British economy. Cotton, Ferguson writes, became the "king of the British economic miracle," with cotton textiles rising from 6 percent of total British exports in the mid-1780s to 48 percent in the mid-1830s.[31] At the same time, the Indian economy, which was dependent on the export of finished cotton products, suffered heavily, with its textile industry destroyed. Sven Beckert's *Empire of Cotton* estimates that the value of cotton cloth exports from Bengal to Britain fell from 1.4 million pounds in 1800–1801 to 330,000 pounds in 1809–1810, and "Indian weavers, who had dominated global cotton textile markets for centuries, went into free fall."[32]

To sum up, here is a direct causal relationship between colonialism (featuring actions by both the British East India Company and the British government), the British Industrial Revolution, and the creation of one of Ferguson's killer apps: consumer society.

In the Indian context, there are other direct links between the rise of Great Britain and colonization. According to Indian economist Dadabhai Naoroji (1825–1917), Britain skimmed something like twenty to thirty million pounds annually from India.[33] How? When Britain employed a public servant in the civil administration or the occupational army, his salary did not come from Britain or other British colonies but from India itself. Thus, the money that the British got out of India through trade and extracting revenue directly or indirectly (through nominally independent "princely states") went toward paying British civil servants and troops. Also, the Indian armed forces supported all kinds of British imperial wars and occupations from Africa to the Middle East to Asia. When the British fought the First and Second World Wars, Indian soldiers played a key role in their battles. Without these troops, British imperialism could not have been sustained. The British could deploy the Indian army to defend and advance their imperialism not only in India but the world over without incurring much cost to themselves. As Princeton scholar Atul Kohli puts it, the British "did not pay a penny."[34] This is another way colonization directly fed the rise of the West, showing how India played a role in Britain becoming the most important military power in the world.

Recent studies by Indian economist Utsa Patnaik have shown the extent of the transfer of wealth from India to Britain during the colonial period. She puts the "drain," or the amount that British colonialism took from India, at 9.2 trillion pounds over the 173-year period between 1765 and 1938. This drain was possible partly due to the British policy of levying high taxes on Indian subjects and using the revenue to buy Indian products for export (this meant the British got the Indian products for "free"). Then the British kept the export earnings, accrued in gold and silver, in Britain, while the local Indian producers were paid in rupees. The overall extraction from India gave a major boost to the British economy. Between 1780 and 1820, the main period of British industrialization, the amount that Britian took from Asia and the West Indies combined was about 6 percent of Britain's GDP, nearly the same as the country's own savings rate.[35]

While some of these figures may be disputed, there is little question that the colonization of India was critical to Britain's ability to maintain its global empire. Lord Curzon, viceroy of India from 1899 to 1905, left little doubt about this: "India is the pivot of Empire," he stated, "by which I mean that outside the British Isles we could, I believe, lose any portion of the dominions of the Queen and yet survive as an Empire; while if we lost India, I maintain that our sun would sink to its setting."[36] At the same time, British rule made India stagnant and impoverished. Not surprisingly, as Kohli points out, after India gained independence in 1947, its annual rate of growth in per capita income shot up from 0.2 percent between 1870 and 1916 to 3 percent from 1950 to 2016. This had much to do with the fact that some 10 to 20 percent of India's savings had been taken out of the country by the British to finance their own needs.[37]

This leads to a very different explanation for Europe's rise than what Ferguson's thesis provides. Ferguson explicitly dismisses the force of European imperialism. Of course, imperialism, as Ferguson rightly points out, is hardly an original European practice. But the European imperialism around the globe after the fifteenth century AD went hand in hand with slavery, which in turn fueled a virulent form of racial prejudice, the scale of which the world had not seen before. In other words, European imperialism, combined with slavery and racism, operating in an emerging capitalist global economy, was different from any previous forms of empire. I call this amalgamation the West's "magic potion," as opposed to Ferguson's killer apps. It was in this magic potion that the killer apps were fermented.

I discuss the other ingredients of this magic potion in subsequent chapters. For now, I will focus on imperialism, the chief ingredient of the brew.

A study by Daron Acemoglu and Simon Johnson of MIT and James Robinson of Harvard, who shared the 2024 Nobel Prize in economics, directly challenges the claim that imperialism had nothing to do with the rise of the West.[38] Their study focuses on what they call "Atlantic Traders," meaning the leading imperial countries such as Britain, France, the Netherlands, Spain, and Portugal that traded with the New World, Africa, and Asia via the Atlantic. Because of this economic activity, which included the slave trade, the Atlantic Traders experienced significant economic growth relative to the rest of Europe. The GDP of the Atlantic Traders doubled between 1500 and 1820, whereas for the rest of western Europe the increase was just under 30 percent, the same rate as in eastern Europe.[39] The study also shows differential growth rates between the Atlantic Trader nations and those inland or on Europe's Mediterranean coast only. The authors conclude that "the rise of Europe between 1500 and 1850 was largely the rise of Atlantic Europe and the rise of Atlantic ports."[40]

These facts, the authors further argue, cast serious doubt on "theories of the origins of European development emphasizing distinctive European characteristics and *purely internal dynamics*" (emphasis added).[41] Remember here Ferguson's claim that the rise of Europe had nothing to do with its imperialism but was largely a European affair resting on internal dynamics, such as competition, work ethic, and consumer society.[42] The study by Acemoglu, Johnson, and Robinson implies that imperialism and the profits made in trade and slavery were indeed central to Europe's rise.[43]

Moreover, the profits made by the Atlantic Traders created differences in institutions, which helped the rise of North America relative to South America. This has to do with the development of property rights, another of Ferguson's killer apps. In his view, in South America, with its abundance of resources and large native population that could be exploited to develop extractive economies, colonialism did not require property rights to constrain the role of the monarchy. In North America, lacking such resources and population, colonizers turned to property rights to constrain the monarchy, and, in the end, this enabled them to do better economically. Property rights accentuated the benefits that the United States got from the Atlantic slave trade as well as from the appropriation of land from the Native Americans.

The role of colonialism also makes it difficult to accept Ferguson's claim that the rise of the West was achieved "more by the word than by the sword."[44] This claim minimizes the militaristic role of the West in advancing and maintaining its position in the world. It is thus impossible to separate colonialism from Western dominance. Nor could colonialism have been possible without the use of massive violence.

A related issue is whether the West's rise preceded or followed colonialism. Ferguson dates the rise of the West to the 1500s. But British economist Angus Maddison estimates that, as late as 1820, China's GDP was 29 percent of the world's GDP and equal to all of Europe's.[45] Before the Opium Wars (1839–1842 and 1856–1860), China was still the leading economy in the world. Maddison also estimates that India and China combined might have been producing 45 percent of the world's GDP, even if neither matched the per capita income of European powers. But this means Europe was not dominant until the nineteenth century, far later than the 1500 benchmark that Ferguson provides.

By the 1800s, what had changed in the world? Three centuries of European colonialism had borne its fruits. The true takeoff point for Europe is almost three hundred years after the European voyages of discovery and colonialism began, starting with the massive looting of resources from South America. The discovery of the Americas allowed the Spanish to extract huge amounts of gold and silver. Fruits and vegetables from the Americas helped to eliminate hunger from the European continent.

Colonialism was of course not just an economic force; it was mainly a political one. When Europeans first came to Asia in visible numbers in the sixteenth century, they signed treaties with local rulers. Initially, these were equal treaties, different from the ones that the British and the other Europeans would force on China after the Opium Wars. These earlier treaties entailed reciprocal obligations, concessions in return for duties, taxes, and so on. But by the nineteenth century, such treaties would disappear, and agreements, if any, would become one-sided or unequal.

Given that, it is difficult to accept the argument that extractive colonialism had nothing to do with the nineteenth-century rise of Europe.

But what motivated European colonization in the first place? And what sustained it? A common argument is that Europe's technological advances made colonization possible. In other words, Europe colonized the Rest because it was technologically able to. But contrary to Ferguson's argument, this killer app did not play an important role in the early stages. The exception could be the fiercely competitive European interstate system, enhanced by the Peace of Westphalia. But many of the innovations associated with colonization—such as the development of steam ships, more automatic infantry guns, railways, and the telegraph—came in the nineteenth century, after the colonization process had started. Although they would play a major role in expanding and sustaining imperialism, making it "easy," these technologies were not the reasons for its initiation.[46]

The economic motive, especially the search for resources by an overpopulated and undernourished western Europe, was no doubt an important reason for the initial search for colonies—not unlike the Greek colonization of the Mediterranean more than two thousand years earlier. Another commonly cited motive is religious: the drive to spread Christianity and combat Islam. Christopher Columbus, in trying to persuade the Spanish monarchy to support his voyage of discovery, argued that the gold he might bring back would be crucial to conquering the Holy Land from the Muslims. In 1452, Pope Nicholas V issued the first papal bull authorizing the king of Portugal to conquer and enslave Muslims and seize their lands and properties. In 1455, Nicholas issued a second papal bull naming Prince Henry the Navigator—a major patron of the Portuguese voyages of discovery—as a soldier of Christ and praising him for his desire to convert infidels to the Catholic faith.[47] And in 1493, a papal bull from Pope Alexander VI divided the right to colonize the world between the Spanish for the Americas and the Portuguese for the East, including Asia. This was to be formalized in the 1494 Treaty of Tordesillas between Spain and Portugal.[48] The spread of Christianity, carried out by hordes of missionaries who traveled to the "heathen" world to save souls, was indistinguishable from the notion of civilization itself. In short, "in the process of empire-building missionaries were nearly as important as merchants and military men."[49]

But while religious conversion, commercial interests, and the quest for gold were important motivations for colonialism, it was not for the most part traders or missionaries who seized and controlled territories, an essential ingredient of imperialist expansion.

There were instances where European powers did acquire territory through peaceful exchange. Perhaps the most famous was the Dutch sale of Manhattan to the British in exchange for the Malukus, or Spice Islands, in what is now Indonesia, which seemed like a very smart bargain then, since Manhattan had no resources comparable to the Malukus. The Louisiana Purchase of 1803, a deal in which the United States acquired 828,000 square miles of territory west of the Mississippi River from France for the sum of fifteen million US dollars, was another grand act of colonial appropriation. But such cases benefited the Western powers at the expense of the native people. In most parts of the world where the Europeans went, they acquired territory by force. Colonial companies might have initially signed agreements and treaties, but their governments, which backed those companies, followed with military expeditions, established extraterritorial rights (as in China), or took over from the companies to establish direct colonial rule (as in India after the 1857 Indian revolt).

While many factors played a role in the rise of Europe and the West, none would be more important than the role of imperialism, especially the colonization and exploitation of the Americas. It stimulated the industrialization of Europe, as Europe supplied manufactured products in exchange for the resources extracted from the Americas. One key element of this was the vast flow of silver mined in South America across the Pacific to China, which was using silver as its currency and where its value was much higher than in other parts of the world, creating opportunities for profit. The bullion trade with China via the Philippines created opportunities for a colonial presence and expansion in Asia. Hence, European colonization was the result of the "stimulating effects of bullion, trade, and opportunity."[50] But as the next two chapters show, it was the result of superior military technology, religious zeal, disease, and brutality.

Chapter 9

The Lost World

The history of Europe's discovery and conquest of the Americas is well-known and continues to be celebrated in Europe and the United States, which still observes a Columbus Day. The encounter between the civilizations of Central and South America and the Europeans who arrived there from the fifteenth century onward was globally transformative. Not to put too fine a point on it, but from the perspective of the indigenous civilizations, the Europeans brought mostly death and destruction on an almost unimaginably grand scale, unprecedented in the meetings of civilizations before then. The European subjugation of indigenous societies and the extraction of their resources were without question the most powerful forces behind Europe's ability to move ahead of the other, more advanced civilizations of Asia and Islam. Hence, European imperialism was at the root of the construction of a world order of global scope.

But this story, whether written by the defenders of the conquerors or their detractors, often misses a key element: the relevance of indigenous societies' political ideas and modes of governance to the emergence of the modern world order. Westerners tend to assume that the pre-Columbian peoples of the Americas were both too culturally different and too geographically isolated to have any relevance for understanding how world orders are created, not to mention to exert any significant influence over the world order that would emerge with Europe's expansion around the globe. In reality, the pre-Columbian civilizations had developed states, empires, and ways of legitimizing and governing them that showed that human beings, despite being geographically distant, could develop similar if not the same ideas and institutions to organize their politics and build world order. To give three main examples, the Maya organized a system of independent city-states, the Aztecs a small but powerful tributary empire, and the Incas a large but decentralized empire. These were similar in some ways to the orders that emerged in other parts of the world, and they add to our understanding of how the contemporary world order came about.

The Maya

By the time the Spanish conquistador Hernán Cortés landed in the Yucatan Peninsula in February 1519, the Mayan civilization was already past its prime. One of the longest lasting among the pre-Columbian civilizations of the Americas, with a span of over three thousand years, the Maya had at different stages covered a large swath of Mesoamerica (*meso* meaning "middle" in Greek), including parts of modern-day Mexico and the countries of contemporary Central America, from Guatemala to Nicaragua.[1] Never developing into a large empire, the Maya reached an advanced period of political organization during the "classic" period, roughly from the mid-third century to the early tenth century AD. In this they were likely to have been influenced by the Olmecs, the earliest known Mesoamerican civilization going back to 1200 BC. The Olmecs not only were responsible for some of the key Mesoamerican innovations—such as the calendar, the ball game, and hieroglyphic script—but also had created the very first polities of the region that engaged in diplomacy, alliances, and long-distance trade.

While the classic age ended in the tenth century AD, when the Spanish arrived five hundred years later, there were still vibrant Mayan centers such as Chichén Itzá. An ancient Mayan text—the Popol Vuh ("council text") of the K'iche' people of the Guatemalan Highlands, one of a

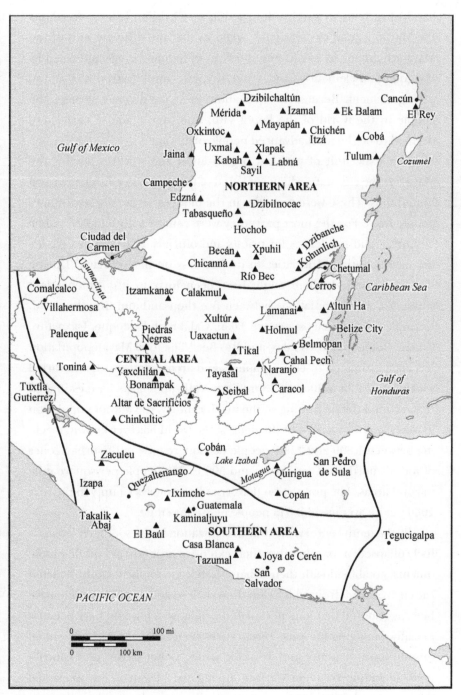

Map 11. Mayan political centers.

handful of texts to survive destruction by Christian priests—recounts the Mayan legend of creation. It suggests that the different eras of the Maya are inhabited by different versions of human beings and ruled by the god of an element—wind, water, fire, etc.—and destroyed by an opposing element. Because of their ability to make divine offerings, the people in the world of the Popol Vuh, who were made of corn, were deemed to be the most advanced people of all time.[2]

The basic unit of political organization and world order for the Maya was the city-state, which consisted of urban centers with large rural hinterlands. These were not cities in the modern sense, where ordinary people lived. For the most part, they were centers with temples, public buildings, and residences for priests and officials. Ordinary people living nearby gathered in cities to do business on market days.[3] During the classic period, there might have been forty to fifty independent city-states, with populations between five thousand and fifty thousand. Examples of these city-states are Tikal, Calakmul, Palenque, Uaxactun, Copán, Bonampak, Dos Pilas, and Río Bec.[4] The total Mayan population has been estimated by ethnographers and archaeologists to have varied widely from 1.25 million to 13 million. Anthropologists have estimated that, around the beginning of the ninth century, the Mayan population in Mesoamerica was one of the densest the world has ever known, reaching between 1,800 and 2,600 people per square mile in the urban zones of today's northern Guatemala, and 500 to 700 people per square mile in rural areas. The population density of Los Angeles County in the year 2000 was an average of 2,345 people per square mile.[5]

By the tenth century, the Mayan civilization in the southern lowlands had collapsed, in part because their extensive program of building monuments, combined with their urban lifestyle generally, steadily depleted the environment from which they drew their sustenance. This might have been aggravated by a long period of drought, which would have been especially damaging for some Mayan states such as Tikal, which depended on rain for agriculture and drinking water.[6] Other factors also contributed, including frequent warfare among the Mayan states, weakened dynasties, and destabilized economic, military, and marriage alliances.

Image 8. The royal palace of the Mayan city of Palenque.

These made a large-scale empire, which might have ensured stability and longevity, impossible.[7] By the time the Spanish arrived in the sixteenth century, Mayan cities had already declined from their highly urbanized form and turned into agricultural villages, with rainforest reclaiming much of what had once existed.[8] The defeat of the K'iche' Maya at the hands of the Spaniards in the Battle of Utatlan in 1524 is considered to be the end of Mayan civilization.[9]

Overall, the Mayan civilization developed attributes that were broadly similar to independent city-state systems in other parts of the world before the Westphalian system emerged in Europe. Although the Mayan states did not maintain standing armies, they were not part of a peace-loving culture, as some early accounts suggested. Warfare motivated by religion, power, and prestige was relatively frequent.[10] While it may be a stretch to compare the Mayan polities with the classical Greek city-states or those of Renaissance Italy, they did have a strong cultural identity and they engaged in constant conflict.[11] Like independent-state systems everywhere, the Mayan states developed a hierarchy, with stronger rulers, or "over kings," extracting allegiance and tribute from weaker ones.[12]

The Aztecs

One of the most insightful assessments of the Aztec civilization, the first empire in the New World to fall to Europeans, comes from the man who was most responsible for its destruction. "Their fashion of living," wrote conquistador Hernán Cortés in a letter to Spanish King Charles V after he took the Aztec capital of Tenochtitlan in 1520, "was almost the same as in Spain, with just as much harmony and order; and considering that these people were barbarous, so cut off from the knowledge of God, and of other civilised peoples, it is admirable to see...what they attained in every respect."[13] It bears stressing that Cortés was talking about civilization, not wealth or territory. Historians dismiss his account because he was a low-class Spaniard, but this is a good reason to trust it even more. He was recording, not interpreting, what he saw of Mexican customs, religion, and government. Christopher Columbus and other conquistadores often exaggerated the bounty of the lands they discovered to impress the Spanish Crown and secure its support or gain political influence. By praising Aztec civilization—such as its "good order and politeness, for they are a people full of intelligence and understanding"—Cortés risked angering the Spanish nobility's sense of cultural superiority, already cemented by the Reconquista (the Spanish victory over the Muslim rulers of Spain).[14] His description was certainly at odds with the views of Spanish priests, who saw Aztecs as little more than bloodthirsty primitives in need of Christian salvation. But, in fact, the Aztecs enjoyed almost universal literacy, perhaps the first civilization to do so, and their "corpus of writings in classical Nahuatl, the language of the [Triple] Alliance, is even larger than the corpus of texts in classical Greek."[15]

The Aztec Empire inherited the legacy of powerful and culturally accomplished civilizations, especially Teotihuacan and the Toltecs. Teotihuacan, in what is now the Valley of Mexico, was probably the largest civilization in the world of its time, but no definitive history has been written showing how it originated, who built it, and why and how it ended, probably sometime in the middle of the eighth century BC. As with the Mayan civilization, environmental degradation is suspected to have been a key factor in Teotihuacan's decline, but signs of wanton destruction of its buildings suggest that an attack or a rebellion might have been the final blow.[16]

The Toltecs took over the former spaces of Teotihuacan and the Mayan cities in Yucatan. The Toltecs are believed to have traded into the southern parts of what is today the United States. But their reign ended around the middle of the twelfth century AD, when Mesoamerica's last indigenous civilization emerged. These were the Aztecs, an obscure tribe from the north who moved to the Valley of Mexico, where the Toltecs tolerated them while deriding them for their "primitive" culture. Eventually, as legend has it, after seeing an eagle perched on a cactus, a sign of divine significance, the Aztecs founded their own capital on an island in the marsh that is today's Mexico City, which the Aztecs believed was the center of the world. To gain legitimacy, the Aztec kings styled themselves as the direct descendants of the earlier Mesoamerican empires, drawing on the prestige of the Toltecs by adopting their artisanal styles and claiming Toltec ancestry.[17]

The Aztec Empire expanded from its central Mexican core and reached its height during the fifteenth and early sixteenth centuries AD. At its peak, it extended over eighty thousand square miles from the Gulf Coast to the Pacific Ocean and south to today's Guatemala.[18] The empire consisted of half a million people divided into several hundred small city-states. It has been described as a "confederation," in which the city-states maintained their political importance and a fair degree of autonomy under imperial rule, controlling the rural zones around them and engaging in trade with nearby cities.[19] In the Aztec political structure, the ruler was chosen by a council of elders from different clans. At the top was the *tlatoani* (speaker), who exercised supreme military and diplomatic authority. Then there was the *cihuacoatl* (snake woman, a symbol of motherhood and fertility in Aztec mythology) in charge of internal affairs. The empire functioned through a tributary system and maintained loose control over its provinces, which ran their own affairs as long as they met their tribute obligations in full. Provinces were organized around *calpulli* (guilds) of interrelated families, each with its headman, who then became members of a city council that ran the city-states. These councils elected a leader and four members (a sort of executive council), drawn from the aristocracy or the military. The cities had their own judicial bodies. The city councils and their leaders in turn were subjected to the empire.[20]

As they began to expand their power, the Aztecs in 1428 formed an alliance with the neighboring city-states of Tlacopan and Texcoco, an arrangement that became known as the Triple Alliance. It carried out warfare and collected tribute.[21] Of particular importance was the ideology that legitimized the Aztec conquests.[22] It was based on a cosmological play of dominance and balance, in which all life on earth depended on an equilibrium among the cosmic forces—represented by the four children of Ometeotl, the deity sustaining the universe—who were in constant struggle. The struggle sometimes led to an uneasy equilibrium, with the four likened by one scholar to sumo wrestlers "sitting motionlessly against each other in the ring."[23] The ascendant of the four either became the sun god Huitzilopochtli himself or, in other versions, simply guided the movement of the sun. In either case, stability among the four allowed the sun to shine and life to be sustained, but it was not permanent. Competition among the brothers would renew, and a new balance had to be found. Moreover, apart from the fraternal struggles, the sun had to battle other cosmic forces, such as the moon and the stars. There was, in other words, a constant competition, a struggle of "light against darkness" in which "each day of sunlight was a victory that must be fought and won again the next day."[24] There was a constant fear that the sun might one day lose the struggle, leading to famine and other calamities that would end life on earth. To prevent this, the sun had to be provided with a continuous supply of energy. And that energy came from blood, through human sacrifice.[25]

The Aztec practice of human sacrifice caught the attention of Europeans and has been a highly controversial, hotly debated topic. There is no question that the practice existed, but there is also no certainty about its extent and purpose. Popular historians have portrayed it as common, involving large numbers of victims, using those numbers to paint a picture of Aztec barbarism. For example, the historian John M. Roberts likens it to "holocaust."[26] One estimate published by the BBC tells of twenty thousand people a year sacrificed in the Aztec Empire, and, according to this account, the numbers went up on special occasions. According to one estimate, the dedication of the temple of Huitzilopochtli in the Aztec capital Tenochtitlan (the Templo Mayor in today's Mexico City) in 1487 might have involved the sacrifice of some 80,400 people.[27]

But the figures of Aztec human sacrifices were exaggerated by Spanish priests to justify their program of religious conversion and to support the Spanish conquest. Cortés estimated three thousand to four thousand sacrifices a year, still a large number but far below the amount claimed by the priests.[28] In a typical double standard, Western historians, while denouncing the barbarism of Aztec sacrifices, often forget to mention the brutal practices and large-scale public executions in other civilizations. One example is the killings in the Roman Colosseum for public entertainment, which some might take to have been a form of human sacrifice.[29] Historians have estimated that seventy-five thousand people were executed in England between 1530 and 1630 AD, which is close to the number of people that Cortés estimated were sacrificed by the Aztec Empire.[30] One might wonder if the same Spanish Catholic priests who found Aztec human sacrifice so barbaric would have felt that the death by torture and impalement widely employed in the Catholic Holy Roman Empire was perfectly fine.

Acquiring captives for sacrifice before the deity was one of the main reasons the Triple Alliance frequently went to war. The wars were cast as struggles against evil, necessary to maintain balance and order in the universe. But there were also economic and political reasons. The Aztecs went to war, for example, when their merchants or ambassadors were killed, or when a neighboring city-state refused passage to Aztec traders, or when a defeated city-state refused to pay tribute. The Aztecs offered warnings to their enemies—three warnings in twenty days, with each accompanied by a gift of weapons—before an attack would take place.

Despite these conflicts, the Aztecs were unable to establish full-scale regional dominance. Some historians have argued that the Aztec's tribute extraction and record of brutality were so harsh that it led neighboring states to join hands with the Spanish invaders. But, while some neighboring states were fed up with the tribute system, this view is at least exaggerated. The Tlaxcalans, the main foes of the Aztecs, initially fought the Spanish and only cooperated once they realized the superiority of the invading European forces.[31]

The Aztec's political cosmology, based on the movement of the sun, has echoes of the chaos-versus-order dualism of other civilizations, including Egypt. Its tributary system also has parallels in history. The Aztecs treated punished enemy rulers who did not submit violently, but their imperialism was based on indirect rule. For the most part, they did not colonize neighbors that paid tribute, and they allowed the defeated rulers that did to remain in control over their land.

The Incas

The Incas were the last to fall among the three civilizations discussed in this chapter. Despite their claim to have brought civilization to the Andes, the Incas were latecomers. They were preceded by the Tiwanaku and Wari (or Huari in Spanish) cultures, and it was the latter who had developed one of earliest empires in the Andes, conquering areas in the central and southern highlands, including Cuzco and the central and southern coasts of modern Peru. The decline of the Wari, whose roads provided the foundation for the famed Incan highway system, set into motion the competition among various states that, after a long and complex struggle, led to the empire of the Incas.[32]

Clues to the origins of the Inca people and their worldview can be found in one of the most popular Incan legends. The god Viracocha ("creator of all things") brought into being a universe with no light,

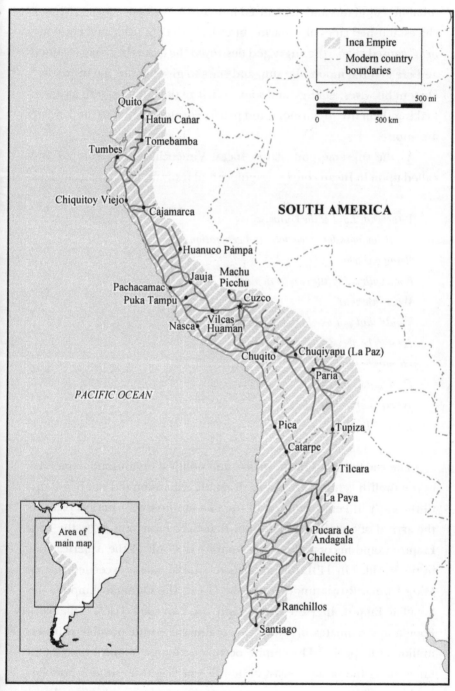

Map 12. Inca Empire.

inhabited by giants and uncivilized humans. To prevent conflict, Viracocha established rules of behavior, but when "vices of pride and covetous-
ness" caused chaos, the angry god destroyed the giants in a massive flood
and created the moon, the sun, and stars to give light to the universe.[33]
He sent his wives, siblings, and sons to civilize the humans, with a view to
making them live in harmony and peace, engage in harvests, and create
an empire.

As the supreme god of the Incas, Viracocha was celebrated and
called upon in Incan court ceremonies and festivals, with poems such as

Viracocha, Lord of the Universe,
. . . [C]ommander of warmth and generation
Being one who
Even with his spittle can work magic.
Where are you?
Would that you would not hide from this your son,
He may be above,
He may be below,
Or alight in the sky,
Where is his council seat,
Hear me![34]

The rudiments of Incan society and political organization emerged
in the twelfth century AD, but its dramatic expansion did not begin until the early fifteenth century. In the one-hundred-year period prior to
the arrival of Spanish conquistador Francisco Pizarro in 1526, the Inca
Empire would become the largest empire not only in the Americas but
in the world.[35] In 1491, the empire's territorial extent exceeded that of
Ming China, Russia under Peter the Great, the Ottoman Empire, the
Songhai Empire in West Africa, and the Aztec-led Triple Alliance.[36]
Population estimates of the Incan realm vary, with possibly thirteen
million at its peak.[37] The empire occupied an area of more than 2,600
miles along the western coast of South America, from what is now Colombia to Chile.[38] The mean features of the empire's sophisticated and

busy highway system were two parallel roads (complete with rock tunnels and suspension bridges supported by vines) in the highlands and on the coast. According to some estimates, the Inca road system, taking into account all its routes and branches, might have covered a total of twenty-five thousand miles.[39] A system of relay messengers transported messages along the main road system at a rate of 150 miles a day. Ironically, the fact that the Incan road system was so well-developed worked to the advantage of the Spanish conquerors.[40]

Incan history has been a matter of much dispute, partly because the Incas lacked a written language and partly because, after the conquest of the Inca Empire, Spanish historians presented the Incas from a biased perspective to serve their own religious and political ends. On the other hand, some narratives of Incan civilization are overly laudatory. One historian, Garcilaso de la Vega, born from a Spanish conquistador father and an Inca princess, portrayed the Incas as virtuous people, their religion sophisticated and their political system highly centralized and well regulated. He even likened the Incan state to ancient Rome. A very different view came from the account of Pedro Sarmiento de Gamboa, written at the behest of the Spanish viceroy Don Francisco de Toledo. By the time Sarmiento entered the picture in the late sixteenth century, the Incan throne was occupied by Inca royalty but under Spanish overlordship. Toledo wanted to destroy the regime of these so-called neo-Incas, whom he viewed as a threat to his authority, and he therefore portrayed them as illegitimate tyrants who had never developed a stable form of government.

Both views are extremes. Garcilaso de la Vega's sympathetic account may seem too utopian. Sarmiento's negative portrayal, directly instigated by Toledo's hostility to native Incan authority, was heavily and unmistakably politicized. Fortunately, there are other accounts of the Incas written by people who served the last generations of Inca rulers and who have provided us with more neutral, objective accounts.

William Hickling Prescott, a noted nineteenth-century American historian and author of *History of the Conquest of Peru*, first published in 1847, observed that the Incan government was one of "unmitigated despotism," comparable to the kind of contemporary "European despot, [who saw] himself the state." Prescott also had no illusion that the Incas were a peaceful people, since it "was by war that their paltry territory had been gradually enlarged to a powerful empire." Nonetheless, the Incas had a reputation for "wise and temperate policy," which "gradually won over the neighboring tribes to their dominion, as these latter became more and more convinced of the benefits of a just and well-regulated government." He further contended that, "far from provoking hostilities," the Incas "allowed time for the salutary example of their own institutions to work its effect, trusting that their less civilized neighbors would submit to their sceptre, from a conviction of the blessings it would secure to them."[41]

In addition to their reputation for fair governance, the Incas, in Prescott's portrayal of them, followed a unique system of religious tolerance with respect to the societies they conquered. Some conquerors elsewhere in the world, like the Persians, allowed their new subjects to practice their own religion; others, including some Islamic conquerors, sought to convert them. The Incas took a middle ground. The people of annexed lands could keep their own religious beliefs as long as they also accepted and worshipped the Inca gods and provided food, land, and labor to the Incan temples and overlord.[42] Inca rule had some notably mild features. Felipe Guamán Poma de Ayala, a distant member of the Inca royal family and a Spanish colonial official, claimed that "no tribute was paid to the Inca [the ruler], his *coya* [queen], or the principal lords....In this kingdom Indian [native] men and women served not captains nor any person."[43] For the average person, the main way of providing tribute or taxation to the state or the temples was in offering one's own labor. The Incas had no slavery in the sense of chattel slavery, where a person could be considered as legal property and owned, bought, and sold. The Inca laborers were free people, and the Incas followed a system of reciprocity, based on *ayni* (the act of giving back) and *mit'a*, a kind of taxation whereby the Inca subjects gave their labor to local chiefs, the temples, and the imperial overlords in Cuzco in return for receiving goods and administrative services.[44]

By the time of the Spanish conquest, the power of the head of the Inca Empire, the Sapa Inca, seemed absolute, but that was not always the case, and the degree of his authority was subject to limits. The Inca Empire had grown from numerous ethnic groups, each with its own chiefs, or "great lords," who could not be easily subordinated. The founder of the empire, Pachacuti, lacked the power to make other chiefs submit to his rule or, more vitally, provide him with labor for building infrastructure except by granting them gifts and favors.

To cope with the latent tendencies toward disunity and fragmentation, the Incas made a number of political innovations to control their territory and legitimize their authority. Specifically, the empire developed a decentralized structure. It was known as the "land of four quarters," based on its division into four parts (*suyu*): northeast (Anti), northwest (Chinchay), southeast (Colla), and southwest (Conti). This allowed for some degree of local autonomy, which helped to secure the loyalty of conquered people without repression. At the same time, it would be an overstatement to call this a federal system. The empire imposed limits to the autonomy of the *suyu* in a variety of ways, including the intimidation, dismissal, or murder of disobedient local chiefs and their replacement by more submissive ones. The Incas also used psychological means to control conquered societies. For example, the Incas would transport a conquered people's chief idols to the capital city of Cuzco, where they were held hostage, to be destroyed if the people in their home province rebelled.

Another technique of empire management was to move conquered peoples to territories already under Incan rule, under the assumption that the "old" subjects, who were familiar with Incan cultural and political norms, would socialize the "new" subjects into accepting Incan authority. This policy also reduced the populations of newly conquered areas, weakening their potential for rebellion. Indeed, this system of forced migration made it difficult for any ethnic group in the Inca Empire to become economically self-sufficient.

The Incas built their empire on warfare, but they followed certain ways in carrying out attacks that eased the suffering of conquered peoples. Prescott claims it was only after efforts "to soften the hearts of the rude tribes around them, and melt them by acts of condescension and kindness," failed that the Incas "employed other measures, but still of a pacific character; and endeavored by negotiation, by conciliatory treatment, and by presents to the leading men, to win them over to their dominion. In short, they practised all the arts familiar to the most subtle politician of a civilized land to secure the acquisition of empire. When all these expedients failed, they prepared for war."[45] The Mongols also gave prior warnings of their attacks, but theirs were not to "soften the hearts" of the rulers and people they were targeting but to remind them of what terrible consequences they might be spared by surrendering.

While there may be some exaggeration in this account, it is generally consistent with the accommodative nature of Incan conquest, such as that described in Garcilaso de la Vega's *Royal Commentaries of the Incas and General History of Peru*. Once the decision to attack was taken, Garcilaso claims, the targets were forewarned and asked to surrender immediately, "one, two or three times." If war did take place and resulted in victory for the Incas, they did not kill the rival chief but carried him and his children to the Incan capital, where they were "treated with kindness" and taught Incan "laws, customs, and correct speech, but also the rites, ceremonies, and superstitions of the Incas." Moreover, the Incas reinstated the vanquished party's own "former laws, liberties, and statutes" and installed the "mild administration of Inca kings."[46]

Internally, Incan society was communitarian, perhaps best illustrated by its system of agriculture. Cultivators first tended to the land belonging to the temple of the sun. Then they turned to the people who—because of old age or sickness or because they were widows, orphans, or soldiers in service—were not able to cultivate land themselves. Only then did cultivators turn to their own lands. Even then, there existed "the general obligation to assist his neighbor, when any circumstance—the burden of a young and numerous family, for example—might demand it." The land belonging to the Inca ruler was cultivated last.[47]

Despite its unique aspects, the Incan imperial system resembled others of the world and included some time-honored ways of building a world order. The leading early example is the Achaemenid Empire of Persia, which showed tolerance toward all religions and cultures within the territories it conquered. The policies of allowing defeated rulers to stay in power and treating the people in conquered lands with kindness echo Kautilya's advice in *Arthashastra*.[48] Granting local autonomy to subject people has been a common practice in pacifying newly conquered lands and managing large empires, whether the ancient Persian and Indian, the medieval Mongolian, or the modern British. The Incan creation narrative, contrasting chaos and order, darkness and light, aggressive giants versus peaceful humans, echoes the legitimizing ideology of rulers and empire builders around the world, including Egypt, Sumer, China, Persia, and India.

Globalization by Theft

The transatlantic slave trade is usually associated with the capture and import of African slaves to the Americas starting in the 1620s, when the Portuguese sent the first slave ships to Brazil. But it began at least decades earlier, in the reverse direction, when some native people from the New World were sent to Europe, though that is just one illustration of the radically one-sided nature of the encounter between the Old World and the New. In fact, it would be difficult to find in all of history an example where one side suffered such disastrous consequences—in the form of death, enslavement, and exploitation—and the other side such staggering advantages in everything from an increase in wealth to a surer, healthier, more varied diet.

What the Spanish found in the Americas, often to their joyous astonishment, was a people whose very culture and nature made them easy victims of depredation, including slavery. None other than Christopher Columbus noted this. Sailing back to Spain in February 1493 after his first voyage to the New World, he conveyed his impression of the native Taíno people of San Salvador Island in a letter written on board his ship to his sponsors, Spanish monarchs Ferdinand and Isabella.

"They have no iron or steel, nor any weapons; nor are they fit thereunto; not because they be not a well-formed people and of fair stature, but that they are most wondrously timorous," as well as "artless and generous with what they have" with a tendency to "show as much lovingness as though they would give their hearts." This touching portrait was not written to persuade the Spanish monarchs of the dignity and humanity of the Taíno but to explain how easy it would be to acquire "slaves as many as they shall order to be shipped."[49]

The conquistadors were also sexual predators. In a letter he wrote during his second voyage to the New World, Christopher Columbus boasted that it was just as easy to recruit Spanish soldiers by giving them native women as by giving land: "A hundred castellanos [one speaking the language of the Castille region of Spain] are as easily obtained for a woman as for a farm, and it is very general, and there are plenty of dealers who go about looking for girls; those from nine to ten are now in demand, and for all ages a good price must be paid."[50] To be sure, the Spanish colonists intermarried with local women, a leading example being Francisco Pizarro taking the daughter of the late Inca emperor Huayna Capac. These interracial marriages have been seen as an example of the "liberal" Spanish policy of assimilation with local people. But it is a fair question how much of this so-called assimilation was voluntary. More likely, these were forced unions, done through abduction and threat by early European colonizers, who were overwhelmingly men.

Aside from promising his soldiers women and land, Columbus had pledged to give the Spanish rulers "as much gold as they may need, with very little aid which their Highnesses will give me." He would have been keen to impress on them that their trust in him to secure the fabulous wealth of the East had been fully vindicated. Columbus had not yet quite realized that what he had found was not India. But he wanted to leave no doubt that the land was wealthy and the natives were simple, generous, and gullible. Columbus was also transporting back twenty-five natives (most likely Lucayan people) to sell them into slavery, although only seven would survive the voyage.[51]

All of these elements of the Spanish invasion of the Americas illustrate the greed and rapacity of Europe's imperial venture into the New World, and, of course, the devastating effect that venture had on indigenous peoples. In prevailing over the native empires and peoples, the Europeans had three major advantages. First, as already noted, infectious diseases brought by the Europeans—such as malaria, smallpox, and measles, against which the native population had no defense—played a decisive role in the defeat and downfall of American civilizations, including their leaders and rulers. Among the most notable victims of European diseases were the Aztecs, the first major standing Native American empire to fall to the Spanish. The nobleman who replaced Aztec leader Montezuma II died of smallpox, which began spreading rapidly, with devastating consequences in the region.[52] The Inca Empire's powerful ruler Huayna Capac died of smallpox around 1525, before conquistador Pizarro finally took the empire through deceit in November 1533.

Second, superior technologies, especially guns, were important in securing European victory over the numerically superior natives. A third factor was infighting among the native ruling families, which Spanish conquistadores like Cortés and Pizarro took full advantage of. For example, supporting Cortés against the Aztecs were local allies, including the Totonacs and Tlaxcalans, These rival groups resented the Aztecs for their demand of resources for tribute and people for sacrifice, although the Tlaxcalans, who played a decisive role in Cortés's victory, were not as eager to side with him as is commonly believed. Internally, advisers to Emperor Montezuma II were divided over whether the Spanish were gods or pillagers. After the Spanish entered the city on the emperor's orders, they massacred hundreds of unarmed Aztec nobles celebrating a festival in the city and later took Montezuma II hostage, creating a leadership vacuum.

Once the Spanish had used these advantages to conquer the indigenous peoples, their new imperial holdings produced a massive flow of wealth to Europe. Between 1503 and 1660, Spain took from its colonies in South America 185,000 kilograms of gold and 16,000,000 kilograms of silver (as measured in imports into Spanish port of Sanlúcar de Barrameda). The amount of silver totaled more than three times all the existing reserves in Europe.[53] The mines of Potosí (now part of Bolivia) were estimated to have yielded some forty thousand metric tons of silver during the colonial period.[54] Gold and silver from South America helped to finance Spain's European and imperial wars. South American vegetables such as potatoes overcame European malnutrition, and medicinal plants such as quinine helped to fight malaria and furthered European colonial advance. Minerals, especially silver obtained through slave labor, provided the riches for Europe to stave off bankruptcy and finance its expansion—just as in an earlier era, Octavian's conquest of Egypt helped to prevent the bankruptcy of the Roman Empire and feed the citizens of Rome. The whole of Western Europe benefited from the plunder; as Uruguayan writer Eduardo Galeano explained: "Spaniards owned the cow, but others drank the milk." Silver and gold flowed directly to Spain's creditors—German, Genoese, Flemish, and Spanish bankers—providing the capital accumulation that sparked European capitalism.[55]

In the process of this massive extraction, the lives of hundreds of thousands of indigenous workers and imported African slaves were lost and the bodies of countless others crippled. By the early seventeenth century, the mines of Potosí, then at peak production, required some 160,000 people, including native Peruvians forced to work there, African slaves, and their Spanish masters. This population exceeded that of London, Milan, or Seville at the time. Potosí's coat of arms read: "I am rich Potosí, treasure of the world, king of all mountains and envy of kings." Yet, conditions for the miners were exceedingly harsh. The difference in temperature between the depth of the mines and outside, poisoning from the mercury used for mining, and cruel treatment by the European masters made the mines deadly for workers. According to Spanish accounts, "If twenty healthy Indians enter on Monday, half may emerge crippled on Saturday." Another account says that, out of a group of 7,000 who went to Potosí, "only some 2,000 people return: of the other 5,000, some die and others stay at Potosí or the nearby valleys because they have no cattle for the return journey."[56] The native people were hunted down like animals and forced to work in the mines. As sixteenth-century priest Fray Rodrigo de Loayza observed, "These poor Indians are like sardines in the sea. Just as other fish pursue the sardines to seize and devour them, so everyone in these lands pursues the wretched Indians."[57]

The flow of gold and silver into Europe created myths and triggered a further rush of imperialist adventurers. After ransoming Inca ruler Atahualpa's life for a room full of gold and silver (gold was to fill half the room) and receiving the loot, Francisco Pizarro and his fellow conquistadores murdered the Inca anyway. They then melted the ransom into thirteen thousand pounds of twenty-two-karat gold and twice that much silver. These stories of stolen riches fed the legend of El Dorado, about lands whose rulers covered themselves in gold, encouraging adventurers from across Europe to traverse the Atlantic and steal what they could for themselves.[58]

While European imperialism in Asia crippled empires, in the Americas it destroyed entire civilizations. European conquest of the New World produced a lost world. But the wholesale destruction inflicted upon indigenous people is only half the story of Mesoamerica. The other half has to do with the contributions of the Americas, however forced and involuntary, to the newly emerging global order. The discovery of the New World ushered in an era of commerce and globalization, which some refer to as the "Columbian exchange," after the infamous Italian explorer. But the terms *theft* or *loot* might best describe what was happening, since *exchange* implies a voluntary and two-sided affair.

What the native population of the New World got from the Columbian exchange was little else but disease, death, and exploitation. The benefits to Europe, on the other hand, included vast tracts of cultivable land, immense quantities of precious minerals and metals, and a whole range of food crops—from staples such as maize, potatoes, sweet potatoes, and cassava to lifestyle-enriching tomatoes, chili peppers, cacao, peanuts, and pineapples—that transformed cuisines and palates all over the world. Some parts of the world even accepted one crop from the New World, tobacco, as currency. Moreover, the fertile fields of the Americas and the Caribbean allowed a dramatic increase in the production of sugar and coffee in plantations owned exclusively by European settlers and farmed by slaves imported from Africa and indentured laborers— that is, workers contracted for a fixed term who could obtain their freedom thereafter—from India, Indonesia, and other places.[59]

The potato illustrates the huge benefits the Europeans reaped from the discovery of the New World. Called "earth apple" (*pomme de terre*) in France, the potato created an agricultural revolution in Europe. It increased Europe's food productivity, dramatically reduced its nutritional deficiency, and protected its people from the familiar scourges of crop failures and famine. Because of the potato, Europe enjoyed higher birth rates and lower mortality, since the new source of nutrition could also alleviate the effects of diseases such as scurvy, measles, and tuberculosis. The Prussian ruler Frederick the Great valued the potato so much that he is "remembered for his feats of guile on both the battlefield and the potato field."[60] In 1774, frustrated by the reluctance of his subjects to grow what they thought was a "tasteless" tuber, Frederick ordered the creation of a royal potato field, heavily guarded so that people would think there was something truly valuable being grown there. But the guards were instructed to allow people to bribe them and steal the plants to grow them on their own land.

Potatoes might have saved Europeans from hunger, and other produce from South America—chili peppers, tomatoes, and cacao—no doubt enhanced the European and global palate. But in most other respects—from the extraction of silver to the appropriation of native land to grow lucrative cash crops like tobacco and sugar—the European impact on the American continents was not so much the globalization of trade as the globalization of theft.

Linking Two Oceans

The impact of the European colonization of the Americas was not limited to the Atlantic region. The example of the Manila galleons shows how the Pacific, too, was brought into the European-led global imperial order. The Manila galleons were Spanish sailing vessels of about two thousand tons used in voyages for 250 years, from 1565 to 1815, across the Pacific between Acapulco, Mexico, and the Spanish possession of Manila, the major port of the Philippine islands. A third of all the silver and gold mined in the Spanish territories in South America was carried by the galleons to Manila, including silver pesos that were minted in Mexico from metal extracted mainly in the former Inca Empire.[61] In all, the Manila galleons carried some seventy-five metric tons of silver every year to Manila, returning to Mexico with a variety of goods from Asia, including Chinese silk and gunpowder, Indian cotton, Southeast Asian spices, and Japanese screens and porcelain.[62]

The journey was often precarious for these four-deck galleons, despite their great size. They fell prey to pirates, natural disasters, and difficult shipping channels, such that some one hundred ships were lost during the years of this trade. And yet, the profit margins were so high—some estimates put them at 100 to 300 percent—that the voyages continued unabated despite the losses.

This huge trade expanded the scope of globalization whose seeds had been planted in the Indian Ocean, the Silk Road, and the Islamic world. And it produced winners and losers. The two-way trade across the Pacific was key to the economic viability of the Spanish colony in the Philippines and of the Spanish Empire as a whole. After being unloaded in Acapulco, 20 percent of the goods from Asia, known as the king's fifth, were transported, first overland across Mexico and then across the Atlantic to Spain. The Manila galleons in this sense were part of a truly global trade network. Previously, goods were mainly transported between China and Europe on the Silk Road. Now the trade still linked China, the world's economic powerhouse, and Europe, the rising trading power, but it included the newly discovered Americas, which had never been part of the global network before.

Although this commerce was Spanish centered, it became a factor in the crisis of the Chinese economy and therefore contributed to the decline of China relative to Europe. During the Ming dynasty (1368–1644), China switched from paper money to silver currency. With a fourth of the world's population, China thus saw a huge rise in the domestic demand for silver. But the massive production of silver in South America and flow of silver to China via the Manila galleon trade caused its value to fall. The resulting inflation caused a major disruption of China's economy around the mid-seventeenth century. The fall of the worldwide value of silver also dealt a powerful blow to Spain, whose rise as a great power had depended on its control of silver from the New World.

The Manila galleons stopped in the early nineteenth century, although the ships were already in decline, as the Bourbon rulers of Spain had allowed competing modes of trans-Pacific shipping in the mid-eighteenth century. The end of the Manila galleons marked a new phase in Europe's rise, built no longer on silver and Spain but on a triangular economic system among Europe, the Americas, and Africa. In this triangle, raw materials and cash crops from the Americas were sent to Europe for consumption and industrial production. This trade generated capital and manufacturing activity for products that could be sold to the African elite. Africa, then, became the chief source of slaves needed to meet the New World's growing plantation economy, since enslaving Christian Europeans was forbidden and Native Americans had become too few or too rebellious to fulfill the demand. A key victim of this new, dominant economic triangle was Africa.

Chapter 10

Africa, Interrupted

In 1324 AD, Musa, the *mansa* (ruler) of Mali, became famous around the world—perhaps the first sub-Saharan African to do so—for spending so much gold when he performed the hajj, the spiritual journey to Mecca, that the price of the metal was deflated throughout the Middle East.[1] This earned Musa a spot—predictably holding up a large nugget of gold—in the *Catalan Atlas* of 1375, one of the most well-known maps of the medieval period. Not surprisingly, historians have pointed to Musa's pilgrimage to illustrate the glories and richness of precolonial Africa.

Few other African rulers enjoyed the same fame as Mansa Musa, even if they did more important and impressive things than shower Cairo with gold. Other rulers of the era included Sundiata Keita, Mansa Musa's great-grandfather or granduncle, who founded the Mali Empire. In 1235, the young Sundiata (known as the Lion Prince) led his Malinke warriors to defeat king Sumanguru of Ghana, who was until then ruling over Mali. One of Sundiata's first acts was to proclaim before a council of nobles a set of rules known as Kouroukan Fouga (literally "clearing on granite rock," so named after the site where it was announced) or the Manden Charter. These principles, though orally transmitted, bore the hallmark of a national constitution, laying out rules for social, economic, and political life and governance in the empire. It was a remarkably liberal document for its time, or any time. Among its provisions, as summarized by UNESCO,

Image 9. Depiction of Mansa Musa, the emperor of Mali, in the *Catalan Atlas*, 1375.

were "advocating social peace in diversity, the inviolability of the human being, education, the integrity of the motherland, food security, the abolition of slavery by razzia (or raid), and freedom of expression and trade."[2] Here are some excerpts from the charter:

> Everybody has a right to life and to the preservation of its physical integrity. Accordingly, any attempt to deprive one's fellow being of life is punished with death.
>
> Women, apart from their everyday occupations, should be associated with all our managements.
>
> Do not ill treat the slaves. You should allow them to rest one day per week and to end their working day at a reasonable time.
>
> Never do wrong to foreigners.

There are five ways to acquire property: the buying, the do-
nation, the exchange, the work and the inheriting. Any other
form without convincing testimony is doubtful.

Before setting fire to the bush, don't look at the ground, rise
your head in the direction of the top of the trees to see if they
don't bear fruits or flowers.[3]

The Manden Charter was proclaimed in the early thirteenth century, around the same time as its far more famed English counterpart,
the Magna Carta. Notably, the Magna Carta, which also recognized the
sanctity of life and property, was underscored by threats of violence by
the privileged nobility against the ruler. In contrast, the Manden Charter rested on the ruler's realization that the principles espoused would
enhance social cohesion and create a framework of moral and effective
governance. And, unlike the Magna Carta, it was not quickly invalidated
by a higher authority, the pope.

African ideals such as respect for life and property, however progressive they may seem even by today's standards, have rarely impressed the
West's leading minds. The most sweeping dismissal of African civilization was from Georg Wilhelm Friedrich Hegel, who wrote in 1837 that
Africa "is no historical part of the World; it has no movement or development to exhibit. Historical movements in it—that is in its northern
part—belong to the Asiatic or European World. Egypt does not belong
to the African Spirit. What we properly understand by Africa, is the Un-
historical, Undeveloped Spirit, still on the threshold of World History."[4]

Influential contemporary writers have upheld Hegel's view. Samuel
Huntington, whose thesis of a "clash of civilizations" caused a global stir
after the end of the Cold War, saw Africa only as "possibly" a civilization,
because "most major scholars of civilization...do not recognize a distinct
African civilization."[5] Most of these "major scholars of civilization" are of
course white Western scholars. Writing in 2014, Kissinger simply omit-
ted Africa in his own history of world order. Niall Ferguson makes little
mention of Africa's contributions to civilization. In his narrative, Africa

counted mainly as a "giant laboratory for Western medicine," enabling European colonizers to experiment with cures for malaria and other diseases and thereby further advance colonization.[6] None of these scholars allow that Africa's role in the origins and spread of human life on this planet, or as the "frontiersmen of mankind," is a great civilizational achievement.[7] And Western writers on world order have had relatively little to say about how African rulers or societies managed their polities and empires and what the modern world order owes to them.

When the size or grandeur of African empires does get acknowledged, it is often credited to foreign influence. Noting that Africa's empires were located on the borders of the Sahara or on the East African coast of the Indian Ocean, the French historian Fernand Braudel contends that these empires were "exceptions rather than the rule," made possible because of "contacts with the outside world," especially Islam but also Christianity.[8] Yet Braudel overstates the case. Ghana and Mali were already proto-imperial in their pre-Islamic stage. Islam was important, but initially in an instrumental way. These empires embraced Islam not because they viewed it as superior to their indigenous religious and cultural beliefs but—much like contemporary Malacca in fifteenth-century-AD Southeast Asia—because of the economic opportunity Arab and other Islamic traders represented. Rather than extinguishing preexisting African beliefs or political systems, Islam in Africa lived with and accommodated indigenous traditions.[9] African societies for the most part remained more African than Islamic and distinctive from their Arabic counterparts in culture, politics, and modes of governance. Sundiata Keita may or may not have converted to Islam, but he kept with his traditional beliefs and worship while adopting a tolerant attitude toward Muslims, which helped the stability of his empire.

Similarly, the rise of Aksum, the rich and highly developed kingdom in today's Eritrea and northern Ethiopia—recognized by Persian sage Mani as one of the four major powers of the third century AD, alongside China, Rome, and Persia—has often been attributed to the arrival of Christianity to sub-Saharan Africa. But Aksum was already a trading hub between Egypt and the western Indian Ocean when Christianity, brought there by traders, arrived and possibly facilitated Aksum's further rise. This pattern is hardly unique. In the eastern Indian Ocean, traders, rather than conquerors or priests, carried Hinduism and Buddhism from India to Southeast Asia, where the imported religions—including Islam, which came later—were grafted onto indigenous traditions and practices.

In sum, the nature and development of African empires had as much, if not more, to do with local resources and leadership than with foreign religious or political influences. In Africa, as in many other societies throughout the world, the foreign worldviews and religion that arrived were remixed with the preexisting culture. In reality, many African polities and empires were products of indigenous thought. African rulers controlled large territories not just through military conquest but through indigenous religious beliefs about the king's connection to the spirits of deceased rulers.

The mindset that credits African achievements to foreign influence extends to other areas. For example, Europeans thought that iron was brought to Africa by the Portuguese, but this is a misconception. In fact, Africa is also a place where iron metallurgy emerged, around 3000 BC. Blacksmiths were regarded as a separate, high class of society. Sub-Saharan Africa was a major exporter of the technology involved in the making of iron, which was central to the eponymous Iron Age.[10]

Billionaire businessman Elon Musk tweeted in 2020 that Egypt's pyramids were built by space aliens.[11] A century and a half earlier, European visitors thought that another of Africa's monuments, the stone edifices of Great Zimbabwe, the trading city that endured from the eleventh to the sixteenth century, had to have been built by someone else. Visiting the area in 1871, German explorer Karl Mauch wrote that a "civilized nation must once have lived there." Less than a decade later, imperialist businessman Cecil Rhodes (after whom the Rhodes scholarship is named) visited Great Zimbabwe to gain control over the minerals in the surrounding region, informing the local chiefs through his henchmen that the purpose of his trip was to see "the ancient temple which once upon a time belonged to white men."[12] British journalist Richard Nicklin Hall was given the job of preserving the site by Rhodes's company in 1902. He dug up the place extensively, thereby causing serious damage, to look for signs of white builders beneath the "filth and decadence of the Kaffir [African Muslim] occupation."[13]

In other words, for early European explorers as much as for later chroniclers of civilizational history, Africa remains the Dark Continent, invisible in the evolution of civilization and world order. Western writers on Africa have ensured what Cornell University Africanist Olúfẹ́mi Táíwò calls "the near-total erasure of Africa; its social, political, and cultural life; its intellectual contributions." African history before European imperialism is ignored or dismissed, while its modern history has been viewed as an "arena of European domination or a sideshow in the drama of emerging maritime empires and global networks."[14]

Many writers have offered explanations for why Africa "lagged behind" the West or even Eurasia as a whole. One of them is Jared Diamond's argument of geographical determinism, which, as discussed in Chapter 8, holds that Africa's north-south orientation prevented the spread of agricultural innovation and domesticated plants and animals, which in turn prevented Africa from producing the agricultural surpluses needed to sustain large empires. Foreign technology, from pottery to printing, was slow to reach Africa for the same reason.

But geography cannot be the only or even the main explanation for European dominance of Africa. The north-south axis of Central and South America did not prevent the development of large empires in the Americas, such as the Incas and the Aztecs, even though they were far more isolated from Eurasia and the rest of the world than Africa was. Empires, like civilizations in general, can grow independent of each other, as well as through interactions and connections.

Other writers argue that Africa was too divided into small cultural zones to develop a shared worldview and stressed how Africa failed to develop "strong" states approximating Europe's Westphalian model.[15] Such views hold that, in Africa, the primary loyalty of people is to family and clan, rather than to some centralized political entity.[16] Africa, in this view, has developed "quasi-states" that are recognized as nations under international law but are barely able to control their borders and exercise sovereignty.[17]

But the historical truth is that, despite what thinkers from Hegel to Huntington have believed, civilization did not bypass Africa—the second largest continent in the world after Asia, three times bigger than Europe. In fact, a major reason Africa has been denied a place in the history of civilizations has to do with Western prejudice and racism. Focusing on issues of geography and environment, à la Jared Diamond, takes attention away from the impact and legacy of Europe's predatory exploitation, territorial slicing, and dismissal of African culture and contributions.

Ironically, anti-racist and sympathetic writings on Africa have contributed to the underestimation of its role in world order. Here, the continent's place in history has been written mainly as a victim, and seldom as a pioneer and creator. Africa certainly was a victim of the transatlantic slave trade and imperialism at the hands of European powers. But the preoccupation with African victimhood has obscured achievements in politics, governance, management of interstate relations, and world-order building before the arrival of the European colonizers. And, even as a victim, Africa contributed powerfully to modernity and world order.

Against this view, I will discuss Africa's world order and its contribution to global civilization in three areas. The first has to do with its states system. I show that the claim about Africa's lack of an imperial tradition is overblown and that size doesn't really matter when it comes to the making of civilization and world order. The second African contribution is its worldview: the collective beliefs about how society is organized and managed, including the relationships between nature and people. The third contribution is intra-African interactions, especially trade. This was important not only in offsetting the effects that small empires and loose polities had but also in forging Africa's role beyond the continent in the making of the modern world order.

Does Size Matter?

Empire is neither necessary nor sufficient a condition for creating a civilization or building a world order. As the cases of Sumer and the Greek city-states show, far from diminishing a civilization, smallness could spur distinctive political and economic inventions, which have been part and parcel of the evolution of world order. The British Empire at its origin was a small and weak state.

Africa historically had political systems of varying sizes and structures, and not all of them were small.[18] Size varied from region to region. Smallness was more common in the Atlantic coast area than the Sahel region (where the empires of Mali and Songhai were located) or around Ethiopia. The average state in Atlantic Africa, according to one estimate, controlled less than six hundred square miles of territory, with twenty thousand to thirty thousand people.[19] Yet, the empire founded by Sundiata, when it reached its zenith under Mansa Musa's reign (1312–1337 AD), covered an area larger than western Europe. The West African empires were also major cultural and educational centers, inviting scholars and establishing centers of learning; Timbuktu in the fifteenth century had a major Islamic university. And they behaved in a perfectly imperial manner. As Arab historian Ibn Khaldun wrote, "The power of Mali became mighty. All the nations of the Sudan stood in awe of Mali."[20] But the Mali Empire was not West Africa's first or last empire. It had been preceded by Ghana (roughly 700–1100 AD) and would be followed by Songhai (roughly 1300–1600 AD), which exceeded Mali's size. The Songhai Empire's territory at its height exceeded one million square miles, making it about the same size as present-day India.

Africans not only built large polities but also colonized other Africans when ambitions swelled and circumstances allowed. The Kushite Empire (in today's Sudan)—whose Nubian ancestors had given ancient Egypt some of its earliest political ideas and institutions, including the personal divinity of the ruler—conquered and ruled upper Egypt in the eighth century BC for about a hundred years. Later, West Africa saw the rise of empires in Ghana, Mali, and Songhai. The Oyo (in today's Nigeria) during its peak in the sixteenth and seventeenth centuries was one such major colonizing power. Additionally, people in northern Nigeria today continue to see themselves as "victims" of colonization by the eighteenth-century Fulani Empire. Another good example is the Asante Empire, which rose from a small area in present-day south-central Ghana

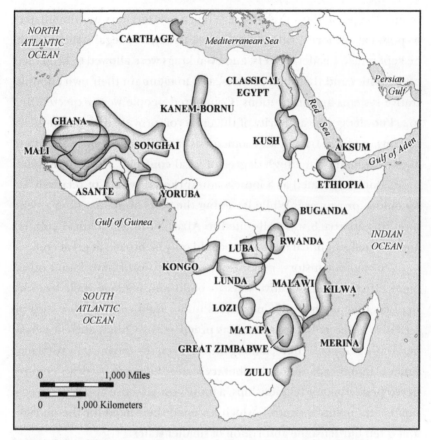

Map 13. Select African empires and states before European colonialism.

and expanded to control much of contemporary Ghana, Ivory Coast, and Togo.

Ethiopia's own empire, which colonized Somalia and Eritrea, is another case in point, far outlasting Italy's five-year colonization of Ethiopia itself. Like other parts of the world, Africa had a varied experience of internal colonization and imperialism, both of which flourished before the arrival of the Europeans.[21]

Similarly, when it came to managing empires, African practices were not all that different from those in other parts of the world. For example, like the Inca Empire, African empires generally showed tolerance to defeated rulers, if not for moral reasons then for strategic ones, so as to reduce the possibility of rebellion. When a new territory was dominated, its political authority, ruling elite, bureaucracy, and legal systems might be kept intact. Leaders, chiefs, and even kings were allowed to keep their official titles and their prerogatives, and to maintain their own administrative systems and institutions. Conquered people were expected first to acknowledge the authority of the emperor, provide him with military recruits, and pay tribute and sometimes taxes, but otherwise they were allowed to maintain a high degree of local control.[22] The Mali Empire, for example, operated as a loosely administered system of relatively autonomous provinces.[23] While lessening the costs of maintaining an empire, this approach was well-suited to Africa's diverse political cultures and became a political model that could only be broken at great cost.

Throughout history, empires all over the world have found other, more efficient and lucrative ways to build and manage their territory than keeping conquerable neighbors under tight control. One such alternative is the tributary system, as practiced by China, ancient Persia, and India's Gupta Empire, among others. Even the territorially voracious Roman Empire maintained tributary states. Likewise, African empires developed tributary relationships, a more cost-effective approach to economic and political control, which lessened their need for the outright and often burdensome absorption of smaller states.

Aksum (also known as Axum), originally a Kush tributary, itself invaded Kush around 350 AD and turned it into a tributary state.[24] Through a mix of direct annexation and tributary relations, the Aksum Empire at different times controlled from upper Nubia down to what is today Sudan and included present-day Ethiopia, Eritrea, Somalia, Yemen, and parts of southern Saudi Arabia. Despite periodic attempts at centralization, the Aksum Empire remained loosely structured.

The West African empires preferred tributary relationships with other states that were economically important, rather than annexing them wholescale. This was a more practical and lucrative way to assert their preeminence. Mali, for example, received tribute from the gold-rich Asante. The tributary relationships also changed direction over time. Mali had once been a tributary of Ghana, but once it achieved

empire status, Mali turned Ghana into a vassal state and extracted tribute from it.[25] The same happened with the Songhai Kingdom, which
seceded from Mali in 1464, when the latter became weak and lost its pre-
dominance.[26] As the Songhai Empire ascended to power, it made Mali a
tributary state.

At times, African rulers tried to change this relatively loose political
order. Muhammad I Askia (1443–1538), the Songhai ruler in West Africa, created a strong centralized government.[27] So did the Akan states,
which covered present-day Ghana, Togo, and large parts of the Ivory
Coast. The Changamire dynasty in central Africa—located between the
Zambezi and Limpopo Rivers (now in Zimbabwe), and lasting roughly
between the fifteenth and early nineteenth centuries—was fairly centralized.[28] Hence, African political history, like that of other parts of
the world, does not show any single pattern of state or empire building.
Africa had small states and tributary polities, but empires also emerged
and flourished across ethnically, linguistically, and culturally diverse areas. This fact challenges the Eurocentric view that only the colonial powers could bring African peoples together by following the model of the
European nation-state.

African World Order

A world order is intimately linked to the shared beliefs of a civilization
about its "creation" and its ways of achieving stability. In most societies,
these beliefs are rooted in religion. Africa's indigenous religions, though
they may seem quite numerous, have many common features, such as the
belief in the existence of a single God with multiple messengers, including ancestors and spirits. Moreover, veneration of land is very widespread
in Africa, especially in West African societies. Christianity and Islam,
although they haven't achieved pan-African status, have played a major
role in bringing together the spiritual outlooks among different parts of
Africa.

While cultural and political differences among African societies
must not be minimized, there is also a shared worldview and an "African

way" of organizing society.[29] One element of this was the institution of divine kingship, wherein kings claimed godly or supernatural attributes and were worshipped as such by their subjects. Such rulers could be found throughout the area of what has been called the "Sudanic civilization," which stretched from the Senegal River in the west to the Red Sea in the east, from the sources of the Nile River in the north to what is now Zimbabwe in the south. A similar system could be found in the Swahili (from the Arabic word meaning "people of the coast") region of East Africa. Divine kingship was also practiced in the western part of the continent. Writing about the people of the kingdom of Kanem-Bornu, which occupied a crescent of territory from what is now southern Libya to eastern Nigeria, the ninth-century AD Arab traveler al-Yaqubi noted, "Their religion is the worship of their kings, for they believe that they who bring life and death, sickness and health."[30] Throughout Africa, as in many other civilizations we have seen, divine kingship and kinship-based rule was commonplace.

Another shared attribute has to do with the importance of the natural environment and humankind's relationship to it. The African worldview, in a manner roughly akin to that of Native Americans, was holistic. One could find a belief across sub-Saharan Africa that the universe consists of "earthly" and "heavenly" elements and was the home of both people and the creator.[31] Moreover, traditional African societies have been communal rather than individualistic, the legacy of which persists today. These values were expressed in forms of mutual assistance based on expectations of reciprocal future assistance. One example is the *osusu* system in Sierra Leone, Benin, and Nigeria, which functioned as a form of microfinancing based on trust and informal arrangements.[32]

Some of the claims about a common African identity were developed during anti-colonial struggles and in the immediate aftermath of independence. There was, of course, a political and instrumental purpose in this: first to develop anti-colonial solidarity and then to secure legitimacy for the ruling regimes, democratic or otherwise. But this does not mean that these ideas were unrelated to traditional cultural elements in Africa. There have been efforts to develop indigenous ideas into a pan-African framework of world order, not unlike recent Chinese efforts to do so with *tianxia* (all under heaven). One example is the collectivist idea of *ubuntu*, popularized in South Africa by, among others, anti-apartheid leader Desmond Tutu. A popular way of understanding it is with the words: "A person is a person through other persons." Variations of the same idea can be found in several countries in southern Africa, including Uganda, Tanzania, and Zimbabwe.[33]

One question that needs to be addressed is whether this combination of harmony with nature, divine kingship, and communitarianism amounts to a totalitarian impulse in African civilization. This is an important question because Western thinkers have made this claim not only about the religious beliefs of Africans but also about the social norms and practices of Africa as a whole. But the evidence shows that these societies were not inherently autocratic; they found ways to limit the power of the ruler and overthrow unjust ones.[34] Take, for example, the political system of Zanj, a term used by Arabs to refer to the Swahili coast. As tenth-century Arab historian al-Masudi noted, "Once the king becomes a tyrant and stops ruling justly, they kill him and refuse to allow his descendants to inherit the throne...because in ceasing to rule justly the king has ceased to be the son of the Supreme Lord, that is to say the God of Heaven and Earth."[35]

This sort of principle did not imply that the state or the empire was weak but that it aspired to justice and fairness toward the subject peoples. British historian of Africa Basil Davidson likens the Zanj system to the Magna Carta, a set of rules proclaimed in 1215 that threatened English King John with overthrow or murder for grossly abusing his power.[36] While the circumstances were different, both implied the right to rebel against and even overthrow an unjust king by his aggrieved subjects. It also has striking echoes of China's mandate of heaven, where the continued authority and legitimacy of the ruler depended on being just and benevolent, failing which rebellion against him is justified. But Africans developed such ideas on their own; there is no evidence of Chinese influence. The point is, contrary to most Western views, Africa did develop cultural beliefs and norms peculiar to it that made up a unique, complex civilization. But culture was not the only ingredient in the evolution of an African worldview and an African world order. As in Europe and Asia, long-distance trading was also a key to African world-order building. In a continent of such immense size and diversity, trade helped to create a degree of connectivity and mitigated the absence of a unifying empire or imperialism on a grand scale.

The three major West African empires, for example, were Ghana, Mali, and Songhai. The first went back to the eighth century, and then the others succeeded it in the interior territory bordering the Sahara Desert. All of these empires were known for their great wealth, and they achieved their prosperity through their control of trans-Saharan trade. The core of this trade was gold from the south, which came from the Asante Empire and upper Senegal and was transferred through Ghana and Mali across the Sahara to North Africa, where it was exchanged for the rock salt of the desert. This was the lifeblood of political organization in that whole area. Ghana was known to the Arabs as the "land of gold," its Soninke people functioning as middlemen for this commerce.

Before the Portuguese reached the Cape of Good Hope, exporting products to West Africa was only achievable via caravan travel through the Sahara. Chinese porcelain, Indian textiles, and Southeast Asian spices would be exported from Egypt to West Africa. The caravans returned with ivory, kola nuts, slaves, and, most importantly, gold. West Africa was very rich with gold, and the empires of Mali and Ghana sent caravans with gold and silver to Tunis, the Arabian Peninsula, Samarkand in central Asia, and China.[37] The kingdom of Zimbabwe controlled gold production on the Zimbabwe Plateau and influenced the gold trade between the interior and the Swahili ports such as Sofala on the eastern coast.[38] Great Zimbabwe was also the gateway that channeled Swahili imports from the Red Sea, Mediterranean, and Indian Ocean.[39]

The African trading network was of truly transcontinental and intercontinental proportions and included a variety of items. The trans-Saharan trade expanded significantly with the introduction of camels in the fourth century AD and subsequently with the entry of Islam into the region in the seventh century, both of which linked the interior of Africa with the Mediterranean world. The camel caravans that carried the trade were not small-scale operations. Ibn Khaldun reported that caravans averaged over one thousand camels, with some ranging up to twelve thousand.[40] The trade network ran both north to south and east to west, reaching its apex around 1500 before it declined as coastal trade with Europeans arose.[41] It influenced both the Mediterranean and the Indian Ocean trade.[42]

Trans-Saharan trade was not just about gold, ivory, salt, and slaves. The southern items that moved north included ostrich feathers, animal hides, and acacia tree gum (known as gum arabic), used for the manufacture of ink, textiles, and pharmaceuticals. Later, Africa would become a major source of medicine for Europeans. Imports into the south consisted of not just Saharan rock salt but also manufactured and luxury items from North Africa, the Mediterranean world, and Europe, such as weapons, silk garments, brocade, glass and porcelain, brass and copper, jewelry, carpets, coffee, tea and sugar, perfumes, paper, and horses.[43]

Moreover, trade linked Africa's interior with other coasts, including the important Indian Ocean coast. For example, the trade route passing through Great Zimbabwe brought ivory and gold from Africa's interior to the southeastern coast, where it became part of the Indian Ocean trade network, which, as previously described, was the largest oceanic artery in the world at that time. This trade network reached the Kilwa Sultanate, located on the southern coast of Tanzania, itself a node of Indian Ocean trade, through which goods traveled to the Arabian Peninsula, India, Southeast Asia, and China. Islamic and Chinese ceramics and glass beads have been found in Great Zimbabwe archaeological sites; these exotic items were likely used as fashion pieces, exchanged in wedding ceremonies by spirit healers, or used to lubricate other trade deals. Beginning in the sixteenth century, the Portuguese, from their colony in Mozambique, sought to control the trade in gold. They tried to force local farmers who mined for gold in the fallow season to shift to full-time gold mining, but they were unsuccessful.[44]

In addition to trade, cultural exchanges are important in building world order. Here, one might note the important role that Islamic Timbuktu played as a center for culture and knowledge. During the fourteenth and fifteenth centuries, relations between Mali and the Arab world were deepened and consolidated. It was also at this time that Mali established the University of Timbuktu, one of the oldest universities in the world, attended by twenty-five thousand students in a city of one hundred thousand, with students coming from many parts of Africa and the Middle East.[45] The city's main library contained hundreds of thousands of manuscripts and scrolls covering a range of subjects such as Islamic theology, philosophy, biography, law, grammar, natural sciences, medicine, history, and politics.[46] Thousands of students studied Islamic theology, the Arabic language, African languages, Sufism, logic, and law.[47] Scholars came to study and teach in Timbuktu, and famous scholars from the city, like Ahmad Baba al-Timbukti, made lasting contributions to Islamic theology.[48]

The Transatlantic Slave Trade

Africa's fate was sealed and the trans-African economy disrupted by the rise of European imperialism, which brought with it two critical developments that severely disrupted Africa's indigenous economy and world order: one was the transatlantic slave trade, the other the colonial partition of the entire continent.

First, the slave trade. Many writers have argued that the capturing or buying of slaves and the selling of them in markets for human beings has been a feature of many civilizations, including in Egypt, Assyria, Athens, Rome, China, and the Islamic world. Importing slaves from Africa was widespread in the Muslim world during the Middle Ages, long before the Europeans arrived.[49] Africans, moreover, were not all silent victims of the transatlantic slave trade; many were active participants in it and even controlled it to a large degree. Africans captured other Africans in raids and organized their detention, transportation, and marketing to Europeans. But they did so mostly because of a mix of economic incentives and intimidation coming from European slave traders, who orchestrated the enterprise. In some ways, this was an extension of traditional African practices—where, again, slavery existed before European colonialism—except that now most of the customers were Europeans.

The distinctive features of the transatlantic slave trade were its scale and its particularly brutal and inhuman form. During the course of the African slave trade, something between ten and twelve million Africans were shipped to the New World. Slave Voyages, a collaborative research project among several US universities on the transatlantic and intra-American slave trade, estimates the number of captive Africans sent to the Americas at about 12.5 million between 1500 and 1840.[50]

Some two million captured Africans might have perished due to the extremely cruel conditions of their transportation aboard slave ships. The large majority of African slaves were sent to Cuba, Jamaica, Barbados, and Saint-Domingue (current-day Haiti and the Dominican Republic) in the Caribbean and to major ports in Brazil (Salvador, Rio de Janeiro, and Recife). From there, they were bought and sold throughout the Americas. The owners of slave ships came from Portugal and Portuguese Brazil, Great Britain, France, Spain and Spanish America, and the Netherlands.[51]

A second difference between the transatlantic trade and other forms of slavery was the purpose of African labor in the Americas. The Islamic slave trade from Africa included women who were not used as laborers or even viewed as property but who served in domestic households and sometimes in the harems of the rich and the powerful. The Islamic slave trade was also often used to recruit warriors for the sultans, and slaves could rise to occupy high civilian positions in the court. This was far from the case in the transatlantic trade, where economic motives were paramount and slaves were thoroughly dehumanized and commodified.

Traditional slavery in Africa retained a social bond between the slave owner and the slave. Previously, slaves were people captured in war or those condemned to slavery due to criminal conduct or failure to repay debts. Usually, the slave owners knew something about their slaves, where they came from, their background, and the reasons they were slaves. This changed with the transatlantic slave trade. The colonial economy "made slaves anonymous—they were so to speak, something bought in a store, selected purely on physical characteristics, like so many cans of soup."[52] The European slave traders, located across the Atlantic, never met the slaves they bought and sold; they "were anonymous units of labor, production inputs on a balance sheet, to be disposed of purely according to an estimate of their future economic value."[53] In the words of an American writer, the transatlantic slave-trafficking system was led by "strangers from across the waters [who] were pitiless hunters—hunters of men." As a result, "the lives of whole communities had been devastated as by volcanic blasts."[54]

The primarily economic nature of the slave trade was in large part a function of the virtual extermination of the native population of the Americas by diseases that the Europeans brought with them and by the devastation wrought by the colonial conquests. The colonists needed imported labor, and this need became more acute as the initial supply of European indentured labor dried up. As the Europeans developed the cultivation of highly lucrative, labor-intensive cash crops such as sugar and coffee, the demand increased.

Given this need, Western imperial powers and profiteers turned to Africa for laborers. Africans were available in large numbers in coastal locations where it was relatively easy to extract them and transport them across the ocean. Other potential sources of slave labor, the Middle East or East Asia, were more difficult in this regard. Only Africa could supply the tens of thousands of slaves needed each year.[55] African elites also profited from the slave trade, receiving guns, food products, and cotton textiles in exchange for the human beings they were able to provide to the European traders.

But while economic factors predominated, the race of the slaves was also an important factor distinguishing the transatlantic slave trade. It was the transatlantic slave trade that led to the identification of black skin color with slavery. In no other civilization was slavery associated with skin color before. This changed with the large-scale import of Africans to the New World, especially the British North American colonies, which created the United States. Here, the Native American people easily fled capture and enslavement; hence the overwhelming number of slaves were Black Africans. Soon, being a slave meant being Black and being Black meant being a slave or having slave heritage. The dark legacy of this, in the form of the widespread racism it produced, remains a defin-ing feature of American society and politics to this day. While Christian-ity forbade enslaving fellow Christians, conversion to Christianity did not protect Black people from being enslaved.

The transatlantic slave trade was also integral to the geopolitical logic of Western imperialism. Competition among European powers was ultimately about political supremacy decided by economic advantage, which in turn depended on the slave trade. Even the end of slavery had a political motive. Although humanitarian motives were not absent, Brit-ain's ban on the slave trade (but not the existing system of slavery in the colonies) in 1807 was aimed at weakening and displacing the French and the Americans, who depended heavily on African slaves for their colo-nies and plantations in West Africa, the Caribbean, and the American South.[56] Britain also sought to gain political advantage over Austria, Prussia, and Russia, whose domestic serfdom it viewed as a form of slav-ery. Despite their supposedly high-sounding motives, the British, when they abolished slavery in 1833, paid compensation not to the slaves but to the slave owners, including (at current rates) a sum of five hundred thou-sand pounds to the Greene King plantations in Montserrat and Saint Kitts.[57]

Moreover, the abolition of slavery simply meant increased reliance by European colonial powers on indentured servitude. When British war-ships "rescued" slaves being transported from Africa to enforce the ban on the transatlantic slave trade, the British did not send them back home to Africa but turned them into indentured labor for the Americas. From 1834—the year after the Slavery Abolition Act that banned slavery in its colonies—to 1920, Britain sent some 1.5 million indentured laborers (85 percent of whom were from India) to its colonies in the Indian Ocean, West Indies, and South Africa. Thus, indentured labor "took over" from slavery.[58] The Dutch used indentured or forced labor on a lesser scale, but its impact on their major colony, Indonesia, was massive nonethe-less. Around the mid-nineteenth century, between half and three-quarters of peasant households in Java, the most populous Indonesian island, were forced to work in agriculture. Between 1863 and 1932, some three hundred thousand Chinese indentured laborers (perhaps a much higher number) came to the Dutch colonies in what is Indonesia today. And in the late nineteenth and early twentieth centuries, over one hundred thousand mainly Javanese indentured laborers might have gone to Malaysia, New Caledonia, and British North Borneo and to Suriname in the Caribbean.[59]

From Africa, the consequences of slavery were both economic and political, including violence and interstate war, which left a lasting impact on the continent. The transatlantic slave trade made violence lucrative for raiders and kidnappers. This led to deep and enduring fractures in Africa's communities. The trade contributed to warfare for control of the slave economy, such as wars between the Oyo Empire of West Africa and the Yoruba states (in today's western Nigeria).[60] Areas that provided more slaves for export experienced more political conflict and violence after the slave trade ended and a higher incidence of corruption and bribery in later times.[61]

The sheer scale and brutality of the transatlantic slave trade is now almost universally recognized. What may be less appreciated is the way it, and colonialism in general, wreaked havoc in Africa, destroying lives and cultures, causing later wars, and justifying it all with its racist demeaning of African civilization. The slave trade came to an end in the nineteenth century, but Europeans soon found other resources to extract from Africa. If anything, colonial exploitation of the continent in the second half of the nineteenth century and after became even more destructive of life and culture than what preceded it.

The Scramble for Africa

In September 1876, King Leopold II of Belgium hosted a meeting of forty Europeans, including explorers, geographers, and philanthropists, at the Palais Royal in Brussels. Henry Morton Stanley's Congo River expedition, which had begun two years earlier, had sparked Leopold's interest in the area. His gathering, known as the Brussels Geographic Conference, had an exciting or even noble purpose, supposedly. It was

to further the exploration of the Congo River region and the humanitarian uplifting of its people, both goals encapsulated in the name of
the organization formed at Leopold's behest, the International Association for the Exploration and Civilization of Central Africa, simplified
as the International African Association. In his novel *Heart of Darkness*,
which takes place on the Congo, Joseph Conrad would call the group the
International Society for the Suppression of Savage Customs.[62]

Despite its high-sounding official title, the real purpose of the organization was to advance Leopold's goal of catching up with the other colonial
powers in what was soon to be called the scramble for Africa. The immediate economic objective was to acquire African resources, mainly natural
rubber, ivory, and palm oil. But this was not like the trade in gold and rock
salt of earlier times; this trade was largely an expropriation based on forced
local labor. African men and women were no longer exported to work on
American and Caribbean plantations, but they were kept at home to work
for the benefit of European colonialists on African plantations, similar to
how Aztecs were forced to labor in Central American gold mines.

Leopold formed a private militia of African soldiers under European commanders, called the Force Publique. Soon after its formation
and through the early 1890s, this militia would pillage, torture, burn,
kidnap, and kill its way through large tracts of the African heartland.
The soldiers held families hostage to force men to work for Leopold's estate. Congolese people had their hands cut off if they resisted. The population of the area where the Force Publique operated would dwindle
from some twenty million to eight million during this murderous period
of Belgian depredation.[63] While there was of course nothing new about
a European nation taking control of a faraway land and creating new
political entities or colonial states, in this case there was a difference.
Everything possessed by the International Congo Society, which was
amalgamated into the Congo Free State in 1885, was Leopold's private
property. An entire vast, resource-rich country roughly ninety times the
size of Belgium technically belonged to a single individual.

In the meantime, the various national committees in Europe set
up to carry out the mission of the International African Association

organized their separate expeditions, despite being a cooperative, international venture. The scramble for Africa, a term coined in 1884 but that reflected a competition that had started over twenty years earlier, was formalized and given legal respectability by an international congress of European powers that met in Berlin from November 15, 1884, to February 26, 1885.[64] The host of this Berlin West Africa Conference (or simply the Berlin Conference), German chancellor Otto von Bismarck, had observed the intense competition among Britain, France, and Belgium and did not want Germany to be left out. Thirteen nations were in attendance: Germany, Austria-Hungary, Denmark, Spain, Belgium, France, Great Britain, Italy, the Netherlands, Portugal, Russia, Sweden-Norway (the two were part of a union then), and the Ottoman Empire. Also present was the United States, thereby making it complicit in the final and total colonization of Africa, though it didn't establish colonies in Africa itself.

In a grand display of liberal conscience, the conference banned slavery in African and Islamic countries, though this was in many ways an empty gesture since the legal slave trade had been abolished decades earlier in Europe. At the same time, the conference formally recognized King Leopold II's territorial possessions as his personal property. The principle of "effective occupation," or recognition of rights over land already occupied or controlled by a European power, was formalized. Based on this principle, the European powers divided African lands among themselves, drawing numerous artificial boundaries, which often went in straight lines without regard to the traditional living spaces and cultural connections among the people who had lived there for millennia. Not a single African was consulted before the conference began, and none was invited to the gathering.[65] Africa was not the only place where the European world order sealed the fate of non-Western civilizations, but it was symptomatic of Europe's global imposition of its standard of civilization, a campaign that became synonymous with imperialism.

Africa was undoubtedly a central arena where Western ascendancy got its oxygen, and it was critical to the West's ability to achieve global dominance in wealth and power. But Western scholars have given little attention to how African rulers or societies—how Africans managed their polities and empires, and thereby contributed to the evolution of modernity and world order. American author Howard French is not far off the mark in saying that "the first impetus for the Age of Discovery was not Europe's yearning for ties with Asia, as so many of us have been taught in grade school, but rather its centuries-old desire to forge trading ties with legendarily rich Black societies hidden away somewhere in the heart of 'darkest' West Africa."[66]

Africa's role in the history of world order is as both a victim and a contributor. Even at the height of European dominance, African slave labor became integral to the emergence of the global economy. Transatlantic slavery engendered a new, more virulent form of racism, in which the supposed inferiority of Africans was given a "scientific" basis, the effects of which are still felt to this day. As Jamaican poet Mutabaruka wrote, "Slavery is not African history. Slavery interrupted African history."[67] But this tragic turn should not blind us to the fact that for most of its history Africa was the birthplace of a variety of political systems—states, tributary systems, and empires—that ruled over vast territories and peoples. African civilizations developed communitarian and humanistic principles—such as those enshrined in the Kouroukan Fouga—that have strong resonances with contemporaneous principles in the Near East, India, and Europe. Africa was an active participant in the global history of empire building and long-distance trade, all essential to the emergence of the modern world order. While Africa is struggling to recover from the shock dealt by European colonization, in the longer play of history, this was an interruption, rather than the end, of Africa's contribution to world order.

Chapter 11

Europe's Double Standard

The 1640s were a fateful decade in the history of world order. They began, in 1641, with the Dutch capture of Malacca, which continued to serve as a key node of Indian Ocean and international trade that the Portuguese had colonized in 1511. This set off a new phase in the European struggle for the dominance of Asia and the world. Following this, European expansion shifted from the initial ad hoc Iberian voyages of discovery to more systematic and organized operations engineered by the northern nations of Europe.

After Alexander the Great was forced to turn back from India by his rebellious troops, who were afraid to venture beyond the Indus, most European visits to Asia had been led not by warriors but by missionaries, merchants, and adventurers. But in 1600 and 1602, the British and Dutch East India Companies were formed, creating government-sanctioned monopolies on trade. This began the process by which Europe would establish outright colonial possession of almost all of South, Southeast, and East Asia (except for Thailand, China, and Japan).

Perhaps it is a coincidence, perhaps not, that the 1640s also saw a momentous shift in power in China, East Asia's largest and richest country. In 1644, the emperor of the Ming dynasty, which had ruled China and dominated the rest of Asia for nearly three hundred years, committed suicide by hanging himself from a tree at the back of the Forbidden

City in Beijing. With that dramatic act of defeat, China came under the control of the Manchus, a group of foreign but Sinicized warriors from the other side of the Great Wall in the Asian northeast. They formed the Qing dynasty, which would rule China for nearly the next three hundred years. This dynasty would initially be strong and expansionist, but it would suffer a serious, fatal decline in the nineteenth century and would go down in history as China's last empire, replaced by a short-lived republic in 1911.

But that was much later. Just four years after the Qing takeover of China, Europe finally settled the Thirty Years' War, the religious-political struggle that ravaged Europe for most of the first half the seventeenth century, killing off as much as half the population of some regions as the various Protestant and Catholic principalities of Germany fought against each other, with France, Spain, the Netherlands, and Sweden taking sides. This was no ordinary war over religion but a struggle for a fundamental political reordering. The two agreements that settled the war, the treaties of Münster and Osnabrück, both concluded in 1648, are together called the Peace of Westphalia. This agreement would go down in history as the formal beginning of the European sovereign state system and the foundation of foreign relations that would undergird the world order until the present era. The basic principle agreed to in the treaty was that the ruler of each state would determine its religion without interference by any other state, though each ruler also agreed to tolerate other religions. This was a major step toward European peace, given the near constant wars of religion that had racked Europe since early in the sixteenth century. By giving each state control over its affairs, the treaty also established a nation's sovereignty as an inviolate principle, which has endured ever since.

But the deeper significance of this era was the birth of a global double standard, or a two-track, European approach to world-order building. One track was the ostensibly anti-hegemonial order based on the Westphalian model of sovereign states who were prohibited, at least theoretically, from subjugating their weaker neighbors. This brought stability to Europe, a fact much celebrated by Western intellectuals led by Kissinger.

Yet, peace in Europe brought calamity for the wider world, including intensified colonization, exploitation, and domination of indigenous peoples. This was the result of the second track, which related to Europe's relations with the rest of the world. The legal and political principles that applied to states within Europe, such as noninterference and equality of states, did not apply to the nations of Asia, Africa, and the Americas. On the contrary, the end of the Thirty Years' War released Europe's competitive energies abroad, intensifying imperial rivalry for control of colonies and their resources. In other words, peace in Europe encouraged and enabled the subjugation of non-European nations. In this way, European expansion and its far-reaching effects on non-European civilizations paved the way for the creation of what could be called the European-led world order, or simply European world order.

European Order, Global Disorder

Early modern western Europe's contribution to world-order building revolved mainly around the Westphalian idea that no higher authority—divine or secular—stood above the state. Until the Peace of Westphalia, European rulers and their subjects in majority Catholic countries theoretically owed allegiance to the pope and the Holy Roman emperor—a title that different rulers at different times in areas that are now Germany, France, Spain, Italy, and Austria had assumed as notional successors to the original Roman Empire. Protestant rulers and their subjects did not recognize the pope, and the growth and expansion of Protestantism was one of the factors that fueled the Thirty Years' War.

The Westphalian system introduced four key elements to the European order. The first, as noted, was the absolute sovereignty of the state, by which there was no longer any authority, such as the pope or the Holy Roman emperor, higher than the ruler. Related to that was the separation of the state, including the Catholic ones, from the Catholic Church, given that each state could now determine for itself whether it would be Catholic or Protestant. Third was the principle of nonintervention; one state could no longer interfere in the internal affairs of another. The fourth principle has to do with the legal equality of all states no matter their differences in power, wealth, size, and territory.

The Peace of Westphalia has been regarded as a defining moment in creating the world order of today. It was the "official birthday of the modern state system," as one writer on the topic has put it.[1] Another described it as a "break point." No longer was religion and its role in Christendom the essential preoccupation of each state. Now nations concerned themselves with the national interest and the larger balance of power.[2] For Henry Kissinger, this was one of the grand ordering moments in world politics, firmly establishing the idea of a system of sovereign, equal, secular states. Thanks to Westphalia, as Kissinger has glowingly written, "the inherent equality of sovereign states, regardless of power or domestic system, was instituted." When it came to sovereignty, each state had the same rights and principles, especially the right not to be dominated by another state.[3] "Beyond the immediate demands of the moment," Kissinger continues, "the principles of 'international relations' were taking shape, motivated by the common desire to avoid the recurrence of total war on the continent." One major consequence of this was the development of international law, "treated as an expandable body of agreed doctrine aimed at cultivation of harmony, with the Westphalian treaties themselves at its heart."[4]

Upon closer analysis, however, the impact of the Peace of Westphalia was more evolutionary than revolutionary.[5] Contrary to the way the agreement is often presented, it did not bring about the end of theology; nor was it the beginning of secular sovereignty. Though Kissinger claims that "the doctrine of sovereign equality reigned," states remained unequal in practice.[6] Westphalia gave France and Sweden (then considered a major European power) the right to interfere in the affairs of other states in order to enforce the peace. It was thus an arrangement of "conditional sovereignty."[7] The peace also limited, but did not eliminate, the authority of the Holy Roman Empire. It gave more autonomy to the empire's German princes, who now had the authority to conduct their own diplomatic affairs, including entering into treaties, but only insofar as their actions did not harm the interests of the empire and the emperor.

The evolutionary nature of Westphalia is important for several reasons having to do with the world order that emerged after 1648, including Europe's domination of the non-European world. For one thing, the post-Westphalian world retained its deep attachment to Christianity and to the European notion of spiritual superiority over the non-Christian world.[8] The idea of a unified or restorable Christendom, of *christianitas* or *res publica Christiana*, would live on as an underlying basis of European Christian identity. The new, supposedly secular European notion of international order granted more primacy to human agency, but it didn't displace the medieval notion of divine agency: that ultimately the world and everything in it was God's doing.[9] Despite their pretense of secular rationalism and scientific inquiry, many modern European thinkers retained a belief in divine creation while elaborating on the possibilities of human agency in law and government. As one scholar has put it, "All significant concepts of the modern theory of the state are secularized theological concepts...whereby, for example, the omnipotent God became the omnipotent lawgiver."[10]

In other words, the revolutionary image of Westphalia creating an entirely new system of equal sovereign states contains a degree of myth.[11] It was not the single, decisive turning point, nor the fundamental break from the past, that it is claimed to be. Europe for the most part continued with pre-Westphalian hierarchical principles of statecraft, including the institution of empire.

One of the most powerful legacies of Westphalia was not in Europe but in the world beyond. The peace addressed a major cause of intra-European wars. In so doing, it released more attention and resources for expansion outside. In other words, as mentioned, peace within Europe directly encouraged imperialism outside it. Now that they were less likely to have to go to war with their neighbors, the European powers could expand their empires and found new colonies.[12] Moreover, the Westphalia settlement encouraged scientific and technological cooperation among European nations in navigation, engineering, medicine, and mapmaking, which would make European colonization more efficient and help it advance to ever more remote places, such as the Congo, while protecting the colonizers from diseases.[13]

Additionally, the Peace of Westphalia created a new hierarchy of powers, both within and outside Europe. This hierarchy would be further developed over the next centuries, finding its full expression in the Concert of Europe. Under this system, there emerged a rank of great powers, who enjoyed more status and authority to manage European affairs and dominated other, lower-ranked European nations. These great powers maintained a balance among them, so that no single country could become more powerful than any combination of others arrayed against it. Gradually, this ordering of Europe would be "projected strongly onto the non-European world," creating an international framework also dominated by the European powers, reducing most of the rest of the world to inferior status but, again, with no European power able to achieve dominance.[14] While this system came at a much later period in history, and was less informal and more multilateral, it also bore a certain resemblance to the ancient Near East's Amarna family of great powers.

A Great Power Club

This managed balance of power system became Europe's signature contribution to the emerging world order. Modern Europe did not invent the system of balancing power. Such systems existed during earlier periods of history in India, China, Greece, and Rome.[15] But it was in modern Europe that the doctrine found its fullest and most durable operation. Balance of power means that no single state is allowed to become dominant: if one tries to gain hegemony, others will pool their resources and form alliances to bring the ambitious state down to their level. This is what the British did against Napoleon, later against Otto von Bismarck, and, still later, against Adolf Hitler.

But through history the emergence of a balance of power system has been neither automatic nor inevitable. It had to be created and managed through coalitions and alliances. This is especially difficult when there are a number of competing great powers involved. In this case, a concert system may emerge if all the great powers share a common interest in the management of order. To do so, they must develop rules and institutions not only to reduce conflicts among themselves but also to manage disputes affecting the international system as a whole. This is where the Concert of Europe—created at the Congress of Vienna in 1815, after the defeat of Napoleon, by Britain, Austria, Prussia, France, and Russia— stood out from previous forms of great power cooperation.

The European concert established the principle that the great powers should enjoy "special status and privileges (but also the 'responsibilities')" in regulating international affairs.[16] It operated on the basis of four principles:

1. reliance on multilateral consultations among the great powers (conference diplomacy) to manage crisis situations;
2. an agreement that there could be no territorial change without great power approval;
3. a commitment to protect all "essential" members of the interstate system; and
4. a recognition that all the great powers must have equal status and that none should be humiliated.[17]

The last of these rules meant that France after the defeat of Napoleon, despite having to make some territorial concessions to the victorious powers, was quickly restored to its position as a member of the club of European powers. The fact that the members of the concert—especially Russia and Austria—were conservative powers, who feared domestic revolutions or another Napoleon-like attempt at regional hegemony, did create a shared interest among them. Applying the above rules, the concert worked well between 1815 and 1823 in keeping the peace in Europe but declined thereafter, eventually collapsing with the Crimean War (1853–1856) between Russia, on the one hand, and a coalition of Britain, France, and the Ottoman Empire on the other, with the Kingdom of Sardinia-Piedmont as a junior partner in the latter. In the long aftermath of the war, great power competition in Europe intensified, leading to the outbreak of World War I. The European concert was less successful than the Amarna system, which, although its most active period was about three decades (1352–1322 BC), contributed to longer term stability in the Near East for two centuries.[18]

Although the Concert of Europe was a milestone in the European world order, its dark sides should not be forgotten. The concert imposed the will of the stronger European powers over the weaker ones. As we have seen, it also gave the European states the internal peace and cooperation that enabled them to pursue their non-European interests, specifically what's been called the "second expansion" that came after the defeat of France in the Napoleonic Wars. The French might have lost their empire in Europe, but they were allowed to keep their colonial possessions in the Caribbean, the Indian Ocean, and in several pockets of West Africa and India. The congress also contributed to a significant expansion of British imperialism. Britain kept most of its colonial possessions and took Malta, Mauritius, Saint Lucia, Tobago, and the Ionian Islands from France; Trinidad from Spain; and Ceylon and the Cape Colony from the Netherlands.[19] By divvying up colonial holdings in this way, the Congress of Vienna was the progenitor of the Berlin Conference, which took place seventy years later and partitioned Africa among the European great powers. The concert has also been praised for contributing to the end of the slave trade, a condition demanded by the British, but, as discussed, this increased the flow of indentured labor.

The Peace of Westphalia and the Concert of Europe are two of Europe's major contributions to world order. Westphalia was not the first model of a system of independent states, but it was the most influential one, with a global imprint that eventually extended to Asia and to the rest of the world. While the European concert system has been recognized as a model for great power cooperation to this day, like the Peace of Westphalia, it had dark sides. The concert was reactionary at home and, like the Peace of Westphalia, encouraged imperialism outside of Europe. In this, both amplified a powerful idea that had emerged in Europe but became globally influential in shaping the European world order: the standard of civilization.

The Dark Standard of Civilization

The standard of civilization is one of the principal ideas behind the emergence of the modern notion of the West and West versus the Rest.

Image 10. Civilization versus barbarism: "From the Cape to Cairo," 1898, by Joseph Udo Keppler, in *Puck Magazine*, 1898.

Its meaning can be confusing, as it had little to do with civilization in the traditional sense, meaning a society's development of writing, agriculture, monuments, social division of labor, urbanization, and so on. Rather, the standard of civilization was a framework developed by the Europeans based on a set of expectations of political, administrative, military, and legal competence. The underlying idea was that, to govern themselves, countries had to meet certain criteria, or a standard, which was derived from the European states' laws, religious practices, property rights, and ways of governance, which were so superior that they served as the benchmark for civilized political life. Also important was the ability to maintain domestic order. This essentially meant protecting the life and property of Europeans living in the territories of non-Western states. It also encompassed the ability to carry out diplomatic relations, fulfilling contractual obligations (again essential to Europeans), and developing defense capabilities. Nations outside Europe usually failed to meet these requirements to the Europeans' satisfaction and were therefore deemed backward or savage and thus fair game for conquest and colonization, or for imposition of unequal treaties allowing extraordinary trade and territorial privileges to the Europeans. Their citizens were considered unworthy of the privileges enjoyed by Europeans around the world. So in the non-European world—whether in Europe's colonies or in countries such as China or Thailand that were not formally colonized—the status of being civilized did not apply. At its extreme, especially for aspiring powers like Japan, meeting the standard of civilization required a capacity to play the game of power politics.

One irony here, given the European definition of the standard of civilization, is that China and many other countries were amply qualified. China created the first centralized bureaucracy in the world, operated through a merit-based examination system, one that Europe had borrowed and adopted. Throughout the history of civilization, non-Western empires around the globe had managed their territories and protected their interests with equal if not more success than European states had done. Though weakened by the nineteenth century, the Moghul empire in India and the Qing Empire in China were still perfectly capable of conducting diplomatic relations. Yet, they were excluded from the club of civilized nations because membership was based on raw power. It had little to do with ideas, norms, or moral principles. Instead, it was a racist legal fiction by which non-Western countries could be deemed uncivilized, mainly because they lacked the power to resist European domination.

As a legal principle, the standard of civilization formed part of the foundation of modern international law, since it was invoked to justify unequal treaties giving Europeans extraterritorial rights, the use of economic sanctions, and even armed intervention and war. It was a concept designed to divide the world into those who had the right to statehood and those who did not, though the latter category took on different forms. In most colonies, the basic duties of government were taken over by the colonizing power. In India, British army officers and civil servants took all the positions of the governing bureaucracy. The powerful Indian Civil Service really opened up to Indians after World War I; until then, the recruitment was conducted in Britain and only a handful of Indians could join. In the meantime, "natives" were trained to occupy lower positions as clerks, soldiers, or police. After China's losses in the Opium Wars opened it up to foreign settlement, the concept of extraterritoriality was used by Europeans to run their own affairs in special foreign settlements, such as the famous French Concession in Shanghai. These European enclaves had their own police and courts, clubs, racecourses, and hospitals, so as not to be under the jurisdiction of the Chinese or even to be in too close contact with them. Given their relative weakness, most non-European nations submitted to these arrangements. But there was one major exception: Japan.

Japan Turns West

In the late nineteenth century, Japan became the first Asian country to successfully modernize itself with a view to meeting the European standard of civilization. The country undertook a set of reforms as part of a larger goal of reviving the power of the Japanese monarchy. And so, under the Meiji emperor, who ruled from 1867 to 1912, Japan abolished the samurai system, built a modern industry, and created a professional army. This was an all-out effort by Japan to emulate Europe economically, culturally, and militarily.

The success of Japan's reforms served as an inspiration to other countries. European thinkers such as Hegel had argued that non-Western countries could not attain civilization on their own and could only become civilized with Western help—that is, under Western colonial tutelage. The Meiji reforms demolished that myth: they proved that an Asian nation could achieve civilization without colonization. This was of no small importance to colonial subjects, especially in Asia.

But soon the dark side of Japan's self-civilizing mission became clear. First, the Meiji reforms stirred a belief among the Japanese elite that, to become more European, Japan had to become less Asian. This meant disowning its Chinese-influenced cultural past and its Asian linkages and heritage. Influential sections of Japan's elite wanted their country to "leave Asia," a wish vividly illustrated in an editorial in the newspaper *Jiji shimpō* in 1885. Though written anonymously, the editorial is widely believed to have been the work of Fukuzawa Yukichi, the newspaper's founder and an early and passionate advocate of westernization of Japan. Fukuzawa was the founder of the prestigious Keio University in Tokyo as well as of the Institute for Study of Infectious Diseases. Perhaps reflecting Fukuzawa's interest in epidemics, the editorial compared the movement of civilization to the spread of measles in Japan, which usually started in Nagasaki in the west and moved eastward. Western civilization was moving toward the East just as unstoppably, but, unlike measles, the benefits of Western civilization would far outweigh its ill effects. Such nearby Asian countries as Korea and China, he wrote, "cannot survive as independent nations with the onslaught of Western civilization to the East." For that reason, he concluded, "it is better for us to leave the ranks of Asian nations and cast our lot with civilized nations of the West."[20]

Second, the economic emulation of Europe was not enough. To gain recognition as a full member of the European-organized club of civilized nations, Japan had to adopt Europe's strategic orientation and capabilities. Hence, Japan's industrialization was accompanied by a massive military buildup. The goal of this was much more than preserving domestic stability; it was meant to contribute to the maintenance of international order. At least that's what the elite of the Meiji era and its immediate successor, the Shōwa under Emperor Hirohito, felt, and the Western powers encouraged and accepted that goal. As a symbol of its acceptance into the club of civilized nations, Japan was allowed to send a contingent of troops to march alongside European and American soldiers deployed to suppress the Boxer Rebellion of 1899–1901, an uprising against the foreign presence in China.

Japan was also inspired to become a military power that could fight and win wars on its own. It demonstrated this ability when it convincingly defeated Russia in the Russo-Japanese War of 1904–1905. This was a turning point, the first time an Asian country had defeated a European one, or, as many saw it, the first time "the yellow race" was victorious over "a major white and Christian Western empire."[21] Asian nationalist leaders—from Sun Yat-sen, the Chinese Republic's first president, to Jawaharlal Nehru, who would become independent India's first prime minister—took note. More dramatically, famed Black intellectual and activist W. E. B. Du Bois said, "The Japanese victory broke the foolish modern magic of the word 'white.'"[22]

In reality, the Russo-Japanese War was not the first Eastern victory over the West. In the seventeenth century, Qing China expelled the Dutch from Taiwan. There was also the Moghul victory over the English in the Child's War of 1690. In 1739, the Maratha Empire, a rival of the Moghuls, drove Portuguese forces out of their garrisons near current-day Mumbai. But most such Eastern victories over Western forces were relatively inconsequential or short-lived. They did not change European power and colonialism in Asia. True, the European imperial powers often had to ally with local rulers and soldiers. For example, the Portuguese collaborated with the king of Kochi to defeat the ruler in Calicut when they first arrived on India's Malabar Coast. The British extensively used local troops, known as sepoys, in India to establish and defend their colonial rule. Still, none of this created an impression of European weakness.

But winning a war against a European power was not enough to satisfy Japan's goal of leaving Asia and joining the West. Just as a condition of membership in the ancient Amarna great power club was to have vassals and subject peoples, joining the European club of civilization could not be complete without imperialism. And so, Japan turned to colonialism, taking over Taiwan, Korea, Manchuria, and later most of Southeast Asia and half of Republican China. The desire for admission into the great powers' club was one of the root causes of Japanese imperialism, which built to its high point in the decades leading to the Second World War. Arguably, there was more to Japan's imperial expansion than a wish to gain status by imitating the West. Some of the motivations were defensive: a desire to counter the threat posed by the white imperial powers and to neutralize the potential threat coming from Korea—famously described by Jakob Meckel, a German military adviser to the Meiji emperor, as a "dagger pointed at the heart of Japan."[23] A related goal was to enhance Japan's bargaining power as it sought to renegotiate treaties it had signed in an earlier, weaker time granting extraterritorial privileges to Western powers.

But Japan did not pursue a policy of imperialism mainly for defensive reasons. Japan may have borrowed extensively from Chinese institutions in the seventh and eighth century, but it had long since rejected any sense of cultural or political inferiority to China. Like Britain and other colonial powers, Japan wanted to project power abroad to protect its domestic markets and to acquire raw materials for its expanding economy. There is no evidence suggesting that Japan's imperial reach was any more defensive in this sense than Britain's and France's. Certainly, the brutality of Japan's colonialism—the draconian measures the colonial regimes adopted and the bloody massacres they committed—is powerful testimony to its nondefensive character. In this regard, Japan's emulation of the European powers and its adoption of its own colonialist ambitions was a remarkable success, but one for which other Asian peoples and, with their defeat in World War II, eventually the Japanese themselves paid dearly.

Invention of Race

Another core feature of the European world order, one that became central to the modern idea of the West, derived from the racism that, as colonialism developed, became indistinguishable from the Western view of the rest of the world. It was one thing to seek colonies for economic benefit, but to add a conviction of racial superiority gave the colonialist powers something more fundamental than mere profit on which to build the edifices of world domination. A belief in the inherent differences between whites and others didn't just justify white supremacy but required it.

To what extent racism is a modern phenomenon is controversial. A kind of proto-racism might have existed in the ancient world, including in ancient Greece and Rome. For example, the Greeks used the term "barbarian" simply to designate people who did not speak the Greek language (derived from the Greek word *barbaroi* or *barbarophonos*, "of incomprehensible speech"). The Roman term *barbarus* applied to anyone who was not from Greco-Roman civilization. While the Greeks and Romans did consider foreigners inferior, barbarian was not a racial notion, certainly not one based on skin color. White Germanic people, such as the Goths, could as easily be called barbarians as Persians or Sudanese. But the fully developed, supposedly scientific or even social idea of race is a modern notion. Indeed, it is highly unlikely that the idea of race in the premodern era—whether in Sumer, India, or Greece—was biologically determined or based on skin color.

Islamic societies did not practice discrimination on the basis of color, although some took into account environmental conditioning. Al-Jahiz, a ninth-century Arab writer born in Basra, wrote, "There are black tribes among the Arabs. White and black are the results of environment, the natural properties of water and soil, distance from the sun, and intensity of heat."[24] Although geography and environmental conditions would also figure in the scientific racism that would later emerge in Europe and the West, there is a major difference. For scientific racists, being European meant having only white and light skin; al-Jahiz makes it clear that Arabs could be both Black and white. Although some form of racist beliefs did exist before, it was not until European thinkers used race to justify the ongoing slave trade and colonialism that the modern concept of racism was invented. Or, as Eric Williams, a scholar and the first prime minister of Trinidad and Tobago, wrote, "Slavery was not born of racism: rather, racism was the consequence of slavery."[25]

Slavery itself was of course not new, but, as noted, the transatlantic slave trade differed from slavery of the past in its volume and its treatment of slaves. A perhaps even more crucial and enduring transformation was the racialization of slavery.

Historically slavery was divorced from color. Slavery in Roman society, for example, included both white slaves and those of darker skin color, probably more of the former. While slavery remained in vogue in Islamic societies, it had nothing to do with skin color, as Arabs took plenty of white slaves. In most ancient or medieval societies—including in Egypt, Persia, India, China, and Europe—slavery was justified as a kind of spoil of war. In the Christian tradition, enslavement of people captured in what was deemed a righteous or just war was quite acceptable and commonplace. Biblical beliefs about Abraham's slaves, in which he and other patriarchs kept slaves without incurring God's disapproval, also had no relation to skin color.[26]

In sum, while a proto-racism might have existed in earlier history, from the fifteenth century onward, race rapidly became the principal framework for organizing world order under European dominance. Racism based on skin color certainly got a powerful boost from the practice of slavery, as European settlers imported African slaves to North and South America as well as the Caribbean. The key motive initially was economic, rather than racial: the colonists could not find Native Americans or Europeans to work in their plantations. Insofar as Native Americans were concerned, while some were captured for slavery, keeping them enslaved proved exceedingly difficult. Being familiar with their own land and environs, they escaped easily and could organize armed resistance against the settlers. Importing European laborers to work in plantations on a large scale was not the solution; they did not "want the job," so to speak. African slaves, on the other hand, were abundant and cheap, once their capture and export to the New World were commercialized. They had nowhere to escape to and were easily recaptured if they did. As transatlantic slavery grew and became institutionalized, racial justifications were brought in as a way of legitimizing a practice that had started for economic and practical reasons. European settlers came to associate slavery with being Black.

While these conditions applied to the whole of the Americas, there were differences. In South America, Spanish settlers quickly intermarried with native women, although, as noted in Chapter 9, this was not always voluntary on the part of the women. Later, a lower proportion of female slaves (compared to North America) and a low birth rate led colonial rulers to allow a wider degree of intermarriage and social mixing

Sale of Prize Slaves.
This Day the 3d of October,
Will be Sold by Public Vendue,
At the Garden of F. Kannemeyer,
SEVENTY prime male and female Slaves,
captured in the French veſſels, La Raiſon-
able and Le Glaucus, and condemned as prize
in the Court of Vice Admiralty.
Cape Town, 28th Sept. 1801.

Image 11. Slave auction notices, Cape Town, 1801. Stellenbosch Village Museum, Stellenbosch, South Africa.

among the natives, imported African slaves, and Europeans. These created new racial categories, such as mestizo (people of indigenous and European ancestry), mulatto (European and African), and zambo (African and indigenous). Slaves in Spanish America also received some protection from the Catholic Church, which came to oppose slavery. Slavery ended earlier in Spanish South America (where, except for Cuba, it was totally abolished by 1850) than in the United States.

In British-dominated areas of North America, by contrast, racial mixing was officially prohibited, although it remained hidden in plain sight. Thomas Jefferson having fathered several children with his Black slave Sally Hemings is one of the most prominent examples. But the net result was large-scale, institutionalized racial separation and formal segregation, continuing well into the latter half of the twentieth century.

This, plus the economic imperative of keeping slavery for the economy of cotton and tobacco in the Southern states, ensured that the concept of race and racism would be a far more robust and durable phenomenon in the United States.

The Caribbean scholar Hilary Beckles identifies the island of Barbados as the place where slavery transitioned to a racialized form. This occurred as white indentured labor was replaced by a chattel slavey system. The word *white*, which meant freedom, was popularized in place of *Christian, English, Irish*, etc. Correspondingly, as juxtaposition to *white*, the term *Black*, implying not free, became more popular, replacing *guinea* or *negroes*, although *negro* remained widely used in the United States. In Barbados, because a white woman could not give birth to an enslaved child, mulatto children (that is, children of white women and Black men) were born into freedom. Slavery was passed through Black women. This model was then transported to the Carolinas by Barbados sugar barons in the 1660s, after the Carolinas were "gifted" to European settlers as a colony by King Charles II.[27] From there, this system spread elsewhere in the United States, explaining, for example, why the children that resulted from Thomas Jefferson's relationship with his slave Sally Hemings were also slaves. Hemings was born of a white father, John Wayles, and his mulatto slave Elizabeth Hemings, and was therefore herself defined as Black.

While Europeans engaged in the slave trade, European philosophers provided intellectual justification for slavery and therefore, indirectly at least, for racism. Among them was John Locke, one of the founding philosophers of liberalism. Based in London, Locke was secretary to Lord Shaftesbury, one of the key colonizers of the Carolinas. (The Carolinas were undivided until 1712 and were known as the Province of Carolina; they covered much of the land between Virginia and Florida.) Locke served as secretary to the Lords Proprietors of Carolina (1668–1671), secretary to the Council of Trade and Plantations (1673–1674), and member of the Board of Trade (1696–1700). He was also an investor in the Royal African Company (1671), which was engaged in the slave trade. He was a drafter of the Fundamental Constitutions of Carolina, which was adopted in 1669 by the eight Lords Proprietors of Carolina (including his employer, Lord Shaftesbury). Its article 110 stated: "Every freeman of Carolina shall have absolute power and authority over his negro slaves, of what opinion or religion soever."[28]

These words mattered because, for the first time, they explicitly and constitutionally identified slavery with a particular race and specified that being a Christian would not exempt a Black person from slavery, despite some past injunctions against Christians enslaving fellow Christians.

Locke's legacy is especially important not only because he is regarded as one of the greatest thinkers of the liberal tradition but also because of his influence on both sides of the Atlantic. When he put the words "Life, Liberty and the pursuit of Happiness" into the Declaration of Independence, Thomas Jefferson was drawing on Locke's *An Essay Concerning Human Understanding*, though Locke's original phrase was "Life, Health, Liberty... [and] Possessions."[29]

Locke's defenders argue that his shares in the Royal African Company were compensation from the English king, who had run out of cash to pay him, and that Locke sold his shares three years after getting them. In his *Second Treatise of Government*, published in 1689 (but perhaps based on earlier work), Locke condemned slavery as "so vile and miserable an institution." After his work on the Carolinas was done, he became the chair of Virginia's Board of Trade, where he opposed Virginia's proslavery laws that granted land to settlers who imported servants and slaves.

But the very fact that Locke, despite considering slavery "vile," worked to help institutionalize it in the Fundamental Constitutions of Carolina shows a striking lack of moral fortitude. Other major figures of the Enlightenment were clearly racist. The German philosopher Immanuel Kant believed that "humanity exists in its greatest perfection in the white race," whereas the "yellow Indians have a smaller amount of talent," and the "Negroes are lower."[30] He insisted, citing another celebrated Enlightenment rationalist philosopher, David Hume, that the "Negroes of Africa have by nature no feeling that rises above the trifling... not a single one was ever found who presented anything great in art or science or any other praiseworthy quality." The differences between the white race and Black Africans "appear to be as great in regard to mental capacities as in color."[31] Kant's invoking of Hume is revealing, showing the tendency among Enlightenment rationalist thinkers to feed on each other's racism.

Kant's racism has often been defended on the grounds that (unlike Locke) he was an anti-imperialist. Yet Kant also believed that nonwhite races must civilize first to the European level before deserving sovereignty. Defenders of Kant also argue that only his writings on geography and anthropology were overtly racist, in contrast to his writings on politics or ethics, which were free from racist remarks. Still, even judged by the standards of their own time, Kant and Locke's tolerance for slavery remains problematic, for the simple reason that some of their contemporaries deeply disagreed with them. Johann Gottfried von Herder, for example, explicitly rejected Kant's scientific racism, arguing that, "notwithstanding the varieties of the human form, there is but one and the same species of man throughout the whole earth."[32] English philosopher and Locke's personal friend James Tyrrell argued in his *Patriarcha non monarcha* that slaves, including those taken in a just war, could justifiably kill their masters if denied "liberty and enjoyment of the ordinary Comforts of Life." And if they were not given such comfort (as in Barbados, which Tyrrell mentioned), they "may lawfully run away if they can."[33]

Still, despite these exceptions, Locke and Kant belonged to a racist and imperialist body of opinion shared by many other thinkers throughout the West, even among those who were political opponents. Some of these figures, including those who otherwise disapproved of colonialism, supported the subjugation of nonwhite people under various pretexts and conditions.[34] John Stuart Mill, for example, developed what has been called "tolerant imperialism," which held that colonization is permissible if it improves the lives of the colonized.[35] The people of India, he believed, would merit independence if and when they adopted the ways of European civilization. Noted British economist J. A. Hobson criticized imperialism as too nationalistic and unprofitable but argued that "all interference on the part of civilized white nations with 'lower races' is not prima facie illegitimate." His objection to imperialism had only to do with the control of the resources of nonwhite countries by the *private enterprise* of white nations: the "civilized Governments [of white nations] may undertake the political and economic control of lower races" on the grounds that such resources were needed for the benefit of the world.[36] Norman Angell, a British liberal thinker, held that British imperialism in India and Egypt was justified because these nations could not develop social and economic cooperation with other countries.[37] Notwithstanding the fact that both countries were known for their robust and long-standing trade and political interactions with other nations, Angell argued that, in such cases, British military conquest had been beneficial. Thanks to British imperialism, the "inferior race [of India] not only survives, but is given an extra lease of life by virtue of the conquest."[38]

Hegel, the German idealist philosopher, constructed racialized categories of reason and consciousness through three stages in world history. He identified the first stage with the despotism and tyranny of the Orient, the second with the imperfect freedom of Greco-Roman civilization (the West at its infancy), and the third stage, the highest stage of knowledge and freedom, with Germanic/European civilization.[39]

The French thinker Alexis de Tocqueville, who was much enamored with American-style democracy, advocated an extremely violent European colonization of Algeria. As he wrote, "Until we have a European population in Algeria, we shall never establish ourselves there [in Africa] but shall remain camped on the African coast. Colonization and war, therefore, must proceed together." The course of action, "after the interdiction of commerce, is to ravage the country." He was specific about how this should be done: "Either by destroying harvests during the harvest season, or year-round by making those rapid incursions called razzias, whose purpose is to seize men or herds." In case this failed, he called upon the Europeans to "destroy everything that resembles a permanent aggregation of population or, in other words, a town."[40]

Jean-Jacques Rousseau, another French philosopher, conjured up the idea of the "noble savage" based on accounts by early European explorers in places like North America. The noble savage was a person at an "early stage" of the "civilizing process," whose mind was "a blank slate upon which civilization will be written. The 'savage' or wild creature is noble because he or she, though unformed, possesses 'natural' human feelings of gentleness and generosity (associated in Europe with the feudal nobility)."[41] Early stereotypes of the "noble savage" placed him or her "at an early stage of evolutionary development leading to the higher stage of European civilization." Such imaginings would later change, and the savages would no longer be considered noble but just savages, with "fixed biological limitation suggestive of the subhuman," destined to remain inferior to white people mentally and culturally.[42]

Racism also found expression in Western stereotypes, some of which continue even today, given the lingering influence of Eurocentric writings and cultural influence. Non-Western societies—including those of China, India, Africa, the pre-Columbian Americas, and Islam—were perceived as irrational, lazy, unproductive, exotic, corrupt, despotic, immature, barbaric, insulated, passive, and feminine, while Western societies were cast as rational, civilized, hardworking, productive, mature, advanced, progressive, democratic, dynamic, and masculine.[43] This tendency of racial stereotyping was pervasive in media, social sciences, and art. Western art was seen as progressive and individualistic, while non-Western art was unchanging, stagnant or repetitive, and collective. Some of these beliefs would persist in the European imagination of the East, as brilliantly captured by Edward Said in his classic book *Orientalism*.[44] In Said's description of the Western view, the East as a whole was "a passive cipher to be governed by an active (and superior) Western civilization."[45] In international affairs, this would be seen as a justification for slavery and colonization, forming the basis of Europe's standard of civilization doctrine.

As colonialism progressed, racism came to be justified on what was widely accepted as a scientific basis. Earlier racism was based on differences in color or culture; now, scientific racism added the belief that people were physically or mentally superior or inferior due to biological or environmental factors. Scientific racism used concepts from the fields of genetics and biology (or eugenics) and categorizations of climate and physical environment to define and classify races.

Racism and its intellectual justifications had powerful consequences in shaping the Western view of world order. Further contributing to this was an influential school of thought about geopolitics that emerged in the late nineteenth and early twentieth centuries. The leading advocates of this point of view included British geographer Halford Mackinder and the American naval officer and writer Alfred Thayer Mahan, both concerned with the protection of the white race against the possibility that the West could be taken over, or at least inundated, by the East Asian "yellow peril."

Mackinder stressed threats posed by land; Mahan emphasized the importance of sea power. Mackinder believed that "European civilization is, in a very real sense, the outcome of the secular struggle against Asiatic invasion."[46] Mahan likened the West—"our not unjustly vaunted European and American civilization"—to an "oasis set in the midst of a desert of barbarism."[47]

Mackinder's "heartland theory" conceived of the world as a series of concentric circles, with eastern Europe and Russia being the "heartland." Any country that could establish control over this geographical region could use it as a "pivot" to control the whole world. Mahan advocated for "sea power" through the building of a strong navy and strategic defense capabilities. He urged control over "chokepoints" in various parts of the world, so as to prevent the East from gaining any sort of foothold. Mahan was especially fearful of the threat posed by China: "Many military men abroad, familiar with Eastern conditions and character, look with apprehension toward the day when the vast mass of China—now inert—may yield to one of those impulses which have in past ages buried civilization under a wave of barbaric invasion."[48]

While Mackinder and Mahan focused on the threat from the East, another group of writers—including Karl Haushofer, Friedrich Ratzel, and Rudolf Kjellén—proposed an "organic-state theory," in which they supported their nationalist leaders by stressing the space required by the state for survival.[49] Haushofer, who influenced Nazi foreign policy, advocated expanding Germany to give it more Lebensraum, or "living space," and in the process "Germanize" both the territory and the peoples of neighboring states.

One place where Europe's mix of expansionism and racism played out is the Pacific islands. Spread across a vast maritime space, the islands did not develop a major empire comparable to the Incas or the West Africans. But to some degree, like African or Native American societies, they were ruled by traditional chiefdoms, sharing a collectivist worldview and strong affinity with the natural environment. At the same time, the Pacific islands were not isolated entities waiting to be discovered by Europeans; they had developed extensive migratory, cultural, and commercial bonds with each other and with Southeast Asia.

As they entered the region, the Europeans regarded its inhabitants as primitive, with some gradations made according to skin color. Melanesia in the western Pacific was even named after the color of its inhabitants, since Melanesia means "black islands" in Greek. In contrast, Polynesia, meaning "many islands," was, as one scholar has put it, "characterized by abundance... and exotica and personified by the Polynesian princess, with all her appealingly savage (semi-naked) and passive femininity."[50] The business of bringing Melanesian workers to work in sugar plantations in Fiji and Queensland was termed "blackbirding."

In his 1697 bestseller, A New Voyage Round the World, the English pirate-explorer William Dampier described western Australia's "aborigines" as "the miserablest People in the World," adding, "They differ but little from Brutes.... They are black...have great Heads, round Foreheads, and great Brows. Their Eyelids are always half closed, to keep the Flies out of their Eyes."[51] The fate of the Australian Aborigines was sealed when Captain James Cook arrived in southeastern Australia's Botany Bay in 1770 and declared the lands as terra nullius, devoid of inhabitants possessing civilization by Europe's criteria (including property ownership and farming), and thus worthy of colonization.[52]

But the Europeans took a different view of the Tahitians of Polynesia, because, aside from having more recognizable (to European eyes) institutions like monarchy and priestly classes, their "physical appearance coincided with European taste."[53] Tahitians also fit well into the European idea of the "noble savage": people living in a peaceful and pristine environment, enjoying happiness, self-sufficiency, and freedom. They were considered different from the barbaric and violent "brutal savages" found elsewhere in the Pacific, such as the "man-eating" Maoris or "head-hunting" Melanesians, although this distinction did not spare the Tahitians from French colonial rule.

The South Seas also followed the pattern, set in the Americas, of indigenous population decline and cultural destruction that accompanied European colonization. Although some writers contend that it was less severe in the Pacific, diseases brought by the Europeans nonetheless exacted a heavy toll.[54] Estimates of the Aboriginal and Torres Strait Islander population before 1788 range from 315,000 to over 1 million, with 750,000 estimated by more recent research. This population "declined dramatically under the impact of new diseases, repressive and often brutal treatment, dispossession, and social and cultural disruption and disintegration."[55] In New Zealand, the indigenous Maori population shrank from about 100,000 in 1769 to 42,000 in 1896. The population of Tahiti was three-quarters down in 1797 compared with when it was discovered by Europeans. Data available from before 1860 shows the population loss in the Pacific islands area—especially Tahiti, Mooréa, and the Marquesas—from European colonization ranged from 20 to 70 percent.[56] Not surprisingly, given the tendency to view the world through a racial prism, Europeans considered the indigenous peoples' failure to withstand the effects of disease a result of their lack of civilization. Thus Dr. Archdall Reid, at a discussion of the Pathological Society of Manchester in 1912, remarked, "Only a race which has undergone evolution against the diseases of crowds is capable of civilization."[57]

Loss of cultural vitality went hand in hand with population decline. To be sure, aspects of the indigenous Pacific civilization, including its collectivist values and emphasis on social relationships, survived in places where the influx of Europeans was less voluminous and permanent. But the introduction of Christianity along with the imposition of European laws and firearms brought about momentous changes in the entire region: the food its inhabitants ate, how they dressed, what they believed, and how they lived. As Captain Cook himself wrote patronizingly, "We debauch their Morals already too prone to vice and we interduce [sic] among them wants and perhaps diseases which they never before knew and which serves only to disturb that happy tranquillity they and their fore Fathers had injoy'd [sic]."[58]

Bad as this may seem, the physical and cultural destruction of the Australian Aborigines was even worse. Edward Wilson, who edited *The Argus* of Melbourne, wrote in his column of March 16, 1856:

> In less than twenty years we have nearly swept them off the face of the earth. We have shot them down like dogs. In the guise of friendship we have issued corrosive sublimate in their damper, and consigned whole tribes to the agonies of an excruciating death. We have made them drunkards, and infected them with disease which has rotted the bones of their adults, and made such few children as are born amongst them a sorrow and a torture from the very instant of their birth. We have made them outcasts on their own land, and are rapidly consigning them to entire annihilation.[59]

To sum up, neither empire nor slavery is a new or unique creation of Europe or the West. What was new were the symbiotic and mutually reinforcing links between those two institutions and racism. Born out of this intersection of empire, slavery, and racism, the standard of civilization doctrine became the main organizing framework of the European world order—in essence, the core of the Western idea that persists to this day.

But the Western world order did not remain a solely European idea. If anything, the notion of the West was strengthened by the rise of the United States to global power. Nor did the West need its traditional colonial empires to persist. In fact, the decolonization process after World War II gave the West a new impetus and cohesion, as Europe and the United States faced challenges not only from the Soviet Union but, even more importantly, from newly independent nations asserting themselves against their former colonial masters.

The Collapse of European Colonialism

Before turning to how the rise of the United States and the postcolonial nations reshaped world order, it is important to take note of the manner in which decolonization occurred. The collapse of European

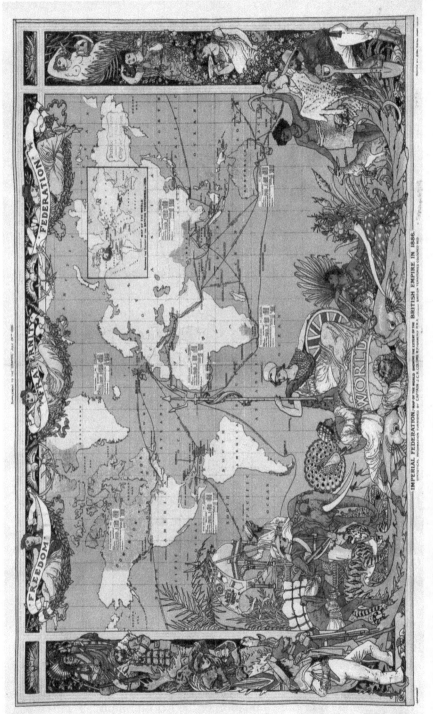

Image 12. Visualization of "British Imperial Federation," 1886.

imperialism was not swift, nor was it widely predicted. In the later part of the nineteenth century, the largest empire, that of Great Britain, seemed alive and well, leading to talk of a British Imperial Federation. There are many explanations for this remarkable phenomenon.

The most conventional explanation centers the exhaustion of European colonial powers from the two world wars, which made it difficult for them to meet the costs of maintaining their overseas empires.[60] Yet, European powers, including Britain, had not given up on empire but were planning to use the colonies to speed up their postwar recovery.[61] This was reinforced by geopolitical reasoning in Britain and France, which feared that, in the emerging bipolar world dominated by the United States and the Soviet Union, if they didn't keep or restore their colonial possessions, they might lose their status as great powers and pave the way for Soviet- and Chinese-backed communist takeovers.[62]

A related explanation has to do with the declining profitability of empire. The eighteenth-century Scottish economist Adam Smith insisted that empires were not profitable. Roughly a century after Smith, British Conservative leader Benjamin Disraeli, an outspoken defender of empire, complained about people saying, "There never was a Jewel in the Crown of England that was so truly costly as the possession of India."[63] While disagreeing with that view, Disraeli's statement acknowledged that the economic and political value of empire was a central factor in the domestic British debate over empire. Still later, British politician Denis Healey (leader of Labour Party from 1980 to 1983) summed up this view: "As early as 1880, the British empire was producing an economic return lower than investment in Britain itself, while to preserve it the British taxpayer was paying two and a half times more for defence than the citizens of other developed countries."[64]

Yet, there remained staunch defenders of colonialism within the European elite and leadership, before and after the two world wars. Most prominent among them was Winston Churchill, who insisted that British imperialism was a bulwark against anarchy and world disorder. As he famously said in 1942, "I have not become the King's First Minister in order to preside over the liquidation of the British Empire."[65] This was a mere five years before Britain had to give up its "jewel," India. But Britain retained dozens of colonies around the world well into the post–World War II period and gave them up only reluctantly. It also kept possession of five Caribbean territories—including that notorious haven for money laundering, the Cayman Islands—as well as Diego Garcia in the Indian Ocean, which Britain leased to the United States to serve as a critical staging point for Western military interventions in the Middle East and Africa. Despite their alleged exhaustion, Western leaders generally wanted to retain their colonial empires or to restore the territories that had been seized by Japan before and during the war. Churchill wanted ardently to hold on to India. The Dutch tried their best to restore their rule in Indonesia, as did the French in Indochina. The British did not give independence to Malaya (comprising Malaysia and Singapore today), once the world's largest source of tin and natural rubber, until 1957, and oil-rich Brunei, a British protectorate, got independence only in 1984.

A third explanation for the end of colonialism has to do with Western moral revulsion against empire. While there was certainly some such feeling in the West, this paints decolonization as if it were a grand act of European charity and benevolence. In reality, sentiment against colonialism was not universally shared in Europe, and most opinions against colonization arose simultaneously with the decline of its perceived material benefits.[66]

Consider the idea of self-determination, the right of people to choose their own statehood and government. This principle is often credited with leading to an acceptance of independence for former colonies. However, it was originally meant to benefit European society and world order. Emerging from the French Revolution, the idea of self-determination helped to stabilize Europe by either unifying disparate territories or dividing them along national and ethnic lines. It also applied to European colonies settled mainly by white people, such as Canada and Australia. It was a deeply racist principle as such, not one meant to give self-governance to non-white people.

Additionally, the mandate system under the League of Nations, set up in 1919 and mostly applied to former territories of the Ottoman

Empire, was for the most part not intended to lead to independence but rather to pass control from the defeated powers to victorious Western ones. The pretext was that these territories were "inhabited by peoples not yet able to stand by themselves under the strenuous conditions of the modern world," and hence should be placed under the "sacred trust of civilization," a more or less direct invocation of the standard of civilization doctrine.[67]

In sum, the European support for decolonization was half-hearted at best. In some cases, European powers saw little choice but to allow independence in their colonies, as the British did in India. But in several other major cases, they were willing to use armed force to suppress anti-colonial struggles: the British in Kenya, the French in Algeria and Vietnam, and the Dutch in Indonesia. Contrary to the conventional view, the United States was not a staunch opponent of colonialism. Despite his public support for decolonization, Franklin D. Roosevelt was unwilling to antagonize Churchill, his greatest wartime ally and staunch defender of the British Empire. In fact, the Charter of the United Nations, drafted in San Francisco under US and Western leadership, was largely silent on colonialism and racism; its major concern was to prevent another world war through collective security and peaceful management of disputes. The reluctance of the United States to oppose European colonialism intensified with the outbreak of the Cold War, when Washington feared that decolonized states would be taken over by Communists or by the Soviet Union. In short, decolonization "was never an overriding principle of American foreign policy before or during the Second World War."[68]

Yet, most of the standard arguments neglect the moral revulsion felt among the colonized themselves and give inadequate credit to their active resistance. It is doubtful that moral revulsion and economic exhaustion in Europe would have ended colonization without the rise of nationalist protests and resistance in the colonies, and without the anti-colonial international coalitions formed in what would come to be known as the Third World. If, as historian John Darwin has argued, "The language of empire and colonial rule had lost almost all its legitimacy in international affairs," the reason for this could be found in places like New Delhi, Bandung, Accra, Cairo, and Belgrade rather than in London, Paris, Washington, DC, or San Francisco.[69] It was in the last of these places that the UN Conference on International Organization was held in 1945 to decide on the post–World War II order, but where colonialism and racism were virtually sidelined by the victorious Western powers. Some of the key norms and institutions of the European world order, especially Westphalian sovereignty, persisted into the world order that emerged from the ashes of the Second World War, but others were challenged. Founded on imperialism, racism, and slavery, the European world order ended largely because of resistance to these forces from *within* the colonies, not from outside. This struggle gave new meaning to the ideas of nationalism, the nation-state, and world order, as we will see in the next chapter.

Chapter 12

The City upon a Hill

The terms *American world order* or *liberal international order* or *liberal world order* in policy debates today conventionally describe the period after World War II when the United States emerged as the world's preeminent economic and military power. But to understand what it means and how it has worked, one has to start from a much earlier period of history, dating back to European colonization, the creation of the United States of America, and its evolution thereafter.

A world order goes through different stages, and so has the American world order. Before World War I, the United States was somewhat inward looking. It had colonized and conquered territories mostly in North America and developed a sphere of influence (under the Monroe Doctrine) over Central America and the Caribbean. After World War I and especially after World War II, the United States enjoyed more relative power and prestige and correspondingly took on a far more active role in global affairs. This is the phase of the liberal order. Here, the word *liberal* does not mean values like democracy and human rights, although these did have their place, but refers to a non-imperial system supported by mechanisms of international cooperation that were theoretically open to equal participation by all nations of the world. Through these international forums, the United States sought to present its own interests and leadership as beneficial to the entire world, and thus make its global dominance more appealing and acceptable. The liberal order, according to proponents, is distinctly American. No other power or powers—including the Europeans—could have made it this way. America, in Kissinger's phrase, is "acting for all mankind."[1]

Indeed, the conventional story about America's emergence as the greatest of the world's great powers stresses its presumed differences not only from western Europe, its cultural progenitor, but also from other great powers before and since its rise. While Europe practiced empire, the story goes, the United States shunned it and supported decolonization. In Europe, democracy, liberty, and equality emerged only after centuries of feudal rule and great power tutelage over smaller nations, but the United States embraced and practiced these values as its founding principles. Unlike Europe, the story goes on, the United States managed the world order not through alliances and power politics but through inclusive, multilateral cooperation, as reflected in its pivotal role in the making of the short-lived League of Nations and the more enduring United Nations. The United States' presumed world ordering has also been expressed in its promotion of democracy around the world, its advocacy of human rights, and its persistent tradition of anti-dictatorial and anti-authoritarian rhetoric, illustrated in such practices as the State Department's annual report on human rights around the world. Freedom is the American secular religion, and the United States is the high priest of the free, open, and inclusive world order humanity has enjoyed since World War II.

But America isn't as exceptional, or a "city upon a hill" as its leaders—from John Winthrop (Massachusetts Bay colony founder) to John F. Kennedy—and other intellectuals have claimed. There are deep continuities between America and old Europe. Like Europe, the United States had a "civilizing mission," which was directed at Native Americans with equally, if not more, brutal consequences than what Europe's colonial subjects endured. US engagement destroyed the Native American civilization, just as the early Spanish conquerors did to the Aztecs and the

Incas. Colonialism and slavery played a big part in the rise of the United States, and slavery lingered much longer than it did in Europe.

While it is true that during the twentieth century the United States, at least in theory, promoted a new, inclusive kind of international cooperation in which all nations of the world could participate, this multilateralism had its limits, reflected in the real-world differences in power and influence among the members of the United Nations. Even though the UN was created at the behest of the Americans, the United States and other great powers remained unwilling to yield any of their real power to that international body. After the start of the Cold War, American military alliances with Europe and other parts of the world quickly became a fundamental part of US world-order building, while the network of multilateral institutions that the United States promoted became instruments of legitimizing its power and advancing its national interests. Moreover, when the United States deemed it essential to act unilaterally or with a small group of allies, it was always ready to jettison multilateralism in favor of self-interest, as it did in various conflicts including the Vietnam War and the invasion of Iraq in 2003. While Americans certainly have a sentimental preference for democracy and often view the world in terms of a conflict between freedom and tyranny (describing rival countries, for example, as "evil empires" or an "axis of evil"), the United States has often found itself tightly bound to dictators in Asia, South America, Africa, and elsewhere. As President Franklin D. Roosevelt is said to have commented about Rafael Trujillo, the dictator of the Dominican Republic, "He may be a bastard, but he's our bastard."[2]

This is not to argue that the United States has never, as Kissinger put it, acted for all mankind, but that, like other countries, it has always put its self-interest first, and in that sense, it has not been all that "exceptional." The liberal world order that it represents has much more continuity with what came before it than many are prone to believe. This includes, perhaps most conspicuously, the treatment of the peoples who already inhabited North America when the Europeans arrived.

A Civilizing Mission

The seeds of the American world order were planted by the first European settlers in the seventeenth century. This world order rode on the back of the outright expansion and colonization characteristic of the European order, with the difference being that the direct colonization took place inside what would become American territory, not in far-flung lands in Africa and Asia. The early colonization of the East Coast in the seventeenth and eighteenth centuries was gradually and inexorably expanded to the west in the nineteenth century, a process that cannot by any stretch of the imagination be seen as a domestic affair.

America's emergence as an independent nation-state and later as a world power evolved in opposition both to British colonial practices and to some European approaches to international order, but the break was not as radical as is often assumed. Both Europe and the United States adopted the standard of civilization doctrine to justify colonialism. Europe imposed its standard of civilization over the rest of the world; America's civilizing mission was directed mainly toward Native Americans.

Estimates of the native population of North America when the Europeans first arrived vary. But the figure of one million cited by some studies is grossly low. A low number served the purpose of justifying colonization, since such a sparsely populated territory was presumed to be terra nullius (land belonging to no one)—there for the taking! Other estimates give a much higher number, ranging from 3.8 million to 20 million.[3] Whatever the exact number, a substantial native population was spread all over the land, leaving no areas uninhabited, as the idea of terra nullius would imply.

This population was subjected from the very early days of the American republic to a "civilizing" policy, led by none other than President George Washington. In his third annual address to Congress, Washington—whom the Native Americans called Conotocarious ("town taker" or "devourer of villages" in Algonquian language), based on the memory of a massacre of chiefs that his great-grandfather had taken part in—asked "that such rational experiments should be made, for imparting to [Native Americans] the blessings of civilization, as may, from time to time, suit their condition."[4]

Nearly a hundred years later, in his State of the Union address on December 4, 1871, President Ulysses S. Grant noted with satisfaction that "the policy pursued toward the Indians has resulted favorably....Many tribes of Indians have been induced to settle upon reservations, to cultivate the soil, to perform productive labor of various kinds, and to partially accept civilization."[5]

Yet these relocations and the resulting changes to the Native American way of life were not induced peacefully but were forced. It meant cultural as well as physical genocide. An integral part of this civilizing mission was the promulgation of laws to regulate or even ban aspects of the Native American traditional way of life. In 1882, Interior Secretary Henry M. Teller called attention to cultural practices regarded as "a great hindrance to the civilization of the Indians."[6] The resulting Code of Indian Offenses of 1883, which remained in effect until 1933, outlawed many traditional customs, including dancing and gift giving, and violations were penalized by imprisonment and the loss of government-provided rations. These laws applied to all tribes except those that were by then considered "civilized": the Cherokee, Chickasaw, Choctaw, Creek (Muscogee), and Seminole, exempted because they had accepted Christianity. The laws were, as one historian has put it, "directly aimed at outlawing Indian culture." Native Americans were confined to reservations that were actually "early examples of internment or concentration camps." Pushed off their traditional hunting grounds, they became dependent on federal rations, even as the government commonly withheld those rations as punishment for alleged violations of the code. "Thus, the federal government's message to tribal Indians in the late nineteenth century was crystal clear—abandon your traditional culture and comply with the Code of Indian Offenses or *starve*."[7]

The ideas of manifest destiny and American exceptionalism are other aspects of the standard of civilization as applied by the United States. Despite, or perhaps because of, its very short history as a nation-state, the United States has never shied away from invoking the distinctiveness and superiority of its culture and institutions. Initially, the American founders associated the country's national culture with its European origin, especially Greco-Roman civilization. Later, the distinctive traits of America were defined in terms of the practices and institutions developed during its early life. The historian Frederick Jackson Turner, among the most influential definers of the special American character, promoted the notion of manifest destiny in nineteenth-century America, and he explained it as a consequence of American exceptionalism. The United States was different from Europe because of the distinctive role of the frontier in the American experience. Certain traits—a "practical, inventive turn of mind," a "masterful grasp of material things," "a restless, nervous energy," "dominant individualism," and the "buoyancy and exuberance which comes with freedom"—were engendered by the settlers who led the American expansion into the west, and these were not dominant traits of European civilization.[8]

As part of the civilizing mission, these traits, especially individualism, were to be passed on to the Native Americans. As John Oberly, commissioner of Indian affairs, noted in his 1888 annual report, "[The Native American] must be imbued with the exalting egotism of American civilization so that he will say 'I' instead of 'We,' and 'This is mine' instead of 'This is ours.'"[9] Part of this strategy was to bar the Native Americans from distributing their property among their kin. Interior Secretary Henry M. Teller denounced the native "custom of destroying or distributing his property [i.e., turning it over to communal ownership] on the death of a member of his family." Individual property ownership was an essential part of the white peoples' custom, and adopting it was deemed necessary to be accepted as civilized. For Native Americans to embrace property rights would have been "a step forward in the road to civilization."[10] While these words were being spoken or written, European settlers throughout the continent had seized and were continuing to seize Native American property as their own.

The laws of European settlers, moreover, were at serious odds with the beliefs and practices of Native American societies, which took a holistic approach to life and cherished their freedom of movement. While beliefs varied, there were shared elements among the native societies in North America. The Great Spirit was the supreme force of the universe, under whose watch all elements—including plants, animals, rocks, and people—were deeply interconnected. To quote Lakota medicine man Lame Deer (English name John Fire), "Being a living part of the earth, we cannot harm any part of her without hurting ourselves."[11] There is evidence that this ecological worldview led to effective ways of protecting the environment, or at least limiting damage to it. Native Americans actively managed their environment through controlled burning (thereby lessening the likelihood of uncontrolled forest fires), planting, hunting, and canal digging to sustain agriculture, regulate movements of species, and create new habitats for people and animals. To be sure, these efforts were not always successful. For example, in the Mississippi area of Cahokia near Saint Louis, the largest Native American settlement north of the Rio Grande, population growth and agricultural practices outstripped the local water supply, leading to a serious drop in some wildlife numbers and land erosion caused by flooding. But in general, the Native Americans maintained a "stable, supple, resilient," and sustainable ecosystem. It was a garden, not a wilderness. It was only with the severe population decline brought by European diseases that such careful management was no longer possible. European colonization thus not only sharply reduced the native population but also triggered a massive ecological disaster, leading to explosive growth of forests and animals. The image of North America as a vast empty space of thundering buffalos was the product of a catastrophic environmental collapse taking place after the Europeans' arrival.[12]

The Native Americans' traditional way of managing their environment was one of the reasons, among others, that they disdained the white man's urban lifestyle. They considered it not only harmful to nature but also a denial of human freedom. "The life of white men is a life of slavery," Sitting Bull (Tatanka Iyotanka), the chief of the Lakota tribe, said. "They are prisoners in towns or farms. The life my people want is a life of freedom." On the confinement of Native Americans on reservations in exchange for food and medical treatment, he said: "They gave us meat, but they took away our liberty. The white men have many things that we wanted, but we could see that they did not have the one thing we liked best—freedom. I would rather live in a tipi and go without meat when game is scarce than give up my privileges as a free Indian."[13]

Despite their contempt for Native American civilization, many European settlers, including political leaders, found the native societies' love of freedom and ability to cooperate admirable. There were European colonizers who were so attracted by the relatively free life of Native American villagers that they joined their communities.[14] In the political realm, the most prominent example of cooperation and freedom was the Iroquois Confederacy (Haudenosaunee), whose origins go back before the arrival of the European settlers in the Americas. Initially composed of five nations—Mohawk, Onondaga, Oneida, Cayuga, and Seneca—the confederacy acquired a sixth member, the Tuscarora, around 1722. Cadwallader Colden, who served as the governor of New York in the 1760s and 1770s, noted that its members "have such absolute Notions of Liberty that they allow no kind of Superiority of one over another, and banish all Servitude from their Territories."[15]

The significance of the Iroquois Confederacy lay in the fact that its oral constitution, known as the Great Law of Peace, regulated relations within and among its members on the basis of equality. At the founding of the confederacy, warriors from the five attending nations were believed to have "buried their weapons," and a tree was planted atop the burial site as a symbol of disarmament and peace.[16] For the European colonists, the Iroquois Confederacy was also a model of unity and collective security, or the idea of "one for all and all for one," which is a core principle of the UN charter. In 1754, a meeting of seven British colonies in Albany, New York, discussed the threat from the French and relations with the Native Americans. At this meeting, known as the Albany Congress, Benjamin Franklin, one of the founding fathers of the United States, proposed a plan of union by which the American colonies would join forces against the French, and he used the Iroquois Confederacy as a model. "It would be a strange thing," he told the congress, "if six nations of ignorant savages should be capable of forming such a union, and yet it has subsisted for ages and appears indissolvable, and yet a like union should be impractical for 10 or a dozen English colonies."[17]

Franklin's plan was rejected by the British colonial government. Yet, on the occasion of the bicentennial of the US Constitution in 1987,

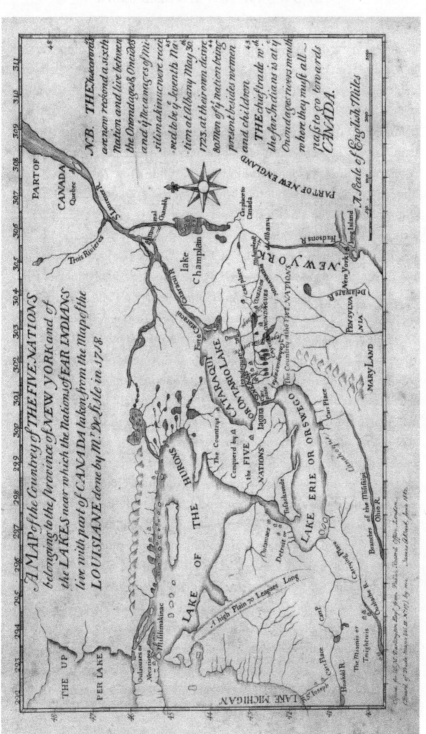

Image 13. The extent of the Iroquois Confederacy in the eighteenth century.

Congress passed a resolution affirming that George Washington and Benjamin Franklin "are known to have greatly admired the concepts, principles and government practices of the Six Nations of the Iroquois Confederacy" and that "the Confederation of the original thirteen colonies into one Republic was explicitly modelled upon the Iroquois Confederacy as were many of the democratic principles which were incorporated into the Constitution itself."[18] While some American historians remain skeptical about the influence of the Iroquois Confederacy on the drafting of the US Constitution, that does not negate the fact that a striking indigenous model of equal states governed by common principles and living in peace existed in North America before the arrival of the Europeans and was recognized by the Constitution's framers.[19]

But the impact of the Iroquois Confederacy on the United States went further. It also played an important role in the American War of Independence. Had the confederacy joined the British, with the British attacking from the east and the Native Americans from the west, the American Revolution might not have succeeded.[20] But the Iroquois hardly get credit for this contribution to the making of the United States.

The fact that, for most of its history, the United States avoided direct colonization of faraway countries has also been deemed an aspect of American exceptionalism and an important difference with Europe. But this, too, is misleading. While the Europeans were colonizing Africa and Asia and other corners of the world, the United States was preoccupied with the colonization of Native Americans, taking over their territories and expelling them to reservations, without or with treaties that the Americans quickly violated. The United States was even better at dominating its own immediate neighborhood, something no European country could do due to Europe's balance of power system. The United States did eventually acquire a few overseas colonies, such as Cuba and the Philippines. But even before that, Washington had been pursuing a long-term policy, begun under President James Monroe in the early nineteenth century, to establish hegemony in Central America and the Caribbean, denying this region to any rival powers.

Rome Reborn?

In organizing its own world order, the American colonization project was much inspired by ancient Rome. This was in part the natural
impulse of the colonists, whose education, even if often not very deep,
stressed the Greco-Roman classics. Eighteenth-century Americans were
deeply familiar with "the ancient authors and the heroic personalities
and events of the ancient world."[21] Edward Gibbon's *The Decline and Fall of
the Roman Empire*, published in 1776, was among the most popular books
of the time. The drafters of the US Constitution not only claimed to have
read Gibbon, but they also often quoted classical writers from Greece
and Rome to make their political points.

The founding fathers, such as John Adams and Thomas Jefferson,
were admirers of the Roman Republic, rather than the Roman Empire.[22]
George Washington himself emulated the legendary Roman general
Cincinnatus, who served briefly as Rome's dictator (not to be confused
with emperor) to defend the republic from the threat posed by the Aequi
tribe. After his reign, Cincinnatus retreated into the countryside (some
say a farm), much like Washington himself. The founders wanted to draw
lessons from the Roman Republic so as not to let the nascent American
republic suffer its fate and succumb to dictatorship. They were admirers
of Cato, Seneca, and Cicero, who opposed tyranny and wished to restore
the Roman Republic even after it degenerated into the empire. They did
not admire Julius Caesar, the lifelong dictator of Rome.

But the American affection for Rome was also a more general admiration of Roman civilization, power, glory, and cultural icons, straddling the republic and the empire. And this made Rome an ambiguous
symbol for the American world order. The Roman Republic, one may be
reminded, was hardly a period of peace and coexistence. Some of the
most intense campaigns behind Rome's rise to power, such as the total
devastation of Carthage or the subjugation of Britain, happened during
the republican period. Similarly, the founders and the leaders of the
United States during its rise to world power did not reject militarism and

expansionism in dealing with adversaries, whether the Native American tribes or foreign nations, especially in its neighborhood.

The founders were also in love with imperial Roman architecture. The buildings of Washington, DC, blend the influences of both Greece and Rome into a neoclassical synthesis. (The Romans themselves had adapted Greek designs.) But the Roman architectural marvels that influenced Washington were built, in most cases, by emperors. Although Capitol Hill is named after ancient Rome's Capitoline Hill, which emerged during the republican period, Jefferson wanted the central dome to look like the Pantheon, built by Emperor Hadrian, rather than follow an alternative design based on Renaissance architecture.[23] Later, the Pantheon would become an inspiration for the design of Jefferson's own memorial. To cite another prominent example, Emperor Constantine built the arch that served as a model for Washington's Union Station.

And then there is the fasces: a bundle of rods bound together with an axe, a symbol of civil authority and a magistrate's power in ancient Rome. Today, two fasces, on either side of the US flag, continue to adorn the walls behind the Speaker's seat in the House of Representatives. This is also where the president gives the annual State of the Union address. On the one hand, the fasces "represent the ideal of American democracy: like the thin rods bound together, the small individual states achieve their strength and stability through their union under the federal government."[24] But the fasces also became a symbol of Mussolini's fascism (a term that derives from *fasces*) and for the contemporary American Far Right.

The symbolic ambiguity of the imperial architecture in America's political center has led Americans to ignore the unsavory and ugly aspects of Greco-Roman history: constant warfare, including civil wars and aggression against neighbors; oppression of subject people; slavery; and cruelty. These elements characterized both the republic and the empire (including in the period of the presumed Pax Romana). It is a fair question whether the general American fascination with Roman civilization might have obscured the basic facts of the Roman Republic, especially that it was not a democracy but an aggressive, expansionist plutocracy.

Nevertheless, Americans have felt that invoking the ideals of the Roman Republic was supposed to make their country more democratic, especially in establishing the system of checks and balances between the presidency, the Congress, and the judiciary.

There is another reason why the image of Roman Empire remains salient in the American mind. The relative, or predicted, decline of America has been likened to the fall of the Roman Empire. In both cases, the decline is attributed to the overextension of military power, domestic disunity, and the rise of rivals—the Germanic tribes in the case of Rome, and China in the case of the United States. But before discussing the debate over America's decline, it is necessary to examine the factors behind its rise to world power.

Rise to World Power

While the subjugation of Native Americans and the usurpation of their territories played a key role in the creation of the United States, racism and slavery were both present at its founding and instrumental in its rise as a world power. The US Constitution inscribed the inferiority of Blacks to whites as the three-fifths compromise, under which only three-fifths of a state's Black population could be counted as part of the state's total population when allocating its congressional seats and share of taxation.

Another striking example of the racism baked into the country's founding can be found in the thinking of Thomas Jefferson, who drafted the Declaration of Independence with the famous words "Life, Liberty and the pursuit of Happiness." Despite this humanistic phrasing, Jefferson believed, although he would call it a "suspicion only," "that the blacks, whether originally a distinct race, or made distinct by time and circumstances, are inferior to whites both in *body and in mind*" (emphasis added).[25] As discussed, major European philosophers such as John Locke and Immanuel Kant, who were very influential in the United States, harbored similar racist convictions. But slavery persisted in the United States much longer than in Europe and played an instrumental role in America's economic rise. Even after Congress banned the import of slaves in 1807, the US economy relied heavily on the abundant domestically born and traded slaves. "The lives and labor of enslaved African-Americans transformed the United States into a world power," reads a poster displayed at the National Museum of African American History and Culture in Washington, DC. By 1860, America's four million slaves (including domestically traded slaves after the US Congress banned the import of slaves in 1807), who were engaged mainly in sugar, cotton, tobacco, and rice cultivation, were producing "well over" 60 percent of the nation's GDP.[26] The cotton industry was crucial to the US economy, accounting for more than half of all exports in the first half of the nineteenth century. And that industry was heavily dependent on slaves. "By 1850, 1.8 million of the 2.5 million enslaved Africans employed in agriculture in the United States were working on cotton plantations."[27] To be sure, the slave trade was also highly beneficial to other sectors of the American economy, including the financial sector (since banks invested in the slave trade) and shipping. But the wealth generated from the cotton industry made the lower Mississippi valley home to most of the millionaires in the United States in 1860. It also made slave labor the American economy's most valuable asset, estimated at $3.5 billion, exceeding the combined worth of all manufacturing and railroads.[28]

All of this economic activity, underpinned by chattel slavery, meant that the United States could steadily expand its territory using force, threats of force, and money throughout the nineteenth century. The acquisition of Louisiana from France in 1803 and Alaska from Russia in 1867 were through purchases, although the sellers had themselves acquired these lands through colonization. Another example is the Oregon Treaty of 1846, under which Britain and the United States settled their disputed border over lands colonized from Native Americans. Another significant expansion involved war, the case being the annexation of Texas in 1845, after its residents declared independence from Mexico and established the Republic of Texas. The United States moved in to negotiate the acquisition of the republic, leading to war with Mexico in 1848, which the Americans won. This secured the United States, under the terms of the Treaty of Guadalupe Hidalgo, approximately 525,000 square miles (55 percent of Mexico's prewar territory) for a price of $15 million and the assumption of $3.25 million worth of Mexican debt.[29] Just like European powers had fought and compromised among themselves to colonize Africa, Asia, and other parts of the world, so did the United States with rival nations in North America.

A parallel element in American expansion concerned the wider Western Hemisphere. The Monroe Doctrine, first enunciated in December 1823 by President James Monroe, forbade European powers from either colonizing or interfering in the affairs of states in America's backyard, meaning the Latin American and Caribbean region, and thereby established American regional hegemony. The Monroe Doctrine created an exclusive sphere of influence, and in so doing, it reproduced in the Americas a time-honored principle and approach to geopolitics in Europe.

The Monroe Doctrine was only possible because of prevailing circumstances. In the early nineteenth century, there was no serious challenge to American power in the Western Hemisphere. With the decline of Spain as a world power and the ongoing rivalry between Britain and France—both in Europe and in the other parts of the world where they were competing for colonies—the United States faced little opposition from European powers in the Western Hemisphere.

The Monroe Doctrine also came during a historic shift in the United States toward international isolationism. From December 1807 to March 1809, Congress had imposed a near total embargo on international commerce, a policy that, along with the 1812 US-British war, both helped the development of US domestic industry and reduced overall American economic interdependence.[30] With less need for foreign trade, the country was less vulnerable to the possibility that European powers, retaliating against the Monroe Doctrine, might cut off America's trade routes. The Monroe Doctrine was also partly an ideological effort to prevent European powers from exporting their monarchical political systems to the Americas.

While the Monroe Doctrine enunciated a sphere of influence, an indirect form of colonialism, the United States also became a direct colonial power. This started soon after the Americans crushed the last of Native American resistance, specifically the defeat in 1890 of the Sioux at Wounded Knee in South Dakota, where US forces killed hundreds of Sioux men, women, and children.[31] With North America now fully colonized and the surviving Native American population confined to reservations, the United States began to acquire its first overseas colonies. Victory in the Spanish-American War of 1898 resulted in the acquisition of the Philippines (formally annexed by an act of Congress in February 1899), Guam, and Puerto Rico. In addition, the United States established a protectorate over Cuba and annexed Hawaii and American Samoa. Of these colonies, only Cuba and the Philippines would gain independence. Still, American officials usually preferred the term "territories" over "colonies." As one official suggested in 1914, "The word colony must not be used to express the relationship which exists between our government and its dependent peoples."[32]

Theodore Roosevelt, president from 1901 to 1909, ruled the country during this remarkable period of imperial assertiveness. He considerably expanded the scope of the Monroe Doctrine, which "provided precedent and support for U.S. expansion on the American continent," as the Department of State put it, and justified American dominance of the Western Hemisphere.[33] The Roosevelt Corollary, announced in 1904, justified unilateral US intervention in Latin America, including to deter a European creditor nation from forcibly collecting debts incurred by a country in the region. For example, Venezuela and the Dominican Republic (then known as Santo Domingo) owed money to European banks, which appealed to their governments for help. Britain and Germany sent warships to the Venezuelan coast. Concerned that such developments were reigniting European military intervention and thus violating the Monroe Doctrine, Roosevelt declared that the United States would itself intervene in any country in the region that was unable to repay its foreign debts due to serious economic difficulties. With this, the United States cemented its sphere of influence in the Americas. Though originally meant to deter European powers seeking economic and strategic influence in the Western Hemisphere, the Roosevelt Corollary and the

Monroe Doctrine in general would become a blanket justification for US intervention in the region during the following decades.[34] It was invoked by President John F. Kennedy during the Cuban missile crisis as he announced a naval blockade of Cuba to remove Soviet missiles on the island.

Theodore Roosevelt won the Nobel Peace Prize in 1906 for his mediation in the Russo-Japanese War. But he also oversaw one of the most aggressive expansions of American strategic reach and military power in the country's history. Indeed, to define Roosevelt's view of Native Americans and the nonwhite world at large as "peaceful" would be a perversion of the term. George Washington had wanted to extend "civilization" to the Native Americans; Roosevelt did not think them worthy of such a mission. What mattered to him was Native American land, which, as he put it, "should be won, for the benefit of civilization and in the interest of mankind." Roosevelt rejected applying "the rules of international morality" to Native Americans as a "false sentimentality," saying that "the most ultimately righteous of all wars is a war with savages, though it is apt to be also the most terrible and inhuman. The rude, fierce settler who drives the savage from the land lays all civilized mankind under debt to him."[35]

Theodore Roosevelt in this sense was influenced by the notion of the civilizing mission as espoused by Rudyard Kipling, a Nobel laureate in literature and a major proponent of imperialist rule. Kipling and Roosevelt met several times before Roosevelt became president—in the spring of 1895 at the Washington zoo, for example—and they corresponded with each other.[36] In September 1898, when Roosevelt was assistant secretary of the navy, Kipling urged him to take full colonial possession of the Philippines from Spain: "Now, go in and put all the weight of your influence into hanging on, permanently, to the whole Philippines. America has gone and stuck a pick-axe into the foundations of a rotten house, and she is morally bound to build the house over, again, from the foundations."[37]

Soon thereafter, Kipling published his famous poem "The White Man's Burden: The United States and the Philippine Islands" in the February 1899 issue of *McClure's Magazine*. Kipling sent Roosevelt an advance copy of the poem, which Roosevelt forwarded to the Massachusetts senator Henry Cabot Lodge, a friend, with the comment that it was "rather poor poetry, but good sense from the expansion point of view."[38]

While insisting that American possession of the Philippines was crucial for the United States to project an image of strength in world affairs, Roosevelt retained a hostile and racist attitude toward the Filipinos themselves. In a letter to Kipling on November 1, 1904, he complained that Americans were "jack fools who seriously think that any group of pirates and head-hunters needs nothing but independence in order that it may be turned forthwith into a dark-hued New England town meeting."[39] He warned Congress in 1901 that "encouragement... to [the Filipino] insurrectos stands on the same footing as encouragement to hostile Indians in the days when we still had Indian wars."[40]

And then there was the building of the Panama Canal. While the canal would serve as a global public good, one must not forget that it was built not through diplomacy but through coercion and threat of force. It was another of Theodore Roosevelt's militant actions. Panama was part of Colombia at the time, and when the latter refused to accept the plan for a canal to link the Pacific and Atlantic Oceans, Roosevelt engineered a political revolution to topple the Colombian government and imposed a naval blockade to prevent Colombian forces from landing in Panama. In 1903, at a cost of $10 million plus an annual payment of $250,000, the United States gained perpetual control of the canal.[41] In 1906, Roosevelt became the first sitting American president to leave the United States when he visited Panama to see the construction of the canal, which, completed in 1914, would not return to Panamanian sovereignty until December 31, 1999.

American World Order 2.0

All of these elements of the American experience—its colonization of Native Americans, its reliance on slavery, and its self-perception as a kind of new Rome—played their role in the formation of the American world order. Still, the international aspects of that world order remained mostly limited to building a sphere of influence in the immediate neighborhood, with the partial exception of establishing direct rule over Hawaii, Puerto Rico, Cuba, and the Philippines. It was only after World War I that the United States turned to full-scale world-order building. In the aftermath of that war, President Woodrow Wilson pushed the nation toward embracing multinational institutions and liberal internationalism and away from America's earlier principles of isolationism and a limited sphere of influence.

Wilson's leading role in the creation of the League of Nations after World War I came against the backdrop of his famous Fourteen Points, which he laid out in a speech in January 1918, while the war was still raging.[42] Among the points were a number of principles, or aspirations, aimed at reorganizing the world order: open diplomacy and rejection of secret treaties among nations, freedom of navigation, free trade, reduction of armaments, the right of self-determination of people under colonial rule, and the establishment of a universal association "for the purpose of affording mutual guarantees of political independence and territorial integrity to great and small states alike." The Fourteen Points endorsed decolonization with the following words: "Free, open-minded, and absolutely impartial adjustment of all colonial claims, based upon a strict observance of the principle that in determining all such questions of sovereignty the interests of the populations concerned must have equal weight with the equitable claims of the government whose title is to be determined."[43]

Not included among the Fourteen Points, but mentioned in the second-to-last paragraph of the text of Wilson's speech was a pledge "to be intimate partners of all the governments and peoples associated together against the Imperialists."[44] Although much shorter in length, Wilson's Fourteen Points speech was to liberal internationalism what Karl Marx and Friedrich Engels's *Communist Manifesto* was to socialist internationalism.

But despite these lofty commitments to freedom, Wilson's internationalism had a dark side. His support for self-determination did not extend to a rejection of racism or the acceptance of racial equality—quite the contrary. During the Versailles conference that came after the war, Wilson used his power as the chairman of the League of Nations commission to kill the inclusion of a racial equality clause in the League of Nations' statement of principles that had been demanded by Japan.[45] It should be noted that Japan's main motive for pushing this clause was not to empower the nonwhite races in general but specifically to secure equal treatment for Japanese people in the United States. Another motive was to place Japan on an equal footing with the Western powers, the original rationale for the Meiji reforms. Some have argued that Wilson's stance was a pragmatic move to prevent the breakup of the conference due to opposition from Britain and Australia to the racial equality clause. Another reason cited was to placate domestic sentiments, especially on the American West Coast, against Japanese immigration.[46] But racist attitudes on the part of Wilson and the US delegation also played a part. William Wiseman was a Briton who participated in the Versailles conference as chief adviser to British foreign secretary Arthur Balfour. He had developed a close liaison with Wilson's adviser Colonel Edward House when he was posted in the United States during the war (he also supposedly met directly with Wilson). "The American hatred of all yellow races is thinly, if at all, disguised," Wiseman wrote. "Any thought of the yellows being brought in to redress the balance of the whites is repugnant to them."[47]

Even if Wilson's motives regarding the racial equality clause cannot be clearly established, there is little question that his actions were consistent with his domestic political stance. Back home, Wilson supported race politics and white supremacy, even showing empathy for the Ku Klux Klan, whose violence against Black people was to Wilson an understandable response to "the sudden and absolute emancipation of the negroes."[48] This is a strong indication that his domestic racism and racist positions in international affairs were closely intertwined. Wilson, whom Kissinger credits for making the United States the "world's conscience,"[49] was also not above using the racist "White Man's Burden" logic in justifying the continued US colonization of the Philippines. The Filipinos, he argued, needed to be taught how to govern before they deserved independence.

The next stage of the history of American world order—what is most commonly called the liberal international order—came with World War II, when the United States emerged as the global hegemon, materially more powerful than any competing power, including the Soviet Union. Even though the world was bipolar in terms of its strategic structure, in every real measure of power—economic, military, and diplomatic—the United States was supreme. The American world order had definitively replaced the European world order.

The key pillars of the liberal international order included support for free trade, democracy promotion, liberal values such as human rights, and multilateral institutions. These are not uniquely American of course. The United States inherited values associated with human rights, participatory political systems, and religious tolerance from Europe, though these also had a basis in other civilizations of the world. For example, the British claimed to have invented and enforced free trade, despite the fact that the practice of open seas and free trade was prevalent in the Indian Ocean before the arrival of European colonial powers. And, of course, Europe had formulated these values even as it practiced wanton imperialism and racism in the wider world. But the American world order gave more stress to some principles that were not fully developed in Europe. These included self-determination and democracy promotion abroad, which had never really been part of the European world order. And it was now in a stronger position than ever before to champion these principles.

Where the American world order was supposedly most distinct from the European world order was in its discarding of the balance of power system, by which states would form coalitions to prevent any one state from becoming hegemonic. It continues to rely on this mechanism to this day, much more so than any genuine multilateral cooperation. The Americans claimed to be more idealistic than the Europeans, believing in a collective security system anchored in multilateral institutions formed at America's behest. While Europe had ruled the world more directly through colonialism, occupation, and empire, the United States, at least in principle, managed global affairs indirectly through multilateral institutions. These institutions were created and maintained by the United States to serve its own purposes, but, as a liberal power, the United States argued that what was in its interest was also in the interest of the world—a view captured by the Western liberal doctrine of "harmony of interest." In reality, this was and remains a self-serving notion, used by the United States and its Western allies to legitimize their dominance of a world order that was designed to benefit them more than other nations.

The American world order did offer some significant benefits to the world. American scholar John Ikenberry, one of the leading supporters of this world order, claims that these benefits included "security provision, maintenance of economic openness and stability, and support for the rules and institutions that formed the order."[50] In September 2010, then US secretary of state Hillary Clinton emphatically and eloquently described the achievements of the American world order: "After the Second World War, the nation that had built the transcontinental railroad, the assembly line and the skyscraper turned its attention to constructing the pillars of global cooperation. The third World War that so many feared never came. And many millions of people were lifted out of poverty and exercised their human rights for the first time. Those were the benefits of a global architecture forged over many years by American leaders from both political parties."[51]

Clinton's remarks are typical of how the defenders of the American world order present their case. They point to the record of economic growth, poverty reduction, and global cooperation achieved under the US-dominated world order. Some economic data bears out her claim. Rough estimates by the World Bank show that extreme global poverty fell 20 percent between 1950 and 1990.[52] A good part of the reason for this is the increasing economic openness of the period, measured by the growth in world trade, which grew forty-five times between 1950 and 2022.[53] This was made possible largely due to measures under the auspices of the General Agreement on Tariffs and Trade (GATT), whose creation was led by the United States, although non-Western nations had also played their part. Established in 1947, it became the World Trade Organization (WTO) in 1995.

But the liberal international order had its limitations and dark sides that are seldom acknowledged by its most notable proponents, such as Clinton and Kissinger. They and others do not mention that the liberal international order was founded upon racism, slavery, and the colonization of Native American land. And they distort the picture when it comes to its main beneficiaries. It was and remains, primarily the West.

Proponents of the American world order argue that, while serving American interests, it also served the interests of the rest of the world.[54] In their view, the postcolonial countries were among its major beneficiaries. The bigger economies and powers of the non-Western world—such as China, India, Brazil, and South Africa—have benefited so much from the US-led order that they would want to keep it going.

There is much truth to this, but it is also overstated. This narrative does not give due credit to the policies of other nations, especially the newly independent countries in maintaining stability, promoting economic development, and providing mechanisms for freedom and justice around the world. But looking into this, one's assessment of the contributions of the American world order should take into consideration who the main beneficiaries were. American participation was key to the defeat of imperial Germany in World War I, making America the savior of Europe. This had some positive effects on the world at large, since the end of the war did break up the largest non-Western imperial power, the Ottoman Empire. But it did not produce the end of European imperialism over non-Western societies, at least not immediately. The US entry into World War II led to the defeat of Nazi Germany, Fascist Italy, and imperial Japan. This was of far greater benefit to non-Western societies, since it facilitated the final retreat of European colonialism. And for the world at large, including the nations of the global South, the system of multilateral institutions the United States promoted was surely a more benign alternative to Europe's imperialism-based world order.

But this world order still left plenty of room for US and Western dominance. The most significant element of the post–World War II American world order was the founding of the United Nations. In a way, the UN was a capstone to the creation of international institutions during the war years; aside from the GATT, it included the International Monetary Fund (IMF) and the World Bank, both with their headquarters in Washington, DC. The United States also developed the WTO. But these institutions were and to some degree remain dominated by the United States and its Western allies. And somewhat contrary to the aspiration for universal collective security, the United States also developed a more parochial system of collective defense, which was limited to alliances with ideologically like-minded countries. This included NATO and, with less teeth, the Central Treaty Organization (CENTO) in the Middle East and the Southeast Asia Treaty Organization (SEATO) in Asia. These are apart from the bilateral alliances the United States developed. The most important among these, surviving the demise of CENTO and SEATO, is NATO, which quickly became the chief instrument of American global security policy after being founded in 1949. NATO is little different in purpose from Europe's alliances, like the Holy Alliance or the Triple Alliance. Targeting America's adversaries like Russia and, increasingly, China, NATO is far from being a multilateral organization meant to develop cooperation over "all mankind," like the United Nations, or even like the Concert of Europe, where all great powers, friend or enemies, met to resolve their differences.

The truth is that the liberal international order has never been genuinely universal or benign to "all of mankind," as Kissinger claimed. As already noted, the American world order functioned as a very selective privileged group of Western nations and their most ardent followers, rather than as an inclusive, global order. Although the collapse of the USSR and the Warsaw Pact and reforms in China and India might have expanded the reach of the liberal international order, its narrow historical base meant these newcomers lacked a sense of ownership. This point was made first by me in my 2014 book *The End of American World Order*, published at the time when the American world order still seemed alive and well to most Western leaders and analysts. In this book I pointed to a "myth" about the American world order, which was about how far it extended and who its main beneficiaries were. I wrote: "The answer is obvious: only a small part of the world was influenced by this concept. The Soviet Bloc, China, India, Indonesia, and a good part of the 'third world' were outside of it. Despite the exalted claims about its power, legitimacy, and public good functions, that order was little more than the US-UK-West Europe-Australasian configuration."[55]

Even Joseph S. Nye, a key defender of American leadership in world-order building, conceded my point when he wrote in a review of my 2014 book that the "American world order did provide shared goods, such as security and prosperity for part of the world, but these were club goods, rather than global public goods. For many non-members of this club such as India, China, Indonesia, Congo, Iran, Guatemala and Chile, among others, the measures taken [by the United States] to provide security and prosperity for the members of the club did not look so benign."[56]

Defenders of the American world order have also given the United States too much credit for the economic growth and development of co-operation after World War II. While the period under US dominance did produce much economic growth, linked to the rise in world trade, this cannot be credited to US leadership and generosity, nor can the role of other nations, including postcolonial ones, be left out of the picture. These postcolonial nations, collectively labeled as the Third World, of course were a varied lot. But there were many who, against heavy odds, did a fair job of advancing themselves and contributing to global cooperation. Those who did well relied on their own leadership. Tiny Singapore steadily became a developed nation, thanks mainly to the leadership of its prime minister Lee Kuan Yew, while another key US ally, the Philippines, failed to do so under its president Ferdinand Marcos. One can also find examples among much bigger nations, especially China and India. After the founding of the US-led liberal international order, China and India not only remained outside of the US system of friends and allies but also faced outright hostility from the United States. They did not grow as rapidly as Singapore or Japan in the beginning, and they faced domestic crises and war, but China and India were nonetheless able to lay the foundation of an educational and industrial system well before the Cold War ended. To credit the postwar economic development to US leadership is to negate how nations were able to make the best of their limited opportunities to advance economically.

The same goes for global cooperation. The United Nations of the 1942–1945 era had a far larger constituency than the US-centric narrative would imply. Scores of diplomats and soldiers from Latin America, Asia, Africa, and the Middle East were already playing and would continue to play an active role in building global cooperation, both through the UN and in their own regions. Among these were Asian and other non-Western contributions to the founding structures of the UN and to work on issues ranging from war-crimes policy to the status of women. Moreover, US support for international cooperation, or multilateralism, which is supposed to be the most distinctive feature of the American world order, has been inconsistent and selective. It expanded and contracted throughout the post–World War II period, reaching new heights during the John F. Kennedy, Bill Clinton, and Barack Obama presidencies but reversing during the Ronald Reagan and George W. Bush years. The United States' refusal to ratify the Law of the Sea treaty and the International Criminal Court and its lukewarm support for UN Security Council reform are notable examples of the limits of American support for multilateralism. Donald Trump's attacks on multilateral organizations during the 2016 presidential election campaign had a part in increasing his popular support; he called out these bodies for giving the United States a "bad deal." He preferred to deal with countries on a bilateral basis, where the United States could have greater leverage.

In sum, while the United States did provide initial leadership, cooperation among nations was not entirely made in America. Non-US allies—India, China, and Latin American nations that have a congenital dislike for US dominance—were deeply involved in developing the global and regional cooperation that created conditions for peace and development around the world. As the US leadership in multilateralism became more selective, these nations stepped in.

Back in Washington, American dominance of the world often bred arrogance and unilateralism, even in administrations ostensibly committed to liberal internationalism. Commenting on US policy toward Iraq in February 1998, Madeleine Albright, the secretary of state under the supposedly multilateral Clinton presidency, noted: "If we have to use force, it is because we are America; we are the indispensable nation. We stand tall and we see further than other countries into the future, and we see the danger here to all of us."[57]

Moreover, the liberal international order was not always peaceful or generous toward its nonmembers or those who enjoyed secondary status. The club promoted its ideology and presumed values—such as capitalism, human rights, and democracy—but it deployed violence, sanctions, coercion, and force, especially against those who took a different ideological path. This undercuts the argument that the American world order enjoyed "the [voluntary] acquiescence and support of other states," especially when the United States tried to bring non-Western countries under its influence.[58] Such American efforts often took the form of interventions, political and military, which produced much violence. Some examples of this include: the overthrow of democratic governments in Iran (1953) and Chile (1973), military interventions against revolutionary governments in Cuba (1961) and North Vietnam (1955–1975), and a pattern of interventions in Latin American and the Caribbean, including in Grenada (1983), Nicaragua (1981–1990), Panama (1989), Guatemala (1954), the Dominican Republic (1965), El Salvador (1981–1992), and Haiti (2004).

This leads to the claim about the American world order's overall stability or peacefulness. Like Pax Romana or Pax Britannica, Pax Americana was an illusory pax, one that was "frightful in its wars" and "even in peace full of horrors," to borrow Tacitus's phrase. To be sure, World War III did not happen. But this was due largely to nuclear deterrence between the United States and the Soviet Union, where the latter, as America's chief adversary, played a key role. Moreover, the "peace" of the American world order accrued mostly to Europe. In the postcolonial countries, the situation was starkly the opposite; they were rife with war and violence. Evan Luard, a British politician and international relations expert, estimated that, out of the 127 "significant wars" that took place in the world between 1945 and 1986, only two occurred in Europe. In other words, the Third World accounted for more than 98 percent of all international conflicts.[59] What is more, these conflicts were often stoked by interventions from outside powers. The United States and the Soviet Union, afraid to engage each other in Europe due to fear of nuclear war, saw fighting proxy wars outside of Europe as permissible. As the India-born scholar Mohammed Ayoob puts it, the two Cold War powers used conflicts in the Third World as "safety valves" to release the tensions of their ideological and strategic rivalry.[60]

Last but not the least, the American world order, despite its supposed liberal values, has been indifferent or even opposed to decolonization. Despite its advocacy of democracy, it supported authoritarian regimes in Pakistan, South Korea, Thailand, Taiwan, Indonesia, Turkey, the Philippines, and other parts of the world. It promoted the exploitation of resources and cheap labor throughout the Third World, especially regarding oil in the Middle East. It opposed regional cooperation in Asia in favor of bilateral arrangements. It was downright hostile to the Nonaligned Movement of Third World nations. Nor did it do a stellar job of preventing and managing violence in the Third World during the Cold War.

The End of American World Order

The American world order reached its climax with the end of the Cold War and the collapse of the Soviet bloc. These momentous events caused Western euphoria and raised expectations that the American-led order would continue indefinitely. Some of its more optimistic proponents argued that the order was so deep-rooted, legitimate, and benign that it might even co-opt its biggest potential challenger, China. It was, as Francis Fukuyama called it, "the end of history." The liberal international order had triumphed so completely that no alternative to it would ever be deemed feasible again.

But in a matter of just two decades or so, that kind of cosmic optimism would be replaced by an almost diametrically opposite conviction, namely that the American-led world order was in decline and would inevitably be replaced by something else. Even at the time of Fukuyama's end-of-history essay, published in 1989, there were already powerful challenges to American supremacy. In 1979, the pro-American shah of Iran was overthrown in a popular uprising and replaced by a theocratic regime that showed little inclination to join the liberal order. For a few years, both Russia and China seemed to be adopting Western ways: Russia replaced communism with what seemed, at least in theory, to be a democracy, with elections and a free press. China moved toward jettisoning state planning and establishing a mostly free-market system. But, contrary to many predictions at the time, both countries turned away from the liberal model and explicitly declared their rivalry with the United States. Then came the terrorist attacks of September 11, 2001, which led to two unsuccessful wars of choice by the United States, in Iraq and Afghanistan. Simultaneously, China became the world's second largest economy and embarked on an ambitious plan of military modernization, aimed at challenging American dominance in the western Pacific. China's one-party rule and its own vision of world order became a competitor to the liberal international order, a fact acknowledged and promoted by both Chinese and the Western analysts.

What does all this mean? In recent years, as the euphoria and optimism of the immediate post–Cold War period has waned, there has been plenty of talk about the decline of the United States. This remains a matter of intense but inconclusive debate, with many pundits and policymakers vigorously contesting the idea of decline.

The debate comes primarily in three varieties, which may be summarized as "crying wolf" syndrome, the "bionic man" argument, and the "Roman Empire" analogy. The crying wolf argument pits those who dismiss the notion of decline because they've heard it all before against those who think that this time the wolf has indeed arrived. The bionic man argument is between those who say the US economy, and hence the country's influence, will recover soon versus those who say that won't matter because the decline is relative and American competitors will do better and catch up faster.

The Roman Empire analogy has been put forward by Joseph Nye, a leading figure in the anti-declinist camp. He argues that the decline of the United States will be like that of the Roman Empire and take a long time, perhaps more than two centuries.[61] The counterargument is this: with the partial exception of Parthia, the Roman Empire did not have any real state competitors. It fell, as Nye correctly points out, to the barbarians through a thousand small cuts, rather than from the rise of a mighty peer—at least until the eastern empire in Constantinople found a rival in the Ottoman Turks and was defeated. Unlike the Roman Empire, the reigning but weakening hegemon today faces some serious challengers, not least China. Its fall may not follow the long Roman example but take place much more quicky—perhaps more like the decline of the British Empire in the twentieth century.

There are other arguments against the decline thesis: that the growing wealth of the emerging countries will not necessarily translate into power or influence; that these powers each have their own economic, military, and political shortcomings; and that the United States still enjoys many fundamental domestic and external strengths, such as its universities, its lead in science and innovation, its openness to immigration, and its alliances around the world. These are all valid arguments, but each of them can be challenged. Put together, they do not seem to warrant the confidence of President Obama's 2012 State of the Union address, where he said, "Anyone who tells you that America is in decline or that our influence has waned doesn't know what they're talking about."[62]

In fact, American economic dominance has been declining since World War II. In 1944–1945, the United States was the largest economy in the world. Estimates of its share of global GDP vary between 35 and 50 percent.[63] Since then, the US share of global GDP has declined, to 32.1 percent by 2001 and 22.3 percent by 2014. China's share grew from 4 percent in 2001 to 13.4 percent in 2014. In 2001, the GDP of the United States was eight times that of China, whereas by 2015, it was only 1.6 times.[64] While China is the main challenger to US economic dominance, other countries such as India and Indonesia are rising as well, contributing to the global shift in economic power.

But my argument is not that the United States will collapse and fall like the Roman Empire did. According to current projections combining different elements of power and influence—economic, military, technological, and cultural, which includes the impact of everything from films to fast food—the United States will likely remain a global superpower, perhaps the only superpower in the world for some time. But this is not comparable to the magnitude of the global hegemony that the United States enjoyed for some time in the aftermath of World War II. The major point here is that even if the United States remains the overall top global power, the world order it built around its vision and values, and above all its leadership of the organizations of global cooperation, will not survive deep into the twenty-first century. That order, whatever one calls it—liberal international order or American world order—is fading rapidly and it is not going to reappear, even if the US economy remains strong and the economic growth of the emerging powers slows down from the pace of recent decades.

The American world order is the last of the Western world orders. The key question for the world, then, is what replaces it. But before discussing answers to this question, one must look at one of the key drivers of any new world order: the return and rise of the Rest.

Chapter 13

The Return of the Rest

On April 18, 1955, Sukarno, the president of Indonesia, opened what he described as "the first intercontinental Conference of coloured peoples in the history of mankind!"[1] At the meeting, in the West Java city of Bandung, were representatives of twenty-nine nations of Asia and Africa. Many of the participants, including host Indonesia, were recently liberated from colonial rule, such as India, Pakistan, Celyon (now Sri Lanka), Burma (now Myanmar), and the Philippines. There were also those who had gained independence a little earlier, such as Saudi Arabia and Iraq (both in 1930s), and nations that had managed to stave off formal colonial rule, including the Ethiopian Empire, the Imperial State of Iran, and the Kingdom of Thailand. The larger nations of the Middle East—Egypt and Turkey—were represented, as was China. This was its first international conference under Communist rule where its then close ally, the Soviet Union, was not present. For Japan, this was its first conference with fellow Asian nations after the fall of its empire in 1945.

To be sure, there had been gatherings against imperialism and racism before, notably the League Against Imperialism and Colonial Oppression, held in Brussels in 1927, and the two Asian Relations Conferences in New Delhi in 1947 and 1949, with the latter focused specifically on Indonesian independence from the Dutch. There had also been the Pan-African Congresses, attended by delegates (mostly but not entirely

Image 14. An informal chat at the Bandung Conference, 1955. In the photo are Indonesia's prime minister Ali Sastroamidjojo, Egypt's president Gamal Abdel Nasser, Indian prime minister Jawaharlal Nehru, Burma's prime minister U Nu, former grand mufti (Islamic jurist) of Jerusalem Amin al-Husseini (attending as an observer), and Indira Gandhi, Nehru's daughter and future Indian prime minister.

Black) from the United States, the Caribbean, Africa, and Europe, as well as a few from Asia. But Bandung was the first intercontinental gathering of non-Western nations held in the territory of one of them. The Bandung Conference, Sukarno said, was attended by participants who "are colonies no more." He added, "Now we are free, sovereign and independent. We do not need to go to other continents to confer."[2]

Faced with such a display of political purpose, the Western powers, led by Britian and the United States, did their best to prevent the conference from being held in the first place and, failing that, to frustrate its political goals. People said that more Western or Western-recruited observers and spies than legitimate official delegates descended on the town during the five days of meetings. The sheer volume of declassified intelligence reports from the United Kingdom, United States, Australia, and Canada I have collected bears out this observation. And these reports are revealing. The British described Bandung as a "mischievous" effort to stir up all the "problems affecting national sovereignty, racialism, and colonialism, on all of which the conclusions reached are likely to be embarrassing to us."[3] The British, who still controlled the foreign relations of Ghana, prevented its leader, Kwame Nkrumah, from attending. South Africa's African National Congress, muzzled by the white apartheid regime, sent two observers. The United States worried that the conference might divert attention from the threat to world peace posed by communist nations such as China and "place the blame for present world tensions on the policies of the United States."[4] Not surprisingly, nations attending the Bandung Conference were subjected to a concerted US-British pressure campaign to support Western objectives, such as downgrading decolonization and denying any support to Communist China.

British and American memos of the period show that the British, with US approval, advised leaders of "friendly" countries such as Ceylon, the Philippines, and Turkey to raise the issue of "communist colonialism" and the absence of religious freedom in the communist world and to reject the Five Principles of Peaceful Coexistence promoted by India and China. A secret telegram sent by the British Foreign Office to governments of friendly nations attending Bandung instructed them to "resist proposals…for extensions of sovereignty," meaning demands for political independence and control over natural resources.[5] Another such memo urged US-UK allies at the conference to cause "maximum embarrassment" to China.[6]

But these efforts largely failed, as official reports from British and American governments would show. The US State Department, then led by the staunchly anti-Bandung John Foster Dulles, wrote an intelligence assessment of the outcome of the conference with the following words: "The nations assembled at Bandung, without little prior experience in running large international conferences and with only decades or less of independent participation in world politics, managed to organize a meeting which rejected the discipline of any of the Conference's five sponsoring powers, yet found its way to common ground with efficiency and dispatch. The Conference succeeded in demonstrating that there is an Asian-African consensus."[7]

In a more patronizing tone, a British diplomat wrote: "The East is no longer age-old, inscrutable, unchanging. It is young, eager, drunk with new nationalism and freedom, but also desperately anxious to behave with maturity and make a good showing before its elders if not betters."[8]

The British conceded that the conference "strengthened the self-confidence" of the participating nations, "gave them a greater sense of their importance in world's affairs," and encouraged them to "evolve policies of their own." An Afro-Asian "common purpose" had been "strengthened," leading to a corresponding "weakening of Western leadership."[9]

The Bandung Conference was not just geared toward ending colonialism and racism and giving a voice to non-Western nations in world affairs; it also provided the first powerful sign of an emerging alternative to the Western-dominated world order, one that rejected superpower dominance, Western or Soviet, and stressed universal human rights and collective security. Above all, Bandung was the first expression of what journalist Fareed Zakaria would later call "the rise of the Rest," one of the most important, if unrecognized, phenomena of the post–World War II world.[10]

Anti-colonialism and the rise to independence of numerous former colonies—along with China's assertion of full sovereignty after a hundred years of foreign control of its treaty ports—was one of the major developments of the postwar world and a leading force trending toward a new world order. Often this historic development, affecting hundreds of millions of people, is attributed to a kind of generosity on the part of the West, where the emergence of newly independent states has been portrayed as the end of a process of tutelage by which the colonialist powers deemed their colonies prepared for self-government. What's missing from this picture, and what will be developed in this chapter, is the other side of the story of the rise of the Rest, which, in the same way as the Bandung Conference, came about not because of Western beneficence but despite it, via a global revolution engineered and executed by the colonized peoples themselves.

This was achieved through both peaceful means and armed struggle. For example, India's anti-colonial struggle was peaceful and violent, represented on the one hand by Mohandas Gandhi and on the other by Bhagat Singh in Punjab, Sri Aurobindo in Bengal, and Subhas Chandra Bose from Odisha and Bengal. The latter even advocated cooperation with Germany and Japan in World War II to further the cause of India's independence.[11] But armed resistance failed spectacularly in India in 1857 in what the British call the "sepoy mutiny" (sepoy being Indian troops in the service of the British), but what Indians recognize as a war of independence, one whose goal was to restore the authority of the Moghul ruler.

Anti-colonial campaigns in Africa ranged from boycotts of colonial products to armed revolution. But militant rejection of colonial rule emerged in all corners of the continent: Ghana, Nigeria, Senegal, Ivory Coast, Benin, Guinea-Bissau, Angola, Libya, Algeria, Tunisia, Morocco, Kenya, Tanzania, Egypt, Sudan, and Somaliland. Even in Francophone Africa—where people of the colonies were nominally accepted as part of French civilization, and a policy of formal assimilation into the French nation was pursued—people violently rejected colonial rule, Algeria being the most prominent example. In Southeast Asia, Indonesia, Vietnam, and Burma pursued armed struggles against their colonial masters, while the Federation of Malaya (which included Singapore) negotiated its independence from the British.

Armed struggle was not always decisive in decolonization. Ethiopia provided a rare example of defeating a colonial power—Italy in 1896— only to see colonization return again under Benito Mussolini, who vengefully occupied the country from 1935 to 1936. Later, the revolutionary organization Viet Minh secured the liberation of Vietnam from French rule, mostly through military success. But for the most part, the retreat of European colonialism was achieved through political means, as the product of a global resistance movement galvanized by key historic figures such as Sukarno, Gandhi, and Nkrumah, as well as Jomo Kenyatta of Kenya, Aung San of Burma, Julius Nyerere of Tanzania, and Nelson Mandela of South Africa. These leaders may have disagreed about the methods to be used and the types of government that should emerge in the former colonies, but they agreed on the critical point: colonialism, the singular driver of Western global dominance, must end.

Westphalia Goes Global

The modern world order was shaped by European power and ideas; it was a force for modernity, but it also came with dark features, such as racism, that were inherited and expanded by the United States. But while this was happening, rudiments of resistance were emerging from the colonized world. Conventional thinking holds that the postcolonial nations merely inherited Western ideals and institutions, such as nationalism, the nation-state, and other elements of Westphalian sovereignty. In fact, the nations that came into being in the process of decolonization have been dynamic actors challenging the Western-dominated world order and developing ideas and approaches to build an inclusive one. Even when they have adopted institutions from the West, including Westphalian sovereignty, they have modified them with their own homegrown ideas, interests, and agendas. Indeed, resistance to Western colonialism generated ideas that have produced a more inclusive world order, challenging Western efforts to secure dominance.

A nation-state is an entity with sovereignty over a clearly defined territory whose citizens are expected to have a shared identity based on history, culture, and language, among other factors. A state is sovereign because its citizens owe allegiance to no higher authority than that state. In a nation-state, territorial boundaries, political organization, and cultural identity are supposed to coincide, though in reality this is very rare. A common belief among Europeans is that their nation-states are authentic expressions of national identity, but the truth is that all nation-states, inside and outside Europe, are artificial creations of territorial adjustments imposed by empires. It is a false claim that only the European nations are authentic while the rest are contrived and imposed.

This misperception lies in the very word "nation," with its roots in the Latin words *natio* (birth), *nasci* (to be born), and *nationem* (origin). As with many such words originating from ancient Greece or Rome, it was adapted into medieval European languages, becoming *nacion* in Old French and *nacioun* in Middle English.[12] Not surprisingly, modern scholarship regards the idea of *nation* as a French or European invention, which Europeans then taught to their colonies around the world, who were until then a disjointed bunch with no sense of unity or identity before the European arrival. According to this notion, the people of the colonies "learnt their notions of nation, self-determination, human rights, and development from their colonial masters, applying the ideas to their own situation, and turning them against their rulers." It was colonial rule itself, this theory insists, that was "the *only* basis for a national culture" (emphasis added). The new states came about because of national borders drawn up by the colonial powers; they didn't reflect some intrinsic national identity.[13] Moreover, the nation-states that emerged after the era of European colonization consisted of "several ethnic groups, each with its own culture, language, history, and of different religious beliefs."[14]

But this explanation misses several points, among them the cultural linkages and identities that existed before European colonialism. It fails to take into account that the sense of shared cultural identity that underpins the territorial and political space of current nation-states derives largely from earlier historical interactions. It ignores countries like Japan, Thailand, and Turkey, which escaped colonial rule but still managed to earn the label of nation-states. And what about China, which was not directly colonized? One might say these states simply looked around and copied the amazing Europeans. But this would be an utterly simplistic view. Nowhere in the world was the process of nation formation unrelated to earlier interactions and identities. China, India, and Japan were all formed after millennia of cultural interactions. Similarly, Korea's sense of cultural unity, and hence its sense of nationhood, was forged through its own cultural and political norms as well as interactions— both pacific and coercive, involving both resistance and adaptation— with its non-Western neighbors, China and Japan.[15]

Similarly, the view that there was no India (also called by its Sanskrit name Bharat in the Indian constitution) before the British Raj is nonsense. It ignores the political, cultural, and economic interactions that existed for millennia, forged through migrations within the subcontinent; the diffusion of religions such as Hinduism, Buddhism, and Jainism; and the political and administrative centralization achieved by empires like those of the Maurya, the Gupta, and the Moghuls. Plenty of ancient literature, including the epics of the *Mahabharata* and *Ramayana*, attest to the idea of India. The Maurya Empire in the third century BC covered much of the same areas—east, west, north, south—that the British Raj "unified" and more than the Republic of India today, thanks to the hasty and genocidal partition of India by the Raj in its dying days.

As noted in Chapter 12, a very fashionable Western explanation of the end of colonialism stresses "the power of an idea: namely that of self-determination," which spread on the back of another powerful idea: nationalism.[16] But why and how nationalism or anti-colonial resistance emerged in the non-Western world is a topic of hot debate. A common answer to this question in the West is that the colonies, or at least their elites, learned of nationalism from their European masters. Many future leaders from these colonies went to Europe for their studies and got exposed to the rising currents of nationalism there. In this view, self-determination, like anti-slavery and anti-racism, was an exemplary contribution of Western civilization. As one scholar has put it, "For protesting colonists, the ideas were nationalism and equality, which they translated into the demand for political independence, Westphalian statehood, for their colony." It was through their absorption of ideas learned in the West that "a small stratum of educated, elite Africans, Asians, and Latin Americans came to desire this statehood."[17]

But this is a rather narrow and Eurocentric view and a huge simplification. Nationalism was not a matter of imitation by local elites, especially those who were educated in the West. Modern nationalism did emerge in Europe, nurtured by the notion of sovereign boundaries imposed by Westphalian principles. One facet of this was the idea that people living within clearly defined boundaries could better organize politically and develop a sense of common identity. The rise of print media within the countries of the Westphalian system also facilitated a sharing of culture and experiences. Political scientist Benedict Anderson has called this the building of "imagined communities."[18] Outside of Europe, however, there were no Westphalian states. Instead, European powers created centralized bureaucracies to govern their conquered territories. Some of them, such as the Dutch in Indonesia, created a national language. This and the arrival of print media in the colonies did play a major role in bringing people of varied ethnic groups and regions together, allowing them to know each other better and develop a sense of common identity.

But this is a one-sided view that obscures the true origins of nationalism in the colonies. Nationalism in the colonies was not a European idea that had to be "taught" to the colonized. Rather, it was born out of revolutionary movements, many of which were led by local leaders and joined by ordinary people. The colonizers' attempts to be more effective in controlling their subjects, more capricious in exploiting their resources, and more brutal in suppressing their rebellions nurtured the growth of national identities among the colonial subjects. For every colonial elite who attended school at Oxford, Cambridge, or the Sorbonne, there were thousands who could not or did not want to. They stayed at home, living the inhumanity of colonial rule most directly. Many never even attended local schools built by colonial powers or joined colonial bureaucracies.

One such person, a fictional one, is Nyai (honorific for an elderly woman or grandmother) Ontosoroh. She is a character in Indonesian writer Pramoedya Ananta Toer's classic novel *This Earth of Mankind*, which astutely reflects the conditions in Java and other parts of what is now Indonesia under Dutch colonial rule. In the story, a Dutch colonial court annuls the marriage of Nyai Ontosoroh's daughter because she was born out of wedlock, her father a Dutchman who had gone missing. Hearing the news of annulment, Nyai Ontosoroh berates her son-in-law, Minke, the main character of the novel, who was educated in the colonial system and worked as a journalist. Her words challenge the fashionable Western view that nation and nationalism emerged in the colonies only because the Western-educated elite learned them from Europe. "I have never been to school," Nyai says. "I have never been taught to admire Europeans.... Those who have been to school are still more fortunate.

At the very least you get to know other races who have their own ways of thieving the property of other peoples."[19]

In short, the European ideas of nationalism and self-determination may have helped to inspire anti-colonial resistance, but in the colonies themselves nationalism arose fundamentally as resistance to foreign rule and dominance. Its substance and content were overwhelmingly local. Behind every José Rizal (the Filipino nationalist who studied in Spain), Jawaharlal Nehru (Cambridge educated), or Sukarno (educated in a Dutch-established engineering college), there were masses of people like Minke's illiterate mother-in-law. Their nationalism was not "imagined" through reading colonial-language books or newspapers but was born out of their real-world experiences, their everyday life of misery and marginalization. The foreign-educated leaders exploited and expanded this nationalism but did not create it. As is the case for the origins of other elements of world order—from humanitarian ethics to free trade— Eurocentrism has obscured aspects of our history and blinded us to the contributions of non-Western people.

Roots of Anti-colonial Movements

There's truth to the often repeated statement that anti-colonialism was built into Western liberalism—and some important Western intellectuals and political figures were fervently anti-colonialist, just as some of their forebears were anti-slavery—but it would be a mistake to say that the notions of nationalism and freedom that spread across the globe in the wake of World War II were mostly the result of Western ideas. In fact, the seeds of a new world order as imagined by anti-colonial leaders grew out of their own societies and civilizations. Nationalism and freedom would not have spread across the world without being mediated by the culture and identity of non-Western societies. The civilizations of the Rest played a critical role.

Anti-colonial leaders in Asia, Africa, and the Middle East invoked their civilizational past, not in any reactionary way but to mobilize their people to confront and overthrow Western imperialism. To be sure, this was not their only weapon. They also relied on modern ideas, including sovereignty, self-determination, and human rights. But there's no question that they looked into their own pasts to replace the racist Western standard of civilization. In building new institutions for domestic governance and foreign policy, they often blended modern principles with their preexisting cultural ideas and practices, both in symbol and substance. This can be seen in the case of India, China, and Turkey, to give examples from three major civilizations.

India's nationalist leaders who fought for independence from Britain used the country's ancient civilization to make the case for national liberation. In 1938, for example, seven years before becoming independent India's first prime minister, Jawaharlal Nehru wrote an article in *Foreign Affairs* aimed at assuaging doubts in both Britain and the United States about whether an independent India would be able to stand on its own feet. "Five to six thousand years ago," Nehru wrote, "the Indus Valley civilization flourished all over northern India and probably extended to the south also.... Since that early dawn of history innumerable peoples, conquerors and settlers, pilgrims and students, have trekked into the Indian plains from the highlands of Asia and have influenced Indian life and culture and art; but always they have been absorbed and assimilated. India was changed by these contacts and yet she remained essentially her own old self."[20]

Independent India, which adopted a Westminster-style parliamentary system, called the two houses of its national parliament Rajya Sabha (upper house) and Lok Sabha (lower house), while the unicameral state legislatures were named Vidhan Sabha. The sabha, or assembly, was an important political institution of Vedic India. Though the government of that time was not a popular democracy, it allowed a wide representation of people in the sabha, including on a nonhereditary basis. Along with *samiti*, another Vedic institution, the sabha sometimes elected the king, who had to defer to these institutions for major matters of state or risk isolation or overthrow.[21] This shows that, while India's modern democratic institutions were influenced by the West, they also drew inspiration from India's classical past. This connection helped make them more appealing to the people of India and may explain why they have proved more durable than in other nations.

China's nationalists—led by Sun Yat-sen, who helped to overthrow his country's imperial system—invoked China's, and indeed Asia's, civilizational past. As Sun put it, "While materially the Orient is far behind the Occident, morally the Orient is superior to the Occident." He contrasted Chinese and Eastern civilization with that of the West: "Oriental civilization is the rule of Right; Occidental civilization is the rule of Might. The rule of Right respects benevolence and virtue, while the rule of Might only respects force and utilitarianism. The rule of Right always influences people with justice and reason, while the rule of Might always oppresses people with brute force and military measures."[22]

Turkey emerged from Ottoman rule with the most secular orientation among Islamic societies. Instead of returning to Islam, Mustafa Kemal Atatürk, founder of modern Turkey who held power from 1923 to 1938, played on Turkey's pre-Islamic multicultural and multicivilizational pasts—including the Hittite, Phrygian, Lydian, and other cultures—as the basis of a new Turkish domestic and foreign policy. Other examples of how civilizational pasts shaped the postcolonial nations' view of world order can be found in regional movements such as Pan-Asianism, Pan-Americanism, Pan-Africanism, and Pan-Arabism. These campaigns had one thing in common: even as political movements, all were based on, or at least tried to construct, a shared civilizational identity. They recognized the limitations and the dark sides of the Western civilization and its idea of modernity.

Take Latin America for example. Latin America is usually regarded as an offshoot of European civilization. But nationalist leaders there recognized and rejected European racism and imperialism no less than their Asian or African counterparts. "The civilization of what is called Latin America," Francisco Javier Yanes, a former secretary-general of the Pan-American Union, wrote in 1914, "began with the first Spanish settlement, the first Indian blood shed by the greed of the white conqueror, and the first attempt to Christianize the inhabitants of the new-found land."[23] At the very least, Latin American elites, partly influenced by the hybrid culture that was shaped by intermarriages between the European settlers and pre-Columbian peoples, were divided between those who saw themselves as children of Europe and those who reject or even denounce their European heritage. But overall, instead of imitating European culture, in the manner of Australians or Canadians, Latin America as a whole developed its own civilizational identity. This identity was initially born out of a struggle to liberate the region from European (mainly Spanish) rule, and then to reject any attempt by European powers to retake the region.[24] Among its first proponents was Simón Bolívar, who dreamed of a union of Latin American states. Although unfulfilled, this ambition was the foundation of Latin American civilizational solidarity.[25] Over the nineteenth century, there emerged a Pan-American movement, challenging not European meddling but US dominance and interventionism, as espoused by the Monroe Doctrine. In 1890, the First International Conference of American States further expressed the Pan-American ideal.

Moreover, a few prominent leaders and intellectuals in the region called for closer integration with pre-Columbian civilizations. These included Víctor Raúl Haya de la Torre (1895–1979) and José Carlos Mariátegui (1894–1930), both from Peru. Haya sought an "Indoamerican" identity and regionalism that recognized the place of the marginalized indigenous people. He fought against what he saw as a subservience in the region to European ideas and institutions. Though a believer in Marxism, he did not accept it as a universal framework that would fit neatly into Latin America. Instead, the ideology had to be adapted to differing conditions. It "is imperative to recognize," Haya wrote, "that the global and simplistic application to our environment of European doctrines and norms of interpretation should be subject to profound modifications."[26]

Pan-Asianism came somewhat later, in the early twentieth century. One early strand of it underpinned Japan's imperial ambitions, calling for Asian unity to fight Western supremacy but under Japan's leadership and dominance. In other words, Japan was fighting Western dominance to create space for its own. But another strand of Japanese Pan-Asianism was more emancipatory, and it was based on intra-Asian civilizational links, as exemplified by Japanese art critic Okakura Kakuzo. Okakura, who famously coined "Asia is one" at the beginning of the twentieth century, developed a strong personal bond with Indian poet Rabindranath Tagore, who himself was a staunch Pan-Asianist.

Asia's first generation of nationalist thinkers and leaders—including Sun Yat-sen, Jawaharlal Nehru, and Aung San—were among those who imagined Asia as a distinct civilization that could be united on the basis of historical links. They saw European imperialism as an outside force that had disrupted those historical links when they carved out different parts of Asia under their colonial empires: the British in India and its neighborhood, the French in Indochina, the Dutch in Indonesia, and the Spanish in the Philippines. But these disruptions, they believed, could now be repaired if not fully restored.

A good example of this could be found in 1947, when Nehru convened the first international conference of Asian countries after World War II in New Delhi in 1947.[27] For that Asian Relations Conference, he organized an "Inter-Asian Art Exhibition" that showcased historical links with Iran, central Asia, China, Burma, Malaya, Siam, Cambodia, Champa (southern Vietnam), and Java, Bali, and Sumatra (parts of contemporary Indonesia).[28]

In China, nationalist leader Sun Yat-sen championed Pan-Asian links, mostly as a strategy of political unity against the European powers that still dominated China. Activists and intellectuals also carried out Pan-Asian projects, such as those from China, Japan, India, Vietnam, and the Philippines who set up the Asian Solidarity Society in Tokyo in 1907 to advocate Pan-Asian unity and cooperation. They recognized José Rizal, executed by the Spanish in 1896 for his anti-colonial stance, as "the quintessential Asian patriot, from whom China and other Asians must learn."[29]

In the Arab world, Pan-Arabism and Pan-Islamism emerged as both political and civilizational concepts. Emerging in the nineteenth century, Pan-Islamism was initially directed at Ottoman rule as well as at European imperialism. A leading figure was Persia-born journalist and political activist Jamal al-Din al-Afghani (1838–1897).[30] Traveling in

India, Egypt, Turkey, London, and Paris, he promoted political ideas that would reconcile Islam with modernity in order to fight Western dominance. His thought would inspire and influence Islamic nationalists in the region, among them Pakistan's founder Muhammad Ali Jinnah.[31]

It may surprise people today, but Pan-Arabism was a mostly secular movement, especially at its birth. One of its early champions, Hussein ibn Ali, the emir of Mecca, downplayed its anti-Western aspects to secure British support against the Ottomans. Lebanese and Syrian intellectuals invoked Pan-Arabism to instigate an Arab revival, using the Arabic language as its secular basis. But both Pan-Arabism and Pan-Islamism rejected the Westphalian nation-state as the dominant political framework for organizing the Islamic world. Pan-Arabism became an international political force under Gamal Abdel Nasser, who served as Egypt's second president from 1954 to 1970 and was a dashing, dynamic figure at the Bandung Conference, his first international conference as Egypt's leader. Once regarded by the Americans as a potential ally, Nasser turned against the West, and pursued both Pan-Arabism and nonalignment.

The Caribbean and Africa also developed their own regional and transnational movements against Western imperialism on the basis of a shared identity. The First Pan-African Conference in London in 1900 combined the Black emancipation movements in the United States, the Caribbean, and other parts of the world and included non-Black delegates from Europe and Asia. Perhaps reflecting this, the Pan-African Conferences (there would be six of them between 1900 and 1945) were not just about promoting the liberation of Africa or Black people around the world. They also aimed to pursue larger causes of building a more just and equitable world order, including ending colonialism and racial discrimination. As W. E. B. Du Bois, the American Black activist who was one of the major voices at the 1900 London conference, put it, "Let the world take no backward step in that slow but sure progress which has successively refused to let the spirit of class, of caste, of privilege, or of birth, debar from life, liberty and the pursuit of happiness a striving human soul. Let no color or race be a feature of distinction between white and black men, regardless of worth or ability."[32]

Du Bois's famous formulation "The problem of the twentieth century is the problem of the color line" summed up the attitude of nationalist leaders around the colonized world.[33] Kwame Nkrumah of Ghana, whom the British had prevented from traveling to the Bandung Conference, became the first president of the first sub-Saharan African country to gain independence. He led the formulation of African ideas about world order, which he modeled after Bandung. These ideas called for rejection of Western dominance and sought African solutions to African problems. In April 1958, Nkrumah hosted the first Conference of Independent African States. Like the Bandung meeting, this association was geared toward not only discussing ways to secure independence from colonial rule but also developing norms of foreign policy conduct, aimed at addressing "the central problem of how to secure peace." As Nkrumah saw it, the conference was the first time that "free Africans were actually meeting together, *in Africa*, to examine and consider African affairs" (emphasis original).[34]

In short, nationalism and the visions of world order that emerged from the colonial world were not taught to them by the colonial powers, but were the result of their resistance to colonialism. Hence, they were not replicas of Western ideals but based on a recognition of the dark truths about the Western-organized world order. They carried a more progressive and universal vision, which took into account the contributions—past and present—of non-Western civilizations. These were the foundations for a world of their own making.

A World of Their Own Making

As they struggled for independence, the postcolonial nations were allowed limited representation and faced heavy odds in making a contribution to the post–World War II order led by the United States. Yet they managed to make themselves heard and laid the groundwork for an alternative, more just, and more inclusive framework of world order.

In the meetings held to draft the UN charter in San Francisco in 1945, the major demands of the postcolonial nations concerned bringing an end to colonialism and racism. But these demands were not allowed by the Western powers to take center stage. In the extensive, monthslong deliberations, there was no mention of "racial equality"—which had been a key point of contention at Versailles in 1919—nor was a link made between racial injustice and colonialism.[35] Gérard E. Lescot, the head of the Haitian delegation, was a rare voice at the San Francisco Conference to have explicitly demanded that racial nondiscrimination be given same weight as "sovereign equality." As for colonialism, it was scarcely discussed or debated, although it was a time when racial discrimination and colonial rule were still rife around the world. A key reason for the lack of focus on colonialism was Churchill: he had refused to allow the mention of colonialism in the Atlantic Charter—the 1941 document outlining the postwar goals of the victorious Allied powers, which was the primary basis of the deliberations leading to the San Francisco Conference.[36]

Why was this the case? Because colonialism, slavery, and racism were too foundational to the world order of the West to be broken at one international conference, no matter how important. To cut off the link to those elements of world order would have been a shameful reminder of an unholy past. Asian and African nations had little representation at the San Francisco Conference and occupied almost no leadership positions.

Instead, the key drafters of the UN charter were from the West, and some were colonialists or racists themselves. Moreover, the creation of the United Nations focused on the immediate context of World War II, including the atrocities committed by the Nazis in Europe, and that was the context for the discussion of human rights.[37] Of course, the Holocaust itself was an extreme form of racism, directed primarily against Jewish people but also targeting the European Roma (Gypsies), and it deserved to be highlighted. But there were countless atrocities claiming millions of lives in the colonies of the Western powers, nurtured by their deeply racist worldview. While promotion of human rights was a central concern of the San Francisco Conference, the conference's records do not acknowledge colonialism as violation of human rights.

While the Western countries were hesitant to confront racism and colonialism, the formerly colonized, newly independent states were not.

They got their best chance in 1955. There were twenty-nine Asian and African countries represented at Bandung that year, compared to the thirteen that were at the San Francisco Conference a decade earlier. Bandung was exclusively an Asian-African affair (including the Middle East), and from the beginning to the end it highlighted the intrinsic links between colonialism, human rights, and racism (which was officially called *racialism*, to capture its broader diplomatic, social, cultural, ideological, and personal dimensions). The conference's final communiqué agreed that "colonialism in all its manifestations is an evil which should speedily be brought to an end," and it affirmed that "the subjection of peoples to alien subjugation, domination and exploitation *constitutes a denial of fundamental human rights, is contrary to the Charter of the United Nations*" (emphasis added). It called for the "recognition of the equality of all races and of the equality of all nations large and small."[38] These exact words would be borrowed by the UN General Assembly in its declaration on colonialism in 1960.[39] With unequivocal statements like that, the Bandung Conference succeeded where the San Francisco Conference had failed.

But the Bandung Conference was not consumed only by negative energy; it offered a positive and forward-looking window into the postcolonial vision of world order: a world of their own making. That vision stressed not only decolonization and racial equality but also human rights, freedom from interference by the great powers (especially the United States and USSR), collective security under the UN rather than through membership in exclusionary military alliances, and comity among the world's civilizations. In fact, the nations that attended the Bandung Conference in 1955 gave more support to expanding the UN's membership than did the United States and United Kingdom, which were resisting decolonization.

This resistance came from British reluctance to suffer further losses of their colonial possessions and American anxiety about the Soviet Union using the newly independent countries to expand communism. The British and Americans had already set up SEATO in September 1954 and CENTO in February 1955, three months before the Bandung Conference. These alliances were not quite as robust as NATO, but they were perceived in the postcolonial world as a new form of Western dominance. Nehru's adviser V. K. Krishna Menon called them "return in a pact form to colonial rule," a comment that American political scientist Rupert Emerson thought reflected a general sentiment about Western military alliances in the postcolonial world.[40] Hence the surest sign of the Bandung Conference's impact in giving voice to postcolonial nations was that any hope for expanding SEATO "vanished" with Bandung, as a secret British assessment noted.[41] Instead, the Bandung Conference paved the way for the emergence of the Nonaligned Movement as an alternative to superpower-led military blocs.

Despite some quarrels engineered by the United States and Britain—especially between bloc members Turkey, the Philippines, and Pakistan on the one hand and "neutralists" (as nonaligned countries were called then) India, Indonesia, and Burma on the other—the conference gave concrete meaning to the idea of a Third World. This term had been coined by French scholar Alfred Sauvy in 1952, who derived it from the French Revolution idea of the "Third Estate," meaning a class of commoners distinct from and inferior to the two other estates, the clergy and the nobility. In international affairs, Third World meant countries that were not part of the US-led capitalist bloc (the First World) or the Soviet-led Communist bloc (the Second World). But while this notion seemed somewhat theoretical when Sauvy coined the term, the Bandung Conference gave it a robust political meaning and voice. It not only signified the group of newly independent nations, most of which were economically poor and politically marginalized; it also came to be associated with anti-colonialism, anti-racism, and demands for economic justice, all of which were key elements of the Bandung platform.

Indeed, the Third World countries made significant contributions to principles of global governance in at least three ways: human rights, international development, and humanitarian intervention and its offshoot, responsibility to protect (R2P).

The Universal Declaration of Human Rights (UDHR) is regarded as the world's foremost statement of human rights standards. Drafted by a committee chaired by Eleanor Roosevelt—wife of US president Franklin D. Roosevelt—it was adopted by the UN in December 1948. But the Latin American states were ahead of the game. After achieving independence, they were subject to continuous intervention by the United States and European powers. Sometimes, these interventions were carried out in the name of protecting the "rights" of US and European nationals living in the region while violating the rights of Latin American people. Hence the independent Latin American nations saw the need for creating a rights framework stressing nonintervention as well as the protection of the individual rights of people of all nations, not just the overseas citizens of Western ones. As early as in 1916, Chilean jurist Alejandro Álvarez (1868–1960) had drafted a Declaration of Rights and Duties of Nations, which specified the "right to life, liberty, and property, without distinction of *nationality*, sex, race, language, or religion" (emphasis added).[42] These principles were later incorporated into the UN charter in 1945. They also formed the basis of the American Declaration of the Rights and Duties of Man, adopted in Bogotá in April 1948, and then six months later into the UDHR, helped by the fact that Latin American states were well represented at the drafting of these later documents.

Peng Chun Chang, a Chinese academic and diplomat (this was before the Communist takeover of mainland China) and Charles Malik, later the foreign minister of Lebanon, served as vice chair and rapporteur, respectively, of the UN's Commission on Human Rights and played a key role in drafting of the UDHR. Chang would urge fellow committee members to "spend a few months studying the fundamentals of Confucianism," as Mrs. Roosevelt would later recall.[43] But the truly unsung hero of the UDHR was India's Hansa Mehta, feminist, nationalist, writer, and member of the commission.[44] The original wording of article 1 of the UDHR, proposed by Britain, France, and Australia (all represented by white men), stated, "All men are created equal," directly borrowing from the US Declaration of Independence. Mrs. Roosevelt, the commission chair, had no problem accepting this. But Mehta argued with her, insisting that the language be changed to "all human beings," words that were used in the final text of the UDHR: "All human beings are born free and equal in dignity and rights."[45]

Mehta's compatriot, lawyer and politician Minocher ("Minoo") Masani, made his own contribution, one that advanced the anti-racism norm in the UDHR. Upon seeing that the original draft of article 2 called for nondiscrimination of people on the basis of race, but not color, Masani argued that "race and colour were two conceptions that did not necessarily cover one another."[46] When told that not even the UN charter had mentioned color and that a reference to race might be understood as subsuming color, Mehta countered that the UDHR should go beyond the UN charter.[47] Thanks to his intervention, color was added to race.[48]

Today, the UN's web page on the UDHR celebrates Mrs. Roosevelt "as the driving force for the Declaration's adoption," while Canadian John Humphrey, who directed the UN secretariat's division for human rights, is cited as having "prepared the Declaration's blueprint," and René Cassin of France is recognized as having "composed the first draft of the Declaration."[49] Mehta and Masani find no space here.

Postcolonial nations also played a crucial role in pushing back against British and American efforts to limit the scope of various human rights agreements, or covenants, that came after the UDHR. At the Bandung Conference, as we have seen, colonialism was recognized as a principal form of human rights violation, one that had found no explicit mention in the UN charter or UDHR. Thus it was left to the postcolonial countries to play the key role in the adoption of the International Covenant on Civil and Political Rights and the International Covenant on Economic, Social, and Cultural Rights, both adopted in 1966. As Australian scholar Christian Reus-Smit points out, "During the negotiation of the two Covenants, newly independent states consistently stressed the primacy of civil and political rights, and the strongest advocates of robust enforcement mechanisms."[50] It was only in the 1990s that Asia's authoritarian nations, such Singapore under Lee Kuan Yew and Malaysia under Mahathir Mohamad, promoted the so-called Asian view of human rights, one that placed collective rights above individual freedom. ("Society over the self," went the refrain.) This has since been substantially discredited as a ruse for authoritarian rule.

International development is another idea where the non-Western nations played a big role, though the conventional view credits Western leaders such as US president Harry Truman as the architect of international development assistance. In 1949, in his presidential inaugural address, Truman stated: "We must embark on a bold new program for making the benefits of our scientific advances and industrial progress available for the improvement and growth of underdeveloped areas."[51] Truman's speech, writes German scholar Wolfgang Sachs, made the term "underdeveloped areas...suddenly, a permanent feature of the landscape, a pivotal concept....For the first time, a new worldview was... announced" that made international development a shared goal of "all the peoples of the earth."[52] However, in the very same speech, Truman also put economic aid to war-devasted Europe as his highest priority, calling it "the greatest cooperative economic program in history," whose purpose was "to invigorate and strengthen democracy in Europe, so that the free people of that continent can resume their rightful place in the forefront of civilization and can contribute once more to the security and welfare of the world."[53] Note especially Truman's reference to European civilization and its role in "security and welfare of the world." This, of course, was the very civilization that had impoverished vast areas of the world with the predatory economic policies that came with colonialism and racism, words that found no mention in Truman's speech.

But the idea of international development as a principle had emerged much earlier, from Asia and Latin America.[54] In 1918, more than thirty years before Truman's speech, Chinese leader Sun Yat-sen published a book in which he proposed an "International Development Organization" in which "various Governments of the Capital-supplying Powers must agree to joint action and a unified policy."[55] Although Sun's main motive was to harness international aid for China's development, the idea that the economic development of an underdeveloped nation, as China was at that point, required multilateral international cooperation was novel for its time. It broke with the pattern of colonial-era economic relations, which were mostly bilateral. These relations also took away rather than gave resources to poorer nations, except when building infrastructure like railways and schools could strengthen the colonial administration, as the British had done in India, for example.

Some of the early and most influential ideas about creating an international development lending institution came out of discussions about an inter-American bank (IAB), in which Latin American nations played the driving role. In contrast to earlier, more limited lending institutions—such as the Bank for International Settlements, established in 1930 with five European nations plus Japan as members—the proposed IAB membership was to be universal—that is, all countries of the region would have borrowing privileges. But the British, still wielding considerable power in global finance, opposed such a body, while the United States, though more receptive, would not commit to joining it. US opposition had a good deal to do with the desire of Latin American nations, especially Mexico, to use the bank as a channel for capital flows to meet their development needs, and this was seen as a threat by the large American banks that had monopolized this role and drew great profits from it. They lobbied the US Congress to kill the proposal. Although the IAB never materialized, US officials would later draw on its ideas when drafting the terms of the International Bank for Reconstruction and Development, a precursor to the World Bank.

In the 1960s, East Asian countries offered the single most important breakthrough in international development by achieving high and sustainable economic growth. Led by Japan, South Korea, Taiwan, Hong Kong, and Singapore, and subsequently by China and the members of the Association of Southeast Asian Nations, this phenomenon came to be known as the East Asian miracle. Neither the Western countries nor the International Monetary Fund nor the World Bank—institutions still controlled by the West—could claim credit for this. Indeed, the East Asian miracle took place in defiance of the standard Western formula of growth through free markets and suggested an alternative pathway in which the state plays a key role, often in close cooperation with the business sector.[56] This was not and still is not the American approach to economic development, and it created much hostility toward Japan, which is now directed against China.

While global institutions such as the World Bank and the IMF are mainly concerned with economic growth and financial stability, a more recent and revolutionary economic idea coming from the non-Western world is human development. It challenges the traditional measurement of economic development based on the size and the growth rate of GDP. Much credit for this idea belongs to Pakistani economist Mahbub ul

Haq, the creator of the idea of human development and the closely related notion of human security.

Instead of GDP growth, human development focuses on expanding human capabilities. Arguing that true development depended not on the rate of economic growth but on its quality and distribution, Haq noted that high economic growth does not always trickle down to the people. Hence, instead of asking, "How much is a nation producing?" the question should be: "How are its people faring?" As Haq put it, "The real objective of development is to enlarge people's choices."[57] In initially developing this idea, he received intellectual support from the Indian economist Amartya Sen. The two were classmates at Cambridge University and would form a lifelong partnership. It was during their conversations at Cambridge when Haq told Sen that measuring development based on one indicator, GDP, was a "silly" idea.[58] Unlike Sen, Haq never won the Nobel Prize in Economics; he was more practical minded than a theoretician like Sen. This reflects much more on the shortcomings of the Nobel award than on the intellect of Mahbub ul Haq.

Can the idea of human development be credited to the Western education of Haq and Sen? To some degree it can be, but the events in their places of birth and upbringing were even more influential. Haq was born in the Indian part of Punjab and came face-to-face with death in the communal violence that took nearly a million lives during the partition of India in 1947. Haq's interest in a people-centric approach to development and security was inspired by that experience, a view confirmed by Sen. According to Sen, Haq's "locality [early childhood experience] must have also played a part."[59]

The term human development became the basis of a global ranking of nations, the Human Development Index, launched in 1990. The UN Development Programme now compiles the index, covering almost all the nations of the world, and donor governments and multilateral banks use it for designing their development assistance programs to poorer nations.

The idea of human security grew out of the idea of human development. Unlike the traditional framework of national security, which prioritizes the security of states or governments, human security stresses the security of people. The state or its government, normally presumed to be the protector of its citizens, can become a threat to their lives and well-being through human rights abuses and genocide. Many developed nations such as Canada, Japan, and Norway soon found the idea of human security attractive and borrowed it to develop a post–Cold War foreign policy approach. Some Western leaders—notably Lloyd Axworthy, Canada's foreign minister from 1996 to 2000—even tried to move the concept away from its economic development roots, its promotion of "freedom from want."[60] These Westerners focused narrowly on the security aspects—which were labeled "freedom from fear"—and gave priority to banning land mines, creating the International Criminal Court, and supporting humanitarian intervention. Although the concept's non-Western proponents, including Sen (Haq died in 1998 before human security acquired global prominence), wanted both aspects to be emphasized; Western policymakers, commanding resources and leadership in international institutions, created the impression that human security and humanitarian intervention were somehow distinctily Western approaches, blurring the contribution of non-Western thinking.

This brings us to a third idea: responsibility to protect, a major new articulation of the principle of humanitarian intervention in the post–Cold War era. Its origin has been credited exclusively to the West. R2P calls for humanitarian intervention in conflicts that take a huge toll in human lives, defying the principle of Westphalian sovereignty. It may seem unbelievable that such a notion has roots in the postcolonial world. The principles of sovereignty and nonintervention are supposed to be vital to these countries, since they had fought to regain their sovereignty after centuries of colonial rule. But gradually, these principles came to be abused by dictators riding roughshod over the rights of their own citizens, or even committing genocide, and continuing to rule with impunity by invoking the principle of nonintervention. For example, when a quarter of Cambodia's population perished during the four years of Khmer Rouge rule in 1975–1979, the international community looked on, and after Communist Vietnam ousted the regime, the West backed a coalition that included the genocidal Khmer Rouge to fight communism in Southeast Asia. But after the end of the Cold War, bloody massacres in Iraq, Bosnia, Rwanda, Burundi, and Kosovo led to the conviction that sovereignty and nonintervention required rethinking.

This was no easy task, as many non-Western countries, including democracies like India and dictatorships like China, held dearly to those principles. Their main concern was that allowing intervention would lead to abuse by powerful Western nations and thus to a new form of colonialism. The challenge was to find a way for the international community to intervene to save lives, while not giving a blank check or allowing the Western powers to abuse that privilege. Somehow, a new formula had to be found that struck a balance between sovereignty and human rights.

Africa's main political cooperation group, the Organization of African Unity (OAU), was established in 1963 and was wedded to the principle of nonintervention. But by the 1980s it has grown frustrated with this norm, which had given it no mandate to handle internal conflicts. Resentful of the inaction of the UN in handling internal massacres in Africa and stymied by nonintervention, the OAU closed shop and remerged as the African Union in 1999. Pushed by African leaders—notably Nelson Mandela, who had begun a five-year term as South Africa's president in 1994—the charter of the new organization included an explicit mandate to intervene in countries experiencing genocide or bloody civil wars. It became the first multilateral organization in the world to explicitly include "humanitarian intervention" in its founding charter, which even the UN charter had failed to do.

Other African leaders and diplomats did much to push this agenda. Notable among them was Francis Deng, a Sudanese and later South Sudanese diplomat. In 1992, the secretary-general of the UN, Boutros Boutros-Ghali, the first African to lead the world body, appointed Deng as the UN's first special representative for internal displacement (later renamed to "internally displaced persons"). Subsequently, Deng took up research positions with think tanks, notably the Brookings Institution in Washington, DC, while also remaining an adviser to the UN.

The product of his work and research was a landmark book, *Sovereignty as Responsibility*, published by Brookings in 1996. The book developed the idea that sovereignty was not an absolute right but a responsibility that must be exercised with due regard to human lives and protected from abuse by dictators. The logic behind this idea was that Africa could not count on outside powers to defend its security, since they would put their own geopolitical interests at the core of any intervention. Africa, Deng believed, "had to find internal solutions, whether domestic or sub-regional or continent-wide."[61] Presenting this view as a new norm of international relations, Deng argues: "The state had to take care of its citizens, but failing that, if its people were suffering and dying, the world should not watch and do nothing. It must intervene." As he puts it, "I do not see sovereignty…as a barricade against the outside world… [but] as a very positive concept of state responsibility for its people. And if it needs support, to call on the international community."[62] While Deng worked collaboratively with fellow experts at Brookings, he was the real face of the idea; responsible sovereignty was his "calling card," as one of his close associates told me. In promoting the idea around the world, he would underplay the intervention part and argue that if a state wants to avoid outside intervention, it must first protect the lives and rights of its own people.

The idea of responsible sovereignty found its fullest expression in the report of the International Commission on Intervention and State Sovereignty. Although Canadian funded and cochaired by Gareth Evans, a former Australian foreign minister, it was hardly a Western product. The other cochair was Mohamed Sahnoun, an Algerian diplomat who served with the OAU, the League of Arab States, and the UN. Western media predictably did not give as much credit to Sahnoun—although Evans personally did so—he had equal influence, as my research found. Another key member of the commission was Indian-born professor Ramesh Thakur, who has done more than most to give the R2P global intellectual visibility. Also missing from the media narrative was the African contribution to the idea of responsible sovereignty. Events in Africa and the support of leaders such as Mandela played a key role in creating the rationale for R2P. Indeed, the emergence of the R2P norm, as Sahnoun put it, was "in many ways an African contribution to [global] human rights."[63]

Non-Western nations also lead the world in providing troops for peacekeeping operations, a principal multilateral mechanism for maintaining stability in the world. In 2023, the top ten nations contributing troops to UN peacekeeping were Bangladesh, Nepal, India, Rwanda, Pakistan, Indonesia, Ghana, China, Egypt, and Morocco.[64] Nigeria and

South Africa are major contributors to the regional peacekeeping missions of the African Union and the Economic Community of West African States. This is of course another example of the contributions of non-Western nations to world order, which the West benefits from, but it does not offset the West's military edge.

These are some of the examples showing that key ideas underpinning world order since World War II were not the West's alone; they were infused with contributions from non-Western countries. New ideas about sovereignty, security, and governance from the Rest have made their impact felt on the way we think about the problems of the world and how to seek solutions to them.

The rise of the Rest or the global South, which has more or less replaced the previously popular term *Third World*, can also be seen in the global diplomatic arena. As one expert has put it, the "countries of the Global South are increasingly organized and taking the stage to say, 'You know what, I'm sorry, enough is enough. We are not going to participate in an international system in which the West calls the shots, sets the rules, and has the leadership in the governance of all the major institutions... and we demand a seat at the table and a role in the governance.'"[65] There are new clubs of emerging nations and multilateral groupings, the best-known of them being the BRICS (originally Brazil, Russia, India, and China). In the decade before 2010, when South Africa joined the grouping, BRICS contributed over a third of world GDP growth and had grown from a sixth of the world economy to almost a quarter in terms of purchasing power parity (PPP).[66] A parade of acronyms followed—CIVETS (Colombia, Indonesia, Vietnam, Egypt, Turkey, and South Africa), MIST (Mexico, Indonesia, South Korea, and Turkey), and IBSA (India, Brazil, South Africa)—though only BRICS has remained influential. In August 2023, the grouping decided to expand its membership, with Iran, the United Arab Emirates, Egypt, Indonesia, and Ethiopia becoming new members, while Argentina pulled out and Saudi Arabia remained undecided.[67] This move, despite the group's internal diversity and conflict (such as between India and China and between Saudi Arabia and Iran), could be more than symbolic. Its expansion comes at a time when the UN Security Council is paralyzed by the Russia-Ukraine war, there are massive US-orchestrated sanctions on Russia, and the West has threatened secondary sanctions on other BRICS members should they assist Russia. This state of affairs could lead to the expansion of the grouping's existing development and financial cooperation mechanisms: the New Development Bank and the Contingent Reserve Arrangement, respectively.

The Group of Twenty (G20) is another institution in which the emerging nations have made their presence felt on the global stage. Representing over 80 percent of the world's population, 90 percent of the world's GDP, 90 percent of the world's finance, and 80 percent of the world's trade, the G20 was established in 1999 but acquired new prominence when it successfully tackled the global financial crisis of 2008. The grouping describes itself as the world's "premier forum for international economic cooperation."[68] The former European Union (EU) foreign policy chief Javier Solana called it the "only forum in which world powers and the emerging countries sit as equals at the same table."[69] Others saw it as having the "potential to alter the international order almost by stealth."[70] Although the G20 has gotten bogged down in the growing US-Russia and US-China rivalry, the leadership of Indonesia and India in 2022 and 2023 saw the group shift gears to address the concerns of developing countries who are not its members. The African Union was invited to join in 2023.

Global Shifts

The West's primacy in the global economy is declining, while the status of the global South rises. In the 1970s, the Group of Seven (G7)—comprising the United States, Germany, Britain, France, Japan, Italy, and Canada—accounted for 65 percent of global GDP. It now stands at 44 percent.[71] Similarly, the share of global South countries in world trade jumped from 35 percent in 2000 to 51 percent in 2012.[72]

China tops the list of challengers to US and Western economic primacy, its recent economic slowdown notwithstanding. According to World Bank data, China's GDP overtook that of the United States in terms of PPP in 2016. In 2023, China's GDP was $34.6 trillion, while that of the United States was $27.3 trillion.[73] While estimates of the economic shift vary and are subject to ongoing and unanticipated global crises, it was evident before the COVID–19 pandemic that the chief trend was the relative decline of Western nations and the rise of others, especially Asian nations. That trend is unlikely to be reversed.

A 2021 US National Intelligence Council report projects that, in nominal terms, US GDP in the year 2040 will account for 20.8 percent of the world total, while China's will be 22.8 percent.[74] It is noteworthy that India, which is showing greater economic dynamism as China's economy slows, has already overtaken the United Kingdom as the world's fifth largest economy, after the United States, China, Japan, and Germany. The EU and the United Kingdom are expected to account for 16.4 percent of the world's GDP by 2040, compared to 20.5 percent in 2020. Overall, the share of global GDP contributed by the United States, United Kingdom, and EU, the traditional core nations of the West, is projected to decline from 44.5 percent in 2020 to 37.2 percent in 2040. During the same period, the combined share of Asian economies—including China and India—is projected to increase from 25.2 percent to 35.1 percent, roughly similar to where they were before the Opium War.

China and India have been the stars of the show. But the economic rise of the Rest is a broader phenomenon, with other non-Western nations also making impressive gains. PricewaterhouseCoopers (PwC), one of the world's largest accounting firms, projects that while China and India could both overtake the United States and become the top two economies in the world by 2050, Indonesia, Brazil, Mexico, and Nigeria will also rise in the rankings. In PwC's estimate, twenty of the thirty-two leading economies in PPP terms will be from the non-Western world by 2050.[75] In PPP terms, developing countries accounted for 58.2 percent of global GDP in 2022 and are expected to contribute 60 percent by 2025.[76] The World Bank estimates that the number of "low income" countries— those with a per capita income of less than $1,036—fell from 30 percent of the total in 1987 to 12 percent in 2022.[77]

All projections about the global economic shift are subject to sudden and unforeseen disruptions, but what is unmistakable is that the leading nations of the global South are clamoring for a greater say at the UN and other multilateral bodies, such as the IMF, World Bank, and WTO.

The growing density and volume of economic exchanges among the global South nations further attests to the power shift from the West to the Rest. Merchandise trade among developing countries, measured as a share of the total world merchandise trade, has now surpassed that among the developed nations: 35 percent to 25 percent.[78] Foreign direct investment flows also suggest a similar trend. In 2020, inflows to developing economies were 66.9 percent of global inflow, marking the first time in modern history that they surpassed inflows to the developed economies. What is more, Asian nations have become major sources of international investment. By 2015, corporations from Asia (excluding Japan) had become the world's largest investing group for the first time, accounting for almost one-third of the world total. In 2017, flows in foreign direct investment from one global South nation to another accounted for about half of the world total.[79] These trends will reshape globalization and ultimately global governance.

The global balance of military power is also shifting, but to a lesser degree and in different ways. China has made impressive gains in military power vis-à-vis the United States. It is now second only to America in terms of annual spending on defense among all nations of the world. The United States increased its military spending by 2.7 percent between 2013 and 2022, whereas China increased its defense budget by 63 percent during the same period.[80] China's navy has overtaken that of the United States to become the largest in the world. As Xi Jinping announced at the centenary of the establishment of the Chinese Communist Party in July 2021, China has vowed to become, by mid-twenty-first century, a "global leader in terms of comprehensive national strength and international influence."[81] China's goal, according to a US Defense Department report, is to be able to "fight and win wars" against a "strong enemy"—a clear reference to the United States.[82]

Rhetoric aside, China is a long way from catching up with the United States or the West militarily. In the words of the above US Defense Department assessment, the Chinese military "feels itself to be behind the world's most capable militaries and that they have not yet achieved that standard." On some counts, China may have more to lose in the event of a military confrontation with the United States. Commerce remains a major basis of China's rise to global prominence, despite ongoing efforts at developing its domestic market. Hence its economic prosperity, domestic social order, political stability, and regime security would be more vulnerable to supply-chain disruption caused by a war. Despite its immense growth in past decades, China's military remains untested in battle.

But China would have some important advantages when it comes to conflicts in its neighborhood. As noted by the RAND Corporation, while "the United States will remain capable of fighting and winning a protracted air and naval battle against China...the two sides might be reaching a series of tipping points, whereby PLA [People's Liberation Army] forces could severely challenge the United States in the initial battles of a war and impose heavy costs on the U.S. military, first in scenarios near the Chinese coast and, later, in more distant locations."[83] China has already matched US capabilities in the Taiwan Strait in air power and gained an advantage in anti-surface ship capability. In the more distant South China Sea, China is closing the military gap, although US forces remain superior.[84]

Moreover, even if China cannot match US military power globally, it can intimidate US allies and constrain operations in the East Asia and the wider Indo-Pacific region, a fact conceded by the commander of the US Pacific Command (now Indo-Pacific Command) as early as in 2010. Having "increased its patrols throughout the region and... [showing] an increased willingness to confront regional nations on the high seas and within the contested island chains," he stated, China could "challenge our freedom of action in the region."[85] China's military capabilities have grown stronger since then.

What about the rest of the world? It is hard to provide a detailed picture of the global military balance in this short space, but some developments are noteworthy. Before the Russia-Ukraine war, Asia had overtaken Europe in defense spending for the first time in modern history.[86] Since the beginning of the conflict, European NATO members have increased their defense spending, but whether this can be sustained remains to be seen. Some non-Western nations—India, North Korea, South Africa, Pakistan, Saudi Arabia, Brazil, Turkey, Iran, and Egypt—have invested considerably in military power. India and Saudi Arabia are among the world's largest defense spenders and importers of armaments. China, India, Brazil, and South Korea manufacture a range of advanced missiles, tanks, aircraft, and naval ships. The advent of drones has expanded the capabilities of non-Western nations like Iran and further dented Western military superiority.

The emergence of new battlefield technologies has implications for the global military balance. Iran and Turkey have become important producers and suppliers of drones, which have demonstrated their importance in recent conflicts, especially in the Armenia-Azerbaijan and Russia-Ukraine wars. Artificial intelligence (AI) has the clear potential to transform future wars, giving both the West and its rivals improved ability to gather and analyze intelligence and attack enemy targets. Here the United States leads for the moment, but as Eric Schmidt, former CEO and chair of Google, warns, the US lead cannot be taken for granted because China is also striving hard to become the global AI leader.[87]

Perhaps the West's main advantage in military power has to do with the fact that most non-Western militaries are too busy fighting domestic enemies and cross-border insurgencies to project power overseas and challenge the West. For example, Nigeria, Africa's most populous nation, is fighting Boko Haram and other insurgent groups; Ethiopia has been bogged down with its civil war in the Tigray region; and Saudi Arabia is preoccupied with Iran-backed Houthi fighters from Yemen. The Pakistani military's main goal is to maintain domestic political control, for which its rivalry with India is an important enabling factor.

Nuclear weapons and ballistic missiles have given countries an increased ability to counter Western intimidation and pressure. Three of the world's six declared nuclear powers are non-Western—India, Pakistan, and North Korea—and a fourth, Iran, is likely to develop such a capability. Meanwhile, the Western ability to intervene militarily in distant theaters is a far cry from the past. As demonstrated by the wars in Vietnam and Afghanistan, the United States has faced significant constraints in fighting insurgencies and extremist groups supported by regional adversaries, such as Iran. Today, the dominance of China in East

Asia suggests that US power projection is likely to be constrained in deterring regional conflicts there. Alliances and partnerships with regional powers—such as NATO in Europe and with Japan, South Korea, Australia, and India in Asia-Pacific—are indispensable for maintaining Western military hegemony.

Against this backdrop, the West's edge in global military technology—including its ability to produce the superior naval platforms and combat aircraft that are key to projecting power to distant areas—may be less decisive than it seems. The West lags in usable military power. As Michael Mazarr, a senior political scientist at the RAND Corporation, told me, "The US will by far remain the world's number one military power, but in areas where it most likely needs to use that power, such as in a conflict with China over Taiwan or in fighting large-scale insurgencies, US military primacy may not be the deciding factor."[88] When it comes to fighting insurgencies, American capabilities depend on political solutions that rest on the ability of local partners to provide effective, legitimate governance. As was seen in cases from Vietnam to Afghanistan, Washington has little control over that. In the meantime, the ability of many non-Western nations to resist American military intervention, or at least increase its cost, has been growing since the late twentieth century. This, together with the expanding economic and diplomatic role of the non-Western nations, might further erode the Western-led world order.

In summary, the period since the end of World War II has seen a remarkable global turnaround. The non-Western nations have not only freed themselves from colonization, but they have also made significant contributions to advancing global economic development, security, and cooperation. They have often done so despite Western indifference or even hostility, a reality that the idea of a benign or inclusive US-led liberal world order fails to capture. While the West still controls the narrative of world order that exalts its ideas and leadership, the Rest has become stronger economically and diplomatically, thereby raising questions about the future of world order, which I will address in the final chapter.

Chapter 14

The Once and Future World Order

In this book, I have made three big claims.

The most important is that building a world order—understood as the power structures, economic links, political ideas, and leadership designed to ensure the stability and peace of the world—is not the monopoly of a single nation or civilization. It is mostly a shared enterprise.

The conventional view of history is that the current world order, which has existed for around three centuries, is an entirely Western creation, that it has mostly been a good thing, and that its decline is deeply worrisome. But this book, which goes back deep in history, shows that many civilizations contributed to the current world order: Sumerian, Egyptian, Persian, Indian, Chinese, Greek, Roman, Islamic, African, Native American, and Western. Ideas about republican government, protection of people from cruel and unjust punishment, personal and collective rights to property, the freedom of all nations to trade in open seas, humanitarian rules of warfare, rational modes of inquiry, and more have come—in their more elementary as well as developed and consequential forms—from multiple places around the world. There have been variations in how they have been developed and applied, as might be expected due to the impact of local conditions. But all in all, the world order of our time is really the creation of many nations and civilizations acting over a long period of time.

This is not to deny that in many aspects of world-order building—whether promoting human rights, democracy, and peaceful commerce or resolving disputes through laws among nations—the West has played a crucial role. But one should not forget, as this book has shown, that the rise of the West also destroyed long traditions of racial coexistence, religious tolerance, social inclusion, peaceful resolution of conflicts, environmental protection, and freedom of seas that already existed in many non-European societies around the world. The West has often been a force for regression, yet its own narratives about world order have focused mostly on its progressive role.

At the same time, the West is far from being the only or main developer of ideas or mechanisms about world order. For example, in the making of world order after the Second World War, while that order is credited almost exclusively to the West, especially to the United States, postcolonial nations played a major role in developing and leading some of its progressive features, including multilateral institutions, such as the UN and its related bodies, norms supporting self-determination and sustainable development, and those against great power rivalry and intervention around the world. They also made their contribution to the creation of global human rights principles—including anti-colonial and anti-racist norms—through the UDHR and subsequent human rights covenants. There was also the consequential 1955 Bandung Conference, when, for the first time, the leaders of all the postcolonial nations gathered in one place and enunciated their vision of world order. This story of the shared creation of the modern world order should be cause for some optimism, since it shows that a humane, stable, and functional world order is possible, even likely, despite the West's decline. There is no good reason to suppose that the nations of the West and the Rest won't uphold fundamental ideas and institutions of world order, since that is what they have been doing for millennia.

This book also shows that the non-Western world has provided alternative and sometimes better ways of organizing world order than what the West has had to offer during the centuries of its global dominance. In fact, as noted, postcolonial nations and their intellectuals have led the way in suggesting ways for ending colonialism and racial discrimination (both hallmarks of the Western-led world order); creating more humane, pacific, and cooperative ways of organizing interstate relations; and tolerating religious and cultural differences. These alternatives can be important in reshaping the contemporary world order as the West declines.

This leads to my second big claim: the coming world order will be multi-civilizational and will not be dominated by any single nation—be it China, India, or a resurgent United States—or any group of nations, such as the West, NATO, EU, or BRICS. To be sure, considering the future of world order must involve a certain amount of speculation. This book does not argue that there are laws governing cycles of history. A return to the past is not what I have in mind. But history such as what this book has covered can be helpful in building a better world order. I agree with Asian historian Wang Gungwu that although "history never really repeats itself," it "enlarges our grasp, of what is possible now and what might arise in the future." This, he adds, "might go some way in preparing ourselves for what individuals and societies might do in the future."[1]

The period before the rise of the West, when the vibrant civilizations of Islam, India, China, Mongolia, and West Africa shaped the destiny of a vast chunk of the world, is a precedent for a multi-civilizational world order. To be sure, any such order will also have to adapt to modern realities, both good and bad, such as the revolutions in transportation and communications, the increasing destructiveness of war, and the existence of international institutions and nongovernmental networks. This is not an easy task—building a world order is never easy—but it is not doomed to fail.

While the future world order will not mean a return to the past, it will look very different from the past three hundred years. It will not have a dominant global power. Neither will it be a multipolar world, where a handful of competing great powers shape security and order on a global scale. Rather, it is best described, as I have noted in the Introduction, as a "global multiplex" in which large, medium, and some innovative smaller nations, as well as people acting through governments, companies, and civil groups powered by social media and employing new forms of interdependence and interactions will shape world order.

This leads to my third claim, which is that this post-Western order will not be the disaster that many in the West insist and fear it will be. No world order—including the one led by the West—has been free from chaos, but maintaining order does not require a supreme power like the United States or a select group of nations like the West. Rather, order rests on underlying ideas and institutions that have emerged from multiple locations around the world. Going a step further, this book argues that the end of Western dominance will actually be a good thing for the world as a whole. The major benefits of the present world order have gone disproportionately to the West at the expense of the Rest, thanks to predatory colonization, violence, racism, and injustice. Centuries of dominance have bred both arrogance and ignorance in the West, in which the ideas and contributions of other civilizations through history have been forgotten or dismissed. A world order that sees the return of the Rest will create a more equitable and mutually respectful global arrangement, one that will temper the worst excesses of Western dominance while satisfying the needs of non-Western nations for development, status, and recognition. Not surprisingly, given the historical advantages that have gone to the West over the past three centuries, the fear of the future is more evident in the United States and Europe than it is in the nations now emerging to challenge Western dominance. While any future world order will reproduce the timeless contest between the forces of order and chaos, there is no reason to think that the decline of the West by itself will ensure that chaos will prevail. The West should embrace its inevitable decline and work with the Rest, whose ideas and approaches could enrich the global knowledge pool, forge genuinely multicultural, mutually tolerant relations among states, and, in so doing, create new conditions and mechanisms for stability, prosperity, and justice.

The School Begins

Understanding the transition to a new world order can be illustrated by an old cartoon, "School Begins," which appeared in the January 25, 1899, issue of *Puck*, America's first humor magazine. The cartoon shows Uncle Sam as the teacher, with four children in the front row: Philippines

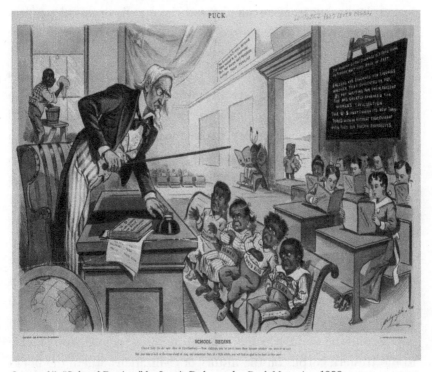

Image 15. "School Begins," by Louis Dalrymple, *Puck Magazine*, 1899.

(whose representative child bears a striking resemblance to the Filipino rebel leader Emilio Aguinaldo), Hawaii, Puerto Rico (spelled Porto Rico), and Cuba. Far away from the group, near the schoolroom entrance, is a Native American child holding an upside-down book labeled "ABC." A Chinese boy with his school bag stands outside the door, while a Black boy cleans a side window. On Uncle Sam's desk is a book titled *U.S. First Lessons in Self-Government*, along with papers labeled with the names of various American states. The original caption reads, "Uncle Sam (to his new class in Civilization). Now, children, you've got to learn these lessons whether you want to or not! But just take a look at the class ahead of you, and remember that, in a little while, you will feel as glad to be here as they are!"[2]

Imagine a contemporary classroom on history, politics, or international affairs in the West today. The pupils in the class would not come from colonies but from ex-colonies and the non-Western independent nations that were never colonized. But some things would not change much. The curriculum would still have a heavy dose of European or Western ideas and history. This would be true even if the class was held in a non-Western country. This is because most textbooks and other items on the required reading list—journal articles and book chapters—are still written and produced in the West. And a vast number of students from non-Western countries go to the West to get their advanced degrees, where they are taught with a curriculum that continues to emphasize the story of Western dominance and theories and concepts derived from it.

The West's hold over world history is such that even when non-Western countries produce history texts or narratives that include the achievements of their own civilizations relative to others, such texts are readily dismissed as propaganda. They are not used in classrooms outside of their countries. Western publishing houses and institutions still hold almost total control over what is taught not only in the West but also around the world. There is certainly nothing remotely comparable to the Western corpus on the history of civilizations, where the books of William McNeill, Henry Kissinger, and Niall Ferguson dominate. No non-Western publisher has produced a history text that is widely used in the West or the Rest. There is no book of comparative history of the world's major civilizations published in the English language, written by a non-Western scholar, and published by a major international press. Ibn Khaldun's may well be the last such work.

Attempts to change or "decolonize" curricula and textbooks and offer a truly global version of world history have been scarce and, when attempted, have met with little success. Western classrooms in social sciences and humanities, such as history, philosophy, and political science, perpetuate a parochial reading of history, where non-Western societies continue to be ignored. A case in point is how Africa has been "dragged into the march of history only through its encounter with Europe," producing "the near-total erasure of Africa; its social, political, and cultural life; its intellectual contributions; and the biographies of its thinkers from the annals of global history."[3] And Africa is not the only place to be forgotten or dismissed. In teaching a first-year undergraduate course in world history and international affairs, I have often seen my largely Western student body express genuine surprise and disbelief—and sometimes admiration—when told about the prohibitions of King Ashoka of India against cruel and unjust punishment of common people; the influence of the Chinese examination system in creating meritocratic civil service recruitment in Europe; the vast, open, and rule-based trading system of the Indian Ocean; the extensive and efficient communication network of the Incas and the Mongols; the rules of Manden Charter (Kouroukan Fouga) of Mali forbidding cruel treatment of slaves and allowing individual property rights; and the indispensable role played by Islamic science and philosophy in making the European Renaissance and Enlightenment possible.

The field of international relations (IR) offers another vivid example of the marginalization of the non-West. As a field of study, IR began in the United Kingdom when it was still the world's largest colonial empire. But the discipline really came of age in the United States, which displaced Britain as the world's leading power. US dominance of the theories, narratives, teaching, and research on IR was so complete that the late Harvard professor Stanley Hoffmann called IR an "American Social Science."[4] Decades later, the epithet still rings true. But the Western-centric narrative of IR is global in scope. A survey published in 2019 of forty-eight "introduction to international relations" syllabi from ten countries found that the geographic focus of more than two-thirds of the readings was on the West (United States and Europe).[5] As one of China's leading scholars of IR, Qin Yaqing, puts it, "No matter what you theorize about [in international relations], its soul is Western."[6]

In short, the "schools" of history, philosophy, political science, and IR still present the West as the creator, leader, and teacher and the non-West as the created, follower, and pupil. They tell a highly selective story of how the present world order came about, who created it, and where it may be heading. This book has called for closing the old school and opening a new one structured around the central arguments about the past and future of world order.

Connecting History

In understanding the history of world order, we need to not just compare civilizations but also connect them.[7] (See Table 14.1.) Without forgetting that civilizations have developed often quite similar ideas and approaches to world order, both independently and through mutual contact and diffusion, this connection can be seen as a two-way street. All civilizations have been both teachers and pupils. In many cases, the West has been the pupil, not the teacher.

Table 14.1 Intercivilizational Learning Before and After the Rise of the West

---

Egypt/Mesopotamia/Persia → Greece: astronomy, chemistry, medicine, mathematics, divine kingship

Phoenicia → Greece: language

Greece → Rome: art, science, philosophy

Greece → Arab-Islamic world/India: art, philosophy, science, medicine

Rome → Europe: law, imperial idea and administration

India → China: Buddhist religion and philosophy

India → Southeast Asia/central Asia/Islamic world: Sanskrit language; epic literature; law; Hindu-Buddhist religion, political ideas, and institutions; "Arabic" numerals

India → rest of Asia/Europe: numerals including zero, cotton textile technology, steel

Persia/Islamic world → India: Islam, administration, food, legal codes, navigation

China → Korea → Japan: Buddhism, Confucianism, art, political ideas and institutions

China → Europe: silk, gunpowder, compass, paper, printing, competitive examinations for civil service

Islamic world → Europe: medicine, chemistry, optics, philosophy (including preserved and expanded Greek philosophy)

Europe → Rest: science, technology, political ideas and institutions

The Rest → the world: anti-imperialism, nationalism, anti-racialism, universal sovereignty

---

Note: → **indicates direction of flow of ideas**

In connecting history, we should not forget that all civilizations are products of synthesis. Borrowing others' ideas and innovations to advance one's civilization and world order does not mean giving up on local ideas, ingenuity, or contributions. All societies are selective in what they take from others, and when they do, they do not displace their own ideas and methods. Instead, they modify, localize, and reconcile foreign ideas to fit local ones, often creating hybrid forms, a phenomenon that can be found in all aspects—religious, economic, and political—of world-order building. The Greeks conjoined Egypt's supreme deity Amun-Re with their own native protector god Zeus, thus giving birth to the hybrid Zeus-Amun, whom Alexander the Great invoked in seeking the status of a universal ruler. Cordoba's Muslim philosopher Ibn Rushd developed the Greek (also Indian) idea that the universe was created by natural forces, rather than by God, a profoundly heretical claim for traditional Muslims and Christians. But far from discarding traditional Islamic beliefs, Ibn Rushd presented God as a facilitator, one that gave the process of creation a decisive push. He thereby created a synthesis that would help west European rationalist philosophy and influence the secular understanding of world order. The Chinese retained and reconciled their Confucian and Daoist beliefs with imported Indian Buddhism. Hence, while the civilizations of Greece, India, China, Africa, Islam, and Europe progressed by borrowing the ideas of outsiders, they kept key elements of their own culture and changed much of what they borrowed to suit their needs. Keeping in mind this continuous blending of foreign and local ideas will go a long way in rejecting parochial views in the West today about the creation of the present world order—i.e., it is mainly the West's handwork—and avoiding the fear that the decline of the West means the collapse of all things.

Moreover, it is important to keep in mind that connections and borrowings are not always good in themselves. In the emergence of new world orders, bad ideas such as racism and authoritarianism travel as easily as good ones. Some of these connections among civilizations have been predatory. The world's biggest connector historically is imperialism, the foremost example being the imperialism of the rising West. The Columbian exchange ought to be called the Columbian looting, or theft, because it was originally a one-way affair whereby gold, silver, animals, fruits, vegetables, and rubber, among other resources, made their way to Europe, to its immediate and immense benefit. Meanwhile, the societies from which these goods came collapsed due to the diseases and exploitation that came with the Europeans. Without this loot, without Indian cotton and tax revenue, the Atlantic slave trade, North American land seizures, and the prior knowledge that came from Islam, China, and India, the West could never have risen as far and as fast as it did. Neither could the West have risen without its magic potion: a blend of imperialism, slavery, and racism.

This does not mean, however, that the process of connecting history through the circulation of ideas and mutual learning is always or inherently conflictual. Although civilizations clash, they can also interact peacefully. The spread of Indian religion and political ideas throughout Asia, especially Southeast Asia and Northeast Asia, was overwhelmingly peaceful, as was, for the most part, the spread of Chinese culture and ideas.

No civilization progresses without learning from others. Once a civilization has learned or "downloaded" (Niall Ferguson's term) what it needs from a previous one, it then "uploads" (my term) its own adaptations and creations for other civilizations to benefit.[8] The Greeks would not have achieved takeoff without borrowing from Sumer, Egypt, and other preceding civilizations. Islam reached greatness first by drawing on the science and philosophy of Greece, India, Persia, and China and then adding its own innovations and exporting them to Europe. Europe would not have emerged from its Dark Ages without borrowing ideas, technologies, and resources from Islam, China, India, the New World, and Africa. It was only then that Europe gained prominence on the world stage and spread its ideas—scientific and political, including ideas of sovereignty and democracy—to the rest of the world through colonization. We may now be seeing a new stage in which the Rest, never a passive learner, is once again becoming a contributor of ideas, leading to a blurring of the West-Rest divide and creating the conditions for a possible global convergence.

Another major point of this book is that we must avoid stereotyping civilizations with extreme, dichotomous categories, including backward versus progressive, cruel versus benevolent, stagnant versus dynamic, scientific versus superstitious, familiar versus exotic, and innocent versus mature. This book has shown that all civilizations, and hence the world orders they create or contribute to, are eclectic. None is purely this or that. This is not a matter of political correctness; it is consistent with historical reality. Take for example the science-versus-superstition dichotomy. Europe—even modern Europe—was quite capable of placing theology and revelation over science and reason, while the so-called superstitious civilizations of India and Islam frequently did the reverse. Islam produced both the revivalist al-Ghazali and the rationalist Ibn Sina and Ibn Rushd. The so-called rationalism of European political institutions—as in Hobbes's *Leviathan* or the Peace of Westphalia—were to some degree inspired by Christian theology.

As another example, in all civilizations compassion and ruthlessness are part of the package. The same Maurya age in India produced the idealist Ashoka and the high priest of imperial ideology, Kautilya. China saw the almost contemporaneous flowering of idealistic Confucianism and Daoism on the one hand, and the ruthless realpolitik of legalism on the other. When it comes to political ideologies as well, all civilizations are eclectic. Greece, India, China, Islam, the pre-Columbian Americas, and Africa all contained diverse or conflicting elements within themselves: idealism with realpolitik, anarchy with hierarchy, and reason with revelation. A future world will retain this eclectic character.

Balance of Fear

With this in mind, my essential argument is that the decline of the West and the rise of non-Western civilizations will not necessarily be a turn for the worse. It may lead to a better long-term future for us. Here I return to a point from the Introduction: certainly, rise of the Rest has produced a corresponding increase in fear in the West of what the next world order might bring. There are many sides to this fear, three of which are especially noteworthy.

First is the fear that "civilization states," accompanied by the rise of authoritarianism, conflict, and chaos, will create a divided and dangerous place to live. Gideon Rachman, the chief foreign affairs commentator for the *Financial Times*, defines a civilization state as "a country that claims to represent not just a historic territory or a particular language or ethnic-group, but a distinctive civilization."[9] The list of such civilization states is topped by China, India, and Turkey. Having embraced the identity of a Eurasian—rather than European—nation and culture, Vladimir Putin's Russia is also among them. The idea here is that the major powerhouses of the non-Western world are working to replace the nation-state model with a return to their traditional values, political systems, and imperial foreign relations, thereby exacerbating conflict with the West and creating world disorder. Rachman argues that the civilization states would reject "universal human rights or common democratic standards."[10] The late British academic Christopher Coker concludes that the civilization states threaten to extinguish the "dream of liberal civilization," which was a "universal value system to which everyone subscribes."[11] Another Western writer, Adrian Pabst, warns that the rise of the civilization states "is not just changing the global balance of power. It is also transforming post–Cold War geopolitics away from liberal universalism towards cultural exceptionalism."[12] These are incredible claims, since they imply that the so-called liberal universalist order did not tolerate or instigate authoritarianism and human rights violations. The history of US support for dictatorships is a long one, covering every part of the non-Western world. This support, moreover, was not only inspired by anti-communism but also by the American search for resources and military bases, the very foundations of the US-led liberal order. Even after the end of the Cold War, the United States has continued to support authoritarian regimes in Egypt, Pakistan, and Saudi Arabia, to mention but a few.

In any case, some top Western leaders have added their own voices to the chorus of fear. Shortly after assuming office, President Trump asked in a speech in Poland: "Do we have the desire and the courage to preserve our civilization in the face of those who would subvert and destroy it?"[13] Two years later, senior US State Department official Kiron Skinner characterized the US relationship with China as "a fight with a really different civilization and a different ideology and the United States hasn't had that before."[14] Yet, predicably, Western analysts are noticeably less concerned when their own leaders invoke civilizational and racist identity, as officials from the United States, Australia, the EU, and NATO have done.[15] In the meantime, conservative forces in the United States would like to turn their country into a civilizational state, with efforts in the Southern states to introduce the Bible in schools.

To be sure, these alarms have been triggered by statements made by the leaders of China, India, Turkey, and Russia. For example, in 2019, Chinese president Xi Jinping called on Asian countries to "strengthen cultural confidence" and use "the foundation of the brilliant achievements obtained by our ancestors" to reach "new glory of Asian civilizations."[16] Like Xi, India's prime minister Narendra Modi has stressed his country's civilizational achievements, dating back to the Indus valley civilization and the subsequent Vedic period.[17]

When, in March 2019, an Australian gunman killed fifty-one Muslims in two mosques in Christchurch, New Zealand, he left a manifesto in which he stressed the demographic and cultural threat to "white nations" from immigrants.[18] Turkey's prime minister, Recep Tayyip Erdoğan, saw this as an attack on Muslim civilization and vowed that the "remnants of the Crusaders cannot prevent Turkey's rise" and "will not be able to make Istanbul Constantinople."[19] Erdoğan had been trying to remake Turkey into an Islamic nation, departing from the secularism that had served as post-Ottoman leader Mustafa Kemal Atatürk's main principle.

The alarm over civilization states resurrects Samuel Huntington's "clash of civilizations" thesis of the 1990s. To recap, Huntington argued that, after the Cold War, the major axis of conflict in world politics would no longer be over ideology or economics but over culture, especially among eight civilizations: Western, Confucian (Chinese), Japanese, Islamic, Hindu, Slavic-Orthodox, Latin American, and "possibly" African. That thesis sparked a global debate that reappears every time there is a major international crisis. While Huntington was criticized for presenting a simplistic and sensationalistic idea, pundits and policymakers in the West have found in his thesis a convenient way to frame international conflict whenever one occurs.[20]

The civilization state concept takes Huntington's thesis to a new level. The West's fear today is greater because China and India were not nearly as powerful when Huntington first outlined his argument as they are now. Moreover, their foreign policies, as well as those of Turkey and Russia, stress their identities as civilizations much more today than they did in the 1990s.

But the rise of civilization states does not inevitably lead to conflict. Nor does it imply a break in cooperation across any civilizational divide. Security and economic ties between India and the United States, between Indonesia and Australia, and between the United States and the Islamic nations of Saudi Arabia and Egypt remain robust and growing. In these and many other cases, pragmatism and expediency trump the clash of civilizations. Non-Western countries may be turning to civilizational nationalism in response to the West's rejection or belittling of their cultures, and their leaders may be using it to mobilize domestic political support, but that does not mean they are rejecting integration with the rest of the world.

Moreover, just because civilization is invoked by certain powerful non-Western leaders does not mean their cultures do not offer universal humanistic values that the West might learn from. Some Westerners fear that China evokes civilization-based concepts like *tianxia* to justify its authoritarian rule and designs for global dominance. But this should not negate the elements of Chinese civilization that genuinely uphold universal ethical principles of justice, benevolence, openness, and humane governance. As this book has shown, there is much to be learned from the ideals of non-Western civilizations, and that risks being obscured by the current discourse of the civilization state. In general, the view that competing civilization states are bent on self-aggrandizement and mischief making rests on exaggeration. It sets up a false binary between the West and the Rest.

A second and more specific fear in the West is the emergence of an alternative, Chinese-built world order. "China is the only country with both the intent to reshape the international order and, increasingly, the economic, diplomatic, military, and technological power to do it," US Secretary of State Antony Blinken said in 2022. "Beijing's vision would move us away from the universal values that have sustained so much of the world's progress over the past 75 years."[21] China presents the greatest challenge to any optimism in the West about the future of world order. To a large extent, this has to do with China's growing economic and military heft, as well as its expanding footprint in the global South, where it presents itself as an alternative to Western-style development. In other words, China's emergence as a world power directly challenges the dominance of the West in many corners of the world. But there is more. The West also sees China's use of technology to surveil its own people, its increasing authoritarianism under its current supreme leader Xi Jinping, its ambitious military buildup, and its aggressive behavior toward Taiwan and in the South China Sea as an effort to reshape the world in a way that would be inimical to liberal and democratic values.

But this reshaping would face severe limits as applied to the entire world. As discussed, while China might replace the United States as the world's biggest economy, it will not do so as the leading military power. It will not have the ability to surpass the United States in power projection or in the control of the global commons, including air and maritime space. Some analysts of China believe that Beijing's goal is to revive the tribute system of centuries past, when China was at the center of the world and the rest paid it a kind of obeisance. A key ground for such suspicion is China's Belt and Road Initiative (BRI), launched by Xi in 2013 as a megaproject for building infrastructure in developing nations with Chinese financial and technical aid as well as the dispatch of Chinese workers. Although its most direct and immediate focus is regional, especially in Eurasia, the BRI's scope extends to all corners of the world. Estimates of its price tag vary widely, from $3 trillion to $6 trillion (the Chinese government is notoriously opaque about costs, and estimates are subject to periodic revisions by the government).[22] Some 150 nations are believed to have signed on to it in some way, although the degree of involvement also varies considerably from nation to nation. In Indonesia, there is a single high-speed rail project from Jakarta to Bandung. On the other end of the scale, there is the star of the show, the China-Pakistan Economic Corridor, a $62 billion sea and land infrastructure development that, among other things, would drastically reduce the distances involved in China's crucial energy imports from the Middle East and speed up the country's connections with Europe.[23]

Whatever its scale and cost, the BRI's effect on Western fears about the rise of China is already substantial. In a special report on the BRI, the *Economist* magazine, one of the most influential defenders of the Western-led world order, noted that China is using the BRI to "reshape a world order more to its liking."[24] China has presented the project as a "benign" way of achieving that goal, specifically by putting it in a "broader historical context: the tributary system of old." In this vision, "China sits at the centre of the world, bringing its wealth and power to bear, first on its near-abroad, and linking people into the concept of China as a beneficent power and an alternative locus to the West. Those who buy into it receive munificence from Beijing. Those who do not will not." China, the *Economist* report concludes, "represents a prototype for an emerging geopolitical bloc at a time when the rules-based order is under shaky American management."

But such words grossly exaggerate the BRI's potential to create a new world order or revive the Chinese tributary system, even if Beijing were willing to undertake such a task.[25] The BRI is bedeviled by corruption, lack of transparency, political instability in many of the partner countries, doubts about whether the projects will benefit local populations, and concerns that they would significantly increase the indebtedness of recipient countries. China's capacity to sustain the initiative in the face of diminishing domestic economic growth rates is increasingly in doubt. More importantly, the BRI has invited backlash, not just from the West but also from China's neighbors. Some spectacular failures—such as in Sri Lanka, which had to turn over its major port to Chinese control to cover its BRI-induced debts—have increased perceptions of the project's predatory nature.

In sum, the BRI places a major burden on China and presents a test for its credibility as a rising power. Beijing is under intense international pressure to deliver results. While the BRI does have its supporters in the global South, failure, or even only partial success, would undercut China's image on the world stage.[26] Keeping in mind that China's historical foreign relations were not peaceful, any attempt by China today to revive its tributary system will be countered by its neighbors and other major powers—such as Japan, the United States, Russia, and India—whereas in the past China faced no major rivals, with the possible exception of Japan and some nomadic/steppe polities. In short, any effort by China to resurrect the tributary system, if in fact it really wants to do so, would be fraught with obstacles and potential for blowback. Many of the factors that create political backlash against US hegemony in the global South could do the same against a hegemonic China.

In addition to the economic and political roadblocks to world dominance, China will not lead in cultural appeal in creating a global civilization, despite the plans outlined by Xi's Global Civilization Initiative. Global civilization, as mentioned in the Introduction, has been proposed by liberal thinkers like Vaclav Havel and Amartya Sen before. These proposals have included ideals of equality and mutual respect among civilizations, which are also prominent in China's initiative. But this cultural project is likely to fail if China's current leadership emerges as its main champion, as it has tried to do by launching the initiative at a 2023 conclave between the Communist Party of China and foreign political parties. Despite China's attempts to own it, global civilization is no more a Chinese idea than it is a Western one.

One related Western fear about the rise of China is that it might spread its ideology and governance model at the expense of "universal values" (which usually refers to Western values). These Chinese values are assumed to be collective interests over individualism, authoritarian governance instead of democracy, and state-led economic development at the expense of the market—in other words, the so-called China model. This fear is largely misplaced. China is not going to become a bastion of democracy and human rights, but this does not mean it can successfully export autocracy or suppress human rights worldwide. Democracy and human rights are in retreat today, both in and outside the West, but this is not due to China and Russia, and it is premature to view this as an irreversible trend. In the West, this is due mainly to domestic forces, especially the rise of right-wing populist movements and political parties. To be sure, these movements have drawn oxygen from growing anger about the Western governments' failure to compete economically with rising powers like China and India. But they come mostly from growing economic inequality, anti-immigrant sentiments, and domestic racial tensions predating the rise of China.[27] While China does showcase its economic achievements and cultural appeal before the world, Beijing has not been in the business of promoting its political ideology since Mao Zedong exported communism. Rather, ideology promotion is a very American way of building world order.

In the coming world order, as in the Western-dominated one that is passing, there will be plenty of authoritarianism, often tolerated and backed by the West. As noted, populism, a cousin of authoritarianism, is on the rise in Europe and the United States. In this climate, the Chinese model of authoritarian rule may be attractive to some nations—such as Cambodia, Hungary, and Singapore—but it would be a considerable stretch to say that the world at large would embrace it. It is noteworthy that China, despite its rise in the past three decades, is surrounded by democracies, however flawed: Japan, South Korea, Taiwan, India, Indonesia, Malaysia, and the Philippines among them. If China's Asian neighbors are not persuaded to adopt its system, why should we expect the rest of the world to do so? Democracy and human rights are not uniquely Western today, if they ever were. Moreover, the other element of the China model, state-led economic development, has been a feature of many other East Asian governments, including Japan, South Korea, Taiwan, and Singapore. In short, these countries were already part of the East Asian miracle before China's bandwagon got rolling.

A third fear in the West about a post-Western world order is of a heightened prospect for chaos, violence, and conflict: a "world on fire" and loss of Western, especially American, leadership to prevent that from happening. We've already seen plenty of signs of this in the past decades, including the 9/11 attacks; the conflicts in Iraq, Afghanistan, Libya, and

Syria; and, more recently, the Russia-Ukraine war and the Israel-Hamas confrontation. Increasingly, there are also rising prospects for war over Taiwan. But this fear needs to be put in perspective. First, no world order is a garden of peace. The Western-dominated world order has seen plenty of wars, and nearly all of them took place in the non-Western world (though the Russia-Ukraine war has now returned major war to the heart of Europe). Second, since most of these wars took place when the West still unequivocally ruled, it is far from clear whether new wars are breaking out because of the decline of the West or because of flawed and failed Western policies. The violence of the colonial era aside, hasty or ill-conceived Western policies have contributed to protracted conflicts in the postcolonial era. Certainly, the US invasion of Iraq in 2003—which cost hundreds of thousands of lives and whose effects persist to this day—was an avoidable war of choice, born out of totally unproven US claims about Iraqi support for terrorism and an alleged program to acquire weapons of mass destruction.

Trends in conflict and violence since the end of the Cold War paint no uniform or linear pattern. Armed conflicts claiming at least one thousand lives declined substantially in the first two decades after the end of the Cold War, then have risen and fallen every few years. While overall conflicts and deaths from conflict have increased with the Russia-Ukraine war, the Israel-Hamas war, and the Myanmar civil war, interstate conflicts in general remain very rare, while intrastate conflicts, with or without foreign intervention, have grown. Yet some highly publicized threats to peace have diminished, especially terrorist attacks, which are a localized threat, confined to a handful of states such as Afghanistan, Iraq, Nigeria, Somalia, and Syria. A related point is that when it comes to disorder, not all parts of the world are alike; the degree of stability varies widely between regions. Some are, and will be, more prone to conflict than others. South America is likely to be more stable than the Middle East; the risk of war will be higher in Northeast Asia than in Southeast Asia. Hence, to speak as if the whole world is on the brink is a gross exaggeration.

No doubt it is for these reasons that fears of a future world order no longer dominated by the West are greater in the United States and

Europe than they are in the global South. Similarly, pessimism about the future of world order is greater in the West than in the Rest. A survey conducted by the Stimson Center in 2023 found that the majority of respondents in China and India believe "things globally are headed in the right direction." The score for China was 82 percent positive to 11 percent negative, and for India 64 percent to 23 percent, the rest being unsure.[28] Even more notable is the finding that there is more optimism about the "state of the world" in the BRICS nations than in the G7 nations. And most importantly, optimism about the future is greater among the younger generation everywhere: when asked whether the world is "doing well," 50 percent of people under forty replied yes, compared to 35 percent of people above that age. When asked whether the world is going in the "right direction," the response was 39 percent positive for people under forty, and 23 percent for people above it.[29]

A Global Multiplex

If Western fears about the new world order are overblown, what exactly will be the shape of the future world? To start with, I call this world order a multiplex, rather than "multipolar," as most pundits and leaders today put it. The two words may sound similar, but there are three crucial differences. First, in multipolarity, conflict and cooperation are shaped by a handful of major powers using their superior military and economic capacity. That's what Britain, France, Russia, Prussia, and Austria-Hungary did in the nineteenth and early twentieth centuries. In the twenty-first century, the candidates for this role will be China, India, the United States, the EU, and Russia. Like a multiplex cinema—where one can watch movies with different producers, directors, actors, and scripts—a multiplex world order is managed by the interaction among many more players, including corporations, foundations, nongovernmental organizations, and people empowered by social media. Second, in a multipolar world, military and economic instruments of power matter most. A multiplex world, on the other hand, takes into account the role of ideas and culture. A third difference is that, in a multiplex world, not only does the number of major powers increase but new forms of leadership and cooperation emerge. The traditional great powers do not, in fact cannot, lead in every area. On the contrary, leadership capacity will vary from issue to issue.

In this world, no state, however powerful, will be able to lead in all areas. In a famous 2014 speech at the West Point Military Academy, then US president Barack Obama said that "America must always lead on the world stage. If we don't, no one else will."[30] But the United States cannot "always" lead the world. This is not because it lacks resources (although it has less economic clout than before) or because of competition from China and Russia, but because an increasingly partisan US Congress, populist leaders like Trump, and a significant chunk of American people disdain global engagement.

At the same time, the multiplex world will not be a leaderless, or "GZERO," world—the zero here referring not just to the absence of G7- or G20-type groupings but to a world without leaders and cooperation.[31] We are entering into a world where there will be more, not fewer, leaders. New forms of cooperation will not rest exclusively with the UN and its agencies, the IMF, the World Bank, the WTO, or the G20. Governments, Western and non-Western, will continue to play a crucial role in fostering cooperation, but they will be joined by a variety of non-state actors, such as private corporations and nonprofit groups dedicated to different causes, ranging from poverty reduction to public health. I call it a G-Plus world.

There are many examples of such G-Plus cooperation already in play. The creation of the International Criminal Court and the treaty to ban land mines were led by advocacy groups, despite the initial opposition of major powers including the United States, China, and Russia. Another example is the Global Fund to Fight AIDS, Tuberculosis, and Malaria, which would not have been possible without support from private sources, led by the Bill & Melinda Gates Foundation. The Internet Corporation for Assigned Names and Numbers, which assigns Internet domain names, was initially organized by the United States, but now it is managed independently by a group of stakeholders that include governments, consumers, and experts. A key force behind global climate change assessment and mitigation is the Intergovernmental Panel on Climate Change, which draws on the expertise of nearly eight hundred scientists. A large number of corporations from the energy, consumer products, and transportation sectors participated in the drafting of the Paris Climate Accords of 2015 and committed themselves to the agreement's implementation by reducing their carbon footprints and stepping up their efforts to use renewable energy. These are non-state groups whose standards have been supported and accepted by governments and international bodies. In a G-Plus world, nongovernmental groups create the momentum for global cooperation and provide the expertise and resources to make it possible.

In a global multiplex, different nations will exercise leadership in different issue areas and locations. For the foreseeable future, the United States will remain the top strategic player globally, especially leading collective defense operations through its alliances such as NATO. But China will also lead, and indeed it has already taken the lead in the trade and development fields. The European Union leads in responding to climate change. India is the world's largest vaccine producer. Japan has been pushed to fourth place as a global economic power but remains a world leader in development assistance.

Leadership depends not just on power and resources but also on ideas and initiatives. In the past, second-tier nations—the so-called middle powers such as Canada, Australia, and Norway—have provided leadership in such areas as peacekeeping, human security, and humanitarian intervention. In a multiplex world, postcolonial nations will join or displace the Western middle powers in providing leadership in these and other areas. Here I am not talking about China—which is not a member of the global South, despite presenting itself as such—or the increasingly assertive India, which aspires to lead the developing world. Rather, countries such as Brazil, South Africa, Nigeria, Mexico, Indonesia, Kenya, Argentina, South Korea, Saudi Arabia, and the United Arab Emirates will become more consequential in global cooperation in different issue areas. Some of these nations and many others, large and small, from Barbados to Botswana to Bangladesh, are deeply involved in building cooperation in their own regions, which is essential to building global peace and development. The Association of Southeast Asian Nations has organized an area of relative peace in that region, where no major conflict has broken out between its members. The African Union has created the world's first regional mechanism for humanitarian intervention, designed and used to protect lives threatened by war, genocide, and government collapse.

This will certainly worry Western nations, who continue to see the postcolonial countries as an unruly herd and a challenge to their own security and to global stability at large. In reality, postcolonial nations have been rule makers, not rule breakers as the West often portrays them. The majority of them voted to condemn the Russian attack that began the war against Ukraine as a violation of international principles of nonaggression and territorial integrity. Regarding Israel's military retaliation against the Hamas October 2023 terrorist attacks, postcolonial nations overwhelmingly supported efforts for ceasefire and to prevent genocide, which the US initially blocked while tens of thousands of Palestinian civilians died.

Postcolonial nations have rebelled when the rules of the Western-led liberal international order (sometimes called the rules-based order) are unfair to them. A good example of this unfairness came during the COVID-19 pandemic, when the rich G7 nations received more than thirty times the allocations made to the world's poorest nations from the IMF's emergency financial reserves. This "grossly unfair" allocation, as the UN secretary-general António Guterres himself admitted, "was done according to the rules." As he pointed out, "There is something morally wrong in the rules that established this kind of procedure."[32]

Global cooperation that brings together both developed and developing nations will become more important. For example, the G20—which emerged as a mechanism to cope with global financial crises, such as those in 1997 and 2008—includes the United States, China, Germany, France, Australia, Russia, India, South Africa, and Brazil, among others. Another example is the world's largest trade grouping, the Regional Comprehensive Economic Partnership, which came into being in 2020 and comprises China, Japan, Australia, and Indonesia. It represents not only different civilizations but also a partnership between Western and non-Western nations.

This leads to another feature of the global multiplex: economic interdependence and globalization will be shaped less by the West and more by the Rest. Since the COVID-19 pandemic, world trade is increasingly dominated by trade among global South nations. In the nineteenth century, trade took place almost exclusively among the rich Western nations, and this trade amounted to some 80 to 90 percent of total global trade. This legacy of the colonial era continued well into decolonization. Even in the early 1990s, trade among rich Western nations still accounted for nearly 60 percent of total world trade. But today, some 35 percent of global merchandise trade is among the countries of the global South, while that among the rich Western nations has fallen to 25 percent.[33]

Next, the global multiplex, as the concept implies, will be one of political and cultural diversity. It will be not a democracy-versus-dictatorship struggle, a simplistic frame often employed by Western leaders such as President Joe Biden. Divergent political systems—authoritarian, democratic, communitarian, and populist—will exist side by side. Many political systems will be hybrid, a reality not fully captured by the current ways of classifying countries' political systems, such as that employed by Western advocacy agency Freedom House.

Last but not least, the influence of the West in shaping global culture will also decline relative to others. This is already seen in films and food. China, which has overtaken the United States as the world's largest box office and for some time has been the biggest foreign market for Hollywood films, is moving away from Western cultural properties. *Oppenheimer* and *Barbie*, two of the biggest Hollywood blockbusters in 2023, did not even make the top thirty in the Chinese box office. This could be due to nationalism or US-China tensions, but it can also be attributed to the fact that China is now matching Hollywood in making diverse and high-quality movies.[34] In India, which produces the largest number of films per year, Hollywood films make up just 12 percent of the box office.[35] India's Bollywood has long been popular in Southeast Asia and even in China. A 2016 survey showed that in six Arab countries in the Middle East, 99 percent of viewers watch TV in Arabic, and only 11 percent also watch TV in English.[36] And here's a little-known fact: Nollywood, the Nigerian film industry, has surpassed Hollywood to become the world's second largest movie industry by volume, right behind Bollywood.

Not only is the global South seeing more of its own movies, but it's exporting more of its culture. K-pop (pop music from South Korea) has become hugely popular around the world, with groups like NewJeans, Fifty Fifty, and Jung Kook (whose song "Seven" became *Billboard*'s number one global song for the summer of 2023) rising to the top of the charts. There is also a diffusion of cuisine. A survey using Instagram hashtags by the *Picky Eater* blog and covering the fifty most visited cities around the world found that while Italian cuisine is the most popular worldwide, Japanese and Indian cuisines are not far behind, and Korean, Mexican, Thai, Chinese, Indonesian, Vietnamese, and Filippino cuisines round out the top ten globally.[37]

To be sure, the global spread of culture and cuisine will not end national rivalries. The idea of global civilization accommodates "divisions as well as the interdependences."[38] But instead of fueling a clash of civilizations on the one hand or creating a single homogenous civilization on the other, this exchange will bring about a "cultural mélange" that may promote understanding and, over time, reduce conflict.[39] This may sound too optimistic, but it is not entirely unfounded, and it should encourage us at least to look at the future with less foreboding and anxiety.

Fear to Hope

A basic premise of this book is that the end of the Western- and US-led order need not mean global collapse and might actually be good for the world. But to ensure stability and prosperity for all of humankind, the West needs to find ways to cooperate with non-Western nations. Instead of giving in to pessimism and fear, and resisting the end of their dominance, the Western nations should adapt and learn to live with the rise of the Rest. Working toward a global project of reconciliation and respect among nations and civilizations would be more productive than a futile last-ditch effort to resist change.

This will involve two closely related tasks. The first has to do with the memory of the past few hundred years. Western nations need to take ownership of their racist colonialism in non-Western societies, as well as address their domestic racism. This might mean underscoring the West's share of responsibility for ongoing conflicts in the world today, such as the India-Pakistan or Israel-Palestine conflicts, both of which emerged from colonial and myopic Western policies. To remember the past as it actually happened would put the West on notice not to repeat the mistake of civilizational hubris: imposing its will, including its arbitrary territorial and political solutions, on people of divergent cultures. While the postcolonial nations may not be totally mollified, this would help to dilute, if not erase, the memories of colonialism and racism in all forms everywhere. At the very least, the postcolonial nations will have less justification to keep blaming their current problems on past Western dominance. They will be reminded of the need to move forward with their task of ensuring economic well-being and political stability for their own citizens and for the world as a whole.

But this is not enough. Equally important is to develop mutual respect between the West and the Rest, partly through a better understanding of the historical contributions of non-Western nations and civilizations to world order, as this book has provided. No civilization is purely benign or purely malign. But the current narratives of history are too partial to Western civilization's benign elements while downplaying or disparaging the ideals and attractions of the Rest. The latter's contributions, and its role in the long history of mutual learning among civilizations, should be brought to the West's classrooms and mainstream media. Many, especially conservative thinkers, lament that Western classrooms are not teaching classical history. But a curriculum that focuses on Greco-Roman achievements—and there are many—while giving short shrift to those of China, India, Islam, Africa, and the pre-Columbian Americas would ill serve the younger generation of students and leaders entering into a brave new world. To recognize these other contributions will not make the world a Kantian paradise of "perpetual peace," but it would address a principal source of division between the West and the Rest.

It would be absurd to end this book with the prediction that all will be well. It won't be. And yet, there is hope, if we take seriously one of the lessons presented in this book. History is not a single, continuous thread of progress leading to the victory of a particular civilization or world order, whether created by the West or others. The end of one history gives rise to another. And the history that is rapidly ending before our eyes is that of the relatively short span of Western hegemony in the long march of civilization.[40] History is now being propelled forward in an entirely new, post-Western, multi-civilizational, and geopolitically multiplex direction.

As this change unfolds, we need to overcome the notion of a West-versus-the-Rest divide. This does not mean wishing for the demise of Western civilization, nor ignoring its contributions to human progress. Rather, it calls for the end of the West as a self-glorifying notion that continues to see itself as racially, politically, and intellectually superior to the rest of the world. As this book has shown, the modern idea of the West was founded on Europe's imperialism, cultural arrogance, and racial exclusion. This not only made the contributions of other civilizations invisible, but also provoked the idea of the Rest, or Third World and then Global South as a movement for resistance and building an alternative world order. In this sense, the decline of Western dominance could alleviate the conflicts and injustice it had caused, help to heal the resentment against it, and thereby make the realization of a global civilization and inclusive world order possible. This book's main lesson—that world order is not the West's monopoly but a shared creation of multiple civilizations over a long span of history—contributes to that goal. This opens up new possibilities for the future, which we must accept and build upon. As Ibn Khaldun would say, "It is as if the entire creation had changed and the whole world been altered, as if it were a new and repeated creation, a world brought into existence anew."[41]

Acknowledgments

Few places can be a more fitting base for writing a five-thousand-year history of world order than a city founded merely 235 years ago. Washington, DC, lives almost entirely in the present, where history often begins and ends with the "made in America" world that its proponents insist has benignly served all humankind since the end of World War II. I have lived and worked in many other places—New Delhi, Beijing, Toronto, Singapore, Bristol, Oxford, and Cambridge (Massachusetts) among them—and traveled to many others. Although these places can inspire and inform, none can match Washington's capacity to provoke the mind, especially when it comes to narratives of world order. By protesting too much against outsiders' views, Washington raises profound suspicions about its own.

I am such an outsider, being in but not of Washington for the past fifteen years. But I have also been lucky to be employed by the School of International Service of American University. Nestled in the garden-like northwestern end of the town, here a diverse and dynamic community of students and faculty have been invaluable companions as my thinking about this book progressed. Whether agreeing or disagreeing with my views, they have been unfailingly curious about alternative ideas about world order, its deep past and long-term future, far beyond what textbooks or the mainstream media tell them. Those in my first-year Civilizations, Empires, and World Orders course in the past decade have given me fair warning but also much hope about how the younger generation in America and the world might take to what I write about in this book.

But crafting a global story of order building would have been impossible without being part of a much larger universe. I had started this journey in Odisha, India, where my first visit to a site of world-order building was actually only a short distance from home. Here, in words carved on the rocks of Dhauli Hills around the mid-third century BC, King Ashoka of the Maurya dynasty had pledged to provide for the "complete welfare and happiness" of all his subjects, just as he would do for his own children, including their protection from "unjust imprisonment or harsh treatment." What made these words particularly striking was that they were written after Ashoka had won a brutal war against Kalinga (the ancient name of Odisha), in which, by his own admission, 100,000 people had been killed and another 150,000 taken as prisoners. But Ashoka never waged war again, and while ruling over the largest empire of ancient India, he launched a peaceful campaign to spread Buddhism all over Asia, the influence of which remains visible to this day. This was a far cry from the way many other rulers—from ancient China, through medieval Arabia, to modern America—managed their empires; it is certainly in marked contrast to the violence and coercion employed by western Europeans to build their world order and spread their beliefs.

This has fascinated me and stoked my lifelong interest in the multiple ways in which world order can be built. They were burnished by my travels to places around the world: from Cairo to Cordoba, Bodh Gaya to Borobudur, Malacca to Machu Picchu, Luoyang to London, and many more than I can possibly mention here. Visiting archaeological sites, monuments, museums, archives, libraries, and research institutes made me increasingly familiar with connections in isolation, similarities amid differences, and order around disorder. These experiences were possible because of my wonderful hosts. They were not only academics, artists, archaeologists, and adventurers but also ordinary folks whose daily lives offer the best window to the civilizations that this book describes. Many of these encounters are truly unforgettable, like the Mayan leader who took me to descend to the tomb of seventh-century ruler of Palenque K'inich Janaab' Pakal, the Sicilian student who drove me around the island to study its colonization by the Carthaginians and Corinthians,

Chinese friends with whom I survived a nasty sandstorm in the dunes of Dunhuang, Egyptian guides who helped me explore Alexander the Great's coronation as the king of the land, Andean companions who walked parts of the Inca Trail with me along the Ecuador-Peru border, and South African students who took me to visit Black townships, Gandhi's ashrams, and Nelson Mandela's birthplace.

My wife Sally and son Arun have been soulmates, sounding boards, morale boosters, and travel companions. They have cheerfully put up with my numerous demands, no matter how unreasonable, and forgiven me when I missed a family event or, worse, a campout or hiking or biking activity that my son was required to complete for his Eagle Scout rank. (He did reach that milestone as this book neared its completion!) The grossest understatement about my life would be to say that I could not have done this book without them.

Distinguished historians of different civilizations were kind enough to comment on draft proposals or chapters of the book. They include Akbar Ahmed (American University), Amin Saikal (Australian National University), Arne Westad (Yale University), Roger Ames (Peking University), Patrick Olivelle (University of Texas, Austin). In addition, seasoned and rising experts—Louis Goodman (American University), Jorge Heine (Boston University), Thomas Tieku (King's University College, University of Western Ontario), and Manjeet Pardesi (Victoria University of Wellington)—significantly enriched my understanding of the non-Western world.

For discussions and suggestions on various themes and chapters, I am especially grateful to John Hobson, Daniel Bell, Tansen Sen, William Bain, Peter Katzenstein, Teresa Vergara, Carmen Escalante, Salimah Cossens, Andrew Hurrell, Louise Fawcett, Ayse Zarakol, Prajakti Kalra, Ken Boutin, and Michael Mazarr.

Institutions around the world facilitated my research at historical sites, museums, and libraries, whether their own or located nearby. My special thanks go to Shandong University, Pontificia Universidad Católica del Perú, Universidad Nacional de San Antonio Abad del Cusco, Universidad Nacional Autónoma de México, FLACSO Ecuador,

University of Catania, Freie Universität Berlin, Rhodes University, Saint Petersburg State University, University College London, Nankai University, Tsinghua University, National Tsing Hua University (Taiwan), Jamia Millia Islamia, Gadjah Mada University, Magadha University, Marmara University, Dunhuang Academy, Sciences Po, Lanzhou University, Oxford University, University College, London, the American University in Cairo, Ritsumeikan University, and Ewha Womans University. For taking me to visit some of the most important historical sites in this book, I am especially grateful to Alessandro Gobbicchi in Rome, Angela Penisi in Sicily, Alejandro Villalobos in Mexico City, Maria Lagutina in Saint Petersburg, Julia Bentley in Canada (who often lived and worked in Asia), Yu Xiaofeng and Falin Zhang in China, Raul Salgado in Ecuador and Peru, Arvind Kumar and Utpal Pati in India, M. Rajarethnam (Raja) in Southeast Asia, Ji Young Kwon in South Korea, and Kevin Marincowitz and Paul Bischoff in South Africa.

I gave several lectures and seminars—both in person and online—to sound out the book's core ideas and arguments. Especially and directly important in shaping the book were lectures delivered at Jamia Millia Islamia in New Delhi (a series of twelve lectures), at University of Catania in Sicily, at the University of British Columbia's Mark Zacher Distinguished Speaker Lecture, at Dunhuang Academy, at Princeton University's Reimagining Word Order project (led by John Ikenberry), and at Oxford Martin School's Changing Global Order project (directed by Louise Fawcett).

A team of rising scholars at American University provided invaluable research assistance for this book. Led by Mohamed Othman, they included Spencer Collins, Noah Rosen, Sisir Bhandari, Sahil Mathur, and Nyandeng V. Gajang. My students Maria Adamou, Yatin Jain, and Ido Leidner offered insightful comments on draft chapters. Critical research support was also provided by Arko Dasgupta in India and Claus Kao-Chu Soong, a Taiwanese scholar who studied with me in Beijing during my sabbatical year there.

My literary agents Peter and Amy Bernstein successfully led the search for a publisher for the book and offered invaluable advice in its framing and completion. Richard Bernstein helped to shape the manuscript for a wider audience. My editor at Basic Books, Michael Kaler, daringly took up a project that challenges so much of the received wisdom about the history of world order and guided me throughout the publishing process. I am grateful to Patti Issacs for help with the maps, Shena Redmond for overseeing the copyediting and page-proofing processes, and Elizabeth Dana for the final edits on the manuscript.

While this book would not have been completed without the help of so many people in so many parts of the world, I alone remain responsible for its content, interpretations, and arguments.

Illustrations

Maps

Images

Notes

Introduction

1. Henry Kissinger, "The Coronavirus Pandemic Will Forever Alter the World Order," *Wall Street Journal*, April 3, 2020, www.wsj.com/articles/the-coronavirus-pandemic-will-forever-alter-the-world-order-11585953005.

2. Robert D. Blackwill and Thomas Wright, *The End of World Order and American Foreign Policy* (New York: Council on Foreign Relations, 2020), www.cfr.org/report/end-world-order-and-american-foreign-policy.

3. "The New World Disorder," *Economist*, June 17, 2020, www.economist.com/leaders/2020/06/18/the-new-world-disorder.

4. Joschka Fischer, "No World Order," *Project Syndicate*, December 18, 2023, www.project-syndicate.org/commentary/russia-ukraine-war-and-middle-east-chaos-symptoms-of-international-breakdown-by-joschka-fischer-2023-12.

5. Francis Fukuyama, "The End of History?," *The National Interest*, no. 16 (Summer 1989): 3–18.

6. National Geographic Society, "Key Components of Civilization," *National Geographic*, last updated March 6, 2024, https://education.nationalgeographic.org/resource/key-components-civilization/.

7. Michael Rundell, ed., *Macmillan English Dictionary*, 2nd ed. (Oxford: Macmillan, 2010), 1634.

8. John King Fairbank, *The Chinese World Order: Traditional China's Foreign Relations* (Cambridge, MA: Harvard University Press, 1968).

9. Henry Kissinger, *World Order* (New York: Penguin Press, 2014), 2.

10. Olúfẹ́mi Táíwò, "It Never Existed," *Aeon*, January 13, 2023, https://aeon.co/essays/the-idea-of-precolonial-africa-is-vacuous-and-wrong.

11. John M. Hobson, *The Eastern Origins of Western Civilization* (Cambridge: Cambridge University Press, 2004); Peter Frankopan, *The Silk Roads: A New*

History of the World (New York: Vintage, 2017); Josephin Quinn, *How the World Made the West: A 4,000 Year History* (London: Penguin Random House, 2024).

12. German Egyptologist Jan Assmann finds parallels between the Egyptian notion of order *(ma'at)* and chaos *(isfet)*—"having set Maat in the place of Isfet"—and similar dualisms in India and Europe. Jan Assmann, "State and Religion in the New Kingdom," in *Religion and Philosophy in Ancient Egypt*, ed. James P. Allen (New Haven, CT: Yale University Press, 1989), 61. I argue that this formulation can also apply to other civilizations, including India, Persia, and the pre-Columbian Americas.

13. G. John Ikenberry, *Liberal Leviathan: The Origins, Crisis, and Transformation of the American World Order* (Princeton, NJ: Princeton University Press, 2011).

14. "Champions of Human Rights: Eleanor Roosevelt (1884–1962)," United for Human Rights, n.d., www.humanrights.com/voices-for-human-rights/eleanor -roosevelt.html.

15. Amartya Kumar Sen, "Universal Truths: Human Rights and the Westernizing Illusion," *Harvard International Review* 20, no. 3 (1998): 42.

16. Yuen Foong Khong, "The American Tributary System," *Chinese Journal of International Politics* 6, no. 1 (March 2013): 1–47.

17. Samuel P. Huntington, "The Clash of Civilizations?," *Foreign Affairs* 72, no. 3 (Summer 1993): 41.

18. Amitav Acharya, *The End of American World Order* (Cambridge: Polity, 2014).

19. Cornelius Tacitus, "The History," in *The Complete Works of Tacitus*, ed. Moses Hadas, trans. Alfred John Church and William Jackson Brodribb (New York: Modern Library, 1942), 420.

20. Václav Havel, "The Search for Meaning in a Global Civilization," *English Academy Review* 16, no. 1 (December 1, 1999): 3–7; Amartya Kumar Sen, "Our Global Civilization," *Procedia Social and Behavioral Sciences* 2, no. 5 (2010), www .researchgate.net/publication/238384820_Our_Global_Civilization.

21. Havel, "The Search for Meaning in a Global Civilization," 3.

22. "It is as if the entire creation had changed and the whole world been altered, as if it were a new and repeated creation, a world brought into existence anew." Ibn Khaldun, *The Muqaddimah: An Introduction to History*, abr. and ed. N. J. Dawood, trans. Franz Rosenthal (Princeton, NJ: Princeton University Press, 2015), 3.

Chapter 1: First Foundations

1. Sumer and Egypt influenced each other in art and metallurgy. The potter's wheel might have reached Egypt from Sumer. Despite being completely

different, Egypt's hieroglyphic language might have been stimulated by contact with Sumer cuneiform. William H. McNeill, *The Rise of the West: A History of the Human Community* (New York: Mentor Books, 1965), 90.

2. John H. Clarke, introduction to *Introduction to African Civilizations*, by John G. Jackson (Secaucus, NJ: Citadel Press, 2001), 4.

3. McNeill, *The Rise of the West*, 64, 66–67.

4. Christopher Ehert, "Africa in World History: The Long, Long View," in *The Oxford Handbook of World History*, ed. Jerry H. Bentley (Oxford: Oxford University Press, 2011), 461.

5. László Török, *The Kingdom of Kush: Handbook of the Napatan-Meroitic Civilization* (Leiden, Netherlands: Brill, 1997), 62.

6. Julian Reade, *Mesopotamia* (London: British Museum Press, 1991), 41–42; *Cone of Entemena*, 2400 BC, terra-cotta, 27 × 12.70 cm, Musée du Louvre, Paris.

7. *The Epic of Gilgamesh*, trans. Andrew George (London: Penguin, 1999), 24, 94–95; *The Epic of Gilgamesh*, trans. N. K. Sandars (Harmondsworth, UK: Penguin Books, 1960), 70–71, 40–41.

8. McNeill, *The Rise of the West*, 67.

9. John Haywood, *The Ancient World* (New York: Metro Books, 2010), 24–25.

10. Cited in Samuel N. Kramer, *The Sumerians: Their History, Culture, and Character* (Chicago: University of Chicago Press, 1963), 84.

11. H. Dieter Viel, trans., *The New Complete Code of Hammurabi* (Lanham, MD: University Press of America, 2012).

12. Albert K. Grayson, "The Empire of Sargon of Akkad," *Archiv für Orientforschung* 25 (1974): 56–64.

13. Irmgard Woldering, *The Art of Egypt: The Time of the Pharaohs* (New York: Crown Publisher, 1963), 36, 49; Bruce G. Trigger, *Understanding Early Civilizations: A Comparative Study* (Cambridge: Cambridge University Press, 2003), 80.

14. Ogden Goelet, "Memphis and Thebes: Disaster and Renewal in Ancient Egyptian Consciousness," *Classical World* 97, no. 1 (2003): 19–29; Maulana Karenga, *Maat, the Moral Ideal in Ancient Egypt: A Study in Classical African Ethics* (New York: Routledge, 2004).

15. Stuart Tyson Smith, *Wretched Kush: Ethnic Identities and Boundaries in Egypt's Nubian Empire* (London: Routledge, 2003), 173.

16. Toby A. H. Wilkinson, ed., *The Egyptian World* (London: Routledge, 2007), 223.

17. Raymond Cohen and Raymond Westbrook, "Introduction: The Amarna System," in *Amarna Diplomacy: The Beginnings of International Relations*, eds. Raymond Cohen and Raymond Westbrook (Baltimore: Johns Hopkins University Press, 2000), 4.

18. Steven R. David, "Realism, Constructivism, and the Amarna Letters," in *Amarna Diplomacy*, eds. Cohen and Westbrook, 54–67.

19. *Amarna Letter: Royal Letter from Ashur-Uballit, the King of Assyria, to the King of Egypt*, ca. 1353–1336 BC, clay, 7.7 × 5.5 cm, Metropolitan Museum of Art, New York, www.metmuseum.org/art/collection/search/544695.

20. Cited in Carlo Zaccagnini, "The Interdependence of the Great Powers," in *Amarna Diplomacy*, eds. Cohen and Westbrook, 149.

21. Cited in ibid., 150.

22. Geoffrey Berridge, "Amarna Diplomacy: A Full-Fledged Diplomatic System?," in *Amarna Diplomacy*, eds. Cohen and Westbrook, 220.

23. Raymond Cohen and Raymond Westbrook, "Conclusion," in *Amarna Diplomacy*, eds. Cohen and Westbrook, 233.

24. Ibid.

25. Adam Watson, *The Evolution of International Society* (New York: Routledge, 1992), 31.

26. Iclal Vanwesenbeeck, "The Kadesh Peace Treaty and Translating Peace: A Conversation with Anthony Spalinger and Veysel Donbaz by Iclal Vanwesenbeeck," *World Literature Today*, June 26, 2019, www.worldliteraturetoday.org /blog/interviews/kadesh-peace-treaty-and-translating-peace-conversation -anthony-spalinger-and-veysel.

27. James Bennett Pritchard, ed., *Ancient Near Eastern Texts Relating to the Old Testament*, 3rd ed. (Princeton, NJ: Princeton University Press, 1992), 199–201.

28. United Nations, "Turkey Gives Peace Treaty Replica to United Nations for Display at Headquarters," news release, September 24, 1970, https://digitallibrary .un.org/record/3813099?v=pdf.

29. McNeill, *The Rise of the West*, 136; Henry W. F. Saggs, "Assyrian Warfare in the Sargonid Period," *Iraq* 25, no. 2 (1963): 145–154.

30. Stephen Bourke, *The Middle East: The Cradle of Civilization Revealed* (London: Thames & Hudson, 2018), 195.

31. A. Leo Oppenheim, *Ancient Mesopotamia: Portrait of a Dead Civilization* (Chicago: University of Chicago Press, 1977), 98.

32. Bourke, *The Middle East*, 174.

33. Ibid., 199.

34. Elias J. Bickerman, "Nebuchadnezzar and Jerusalem," *Proceedings of the American Academy for Jewish Research* 46, no. 1 (1979): 69–85.

35. *The Map of the World*, sixth century BC, clay tablet, 12.20 × 8.20 cm, British Museum, London, www.britishmuseum.org/collection/object/W_1882-0714 -509.

36. Pierre Briant, *Alexander the Great and His Empire: A Short Introduction* (Princeton, NJ: Princeton University Press, 2010).

37. James Hall, *A History of Ideas and Images in Italian Art* (New York: Harper & Row, 1983), 47–48.

Chapter 2: Greek Myths and Persian Power

1. Aristotle, *Politics*, trans. Benjamin Jowett (Kitchener, Ontario: Batoche Books, 1999), 161–162.

2. Fernand Braudel, *The Mediterranean in the Ancient World* (London: Penguin Books, 2001), 259.

3. Pavel Oliva, *The Birth of Greek Civilization* (London: Orbis Books, 1981), 105.

4. Fernand Braudel, *Memory and the Mediterranean* (New York: Vintage, 2002), 254; Braudel, *Mediterranean in the Ancient World*, 289.

5. Josiah Ober, *The Rise and Fall of Classical Greece* (Princeton, NJ: Princeton University Press, 2015), 41–42.

6. Braudel, *Mediterranean in the Ancient World*, 289.

7. Leonard Cottrell, *The Anvil of Civilization* (New York: Mentor Books, 1957), 179–180.

8. Eric W. Robinson, *Democracy Beyond Athens: Popular Government in the Greek Classical Age* (Cambridge: Cambridge University Press, 2011).

9. John Thorley, *Athenian Democracy*, 2nd ed. (London: Routledge, 2004), 79.

10. Braudel, *Mediterranean in the Ancient World*, 272.

11. Thucydides, *History of the Peloponnesian War*, trans. Rex Warner (London: Penguin Books, 1954), 145–147.

12. Jawaharlal Nehru, *The Discovery of India* (New Delhi, India: Penguin Books, 2004), 550.

13. Arlene W. Saxonhouse, "Democratic Origins," in *Encyclopedia of Democratic Thought*, eds. Paul B. Clarke and Joe Foweraker (London: Taylor & Francis, 2001), 246.

14. Robert W. Wallace, "Law, Freedom, and the Concept of Citizens' Rights in Democratic Athens," in *Demokratia: A Conversation on Democracies, Ancient and Modern*, eds. Josiah Ober and Charles Hedrick (Princeton, NJ: Princeton University Press, 1996), 115.

15. Aristotle, *The Athenian Constitution*, trans. Harris Rackham (Cambridge, MA: Harvard University Press, 1935), ch. 2, section 2.

16. Herbert J. Muller, *The Uses of the Past* (New York: Oxford University Press, 1957), 118–119. The Greeks also lacked the connectivity or transportation system of the kind the Persian, Romans, Mongols, and the Incas had.

17. Thucydides, *History of the Peloponnesian War*, 49.

18. Graham T. Allison, *Destined for War: Can America and China Escape Thucydides's Trap?* (New York: HarperCollins, 2017).

19. D. D. Kosambi, *The Culture and Civilisation of Ancient India in Historical Outline,* 2nd ed. (London: Routledge & Kegan Paul, 1965), 141.

20. Charles C. Mann, *1491: New Revelations of the Americas Before Columbus,* (New York: Vintage, 2011), 137.

21. Tamar Hodos, *Local Responses to Colonization in the Iron Age Mediterranean* (London: Routledge, 2006), 89–90.

22. Lorena Jannelli and Fausto Longo, *The Greeks in Sicily* (Venice, Italy: Arsenale Editrice, 2004), 6.

23. Ober, *Rise and Fall,* 41.

24. Edward A. Freeman, *The History of Sicily from the Earliest Times* (Oxford: Clarendon Press, 1891), 1:320.

25. There's no solid academic consensus on when Zoroaster lived. See: Mary Boyce, *A History of Zoroastrianism,* vol. 1, *The Early Period* (Leiden, Netherlands: Brill, 1996), 189–191; Solomon Alexander Nigosian, *The Zoroastrian Faith: Tradition and Modern Research* (Montreal: McGill-Queen's University Press, 1993), 15–16.

26. Reza Aslan, *God: A Human History* (New York: Random House, 2018), 95–97.

27. Ibid., 97–98.

28. John O. Hyland, *Persian Interventions: The Achaemenid Empire, Athens, and Sparta, 450–386 BCE* (Baltimore: Johns Hopkins University Press, 2018), 5.

29. Herodotus, *The Histories,* trans. Aubrey De Selincourt (Harmondsworth, UK: Penguin Books, 1972).

30. Robin Lane Fox, *The Classical World: An Epic History of Greece and Rome* (London: Penguin, 2006), 101.

31. Ibid., 107.

32. *Encyclopaedia Britannica Online,* s.v. "Darius I," by J. M. Munn-Rankin, February 26, 2024, www.britannica.com/biography/Darius-I.

33. Herodotus, *Histories,* 398.

34. Thucydides, *History of the Peloponnesian War,* 408.

35. Dinah Shelton, ed., *Encyclopedia of Genocide and Crimes Against Humanity* (Detroit: Macmillan Reference, 2005), 95.

36. Ibid., 94.

37. Plato, *Laws,* Volume I: Books 1–6, trans. R. G. Bury (Cambridge, MA: Harvard University Press, 1926), 225, www.loebclassics.com/view/LCL187/1926/volume.xml.

38. *The Cyrus Cylinder,* c. 539 BC, fired clay, British Museum, London, www.britishmuseum.org/collection/object/W_1880-0617-1941; *Encyclopaedia Britannica*

Online, s.v. "Cyrus the Great," by Richard N. Frye, February 26, 2024, www.britannica .com/biography/Cyrus-the-Great.

39. "Cyrus Cylinder: How a Persian Monarch Inspired Jefferson," BBC, March 11, 2013, www.bbc.com/news/world-us-canada-21747567.

40. Robin Lane Fox, who argues that a Persian victory over the Greeks would have "curbed" Greek philosophical and artistic accomplishments, nevertheless dates the origins of Greek philosophy to the period between 580 BC and 500 BC, which straddles the onset of Persian conquest of Anatolia. It was during this period that "we first hear of a new Greek innovation: philosophy. Some of it also qualifies as the world's first scientific thought." Fox, *Classical World*, 84, 106.

41. *Encyclopaedia Britannica Online*, s.v. "ancient Greek civilization," by Simon Hornblower, August 13, 2024, www.britannica.com/place/ancient-Greece.

42. Adam Watson, *The Evolution of International Society* (New York: Routledge, 1992), 58.

43. William C. Wohlforth et al., "Testing Balance-of-Power Theory in World History," *European Journal of International Relations* 13, no. 2 (June 1, 2007): 165, https://doi.org/10.1177/1354066107076951.

44. Braudel, *Mediterranean in the Ancient World*, 256.

45. Watson, *Evolution of International Society*, 47.

46. Hyland, *Persian Interventions*, 5.

47. Susan Wise Bauer, *The History of the Ancient World: From the Earliest Accounts to the Fall of Rome* (New York: W. W. Norton, 2007), 527.

48. Although the Achaemenid Empire was destroyed by Alexander, Persian civilization and Persia's political system did not die with it. The Persian Empire was reincarnated several times. After the Roman conquest of the Greek city-states, for example, the Parthians, a powerful Persian civilization in northeast Iran, became Rome's biggest scourge next to Hannibal of Carthage. Maria Brosius, *The Persians: An Introduction* (New York: Routledge, 2006), 91–92. Later the Sassanids (224–651 AD) built another vast empire, which at its height was as extensive as that of Darius the Great. Founded by Ardashir I (180–242 AD), the Sassanids saw themselves as the heirs to the Achaemenids of Cyrus the Great. Thus the Persian Empire actually lasted longer than the ancient Greek political system, which was absorbed into the Roman Empire.

49. Peter Green, *Alexander the Great* (New York: Praeger, 1970), 144.

50. Arrian, "The Campaigns of Alexander," in *The Landmark Arrian*, ed. James S. Romm, trans. Pamela Mensch (New York: Anchor Books, 2012), 104.

51. Charles A. Robinson Jr., "The Extraordinary Ideas of Alexander the Great," *American Historical Review* 62, no. 2 (January 1957): 326–344, 331, https://doi.org/10.1086/ahr/62.2.326.

52. Arrian, "Campaigns of Alexander," 106.

53. Green, *Alexander the Great*, 144.

54. Arrian, "Campaigns of Alexander," 81.

55. J. P. V. D. Balsdon, "The 'Divinity' of Alexander," *Historia: Zeitschrift für Alte Geschichte* 1 (1950): 363–388.

56. Isocrates, "To Philip, II," letter 3, *Isocrates*, vol. 1, ed. and trans. George Norlin (Cambridge, MA, Harvard University Press, 1980; Perseus Digital Library), www.perseus.tufts.edu/hopper/text?doc=Perseus%3Atext%3A1999.01.0246%3 Acollection%3Dl.%3Aletter%3D3.

57. He is believed to have so treasured Aristotle's teachings that he protested his publishing them. "What advantage shall I have over other men if these theories in which I have been trained are to be made common property?" he asked in a letter to Aristotle. Plutarch, *The Age of Alexander: Nine Greek Lives*, trans. Ian Scott-Kilvert (London: Penguin Books, 1973), 259.

58. *Encyclopaedia Britannica Online*, s.v. "Aristotle," by Anselm H. Amadio and Anthony J. P. Kenny, January 5, 2024, www.britannica.com/biography /Aristotle.

59. D. Brendan Nagle, "Alexander and Aristotle's 'Pambasileus,'" *L'Antiquité Classique* 69 (2000): 129.

60. Justin D. Lyons, *Alexander the Great and Hernán Cortés: Ambiguous Legacies of Leadership* (Lanham, MD: Lexington Books, 2015), 31.

61. P. J. Rhodes, *A History of the Classical Greek World, 478–323 BC*, 2nd ed. (Hoboken, NJ: Wiley-Blackwell, 2010), 367.

62. Stephen Bourke, *The Middle East: The Cradle of Civilization Revealed* (London: Thames & Hudson, 2018), 161.

63. William W. Tarn, *Alexander the Great*, vol. 1, *Narrative* (Cambridge: Cambridge University Press, 1948).

64. Arrian, "Campaigns of Alexander," 314, 382. See also, Plutarch, *Age of Alexander*, 312.

65. Quintus Curtius Rufus, *The Complete Works of Quintus Curtius Rufus*, trans. J. C. Rolfe (Hastings, UK: Delphi Classics, 2017).

66. Arrian, "Campaigns of Alexander," 166–168.

67. C. Suetonius Tranquillus, *The Lives of the Twelve Caesars* (New York: Modern Library, 1931), 63.

68. Romila Thapar, *Ashoka and the Decline of the Mauryas*, 3rd ed. (New Delhi, India: Oxford University Press, 2012), 268.

69. Plutarch, *Age of Alexander*, 320.

Chapter 3: Conquest and Compassion

1. Rohan Venkataramakrishnan, "Who Was Here First? A New Study Explains the Origins of Ancient Indians," *Quartz*, April 3, 2018, https://qz.com/india/1243436/aryan-migration-scientists-use-dna-to-explain-origins-of-ancient-indians/.

2. There are four Vedas, which were initially orally transmitted as hymns. They are the *Rig Veda* (the knowledge of verses, the earliest of the four), the *Yajurveda* (sacrificial formulas), the *Samveda* (chants), and the *Atharvaveda* (procedures of everyday life, the last of the four). The Vedas are the earliest known body of religious, philosophical, and ritual knowledge in Hinduism, although they might have absorbed the beliefs and practices of India's earlier inhabitants, including from the Indus valley civilization.

3. John Haywood, *The Ancient World* (London: Quercus, 2010), 58.

4. Arthur L. Basham, *The Wonder That Was India: A Survey of the History and Culture of the Indian Sub-Continent Before the Coming of the Muslims*, 3rd ed. (London: Picador, 2004), 97.

5. K. A. Nilakants Sastri, *Age of the Nandas and Mauryas*, 2nd ed. (Delhi, India: Motilal Banarsidass, 1967), 173.

6. Basham, *Wonder That Was India*, 34.

7. Romila Thapar, *Early India: From the Origins to AD 1300* (Berkeley: University of California Press, 2004), 148.

8. Ibid., 149–150.

9. The four castes in Hinduism are Brahmans (priests, religious leaders), Kshatriyas (warriors, rulers, and aristocrats), Vaishyas (merchants and farmers), and Sudras (laborers and artisans).

10. Hermann Kulke and Dietmar Rothermund, *A History of India*, 6th ed. (London: Routledge, 2016), 63.

11. Ram Sharan Sharma, *Aspects of Political Ideas and Institutions in Ancient India*, 4th ed. (New Delhi, India: Motilal Banarsidass, 1996), 122.

12. D. D. Kosambi, *An Introduction to the Study of Indian History* (Bombay, India: Popular Prakashan, 1975), 55.

13. *Shastra* (also written as *sastra*) generally refers to a body (or a text or a manual) of specialized knowledge. *Artha* can narrowly mean wealth or material gain, but in its broader sense conveys both political and economic purpose. Indian Hindu philosophy distinguishes between four main types of human purpose or activity: *dharma* (virtue or morality), *kama* (sensual pleasure), *moksha* (liberation), and *artha* (material, political, and economic aspects of living).

According to another of its translators, *Arthashastra* refers to the "science of politics" and the "art of government in its widest sense." Kautilya, *The Arthashastra*, ed. and trans. L. N. Rangarajan (New Delhi: Penguin Books India, 1992), 15.

14. After disappearing for ages, the text of the *Arthashastra* was discovered in the southern Indian city of Mysore (now in Karnataka state) in 1905. The dating of its first composition ranges from the fourth century BC, around the time of the Maurya dynasty, to the third century AD. Another view holds that the first written version of the *Arthashastra* was done around the middle of the first century AD, but that this text incorporated oral (and possibly written) sources from previous centuries. The text is also believed to have undergone revisions in later periods. The text, as it was found in 1905, might not have been the work of a single individual; at least it reflected the views of several authors and commentators, making it the manifesto of a school of politics. I am grateful to Patrick Olivelle, translator of the *Arthashastra*, for his insights into its origins.

15. The ordering principle of the mandala scheme is: "Direct neighbour equals to enemy, and indirect neighbour equals to friend.... However, beyond friends and enemies, there are middle states (*madhyama*), bordering the 'activist' state and its allies as well as its enemies. And, there are distant powerful or neutral states (*udāsīna*), which (at least temporarily) stay out of the conflicts in which the 'activist' state is involved." Michael Liebig and Saurabh Mishra, introduction to *The Arthaśāstra in a Transcultural Perspective: Comparing Kauṭilya with Sun-Zi, Nizam al-Mulk, Barani and Machiavelli* (New Delhi, India: Pentagon Press, 2017), 9.

16. Kautilya, *Arthashastra*, trans. R. Shamashastry (Bangalore: Government Press, 1915), book 7, https://franpritchett.com/00litlinks/kautilya/book07.htm.

17. Deepshikha Shahi, "'Arthashastra' Beyond Realpolitik: The 'Eclectic' Face of Kautilya," *Economic and Political Weekly* 49, no. 41 (2014): 72.

18. Kautilya, *The Kautilya Arthasastra*, Part 2, trans. R. P. Kangle (New Delhi: Motilal Banarsidass, 2010), 319, https://archive.org/details/OdAH_artha-shastra-part-2-r.-p.-kangle/page/n7/mode/1up?view=theater.

19. Ibid., 314.

20. Ibid., 492. See also, Shahi, "'Arthashastra' Beyond Realpolitik," 72.

21. Nayanjot Lahiri, *Ashoka in Ancient India* (Cambridge, MA: Harvard University Press, 2015), 101–102.

22. Romila Thapar, "A Translation of the Edicts of Asoka," in *Asoka and the Decline of the Mauryas*, 3rd ed. (New Delhi, India: Oxford University Press, 2012), 382.

23. Ibid., 384.

24. Gerald Draper, "The Contribution of the Emperor Asoka Maurya to the Development of the Humanitarian Ideal in Warfare," *International*

Review of the Red Cross 35, no. 305 (April 1995): 192–206, https://doi.org/10.1017/S0020860400090604.

25. Ibid.

26. Thapar, "Translation of the Edicts of Asoka," 385.

27. S. Dhammika, trans., *The Edicts of King Ashoka* (Kandy, Sri Lanka: Buddhist Publication Society, 1993), www.cs.colostate.edu/~malaiya/ashoka.html. Thapar's translation of the same edicts reads: "City magistrates should at all times see to it that men are never imprisoned or tortured without good reason." Thapar, "Translation of the Edicts of Asoka," 385.

28. Thapar, *Asoka and the Decline of the Mauryas*, 214.

29. Amartya Kumar Sen, "Universal Truths: Human Rights and the Westernizing Illusion," *Harvard International Review* 20, no. 3 (1998): 42.

30. As translated in Patrick Olivelle, "Appendix: Ashoka's Inscriptional Corpus," in *Ashoka: Portrait of a Philosopher King* (New Delhi, India: HarperCollins, 2023).

31. Thapar, "Translation of the Edicts of Asoka," 383.

32. Stanley J. Tambiah, *World Conqueror and World Renouncer: A Study of Buddhism and Polity in Thailand Against a Historical Background* (Cambridge: Cambridge University Press, 1976), 46–47.

33. John S. Strong, *The Legend of King Ashoka: A Study and Translation of the Aśokāvadāna* (New Delhi, India: Motilal Banarasidass, 1989), 6:50.

34. Kautilya, *The Kautilya Arthasastra*, trans. R. P. Kangle, 389.

35. Basham, *Wonder That Was India*, 8–9.

36. As second-century AD Greek geographer Pausanias noted: "I know that the Chaldeans and Indian sages were the first to say that the soul of man is immortal, and have been followed by some of the Greeks, particularly by Plato the son of Ariston," Pausanias, *Description of Greece*, Aikaterini Laskaridis Foundation, https://topostext.org/work/213.

37. Third Geneva Convention, art. 3, no. 1, https://ihl-databases.icrc.org/en/ihl-treaties/gciii-1949/article-3.

38. F. Max Müller, ed., *The Sacred Books of the East*, vol. 1 (Oxford: Clarendon Press, 1886), 231.

39. "That one is mine and the other a stranger is the concept of little minds. But to the large-hearted, the world itself is their family." "Text of President Barack Obama's Address to India's Parliament," *Times of India*, November 8, 2010, https://timesofindia.indiatimes.com/india/Text-of-President-Barack-Obamas-address-to-Indias-parliament/articleshow/6889675.cms. But the phrase also has a dark meaning. In Indian folklore, a cunning jackal used it to lure and kill a naive deer; hence some see these words as hiding one's true intentions before causing harm.

40. Wendy Doniger O'Flaherty, trans., *The Rig Veda* (London: Penguin Books, 1981), 25.

41. Damodar P. Singhal, *India and World Civilization* (New Delhi, India: Rupa Publications, 2014), 1:25.

42. The term *Sankhya* or *Samkhya* is associated with reasoning, investigation, analysis, calculation, interpretation, and ratiocination (exact thinking). Gerald James Larson, *Classical Sāṃkhya: An Interpretation of Its History and Meaning* (Delhi, India: Motilal Banarsidass, 1998), 1–3; Gerald James Larson, "Introduction to the Philosophy of Samkhya," in *The Encyclopedia of Indian Philosophies*, ed. Gerald James Larson and Ram Shankar Bhattacharya (Princeton, NJ: Princeton University Press, 2014), 4–5.

43. Some scholars have likened *prakriti* to the primeval matter from which the big bang occurred (which is yet to be "seen" or proven by modern science), and as an early model of evolution from a nonconscious or nonliving to a conscious or living entity, which Charles Darwin's theory did not cover. Somparn Promta, *Classical Indian Philosophy: A Critical Introduction* (Bangkok, Thailand: Chulalongkorn University Press, 2011), 173–174.

44. Singhal, *India and World Civilization*, 1:159.

45. Ibid., 1:158.

46. Ibid.

47. S. Radhakrishnan, *Eastern Religions and Western Thought* (New Delhi, India: Oxford University Press, 1940), 294.

48. See note 36.

49. These avatars can take human, animal, or mixed form. The ten avatars are fish, tortoise, boar, Narasimha (half man, half lion), dwarf, Parashurama (warrior Brahman), Rama (the hero of the epic *Ramayana*), Krishna (in human form but with divine powers, who is a leading character in the epic *Mahabharata*), Buddha, and Kalki (the future tenth incarnation, who is supposed to end the present epoch of Kali).

50. Thapar, *Early India*, 99.

51. Ibid., 100.

52. Julian E. Reade, "The Indus-Mesopotamia Relationship Reconsidered," in *Intercultural Relations Between South and Southwest Asia*, ed. Eric Olijdam and Richard H. Spoor (Oxford: Archaeopress, 2008), 12–18.

53. Erik Zürcher, "The Buddhist Conquest of China: The Spread and Adaptation of Buddhism in Early Medieval China," *Sinica Leidensia* 11 (2007): 23.

54. Margarita Angelica Delgado Creamer, "The Funerary Buddha: Material Culture and Religious Change in 'The Introduction of Buddhism to China'" (doctoral diss., University of Pittsburgh, 2016), 31–36.

55. George Coedes, *The Indianized States of Southeast Asia*, ed. Walter F. Vella, trans. Sue Brown Cowing (Honolulu: University of Hawaii Press, 1968); Ian W. Mabbett, "The 'Indianization' of Southeast Asia: Reflections on the Prehistoric Sources," *Journal of Southeast Asian Studies* 8, no. 1 (1977): 1–14.

56. Jacob C. van Leur, *Indonesian Trade and Society: Essays in Asian Social and Economic History*, trans. James S. Holmes and A. van Marle (The Hague, Netherlands: W. van Hoeve, 1955), 103–104.

57. Abraham Eraly, *The First Spring: The Golden Age of India* (New Delhi: Penguin Books India, 2011), 102.

Chapter 4: Heaven's Way

1. "The Chinese nation does not carry aggressive or hegemonic traits in its genes." Xinhua, "Xi Focus-Quotable Quotes: Highlights of Xi Jinping's Remarks at CPC Centenary Ceremony," 100th Anniversary of the Founding of the Communist Party of China, July 7, 2021, www.xinhuanet.com/english/special /2021-07/01/c_1310038364.htm.

2. Charles P. Fitzgerald, *The Southern Expansion of the Chinese People: "Southern Fields and Southern Ocean"* (London: Barrie & Jenkins, 1972).

3. Ancient Chinese texts place the Xia, based around the Yellow River in North China, to about 2205–1766 BC. Edwin O. Reischauer and John K. Fairbank, *East Asia: The Great Tradition* (Boston: Houghton Mifflin, 1960), 38–39; Claudio Cioffi-Revilla and David Lai, "War and Politics in Ancient China, 2700 BC to 722 BC: Measurement and Comparative Analysis," *Journal of Conflict Resolution* 39, no. 3 (September 1995): 467–494. But doubts over the existence of the Xia persist because they were mentioned only in Chinese literary sources written much later, from the Zhou dynasty (1046–256 BC) onward. Excavations in the late 1950s on the south bend of the Yellow River in Erlitou, near Loyang, revealed palace-like structures that some experts associate with the Xia, but this has not closed the debate. Just as nationalism has clouded the debate over the origins of the Indian civilization, in the case of China, "theoretical flaws, nationalism, and disciplinary limits have obscured the complexities" of research on the origin of the state, including the existence of the Xia as the founding dynasty of China. Xu Hong and Yin Zhang, "An Archaeological Proposal of the Origin of State in China," *Journal of Chinese Humanities* 5, no. 1 (November 28, 2019): 43. See also, Qi Sun, "Editor's Preface," *Journal of Chinese Humanities* 5, no. 1 (November 28, 2019): 3–5.

4. John K. Fairbank, *China: A New History* (Cambridge, MA: Belknap, 1994), 37–38.

5. It is important to keep in mind that the Chinese notion of heaven is a vague term combining nature, culture, ancestors, and local gods that needs to be distinguished fundamentally from the Abrahamic notion of a transcendent, self-sufficient location with a creator deity; one must not conflate the deities of the Chinese heaven with the Old Testament God. I am grateful to Professor Roger Ames of Peking University for clarifying this distinction.

6. "Ode 260," in *A Source Book in Chinese Philosophy*, ed. and trans. Wing-tsit Chan (Princeton, NJ: Princeton University Press, 1969), 5.

7. "Ode 267," in Chan, *Source Book*, 6.

8. Zhao Tingyang, "Redefining the Concept of Politics via 'Tianxia': The Problems, Conditions and Methodology," ed. Sun Lan, trans. Lu Guobin, *World Economics and Politics (Beijing)*, no. 6 (2015): 4–22; Zhao Tingyang, "A Political World Philosophy in Terms of All-Under-Heaven (Tian-Xia)," *Diogenes*, no. 221 (2009): 5–18.

9. Feng Zhang, "The Tianxia System: World Order in a Chinese Utopia," *China Heritage Quarterly*, no. 21 (March 2010), www.chinaheritagequarterly.org /tien-hsia.php?searchterm=021_utopia.inc&issue=021.

10. William A. Callahan, "Chinese Visions of World Order: Post-Hegemonic or a New Hegemony?," *International Studies Review* 10, no. 4 (December 2008): 749–761.

11. Li Feng, *Early China: A Social and Cultural History* (Cambridge: Cambridge University Press, 2013).

12. Yan Xuetong, *Ancient Chinese Thought, Modern Chinese Power*, ed. Daniel A. Bell and Sun Zhe, trans. Edmund Ryden (Princeton, NJ: Princeton University Press, 2013), 44–45, 49, 54, 64–65.

13. Cited in Daniel A. Bell, "Just War and Confucianism: Implications for the Contemporary World," in *Beyond Liberal Democracy: Political Thinking for an East Asian Context* (Princeton, NJ: Princeton University Press, 2006), 39.

14. John Haywood, *The Ancient World* (London: Quercus, 2010), 106.

15. *The Book of Lord Shang*, cited in Yuri Pines, "Legalism in Chinese Philosophy," *Stanford Encyclopedia of Philosophy* (Winter 2018), https://plato.stanford.edu /archives/win2018/entries/chinese-legalism/.

16. Ibid.

17. Hanfeizi, cited in Jianying Zha, "China's Heart of Darkness: Prince Han Fei and Chairman Xi Jinping: Part III: The Revenant Han Fei," *China Heritage*, July 20, 2020, https://chinaheritage.net/journal/chinas-heart-of-darkness-part-iii/.

18. Current Chinese leader Xi Jinping has cited Hanfeizi to justify the need for China to have strong leaders upholding the law (rule *by* law, rather than rule

of law). Chris Buckley, "Leader Taps into Chinese Classics in Seeking to Cement Power," *New York Times*, October 11, 2014, www.nytimes.com/2014/10/12/world /leader-taps-into-chinese-classics-in-seeking-to-cement-power.html.

19. Yan, *Ancient Chinese Thought*, 39.

20. Ibid., 218.

21. Ge Zhaoguang, *What Is China? Territory, Ethnicity, Culture, and History*, trans. Michael Gibbs Hill (Cambridge, MA: Harvard University Press, 2018), 44–46.

22. Tansen Sen, *Buddhism, Diplomacy, and Trade: The Realignment of Sino-Indian Relations, 600–1400* (Honolulu: University of Hawaii Press, 2003), 97.

23. Fairbank, *China*, 112.

24. Warren I. Cohen, *East Asia at the Center: Four Thousand Years of Engagement with the World* (New York: Columbia University Press, 2000), 26.

25. Gakusho Nakajima, "The Structure and Transformation of the Ming Tribute Trade System," in *Global History and New Polycentric Approaches: Europe, Asia and the Americas in a World Network System*, ed. Manuel Perez Garcia and Lucio De Sousa (Singapore: Springer Nature Singapore, 2018), 137–162.

26. Cohen, *East Asia at the Center*, 151.

27. Geoff Wade, "The Zheng He Voyages: A Reassessment," *Journal of the Malaysian Branch of the Royal Asiatic Society* 78, no. 1 (2005): 37–58.

28. Letter from Emperor Yongle to King Borommarachathirat of Siam in the early fifteenth century, cited in Geoff Wade, "The Ming Shi-Lu as a Source for Thai History—Fourteenth to Seventeenth Centuries," *Journal of Southeast Asian Studies* 31, no. 2 (September 2000): 253.

29. Reischauer and Fairbank, *East Asia*, 319.

30. Zhang Feng, "Rethinking the 'Tribute System': Broadening the Conceptual Horizon of Historical East Asian Politics," *Chinese Journal of International Politics* 2, no. 4 (Winter 2009): 560–561, https://doi.org/10.1093/cjip/pop010.

31. Qin Yaqing, "Why Is There No Chinese International Relations Theory?," *International Relations of the Asia-Pacific* 7, no. 3 (September 1, 2007): 323, https://doi.org/10.1093/irap/lcm013.

32. Kurt A. Raaflaub, "Introduction: Searching for Peace in the Ancient World," in *War and Peace in the Ancient World* (Oxford: Blackwell, 2007), 22.

33. Peter C. Perdue, *China Marches West: The Qing Conquest of Central Eurasia* (Cambridge, MA: Harvard University Press, 2005), 285.

34. Edward L. Dreyer, *Zheng He: China and the Oceans in the Early Ming Dynasty, 1405–1433* (New York: Pearson, 2006).

35. Cohen, *East Asia at the Center*, 160–161.

36. Wade, "Zheng He Voyages," 37–58.

37. Ibid. In this respect, China's role was similar to Rome, but the degree of coercion in Roman imperialism was far greater than under the Chinese tributary order.

38. Tansen Sen, "Zheng He's Military Interventions in South Asia, 1405–1433," *China and Asia* 1, no. 2 (December 20, 2019): 159, https://doi.org/10.1163/2589465X-00102003.

39. John Man, *Kublai Khan: The Mongol King Who Remade China* (London: Bantam, 2007), 281.

40. Yingcong Dai, "A Disguised Defeat: The Myanmar Campaign of the Qing Dynasty," *Modern Asian Studies* 38, no. 1 (February 2004): 145.

41. Cohen, *East Asia at the Center*, 243–244.

42. Zhang, "Rethinking the 'Tribute System.'"

43. Ibid., 556.

44. Ibid.

45. Ibid., 555.

46. Wang Gungwu, cited in ibid., 567.

47. Zhang, "Rethinking the 'Tribute System,'" 569.

48. Ibid., 566.

49. Charles Holcombe, *The Genesis of East Asia: 221 B.C.–A.D. 907* (Honolulu: University of Hawaii Press, 2001), 56–57.

50. Michael J. Seth, *A History of Korea: From Antiquity to the Present* (Lanham, MD: Rowman & Littlefield, 2011), 4–5.

51. Holcombe, *Genesis of East Asia*, 58–59.

52. *Samguk yusa* [Memorabilia of the three kingdoms], trans. Tae-Hung Ha and Grafton K. Mintz (Seoul, Korea: Yonsei University Press, 1972), 2.

53. Reischauer and Fairbank, *East Asia*, 476.

54. Hyman Kublin, *Japan: Selected Readings* (Boston: Houghton Mifflin, 1968), 31–34.

55. Kamata Toji, *Myth and Deity in Japan: The Interplay of Kami and Buddhas*, trans. Gaynor Sekimori (Tokyo: Japan Publishing Industry Foundation for Culture, 2017), 30–31.

56. Liu Haifeng, "Influence of China's Imperial Examinations on Japan, Korea and Vietnam," *Frontiers of History in China* 2, no. 4 (2007): 493–512.

57. Youru Wang, *Historical Dictionary of Chan Buddhism* (Lanham, MD: Rowman & Littlefield, 2017).

58. George Coedes, *The Indianized States of Southeast Asia*, ed. Walter F. Vella, trans. Sue Brown Cowing (Honolulu: University of Hawaii Press, 1968), 34.

59. Craig A. Lockard, "Chinese Migration and Settlement in Southeast Asia Before 1850: Making Fields from the Sea," *History Compass* 11, no. 9 (September 2013): 765–781.

60. William H. McNeill, *The Rise of the West: A History of the Human Community* (New York: Mentor Books, 1965), 777.

61. Citied in John M. Hobson, *The Eastern Origins of Western Civilization* (Cambridge: Cambridge University Press, 2004), 194.

62. Cited in Liang-li T'ang, *The Foundations of Modern China* (London: Nole Douglas, 1928), 198.

63. "The Ancient Chinese Exam That Inspired Modern Job Recruitment," BBC, July 23, 2013, www.bbc.com/news/magazine-23376561.

64. Ssu-yu Teng, "Chinese Influence on the Western Examination System," *Harvard Journal of Asiatic Studies* 7, no. 4 (September 1943): 308.

65. *The Executive Documents: Senate of the United States, for the First Session of the Forty-Third Congress, 1873–74* (Washington, DC: US Government Printing Office, 1874), 2:24.

Chapter 5: The Wrath of Rome

1. Michael Koortbojian, *The Divinization of Caesar and Augustus: Precedents, Consequences, Implications* (New York: Cambridge University Press, 2013), 84.

2. Plutarch, *Fall of the Roman Republic*, ed. Robin Seager, trans. Rex Warner, rev. ed. (Harmondsworth, UK: Penguin Books, 1972), 307.

3. Henry F. Burton, "The Worship of the Roman Emperors," *Biblical World* 40, no. 2 (August 1, 1912): 80–91, 83.

4. Gwynaeth McIntyre, *Imperial Cult* (Leiden, Netherlands: Brill, 2019).

5. This was true in Egypt as well. For example, Egyptians constructed mortuary temples where people continued to worship after the pharaoh's death.

6. Lily Ross Taylor, *Roman Voting Assemblies: From the Hannibalic War to the Dictatorship of Caesar* (Ann Arbor: University of Michigan Press, 1990).

7. Harriet I. Flower, *Roman Republics* (Princeton, NJ: Princeton University Press, 2011), 210.

8. Mark Cartwright, "Etruscan Civilization," *World History Encyclopedia*, February 24, 2017, 24, www.worldhistory.org/Etruscan_Civilization/; for more on Etruscan assimilation into Rome, see John Franklin Hall, ed., *Etruscan Italy: Etruscan Influences on the Civilizations of Italy from Antiquity to the Modern Era* (Provo, UT: Brigham Young University and Museum of Art, 1996).

9. Aristotle, *Politics*, trans. Benjamin Jowett (Kitchener, Ontario: Batoche Books, 1999), 139.

10. Alan Lloyd, *Destroy Carthage! The Death Throes of an Ancient Culture* (London: Souvenir Press, 1977), 178. The estimate of one hundred thousand is Braudel's. Fernand Braudel, *The Mediterranean in the Ancient World* (London: Penguin Books, 2001), 224.

11. Polybius, *The Histories of Polybius*, trans. Evelyn S. Shuckburgh, vol. 2 (London: Macmillan and Co., 1889), book 38, 516.

12. William D. Rubinstein, *Genocide* (London: Routledge, 2014).

13. According to estimates from Caesar himself. Historian David Henige argues that these numbers were likely inflated: David Henige, "He Came, He Saw, We Counted: The Historiography and Demography of Caesar's Gallic Numbers," *Annales de Démographie Historique*, no. 1 (1998): 215–242.

14. *Encyclopaedia Britannica Online*, s.v., "imperium," June 20, 2017, www .britannica.com/topic/imperium-Roman-law.

15. Ibid.

16. Erich S. Gruen, "Augustus and the Making of the Principate," in *The Cambridge Companion to the Age of Augustus*, ed. Karl Galinsky (Cambridge: Cambridge University Press, 2005), 38–39.

17. Adrian Goldsworthy, *Pax Romana: War, Peace and Conquest in the Roman World* (New Haven, CT: Yale University Press, 2016).

18. Paul W. Blank, "The Pacific: A Mediterranean in the Making?," *Geographical Review* 89, no. 2 (April 1999): 270.

19. C. Suetonius Tranquillus, *The Lives of the Twelve Caesars* (New York: Modern Library, 1931), 113.

20. This is known as the "hegemonic stability theory," which refers to how a dominant power provides benefits to all in areas such as security, free trade, and protection of air and sea space. It was developed by international relations scholars in the United States out of the work of American economist Charles P. Kindleberger. Charles P. Kindleberger, *The World in Depression, 1929–1939* (Berkeley: University of California Press, 2013). For criticism of this theory, see: Duncan Snidal, "The Limits of Hegemonic Stability Theory," *International Organization* 39, no. 4 (1985): 579–614.

21. Gaius Stern, "Women, Children, and Senators on the Ara Pacis Augustae: A Study of Augustus' Vision of a New World Order in 13 BC" (PhD diss., University of California, Berkeley, 2006), www.proquest.com/dissertations-theses /women-children-senators-on-i-ara-pacis-augustae/docview/305365124/se-2.

22. Martin Goodman, *The Roman World: 44 BC–AD 180* (London: Routledge, 1997), 110–112.

23. Neville Morley, *The Roman Empire: Roots of Imperialism* (London: Pluto Press, 2010), 69.

24. Cornelius Tacitus, *The Agricola and Germania*, trans. R. B. Townshend (London: Aberdeen University Press, 1894), 33–34. These words were of course paraphrased by Tacitus (a common practice among classical historians) and their authenticity can be disputed. But Tacitus, one of the greatest historians of ancient Rome, happened to be Agricola's son-in-law and therefore could have sanitized narrative. The fact that he did not is a powerful testament to the brutality of Roman imperialism as felt by its victims.

25. These estimates, from Roman historian Cassius Dio, are reported in Thorsten Opper, ed., *Hadrian: Empire and Conflict* (Cambridge, MA: Harvard University Press, 2008), 95. The book was published to officially accompany an exhibition (which I visited) with the same title at the British Museum, July 24–October 26, 2008.

26. The quote is from the biography of Hadrian in *Historia Augusta* written by Aelius Spartianus. Cited in Opper, *Hadrian*, 26.

27. Souren Melikian, "The 'Peaceful' Hadrian and His Endless Wars," *New York Times*, August 22, 2008, www.nytimes.com/2008/08/23/arts/23iht-melik23 .1.15537945.html.

28. Morley, *Roman Empire*, 69.

29. Goodman, *Roman World*, 159.

30. Francois P. Retief and Louise Cilliers, "Causes of Death Among the Caesars (27 BC–AD 476)," *Acta Theologica Supplementum* 26, no. 2 (2010): 89–106. Another estimate is that some 20 percent of Rome's eighty-two emperors were assassinated: Cornelius Christian and Liam Elbourne, "Shocks to Military Support and Subsequent Assassinations in Ancient Rome," *Economics Letters* 171 (October 1, 2018): 79–82, https://doi.org/10.1016/j.econlet.2018.06.030.

31. Kyle Harper estimates between 2.3 and 9.6 million slaves during the late empire period (260–425 AD), about 4.5 to 19.5 percent of the overall Roman population. Kyle Harper, *Slavery in the Late Roman World, AD 275–425* (New York: Cambridge University Press, 2011), 59.

32. Walter Scheidel, "Human Mobility in Roman Italy, II: The Slave Population," *Journal of Roman Studies* 95 (2005): 67.

33. Julian Bennett, *Trajan: Optimus Princeps* (London: Routledge, 1997), 104.

34. John G. Jackson, *Introduction to African Civilizations* (Secaucus, NJ: Citadel Press, 2001), 160; Damodar P. Singhal, *India and World Civilization* (New Delhi, India: Rupa Publications, 2014), 84.

35. Myles Lavan, "The Spread of Roman Citizenship, 14–212 CE: Quantification in the Face of High Uncertainty," *Past & Present* 230, no. 1 (February 2016): 3–46.

36. Susan Wise Bauer, *The History of the Ancient World: From the Earliest Accounts to the Fall of Rome* (New York: W. W. Norton, 2007), 761.

37. Goodman, *Roman World*, 141.

38. Singhal, *India and World Civilization*, 84.

39. Cristin O'Keefe Aptowicz, "Could You Stomach the Horrors of 'Halftime' in Ancient Rome?," *Live Science*, July 21, 2022, www.livescience.com/53615-horrors-of-the-colosseum.html.

40. Richard A. Bauman, *Crime and Punishment in Ancient Rome* (London: Routledge, 2002), 23–24.

41. Polybius, *Histories*, 1.

42. Tacitus, *The History*, 2.38, in *Complete Works of Tacitus*, 499.

43. George W. Botsford, "Roman Imperialism," *American Historical Review* 23 (October 1917–July 1918, repr. 1982): 773.

44. David Potter, *Rome in the Ancient World: From Romulus to Justinian* (London: Thames & Hudson, 2009), 142–143.

45. Gotthard Karl Galinsky, *Augustus: Introduction to the Life of an Emperor* (New York: Cambridge University Press, 2012), 56.

46. Goodman, *Roman World*, 257.

47. For example, Emperor Tiberius "pronounced a very sharp censure on [a senator's] visit to Alexandria without the emperor's leave, contrary to the regulations of Augustus." Cornelius Tacitus, "The Annals," 2.59, in *Complete Works of Tacitus*, 87.

48. Walter Scheidel, "The Road from Rome," *Aeon*, April 15, 2021, https://aeon.co/essays/how-the-fall-of-the-roman-empire-paved-the-road-to-modernity.

49. Jan Nelis, "Constructing Fascist Identity: Benito Mussolini and the Myth of 'Romanità,'" *Classical World* 100, no. 4 (July 2007): 403.

50. Emma Yeomans, "The Far Right Is Using Antiquity to Re-Brand Itself—but Classicists Are Fighting Back," *New Statesman*, July 4, 2018, www.newstatesman.com/science-tech/2018/07/far-right-using-antiquity-re-brand-itself-classicists-are-fighting-back; Sean Illing, "Why the Alt-Right Loves Ancient Rome," *Vox*, November 6, 2019, www.vox.com/2019/11/6/20919221/alt-right-history-greece-rome-donna-zuckerberg.

51. Philip Burton, "The Values of a Classical Education: Satirical Elements in Robert Graves's Claudius Novels," *Review of English Studies* 46, no. 182 (May 1995): 192–193.

52. "America: An Empire to Rival Rome?," BBC, January 26, 2004, http://news.bbc.co.uk/2/hi/americas/3430199.stm.

53. Moises Mendez II, "According to a New TikTok Trend, Men Think About the Roman Empire All the Time," *Time*, September 15, 2023, https://time.com /6314544/tiktok-roman-empire-trend.

Chapter 6: Rejuvenating the World

1. *The Oxford Dictionary of Islam*, ed. John L. Esposito (New York: Oxford University Press, 2003), s.v. "Dar Al-Harb."

2. Albert Hourani, *A History of the Arab Peoples* (Cambridge, MA: Belknap, 1991), 83.

3. Albert Hourani, *Arabic Thought in the Liberal Age 1798–1939* (New York: Cambridge University Press, 1983), 7.

4. Ibid.

5. *Oxford Dictionary of Islam*, s.v. "ummah."

6. Karen Armstrong, *Islam: A Short History* (New York: Modern Library, 2002), 30.

7. Ali Murat Kurşun, "Deconstructing the Sykes-Picot Myth: Frontiers, Boundaries, Borders and the Evolution of Ottoman Territoriality," *All Azimuth* 9, no. 1 (2020): 83–104.

8. Selim Deringil, *The Well-Protected Domains: Ideology and the Legitimation of Power in the Ottoman Empire, 1876–1909* (London: I.B. Tauris, 1998).

9. Cited in Bernard Lewis, *The Multiple Identities of the Middle East* (New York: Knopf, 2001), 120.

10. Ibid., 120.

11. Ibid., 122.

12. Ibid., 119.

13. Ibid.

14. *Encyclopaedia Britannica Online*, s.v. "jihad," by Asma Afsaruddin, February 4, 2024, www.britannica.com/topic/jihad.

15. Ibid.

16. Mohammed Ayoob, *The Many Faces of Political Islam: Religion and Politics in the Muslim World* (Ann Arbor: University of Michigan Press, 2008), 8.

17. Yousuf H. Aboul-Enein and Sherifa Zuhur, *Islamic Rulings on Warfare* (Carlisle, PA: US Army War College Press, 2004), 22.

18. Megan Specia, "Who Are Sufi Muslims and Why Do Some Extremists Hate Them?," *New York Times*, November 24, 2017, www.nytimes.com/2017/11/24/world /middleeast/sufi-muslim-explainer.html.

19. *The Imperial Gazetteer of India*, vol. 2, *Descriptive* (Oxford: Clarendon Press, 1909), 366.

20. William D. Rubinstein, *Genocide* (London: Routledge, 2014).

21. Thomas Swan, "40 Facts About Tamerlane—Timur the Lame," UK Disability History Month, last modified April 19, 2015, https://ukdhm.org/40-facts-about -tamerlane-timur-the-lame/#:~:text=It%20is%20estimated%20that%20his,Khan's %20descendents%2C%20the%20Borjigin%20clan; John Joseph Saunders, *The History of the Mongol Conquests* (Philadelphia: University of Pennsylvania Press, 2001), 174.

22. Alexander Gillespie, *The Causes of War: Volume IV: 1650–1800* (New York: Bloomsbury, 2021), 401.

23. Fernand Braudel, *A History of Civilizations*, trans. Richard Mayne (New York: Penguin Books, 1995), 232.

24. Dara Shukoh, *Majma 'Ul-Bahrain: The Mingling of the Two Oceans* (Morrisville, NC: Lulu.com, 2022).

25. Braudel, *History of Civilizations*, 41.

26. *Oxford Dictionary of Islam*, s.v. "ijtihad."

27. John M. Hobson, *The Eastern Origins of Western Civilization* (Cambridge: Cambridge University Press, 2004), 178.

28. Braudel, *History of Civilizations*, 76.

29. Jonathan Lyons, *The House of Wisdom: How the Arabs Transformed Western Civilization* (London: Bloomsbury, 2010).

30. "Centuries in the House of Wisdom," *Guardian*, September 22, 2004, www.theguardian.com/education/2004/sep/23/research.highereducation1.

31. Jared M. Diamond, *Guns, Germs, and Steel: The Fates of Human Societies* (New York: W. W. Norton, 1999), 253.

32. Cited in Hourani, *History of Arab Peoples*, 76.

33. Dimitri Gutas, "Ibn Sina [Avicenna]," *Stanford Encyclopedia of Philosophy*, Fall 2024 edition, https://plato.stanford.edu/archives/fall2024/entries/ibn-sina/.

34. Arun Bala, *The Dialogue of Civilizations in the Birth of Modern Science* (New York: Palgrave Macmillan, 2006), 53–62.

35. Hobson, *Eastern Origins*, 178–180.

36. Hans Belting, *Florence and Baghdad: Renaissance Art and Arab Science*, trans. Deborah Lucas Schneider (Cambridge, MA: Belknap, 2011); Bob Duggan, "Did the Italian Renaissance Begin in Baghdad?," *Big Think*, October 20, 2011, https:// bigthink.com/guest-thinkers/did-the-italian-renaissance-begin-in-baghdad/.

37. Prince of Wales, "Islam and the West," October 27, 1993, Sheldonian Theatre, Oxford, transcript, https://eweb.furman.edu/~ateipen/pr_charles _speech.html.

38. Ibid.

39. Lyons, *House of Wisdom*, 174.

40. Nicolas Pelham, "The People Who Shaped Islamic Civilisation," *1843 Magazine*, December 5, 2016, www.economist.com/1843/2016/12/05/the-people -who-shaped-islamic-civilisation.

41. Kenneth Seeskin, "Maimonides," *Stanford Encyclopedia of Philosophy*, last modified February 4, 2021, https://plato.stanford.edu/entries/Maimonides.

42. Akbar S. Ahmed, *The Flying Man: Aristotle, and the Philosophers of the Golden Age of Islam* (Beltsville, MD: Amana Publications, 2021).

43. Arnold J. Toynbee, *A Study of History* (London: Oxford University Press, 1934), 3:322.

44. Ibn Khaldun, *The Muqaddimah: An Introduction to History*, ed. N. J. Dawood, trans. Franz Rosenthal (Princeton, NJ: Princeton University Press, 2015), 133.

45. Hobson, *Eastern Origins*, 48–49. In this context, one should note that the Mongol Empire, which is often viewed as a destructive force, also provided a pacified area in which long-distance trade would flourish between China and Europe.

46. Diamond, *Guns, Germs, and Steel*, 253.

47. Hobson, *Eastern Origins*, 32.

48. James Piscatori and Amin Saikal, *Islam Beyond Borders: The Umma in World Politics* (New York: Cambridge University Press, 2019).

Chapter 7: The World Connectors

1. Jack Weatherford, *Genghis Khan and the Making of the Modern World* (New York: Three Rivers Press, 2004), 115–118.

2. Brian Baumann, "By the Power of Eternal Heaven: The Meaning of Tenggeri to the Government of the Pre-Buddhist Mongols," *Extrême-Orient Extrême-Occident* 2013, no. 35 (May 1): 251.

3. Urgunge Onon, ed., trans., *The Secret History of the Mongols: The Life and Times of Chinggis Khan* (London: Routledge, 2001), 93.

4. Ayse Zarakol, *Before the West: The Rise and Fall of Eastern World Orders* (Cambridge: Cambridge University Press, 2022), 77.

5. Cited in Weatherford, *Genghis Khan*, 105.

6. Prajatki Kalra, *The Silk Road and the Political Economy of the Mongol Empire* (London: Routledge, 2021), 119.

7. David O. Morgan, *The Mongols*, 2nd ed. (Oxford: Blackwell, 2007), 40.

8. Erik Ringmar, *History of International Relations: A Non-European Perspective* (Cambridge: Open Book Publishers, 2019), 116–119, www.openbookpublishers .com/reader/228#page/150/mode/2up.

9. William H. McNeill, *Plagues and Peoples* (Garden City, NY: Anchor Books, 1976), 134.

10. Sam Safavi-Abbasi et al., "The Fate of Medical Knowledge and the Neurosciences During the Time of Genghis Khan and the Mongolian Empire," *Neurosurgical Focus* 23, no. 1 (2007): 1–6, https://doi.org/10.3171/foc.2007.23.1.13.

11. Janet Abu-Lughod, *Before European Hegemony* (New York: Oxford University Press, 1989), 158.

12. Peter Frankopan, *The Silk Roads: A New History of the World* (New York: Vintage, 2017), 178.

13. Vikram Doctor, "The Naming of Seas: The Associated Problems and Their Resolutions," *Economic Times*, August 5, 2017, https://economictimes.indiatimes.com/news/politics-and-nation/heres-how-seas-receive-names-and-the-associated-problems-and-resolutions/articleshow/59922770.cms.

14. *Encyclopaedia of Islam Online*, s.v. "Baḥr Al-Hind," by R. Hartmann and D. M. Dunlop, April 24, 2012, https://referenceworks.brillonline.com/entries/encyclopaedia-of-islam-2/bahr-al-hind-SIM_1060.

15. *Online Etymology Dictionary*, s.v. "Indian Ocean," last modified October 10, 2017, www.etymonline.com/word/indian%20ocean.

16. Abdul Sheriff, "Globalisation with a Difference: An Overview," in *The Indian Ocean: Oceanic Connection and the Creation of New Societies*, ed. Abdul Sheriff and Engseng Ho (London: Hurst, 2014), 20.

17. William J. Bernstein, *A Splendid Exchange: How Trade Shaped the World* (New York: Grove Press, 2008), 155–156.

18. Cited in Edward A. Alpers, *The Indian Ocean in World History* (Oxford: Oxford University Press, 2014), 93.

19. Cited in *The New Cambridge History of India*, vol. II. 5, *European Commercial Enterprise in Pre-Colonial India*, by Om Prakash (Cambridge: Cambridge University Press, 1998), 140.

20. K. N. Chaudhuri, *Trade and Civilisation in the Indian Ocean: An Economic History from the Rise of Islam to 1750* (Cambridge: Cambridge University Press, 1985), 112.

21. Tome Pires, *The Suma Oriental of Tome Pires, and the Book of Francisco Rodrigues*, ed. Armando Cortesão, vol. 2 (New Delhi, India: Asian Educational Services, 2005), 285–287.

22. Chaudhuri, *Trade and Civilisation*, 112 –113; *Undang-Undang Laut Melaka* (Kuala Lumpur: Multimedia University, 2019/2020), https://www.studocu.com/my/document/multimedia-university/malaysian-legal-history/undang-undang-laut-melaka/8222382; Manjeet S. Pardesi, "Decentering Hegemony and 'Open' Orders: Fifteenth-Century Melaka in a World of Orders," *Global Studies Quarterly* 2, no. 2 (October 2022), https://doi.org/10.1093/isagsq/ksac072.

23. Paul W. Blank, "The Pacific: A Mediterranean in the Making?," *Geographical Review* 89, no. 2 (April 1999): 276.

24. Tansen Sen, "Zheng He's Military Interventions in South Asia, 1405–1433," *China and Asia* 1, no. 2 (December 20, 2019): 161, https://doi.org/10.1163/2589465X-00102003. Sen and American historian Victor Mair further contend that the Ming admiral's voyages consolidated links among the Indian Ocean's maritime networks, which would later prove "beneficial to European commercial enterprises, whose ships travelled through these same networks to colonize most of Asia not long after the Zheng He voyages ended." Tansen Sen and Victor H. Mair, *Traditional China in Asian and World History* (Ann Arbor, MI: Association for Asian Studies, 2012), 78.

25. Wang Gungwu, *The Nahai Trade: The Early History of Chinese Trade in the South China Sea* (Singapore: Eastern Universities Press, 2003), 56, 62.

26. Manuel Joaquim Pintado, trans., *Portuguese Documents on Malacca*, vol. 1 (Kuala Lumpur: National Archives of Malaysia, 1993), 341.

27. Alpers, *Indian Ocean in World History*, 86.

28. Bernstein, *Splendid Exchange*, 155.

29. Alpers, *Indian Ocean in World History*, 80–81.

30. Ibid., 83.

31. Ruby Maloni, "Control of the Seas: The Historical Exegesis of the Portuguese 'Cartaz,'" *Proceedings of the Indian History Congress* 72 (2011): 476–484.

32. Bernstein, *Splendid Exchange*, 194.

33. Ibid., 196–197.

34. Alpers, *Indian Ocean in World History*, 111.

35. Charles H. Alexandrowicz, *An Introduction to the History of the Law of Nations in the East Indies (16th, 17th and 18th Centuries)* (Oxford: Oxford University Press, 1967), 65.

36. Percy Thomas Fenn, "Justinian and the Freedom of the Sea," *American Journal of International Law* 19, no. 4 (October 1925): 716–727.

37. Alexandrowicz, *Law of Nations in the East Indies*, 65. It is important to note that Grotius's book on free seas (*Mare Liberum*) is subtitled: *"De ivre qvod Batavis competit ad Indicana commercia*: "The right which belongs to the Dutch to take part in the East Indian trade"; see Hugo Grotius, *The Freedom of the Seas*, ed. James Brown Scott, trans. Ralph van Deman Magoffin (New York: Oxford University Press, 1916), accessed September 14, 2024, https://oll.libertyfund.org/title/scott-the-freedom-of-the-seas-latin-and-english-version-magoffin-trans. This clearly shows that he took inspiration from Indian Ocean events. As the Dutch scholar Peter Borschberg confirms, Grotius did receive documents on Portuguese

maritime affairs in the Indian Ocean from the VOC when he turned his legal brief into a book. Peter Borschberg, "Hugo Grotius' Theory of Trans-Oceanic Trade Regulation: Revisiting Mare Liberum (1609)" (IILJ working paper no. 2005/14, Institute for International Law and Justice, New York, 2005). Moreover, that there was such freedom of seas in the Indian Ocean can be established from other accounts, including those of Muslim travelers such as Ibn Battuta.

38. Borschberg, "Hugo Grotius," 3.

Chapter 8: The Rise of the West

1. Marcin Wojciech Solarz, "'Third World': The 60th Anniversary of a Concept That Changed History," *Third World Quarterly* 33, no. 9 (October 2012): 1561–1573.

2. Daron Acemoglu, Simon Johnson, and James Robinson, "The Rise of Europe: Atlantic Trade, Institutional Change, and Economic Growth," *American Economic Review* 95, no. 3 (June 2005): 546. The Great Divergence is sometimes divided into two stages, the first between 1500 and 1800, and the second during the nineteenth century.

3. David S. Landes, *The Wealth and Poverty of Nations: Why Some Are So Rich and Some So Poor* (New York: W. W. Norton, 1998).

4. Philip T. Hoffman, *Why Did Europe Conquer the World?* (Princeton, NJ: Princeton University Press, 2015).

5. Ian Morris, *Why the West Rules—For Now: The Patterns of History, and What They Reveal About the Future* (New York: Farrar, Straus and Giroux, 2010).

6. Mark Elvin, *The Pattern of the Chinese Past: A Social and Economic Interpretation* (Stanford, CA: Stanford University Press, 1973).

7. Jared M. Diamond, *Guns, Germs, and Steel: The Fates of Human Societies* (New York: W. W. Norton, 1999), 253.

8. Ibid., 414.

9. Ibid.

10. Kenneth Pomeranz, *The Great Divergence: China, Europe, and the Making of the Modern World Economy* (Princeton, NJ: Princeton University Press, 2000).

11. Eric L. Jones, *The European Miracle: Environments, Economies, and Geopolitics in the History of Europe and Asia*, 2nd ed. (Cambridge: Cambridge University Press, 2003).

12. Niall Ferguson, *Civilization: The Six Killer Apps of Western Power* (London: Penguin Books, 2012). The same book was published under a different subtitle, *The West and the Rest*, by Penguin.

13. Ibid., 8.

14. Niall Ferguson, "The 6 Killer Apps of Prosperity," July 2011, Edinburgh, Scotland, TED video, 20:02, www.ted.com/talks/niall_ferguson_the_6_killer _apps_of_prosperity?language=en.

15. One of the strongest criticisms of Ferguson's *Civilization* was by Pankaj Mishra, a London-based Indian writer ("Watch This Man," *London Review of Books* 33, no. 21 [November 2011]), which Ferguson found "libellous." Mishra's review and Ferguson's reply and their subsequent exchange can be found at www.lrb.co.uk/the-paper/v33/n21/pankaj-mishra/watch-this-man.

16. John M. Hobson, *The Eastern Origins of Western Civilization* (Cambridge: Cambridge University Press, 2004).

17. Ferguson, *Civilization*, 146.

18. Ibid., 170.

19. Ibid., 176.

20. Jamie E. Ehrenpreis and Eli D. Ehrenpreis, "A Historical Perspective of Healthcare Disparity and Infectious Disease in the Native American Population," *American Journal of the Medical Sciences* 363, no. 4 (April 1, 2022): 288–294, https://doi.org/10.1016/j.amjms.2022.01.005.

21. Ferguson, *Civilization*, 198.

22. "The demand side of the Industrial Revolution was driven by the seemingly insatiable appetite human beings have for clothes. Nothing did more to stimulate that appetite than the large-scale import of Indian cloth by the East Indian Company, beginning in the seventeenth century." In Ferguson, *Civilization*, 201.

23. Sven Beckert, *Empire of Cotton: A Global History* (New York: Vintage, 2014), 46.

24. Cited in Dieter Schlingloff, "Cotton-Manufacture in Ancient India," *Journal of the Economic and Social History of the Orient* 17, no. 1 (1974): 81–90.

25. April Munday, "Medieval Linen," *A Writer's Perspective* (blog), March 3, 2019, https://aprilmunday.wordpress.com/2019/03/03/medieval-linen/.

26. Cited in "Manufacture of Cotton in India," in *Fisher's National Magazine and Industrial Record*, vol. 3 (New York: Redwood Fisher, 1846), 126.

27. Beckert, *Empire of Cotton*, 45. Beckert quotes Indian sources on this.

28. Ferguson, *Civilization*, 201.

29. Beckert, *Empire of Cotton*, 47–48.

30. Ibid., 48.

31. Ferguson, *Civilization*, 201. In the same paragraph, Ferguson further notes that imported manufactured cotton textiles from places like India fueled not only Britain's but all of Europe's consumer society, another of his "killer apps": "Europeans acquired a taste for cheap factory-made cloth well before they learned how to produce it themselves" (201–202).

32. Beckert, *Empire of Cotton*, 75.

33. Birendranath Ganguli, *Dadabhai Naoroji and the Drain Theory* (New York: Asia Publishing House, 1965).

34. Atul Kohli, *Imperialism and the Developing World* (New York: Oxford University Press, 2021), 199.

35. Ajai Sreevatsan, "British Raj Siphoned out $45 Trillion from India: Utsa Patnaik," *Mint*, November 21, 2018, www.livemint.com/Companies/HNZA71LN VNNVXQ1eaIKu6M/British-Raj-siphoned-out-45-trillion-from-India-Utsa -Patna.html; Shubhra Chakrabarti and Utsa Patnaik, eds., *Agrarian and Other Histories: Essays for Binay Bhushan Chaudhuri* (New Delhi, India: Tulika Books, 2017).

36. *Speeches by Lord Curzon of Kedleston, 1898–1900*, vol. 1 (Calcutta, India: Office of the Superintendent of Government Printing, 1900), xxiv.

37. Kohli, *Imperialism and the Developing World*, 163, 168.

38. Acemoglu, Johnson, and Robinson, "Rise of Europe."

39. Ibid., 548.

40. Ibid., 572.

41. Ibid.

42. It should be noted that Ferguson's thesis goes beyond the mid-nineteenth century and may apply more to the second Great Divergence (although Ferguson does not make such a distinction), which occurred during the nineteenth century. But even then, the killer apps that emerged during the second Great Divergence were possible because of prosperity (and the expansion of research and learning) enabled by the rapid economic growth of the first Great Divergence period (1500–1800), which had to do with Atlantic Traders' colonialism and slave trade.

43. Acemoglu, Johnson, and Robinson, "Rise of Europe," 549–550.

44. Ferguson, *Civilization*, 5.

45. Angus Maddison, *The World Economy: A Millennial Perspective* (Paris: OECD Development Centre Studies, 2001), 215.

46. Azar Gat, *War in Human Civilization* (Oxford: Oxford University Press, 2008), 543–544; Gat cites the work of Daniel Headrick, *Tools of Empire: Technology and European Imperialism in the Nineteenth Century* (Oxford: Oxford University Press, 1981).

47. Hobson, *Eastern Origins*, 136.

48. National Geographic Society, "June 7, 1494 CE: Treaty of Tordesillas," *National Geographic*, last modified October 19, 2023, https://education.nationalgeo graphic.org/resource/treaty-tordesillas/.

49. Ferguson, *Civilization*, 142.

50. J. H. Elliott, *The Old World and the New: 1492–1650* (Cambridge: Cambridge University Press, 1992), 59.

Chapter 9: The Lost World

1. Although the Mayan culture and its distinctive agriculture, such as the cultivation of corn, goes back to a much earlier period, as a civilization with states and urban centers, the Maya emerged in 2000–1500 BC. Historians divide the growth and decline of the Mayan civilization into three periods: preclassic, 2000 BC–250 AD; classic, 250–909; and postclassic, 909–1697. John Haywood, *The Ancient World* (London: Quercus, 2010), 180. There are minor variations on the exact beginning and end of each period: preclassic: 1800 BC–250 AD; classic: 250–900 AD; and postclassic: 950–1500 AD.

2. Allen J. Christenson, trans., *Popol Vuh: The Sacred Book of the Maya: The Great Classic of Central American Spirituality, Translated from the Original Maya Text* (Winchester, UK: O Books, 2007).

3. Ignacio Bernal, *Mexico Before Cortez: Art, History and Legend*, trans. Willis Barnstone (Garden City, NY: Anchor Books, 1975), 39–40.

4. Rober J. Sharer and Loa P. Traxler, *The Ancient Maya*, 6th ed. (Stanford, CA: Stanford University Press, 2006).

5. Michon Scott, "Mayan Mysteries," NASA Earth Observatory, August 24, 2004, https://earthobservatory.nasa.gov/features/Maya.

6. Ibid.

7. Sharer and Traxler, *Ancient Maya*, 499–505.

8. Ibid.

9. Ibid., 764.

10. "Mayan Government," Mayan Architecture of the Yucatan Peninsula, University of Idaho, accessed January 24, 2021, www.webpages.uidaho.edu/arch499/nonwest/mayan/agriculture.htm.

11. Haywood, *Ancient World*, 184.

12. Antonia E. Foias, *Ancient Maya Political Dynamics* (Gainesville: University Press of Florida, 2013); Haywood, *Ancient World*, 184.

13. Hernán Cortés, *Letters of Cortes: The Five Letters of Relation from Fernando Cortes to the Emperor Charles V*, vol. 1, ed. and trans. Francis Augustus MacNutt (New York: G. P. Putnam, 1908), 263.

14. Ibid., 210.

15. Charles C. Mann, *1491: New Revelations of the Americas Before Columbus* (New York: Vintage, 2011), 137.

16. Sarah C. Clayton, "After Teotihuacan: A View of Collapse and Reorganization from the Southern Basin of Mexico," *American Anthropologist* 118, no. 1 (March 2016): 104–120.

17. Patricia Rieff Anawalt, "The Emperors' Cloak: Aztec Pomp, Toltec Circumstances," *American Antiquity* 55, no. 2 (April 1990): 291–307.

18. Michael E. Smith, *The Aztecs*, 3rd ed. (Hoboken, NJ: Wiley-Blackwell, 2012).

19. Michael E. Smith, "Aztec City-States," in *A Comparative Study of Thirty City-State Cultures: An Investigation*, ed. Mogens Herman Hansen (Copenhagen, Denmark: Royal Danish Academy of Sciences and Letters, 2000), 581–596.

20. Ibid., 589.

21. Ibid., 585.

22. Mann, *1491*, 134.

23. Ibid., 135.

24. Ibid.

25. John M. Ingham, "Human Sacrifice at Tenochtitlán," *Comparative Studies in Society and History* 26, no. 3 (1984): 379–400.

26. John M. Roberts, *The New Penguin History of the World*, 5th ed. (London: Penguin Books, 2007), 486.

27. "How Many People Did the Aztecs Sacrifice?," HistoryExtra, *BBC History Revealed*, August 27, 2018, www.historyextra.com/period/ancient-history/how-many-people-did-the-aztecs-sacrifice/.

28. Mann, *1491*, 136.

29. Damodar P. Singhal, *India and World Civilization* (New Delhi, India: Rupa Publications, 2014), 84.

30. Mann, *1491*, 137.

31. Camilla Townsend, *Fifth Sun: A New History of the Aztecs* (New York: Oxford University Press, 2019).

32. Gordon F. McEwan, *The Incas: New Perspectives* (New York: W. W. Norton, 2008), 42.

33. Pedro Sarmiento De Gamboa, *The History of the Incas*, trans. Clements Markham (Cambridge: Hakluyt Society, 1907), 28–58, www.sacred-texts.com/nam/inca/inca01.htm. Pedro Sarmiento De Gamboa was a Spanish author who lived in Cuzco not long after the Spanish conquest and completed this account in 1572, drawing from indigenous sources.

34. Cited in Victor Wolfgang von Hagen, *The Realm of the Incas* (New York: New American Library, 1957), 210. Von Hagen's source for this passage was

American anthropologist Philip Ainsworth Means, "Pre-Spanish Navigation off the Andean Coast," *American Neptune*.

35. Heather Pringle, "The Lofty Ambitions of the Inca," *National Geographic*, April 2011, www.nationalgeographic.com/magazine/article/inca-empire.

36. Mann, *1491*, 74.

37. McEwan, *The Incas*, 95.

38. Charles Stanish, "Regional Research on the Inca," *Journal of Archaeological Research* 9, no. 3 (September 2001): 213.

39. Doug Bonderud, "Navigating the Inca Road System That United an Empire," *Now*, March 5, 2021, https://now.northropgrumman.com/navigating-the-inca-road-system-that-united-an-empire.

40. Joshua Rapp Learn, "How the Inca Road System Tied Together an Empire and Facilitated Its Fall," *Discover*, December 14, 2020, www.discovermagazine.com/planet-earth/how-the-inca-road-system-tied-together-an-empire-and-facilitated-its-fall.

41. Wiliam H. Prescott, *History of the Conquest of Peru* (London: J. M. Dent and Sons, 1908), 7–8, 42–43. Critics take Prescott's view here as overly romanticized, although he did not consider Incas a peace-loving people.

42. Robert M. Hayden and Timothy D. Walker, "Intersecting Religioscapes: A Comparative Approach to Trajectories of Change, Scale, and Competitive Sharing of Religious Spaces," *Journal of the American Academy of Religion* 81, no. 2 (June 2013): 403.

43. Felipe Guamán Poma de Ayala, *The First New Chronicle and Good Government*, trans. Ronald Hamilton (Austin: University of Texas Press, 2009), 269. Ayala is believed by contemporary Peruvian scholars to be among the more reliable sources on Inca history, despite some of its exaggerations (interview with Dr. Carmen Escalante, Universidad Nacional de San Antonio Abad del Cusco, May 20, 2023). The book was completed around 1615 and sent to the Spanish monarch, who never received it, but it was found in Copenhagen in 1908.

44. Francisco Garrido and Diego Salazar, "Imperial Expansion and Local Agency: A Case Study of Labor Organization Under Inca Rule," *American Anthropologist* 119, no. 4 (December 2017): 631–644.

45. Prescott, *History of the Conquest of Peru*, 43. See also, Geoffrey W. Conrad and Arthur Andrew Demarest, *Religion and Empire: The Dynamics of Aztec and Inca Expansionism* (Cambridge: Cambridge University Press, 1984).

46. Garcilaso de la Vega, *Royal Commentaries of the Incas and General History of Peru*, ed. Karen Spalding, trans. Harlod V. Livermore (Indianapolis, IN:

Hackett Publishing, 2006), 33; Justin Jennings, "The Fragility of Imperialist Ideology and the End of Local Traditions, an Inca Example," *Cambridge Archaeological Journal* 13, no. 1 (2003): 107–120.

47. Prescott, *History of the Conquest of Peru*, 30.

48. One is also reminded of Alexander the Great's action in sparing the life of King Poros on the Indian frontier and giving him back his kingdom with some additional territory.

49. Christopher Columbus, *The Spanish Letter of Columbus to Luis de Sant Angel, February 15, 1493* (London: Ellis & Elvey, 1889), 35, 37.

50. Christopher Columbus, "Letter of Columbus to the Nurse of Prince John, c. 1500," in *The Northmen, Columbus and Cabot, 985–1503 [and] the Voyages of Columbus and of John Cabot*, eds. Julius E. Olson and Edward Gaylord Bourne (New York: Charles Scribner's Sons, 1906), 378.

51. Spencer McDaniel, "Why Are We Still Celebrating 'Columbus Day'?," *Tales of Times Forgotten* (blog), October 12, 2018, https://talesoftimesforgotten .com/2018/10/12/why-are-we-still-celebrating-columbus-day/.

52. Anthony Brandt, "Perfect Storm at Tenochtitlan 1521," *HistoryNet*, April 5, 2017, www.historynet.com/perfect-storm-tenochtitlan-1521/.

53. Eduardo Galeano, *Open Veins of Latin America: Five Centuries of the Pillage of a Continent* (New York: Monthly Review Press, 1973), 23.

54. Juan Forero, "In Bolivia, Miners Pick Away at Storied Rich Mountain, but It Takes a Toll," *Washington Post*, September 25, 2012, www.washingtonpost.com /world/the_americas/in-bolivia-miners-pick-away-at-rich-mountain-but-it-takes -back-its-own-toll/2012/09/25/5f6aac74-01d0-11e2-bbf0-e33b4ee2f0e8_story .html.

55. Galeano, *Open Veins of Latin America*, 23.

56. Patrick Greenfield, "Story of Cities #6: How Silver Turned Potosí into 'the First City of Capitalism,'" *Guardian*, March 21, 2016, www.theguardian .com/cities/2016/mar/21/story-of-cities-6-potosi-bolivia-peru-inca-first-city -capitalism.

57. Cited in Galeano, *Open Veins of Latin America*, 40.

58. Christopher Minster, "Where Is the Lost Treasure of the Inca?," *ThoughtCo*, July 19, 2019, www.thoughtco.com/lost-treasure-of-the-inca-2136548.

59. Nathan Nunn and Nancy Qian, "The Columbian Exchange: A History of Disease, Food, and Ideas," *Journal of Economic Perspectives* 24, no. 2 (May 1, 2010): 163.

60. Christoph Niemann, "The Legend of the Potato King," *New York Times*, October 10, 2012, https://archive.nytimes.com/niemann.blogs.nytimes.com/2012/10/11 /the-legend-of-the-potato-king/.

61. Ellsworth Boyd, "The Manila Galleons: Treasures for the 'Queen of the Orient,'" National Underwater and Maritime Agency, July 2, 2012, https:// numa.net/2012/07/the-manila-galleons-treasures-for-the-queen-of-the-orient/.

62. Javier Mejia, "The Economics of the Manila Galleon," *Journal of Chinese Economic and Foreign Trade Studies* 15, no. 1 (2022): 35–62.

Chapter 10: Africa, Interrupted

1. See for example: Barbara Krasner, *Mansa Musa: The Most Famous African Traveler to Mecca* (New York: Rosen, 2017).

2. "Manden Charter, Proclaimed in Kurukan Fuga," UNESCO, accessed July 13, 2024, https://ich.unesco.org/en/RL/manden-charter-proclaimed-in -kurukan-fuga-00290.

3. This text is from a version of the Manden Charter compiled in Guinea during a meeting between traditional and modern Kankan (communicators), during March 3–12, 1998. Mangoné Niang, "The Kurukan Fuga Charter: An Example of an Endogenous Governance Mechanism for Conflict Prevention," in *Intergenerational Forum on Endogenous Governance in West Africa*, vol. 2 (Paris: Sahel and West Africa Club and OECD, 2006), annex 1, 75–77.

4. Georg W. F. Hegel, *The Philosophy of History*, trans. J. Sibree, reprint (Kitchener, ON: Batoche Books, 2001), 117.

5. Samuel P. Huntington, *The Clash of Civilizations and the Remaking of World Order* (New York: Simon & Schuster, 1996), 47.

6. Niall Ferguson, *Civilization: The Six Killer Apps of Western Power* (London: Penguin Books, 2012), 170.

7. John Iliffe, *Africans: The History of a Continent* (Cambridge: Cambridge University Press, 2007), 1.

8. Fernand Braudel, *A History of Civilizations*, trans. Richard Mayne (New York: Penguin Books, 1995), 126.

9. John M. Roberts, *The New Penguin History of the World*, 5th ed. (London: Penguin Books, 2007), 480.

10. Richard Olaniyan, "African History and Culture: An Overview," in *African History and Culture*, ed. Richard Olaniyan (Lagos: Longman Nigeria, 1982), 14–15.

11. Tweet by Musk at https://x.com/elonmusk/status/1289051795763769345; BBC, "Egypt Tells Elon Musk Its Pyramids Were Not Built by Aliens," August 2, 2020, www.bbc.com/news/world-africa-53627888.

12. Mawuna Koutonin, "Lost Cities #9: Racism and Ruins—the Plundering of Great Zimbabwe," *Guardian*, August 18, 2016, www.theguardian.com/cit ies/2016/aug/18/great-zimbabwe-medieval-lost-city-racism-ruins-plundering;

Peter Tyson, "Mysteries of Great Zimbabwe," *NOVA*, February 22, 2000, www.pbs .org/wgbh/nova/article/mysteries-of-great-zimbabwe/.

13. Koutonin, "Lost Cities #9."

14. Olúfẹ́mi Táíwò, "Out of Africa," *Foreign Affairs* 11, no. 3 (June 2022): 182.

15. Carolyn M. Warner, "The Rise of the State System in Africa," *Review of International Studies* 27, no. 5 (2001): 65–89.

16. Aidan Southhall, "The Segmentary State in Africa and Asia," *Comparative Studies in Society and History* 30, no. 1 (January 1988): 52–82.

17. Robert H. Jackson, *Quasi-States: Sovereignty, International Relations and the Third World* (Cambridge: Cambridge University Press, 1990).

18. Jolayemi Solanke, "Traditional Social and Political Institutions," in *African History and Culture*, 32–35.

19. John Thornton, *Africa and Africans in the Making of the Atlantic World, 1400–1800*, 2nd ed. (Cambridge: Cambridge University Press, 1998), 105.

20. Ibn Khaldun, cited in Basil Davidson, Francis Kwanina Buah Ma, and Jacob Festus Ade Ajayi, "A History of West Africa 1000–1800," in *The Growth of African Civilization*, 9th ed. (Harlow, UK: Longman, 1996), 42.

21. Olúfẹ́mi Táíwò, "It Never Existed," *Aeon*, January 13, 2023, https://aeon .co/essays/the-idea-of-precolonial-africa-is-vacuous-and-wrong.

22. Michał Tymowski, "Early Imperial Formations in Africa and the Segmentation of Power," in *Tributary Empires in Global History*, ed. Peter Fibiger Bang and C. A. Bayly (London: Palgrave Macmillan UK, 2011), 109–110.

23. *Encyclopaedia Britannica Online*, s.v. "Sundiata Keita," January 1, 2023, www.britannica.com/biography/Sundiata-Keita.

24. Stanley M. Burstein, "Axum and the Fall of Meroe," *Journal of the American Research Center in Egypt* 18 (1981): 47–50, https://doi.org/10.2307/40000342.

25. Michael Gomez, *African Dominion: A New History of Empire in Early and Medieval West Africa* (Princeton, NJ: Princeton University Press, 2019), 81.

26. Patricia McKissack and Fredrick McKissack, *The Royal Kingdoms of Ghana, Mali, and Songhay: Life in Medieval Africa* (New York: Henry Holt, 2016), 88.

27. Ibid., 99.

28. Roland Oliver and Anthony Atmore, *Medieval Africa, 1250–1800* (Cambridge: Cambridge University Press, 2001), 209.

29. Gabriel E. Idang, "African Culture and Values," *Phronimon* 16, no. 2 (January 2015): 97–111, https://journals.co.za/doi/10.10520/EJC189182.

30. Cited in Mark Cartwright, "Kingdom of Kanem," *World History Encyclopedia*, April 23, 2019, www.worldhistory.org/Kingdom_of_Kanem/.

31. Olaniyan, "African History and Culture: An Overview," 8.

32. Idang, "African Culture and Values"; E. O. Ugiagbe and G. Vincent-Osaghae, "An Evaluation of the Indigenous Practice of Osusu Cooperatives Among the Benins of South-South, Nigeria," *AFRREV IJAH* 3, no. 1 (April 25, 2014): 1–17.

33. John Scharges, "…Ubuntu?," CapeTownMagazine.Com, accessed July 13, 2024, www.capetownmagazine.com/whats-the-deal-with/ubuntu/125_22_17348.

34. Idang, "African Culture and Values."

35. Basil Davidson, *A History of East and Central Africa to the Late Nineteenth Century* (New York: Anchor Books, 1969), 28–29.

36. Ibid., 29–30.

37. Dirk Hoerder, *Cultures in Contact: World Migrations in the Second Millennium* (Durham, NC: Duke University Press, 2002), 36.

38. Martin Hall and Rebecca Stefoff, *Great Zimbabwe* (New York: Oxford University Press, 2006), 37.

39. Ibid.

40. Ibn Khaldun, cited in Jacqueline Passon et al., "Traders, Nomades and Slaves," in *Across the Sahara: Tracks, Trade and Cross-Cultural Exchange in Libya*, eds. Klaus Braun and Jacqueline Passon (Cham, Switzerland: Springer International Publishing, 2020), 61, https://doi.org/10.1007/978-3-030-00145-2_3.

41. Davidson, Ma, and Ajayi, "History of West Africa," 25.

42. Roberts, *New Penguin History of the World*, 479.

43. David C. Conrad, *Empires of Medieval West Africa: Ghana, Mali, and Songhay* (New York: Chelsea House, 2010), 26.

44. Shadreck Chirikure, "New Perspectives on the Political Economy of Great Zimbabwe," *Journal of Archaeological Research* 28, no. 2 (2020): 139–186.

45. David N. Abdulai, *African-Centred Management Education: A New Paradigm for an Emerging Continent* (London: Routledge, 2016), 26.

46. Abdel Kader Haidara, "The State of Manuscripts in Mali and Efforts to Preserve Them," in *The Meanings of Timbuktu*, eds. Shamil Jeppie and Souleymane Bachir Diagne (Cape Town, South Africa: HSRC Press, 2008), 265–269.

47. Ousmane Kane, *Beyond Timbuktu: An Intellectual History of Muslim West Africa* (Cambridge, MA: Harvard University Press, 2016), 76–77.

48. Timothy Cleaveland, "Ahmad Baba Al-Timbukti and His Islamic Critique of Racial Slavery in the Maghrib," *Journal of North African Studies* 20, no. 1 (January 1, 2015): 42–64, https://doi.org/10.1080/13629387.2014.983825.

49. J. Alexander, "Islam, Archaeology and Slavery in Africa," *World Archaeology* 33, no. 1 (2001): 44–60.

50. SlaveVoyages, Rice University, accessed July 13, 2024, www.slavevoyages.org.

51. The main points of arrival were Brazil (45 percent); the Caribbean colonies of Britain, France, the Netherlands, and Denmark (37 percent); Spanish America (11 percent); and North America (4 percent). Among the suppliers of slave ships, Portugal and Portuguese Brazil led the way (47.6 percent), followed by Great Britain (25.5 percent), France (10.8 percent), Spain and Spanish America (8.2 percent), the Netherlands (4.4 percent), colonial North America and the United States (2.3 percent), and Denmark and the Baltic states (0.8 percent). *Digital Encyclopedia of European History*, s.v. "the Atlantic slave trade," by Pieter Emmer, February 5, 2021, https://ehne.fr/en/node/21292.

52. Charles C. Mann, *1493: Uncovering the New World Columbus Created* (New York: Knopf, 2011), 338.

53. Ibid.

54. Stanton A. Coblentz, *The Long Road to Humanity* (New York: Thomas Yoseloff, 1959), 325.

55. Luis Angeles, "On the Causes of the African Slave Trade," *Kyklos* 66, no. 1 (February 2013): 5.

56. Robert Tombs, *The English and Their History* (New York: Knopf, 2014), 550–553.

57. Kevin Rawlinson, "Lloyd's of London and Greene King to Make Slave Trade Reparations," *Guardian*, June 17, 2020, www.theguardian.com/world/2020/jun/18/lloyds-of-london-and-greene-king-to-make-slave-trade-reparations.

58. Virginie Chaillou-Atrous, "Indentured Labour in European Colonies During the 19th Century," *Digital Encyclopedia of European History*, accessed July 21, 2024, https://ehne.fr/en/encyclopedia/themes/europe-europeans-and-world/forced-migration-and-work-in-european-colonies/indentured-labour-in-european-colonies-during-19th-century.

59. Thio Termorshuizen, "Indentured Labour in the Dutch Colonial Empire 1800–1940," in *Dutch Colonialism, Migration and Cultural Heritage*, ed. Gert Oostindie (Leiden, Netherlands: KITLV Press, 2008), 261–314.

60. Olatunji Ojo, "The Atlantic Slave Trade and Local Ethics of Slavery in Yorubaland," *African Economic History* 41 (2013): 73–100.

61. Nonso Obikili, "The Trans-Atlantic Slave Trade and Local Political Fragmentation in Africa," African Economic History Network, September 12, 2016, www.aehnetwork.org/blog/the-trans-atlantic-slave-trade-and-local-political-fragmentation-in-africa/.

62. Joseph Conrad, *Heart of Darkness* (Boston: Bedford Books of St. Martin's Press, 1996), 74.

63. *Encyclopaedia Britannica Online*, s.v. "Congo Free State," November 3, 2023, www.britannica.com/place/Congo-Free-State.

64. *Encyclopedia of Africa*, eds. Kwame Anthony Appiah and Henry Louis Gates (Oxford: Oxford University Press, 2010), s.v. "Scramble for Africa."

65. *Encyclopaedia of Africa*, s.v. "Berlin Conference of 1884–1885."

66. Howard W. French, *Born in Blackness: Africa, Africans, and the Making of the Modern World, 1471 to the Second World War* (New York: Liveright, 2021), 2.

67. Delano George Bell, "10 Quotes by Jamaican Poet Mutabaruka You Should Know," Jamaicans.com, accessed July 19, 2024, https://jamaicans.com /10-quotes-by-jamaican-dub-poet-mutabaruka-you-should-know/.

Chapter 11: Europe's Double Standard

1. Kalevi J. Holsti, *Peace and War: Armed Conflicts and International Order, 1648–1989* (Cambridge: Cambridge University Press, 1991), 20–21.

2. Stephen Krasner, *Sovereignty: Organized Hypocrisy* (Princeton, NJ: Princeton University Press, 1999), 82.

3. Henry Kissinger, *World Order* (New York: Penguin Press, 2014), 26.

4. Ibid., 27.

5. Andreas Osiander, "Sovereignty, International Relations, and the Westphalian Myth," *International Organization* 55, no. 2 (2001): 251–287.

6. Kissinger, *World Order*, 31.

7. Alan Philps, "Why the Peace Treaty of 1648 Merits Scrutiny Today," *National*, January 28, 2016, www.thenationalnews.com/opinion/why-the-peace-treaty-of -1648-merits-scrutiny-today-1.203678.

8. William Bain, *Political Theology of International Order* (Oxford: Oxford University Press, 2020), 60. See also, James H. Burns, introduction to *The Cambridge History of Political Thought, 1450–1700* (Cambridge: Cambridge University Press, 1991), 2–3.

9. Bain, *Political Theology*, 115.

10. Carl Schmitt, *Political Theology: Four Chapters on the Concept of Sovereignty*, trans. George Schwab (Chicago, IL: University of Chicago Press, 1985), 36.

11. Osiander, "Sovereignty, International Relations."

12. University of Münster, "The Peace of Westphalia Also Had Its Dark Side," news release, September 19, 2018, www.uni-muenster.de/Religion-und-Politik/en /aktuelles/2018/sep/PM_Westfaelischer_Frieden_hatte_auch_Schattenseiten.html.

13. Ibid.

14. Ibid.

15. William C. Wohlforth et al., "Testing Balance-of-Power Theory in World History," *European Journal of International Relations* 13, no. 2 (June 1, 2007): 165, https://doi.org/10.1177/1354066107076951. Stuart J. Kaufman, Richard Little, and William C. Wohlforth, *Balance of Power in World History* (London: Palgrave Macmillan, 2007).

16. Benjamin Miller, "A 'New World Order': From Balancing to Hegemony, Concert or Collective Security?," *International Interactions* 18, no. 1 (1992): 10.

17. Richard Elrod, "The Concert of Europe: A Fresh Look at an International System," *World Politics* 28, no. 2 (1976): 163–167.

18. Raymond Cohen and Raymond Westbrook, "Introduction: The Amarna System," in *Amarna Diplomacy: The Beginnings of International Relations*, eds. Raymond Cohen and Raymond Westbrook (Baltimore: Johns Hopkins University Press, 2000), 11.

19. Melvin E. Page and Penny M. Sonnenburg, eds., *Colonialism: An International, Social, Cultural, and Political Encyclopedia*, vol. 2 (Santa Barbara, CA: ABC-CLIO, 2003), 614.

20. Fukuzawa Yukichi, "Datsu-A Ron 'On Leaving Asia'—from the *Jiji shinpō* Newspaper, March 16, 1885," *Education About Asia* 21, no. 1 (Spring 2016), accessed July 25, 2024, www.asianstudies.org/publications/eaa/archives/lesson-plan-on-leaving-asia-primary-source-document/.

21. Cemil Aydin, "A Global Anti-Western Moment? The Russo-Japanese War, Decolonization, and Asian Modernity," in *Competing Visions of World Order: Global Moments and Movements, 1880s–1930s*, eds. Sebastian Conrad and Dominic Sachsenmaier (New York: Palgrave Macmillan, 2007), 213, https://doi.org/10.1057/9780230604285_8.

22. Cited in Reginald Kearney, "The Pro-Japanese Utterances of W. E. B. Du Bois," *Contributions in Black Studies*, 13/14 (1995/1996): 201, https://scholarworks.umass.edu/cgi/viewcontent.cgi?article=1128&context=cibs.

23. Cited in Peter Duus, *The Abacus and the Sword: The Japanese Penetration of Korea* (Berkeley: University of California Press, 1998), 49.

24. Abû Ûthmân al-Jâhiz, "On the Zanj ['Black Africans']," in *The Essays* (c. 860 AD), Internet Medieval Sourcebook, Fordham University, last modified June 28, 2024, https://sourcebooks.fordham.edu/source/860jahiz.asp.

25. Eric Williams, *Capitalism and Slavery* (Chapel Hill: University of North Carolina Press, 1994), 7.

26. Genesis 21:9–10; Samuel Sewall, "The Selling of Joseph: A Memorial," 1700, Electronic Texts in American Studies, University of Nebraska, Lincoln,

July 5, 2007, https://digitalcommons.unl.edu/cgi/viewcontent.cgi?article=1026 &context=etas. The first well-known anti-slavery writing in colonial North America examined four justifications of slavery: civilizing people by enslaving and baptizing them, just war, the curse of Ham, and Abraham's slaves.

27. Email correspondence with Sir Hilary Beckles, July 2, 2020. His analysis can be found in Hilary Beckles, *The First Black Slave Society: Britain's "Barbarity Time" in Barbados, 1636–1876* (Kingston, Jamaica: University of the West Indies Press, 2016).

28. The Fundamental Constitutions of Carolina, March 1, 1669, Avalon Project, Yale Law School, 2008, https://avalon.law.yale.edu/17th_century/nc05.asp.

29. For the original Jefferson draft, see Thomas Jefferson, "Draft of Declaration of Independence," 1776, Library of Congress, www.loc.gov/exhibits/jefferson /jeffdec.html#049.

30. Cited in David McCabe, "Kant Was a Racist. Now What?," *American Philosophical Association* 18, no. 2 (2019): 2.

31. Immanuel Kant, *Observations on the Feeling of the Beautiful and Sublime*, cited in McCabe, "Kant Was a Racist," 3. Kant also wrote in 1764: "This fellow was quite black...a clear proof that what he said was stupid"; cited in Ali Rattansi, *Racism: A Very Short Introduction* (Oxford: Oxford University Press, 2020), 14.

32. Cited in Raphael Falk, "Genetic Markers Cannot Determine Jewish Descent," *Frontiers in Genetics* 5 (January 21, 2015): 3, https://doi.org/10.3389/fgene .2014.00462.

33. Cited in Robert Bernasconi, "Proto-Racism: Carolina in Locke's Mind," in *Racism and Modernity: Festschrift for Wulf D. Hund*, eds. Iris Wigger and Sabine Ritter (Münster, Germany: Lit Verlag, 2011), 75.

34. Partha Chatterjee, "Empires, Nations, Peoples: The Imperial Prerogative and Colonial Exceptions," *Thesis Eleven* 139, no. 1 (April 1, 2017): 84–96, https:// doi.org/10.1177/0725513617700040.

35. Mark Tunick, "Tolerant Imperialism: John Stuart Mill's Defense of British Rule in India," *Review of Politics* 68, no. 4 (2006): 586–611.

36. John A. Hobson, *Imperialism: A Study* (Ann Arbor: University of Michigan Press, 1965), 232.

37. Norman Angell, *The Great Illusion* (London: G. P. Putnam and Sons, 1913), 146, 236–237.

38. Ibid., 236–237.

39. Shawn Kelley, *Racializing Jesus: Race, Ideology, and the Formation of Modern Biblical Scholarship* (London: Routledge, 2002), 49.

40. Alexis de Tocqueville, "Essay on Algeria," in *Writings on Empire and Slavery*, ed. and trans. Jennifer Pitts (Baltimore, MD: Johns Hopkins University Press, 2001), 59–116.

41. Mark Antliff and Patricia Leighten, "Primitive," in *Critical Terms for Art History*, eds. Robert S. Nelson and Richard Shiff, 2nd ed. (Chicago: University of Chicago Press, 2003), 225.

42. Ibid., 226.

43. John M. Hobson, *The Eastern Origins of Western Civilization* (Cambridge: Cambridge University Press, 2004), 7.

44. Edward W. Said, *Orientalism* (New York: Vintage, 1979).

45. Antliff and Leighten, "Primitive," 224.

46. Halford J. Mackinder, "The Geographical Pivot of History," *Geographical Journal* 23, no. 4 (1904): 423.

47. Alfred Thayer Mahan, *The Interest of America in Sea Power and Future* (Boston: Little, Brown, 1897), 118.

48. Ibid., 31.

49. James A. Tyner, "The Geopolitics of Eugenics and the Exclusion of Philippine Immigrants from the United States," *Geographical Review* 89, no. 1 (1999): 58.

50. Tracey Banivanua-Mar, *Violence and Colonial Dialogue: The Australian-Pacific Indentured Labor Trade* (Honolulu: University of Hawaii Press, 2007), 23.

51. Cited in Richard Lansdown, introduction to *Strangers in the South Seas: The Idea of the Pacific in Western Thought* (Honolulu: University of Hawaii Press, 2006), 12–16, 21.

52. Lansdown, *Strangers in the South Seas*, 18.

53. Ibid.

54. Ibid., 24.

55. Australian Bureau of Statistics, "Aboriginal and Torres Strait Islander Population," *Year Book of Australia 2008*, www.abs.gov.au/ausstats/abs@.nsf/0/68AE74ED632E17A6CA2573D200110075?opendocument.

56. Lansdown, *Strangers in the South Seas*, 19; Robert Johnson, *British Imperialism* (New York: Bloomsbury, 2017), 69; B. S. Penman, S. Gupta, and G. D. Shanks, "Rapid Mortality Transition of Pacific Islands in the 19th Century," *Epidemiology and Infection* 145, no. 1 (January 2017): 1–11, https://doi.org/10.1017/S0950268816001989.

57. "Discussion on Heredity and Disease at the Pathological Society of Manchester," *British Medical Journal* 2, no. 2706 (November 9, 1912): 1319.

58. Cited in Kerry R. Howe, "The Fate of the Savage in Pacific Historiography," *New Zealand Journal of History* 11, no. 2 (October 1977): 138.

59. Edward Wilson, "The Aborigines," *Argus*, March 16, 1856, 4.

60. Niall Ferguson, *Empire: The Rise and Demise of the British World Order and the Lessons for Global Power* (New York: Basic Books, 2004), 300.

61. Robert H. Jackson, "The Weight of Ideas in Decolonization: Normative Change in International Relations," in *Ideas and Foreign Policy: Beliefs, Institutions, and Political Change*, eds. Judith Goldstein and Robert O. Keohane (Ithaca, NY: Cornell University Press, 1993), 128.

62. Ibid., 227–228.

63. Benjamin Disraeli, address delivered at the Crystal Palace, London, 1872, transcript, Medium, June 13, 2022, https://medium.com/@Pechhacker/the-maintenance-of-empire-1872-by-benjamin-disraeli-7d4082e7d8fd.

64. Cited in Avner Offer, "The British Empire, 1870–1914: A Waste of Money?," *Economic History Review* 46, no. 2 (May 1993): 215.

65. "From the Archive: Mr. Churchill on Our One Aim," *Guardian*, November 11, 1942, republished November 11, 2009, www.theguardian.com/theguardian/2009/nov/11/churchill-blood-sweat-tears.

66. Jürgen Osterhammel, *The Transformation of the World*, trans. Patrick Camiller (Princeton, NJ: Princeton University Press, 2014), 917–918.

67. Covenant of the League of Nations, art. 22, www.ungeneva.org/en/about/league-of-nations/covenant.

68. Robert J. McMahon, *Colonialism and Cold War: The United States and the Struggle for Indonesian Independence, 1945–49* (Ithaca, NY: Cornell University Press, 1981), 45.

69. John Darwin, *After Tamerlane* (New York: Bloomsbury Publishing, 2008), 442, 504–505.

Chapter 12: The City upon a Hill

1. Henry Kissinger, *World Order* (New York: Penguin Press, 2014), 234.

2. Cited in Phil Cerny, letter to the editor, *International Herald Tribune*, May 9, 2002, www.nytimes.com/2002/05/09/opinion/IHT-america-in-the-world-letters-to-the-editor.html.

3. Jared M. Diamond, *Guns, Germs, and Steel: The Fates of Human Societies* (New York: W. W. Norton, 1999), 210–212.

4. James Daniel Richardson, *A Compilation of the Messages and Papers of the Presidents* (Washington, DC: Government Printing Office, 1897), 1:104–105. Conotocarious was the name the Susquehannah tribe had given to Washington's great-grandfather John Washington after he took part in a colonist massacre of five Native chiefs. When Washington met the Native Americans in 1753, they

also called him by the same name, and Washington used the name in some correspondence with the Oneida tribe in 1755. "Conotocarious," George Washington Presidential Library, accessed July 27, 2024, www.mountvernon.org/library /digitalhistory/digital-encyclopedia/article/conotocarious/.

5. Ulysses S. Grant "Third Annual Message," December 4, 1871, American Presidency Project, www.presidency.ucsb.edu/documents/third-annual -message-11.

6. Hiram Price, "Rules Governing the Court of Indian Offenses," March 30, 1883, 1, University of North Dakota Scholarly Commons, https://commons.und .edu/indigenous-gov-docs/131/.

7. Robert N. Clinton, "Code of Indian Offenses," *For the Seventh Generation* (blog), February 24, 2008, http://tribal-law.blogspot.com/2008/02/code-of-indian -offenses.html.

8. Frederick J. Turner, "The Significance of the Frontier in American History," January 1, 1893, American Historical Association, www.historians.org /resource/the-significance-of-the-frontier-in-american-history/.

9. Cited in David Eugene Wilkins and K. Tsianina Lomawaima, *Uneven Ground: American Indian Sovereignty and Federal Law* (Norman: University of Oklahoma Press, 2001), 116.

10. Price, "Rules Governing the Court of Indian Offenses," 2.

11. Cited and discussed in Jack D. Forbes, "Indigenous Americans: Spirituality and Ecos," *Daedalus* 130, no. 4 (Fall 2001): 283–300. Forbes was professor of Native American studies at University of California, Davis.

12. Charles C. Mann, *1491: New Revelations of the Americas Before Columbus* (New York: Vintage, 2011), 295–301, 363–367.

13. Gerald McMaster and Clifford E. Trafzer, eds., "Sitting Bull (Tantanka Yotanka)," in *Native Universe: Voices of Indian America* (Washington, DC: National Museum of the American Indian, 2008); McMaster and Trafzer, "This Land Belongs to Us," in *Native Universe*, 192.

14. Charles C. Mann, "The Founding Sachems," *New York Times*, July 4, 2005, www.nytimes.com/2005/07/04/opinion/the-founding-sachems.html.

15. Cadwallader Colden, *The History of the Five Indian Nations of Canada Which Are Dependent on the Province of New York* (New York: New Amsterdam Book Company, 1902), www.loc.gov/item/02030132/.

16. Iroquois Confederacy of Nations, *Hearing Before the Select Committee on Indian Affairs, United States Senate*, 100th Cong., December 2, 1987 (Washington, DC: U.S. Government Printing Office, 1988), 7, 13.

17. Cited in "Iroquois Constitution: A Forerunner to Colonists' Democratic Principles," *New York Times*, June 28, 1987, www.nytimes.com/1987/06/28/us/iroquois-constitution-a-forerunner-to-colonists-democratic-principles.html.

18. "Haudenosaunee Impact Recognized by Congress," Oneida Indian Nation, accessed July 13, 2024, www.oneidaindiannation.com/haudenosaunee-impact-recognized-by-congress/.

19. Bruce E. Johansen, *Forgotten Founders: Benjamin Franklin, the Iroquois and the Rationale for the American Revolution* (Ipswich, MA: Gambit Incorporated, 1982), https://ratical.org/many_worlds/6Nations/FF.html.

20. Iroquois Confederacy of Nations, *Hearing Before the Select Committee*, 11.

21. Bernard Bailyn, *The Ideological Origins of the American Revolution* (Cambridge, MA: Harvard University Press, 2017), 24.

22. Carl J. Richard, "A Dialogue with the Ancients: Thomas Jefferson and Classical Philosophy and History," *Journal of the Early Republic* 9, no. 4 (1989): 431–455, https://doi.org/10.2307/3123751.

23. Jackie Craven, "The Public Architecture of Washington, DC," *ThoughtCo*, last modified July 3, 2019, www.thoughtco.com/diverse-architecture-of-washington-dc-4065271.

24. "House Rostrum," History, Art & Archives, US House of Representatives, https://history.house.gov/Education/Fact-Sheets/Rostrum-Fact-Sheet2/.

25. Thomas Jefferson, "Notes on the State of Virginia, Query 14, 1781–1782 (excerpt)," ed. Zachary M. Schrag (History 120, George Mason University, Fairfax, VA, 2005), https://mason.gmu.edu/~zschrag/hist120spring05/jeffersonquery14.htm. Although Jefferson condemned slavery, he also admitted that the value of his Monticello estate gained 4 percent annually by having Black children born there who could be sold for profit. Hence he thought of breeding slaves, like cattle, as an "investment strategy," and he recommended it not only to friends but also to George Washington, who was supposed to have been "disgusted" by the suggestion. Henry Wiencek, "The Dark Side of Thomas Jefferson," *Smithsonian Magazine*, October 2012, www.smithsonianmag.com/history/the-dark-side-of-thomas-jefferson-35976004/.

26. Galleries of National Museum of African American History, Washington, DC (personal visit, July 30, 2017).

27. "How Slavery Helped Build a World Economy," *National Geographic*, January 3, 2003, https://api.nationalgeographic.com/distribution/public/amp/news/2003/1/how-slavery-helped-build-a-world-economy.

28. Ta-Nehisi Coates, "Slavery Made America," *Atlantic*, June 24, 2014, www.theatlantic.com/business/archive/2014/06/slavery-made-america/373288/.

Coates cites these figures from Yale professor David W. Blight's course, the Civil War and Reconstruction Era, 1845–1877.

29. "The Annexation of Texas, the Mexican-American War, and the Treaty of Guadalupe-Hidalgo, 1845–1848," Office of the Historian, US State Department, accessed July 13, 2023, https://history.state.gov/milestones/1830-1860 /texas-annexation.

30. J. Van Fenstermaker and John E. Filer, "The U.S. Embargo Act of 1807: Its Impact on New England Money, Banking, and Economic Activity," *Economic Inquiry* 28, no. 1 (1990): 163–184; Joshua L. Rosenbloom, "Path Dependence and the Origins of Cotton Textile Manufacturing in New England" (NBER working paper no. 9182, National Bureau of Economic Research, Cambridge, MA, September 2002), http://doi.org/10.3386/w9182.

31. Dee Brown, *Bury My Heart at Wounded Knee: An Indian History of the American West* (New York: Holt, Rinehart & Winston, 1971).

32. Cited in Daniel Immerwahr, *How to Hide an Empire: A History of the Greater United States* (New York: Farrar, Straus and Giroux, 2019).

33. "Monroe Doctrine, 1823," US Department of State Archive, accessed July 13, 2024, https://2001-2009.state.gov/r/pa/ho/time/jd/16321.htm.

34. "Roosevelt Corollary to the Monroe Doctrine, 1904," Office of the Historian, US State Department, accessed July 13, 2024, https://history.state.gov /milestones/1899-1913/roosevelt-and-monroe-doctrine.

35. Theodore Roosevelt, cited in Howard K. Beale, *Theodore Roosevelt and the Rise of America to World Power* (Baltimore, MD: Johns Hopkins University Press, 1956), 160–161.

36. Christopher Benfey, "America: Beaver or Bear?," *New York Review of Books*, July 4, 2015, www.nybooks.com/online/2015/07/04/america-beaver-bear-roosevelt -kipling/.

37. Rudyard Kipling, *The Letters of Rudyard Kipling*, ed. Thomas Pinney (London: Palgrave Macmillan, 1990), 2:350.

38. Martin F. Nolan, "American Empire / The Day Teddy Roosevelt, Admiral Dewey and 'Bayonet Rule' Converged in S.F.," *SFGATE*, May 11, 2003, www.sfgate .com/opinion/article/American-Empire-The-day-Teddy-Roosevelt-2649139 .php. See also, Stephen Kinzer, *The True Flag: Theodore Roosevelt, Mark Twain, and the Birth of American Empire* (New York: Henry Holt and Company, 2017), 120.

39. Theodore Roosevelt, *Letters and Speeches* (New York: Library of America, 2004); Patrick Brantlinger, "Kipling's 'The White Man's Burden' and Its Afterlives," *English Literature in Transition, 1880–1920* 50, no. 2 (2007): 177.

40. Brantlinger, "Kipling's 'The White Man's Burden,'" 176.

41. Sidney Milkis, "Theodore Roosevelt: Foreign Affairs," Miller Center of Public Affairs, University of Virginia, accessed October 4, 2016, https://millercenter.org/president/roosevelt/foreign-affairs.

42. Woodrow Wilson, "President Woodrow Wilson's Fourteen Points," January 8, 1918, Avalon Project, Yale Law School, 2008, https://avalon.law.yale.edu/20th_century/wilson14.asp.

43. Ibid.

44. Ibid.

45. Kristofer Allerfeldt, "Wilsonian Pragmatism? Woodrow Wilson, Japanese Immigration, and the Paris Peace Conference," *Diplomacy & Statecraft* 15, no. 3 (2004): 545–572.

46. Ibid.

47. Cited in Naoko Shimazu, "Japan at the Paris Peace Conference of 1919: A Centennial Reflection," *Japan Review* 3, no. 1 (2019): 4.

48. Woodrow Wilson, "The Reconstruction of the Southern States," *Atlantic*, January 1, 1901, www.theatlantic.com/magazine/archive/1901/01/the-reconstruction-of-the-southern-states/520035/.

49. Henry Kissinger, *World Order* (New York: Penguin Press, 2014), 256.

50. G. John Ikenberry, *Liberal Leviathan: The Origins, Crisis, and Transformation of the American World Order* (Princeton, NJ: Princeton University Press, 2011), 26–27, 142.

51. Cited in Andrew J. Bacevich, "Hillary Clinton's 'American Moment' Was Nothing but American Blather," *New Republic*, September 13, 2010, https://newrepublic.com/article/77612/hillary-clintons-american-moment-was-nothing-american-blather.

52. Nishant Yonzan et al., "Estimates of Global Poverty from WWII to the Fall of the Berlin Wall," *Data Blog*, World Bank, November 23, 2022, https://blogs.worldbank.org/opendata/estimates-global-poverty-wwii-fall-berlin-wall.

53. "Evolution of Trade Under the WTO: Handy Statistics," World Trade Organization, accessed July 13, 2024, www.wto.org/english/res_e/statis_e/trade_evolution_e/evolution_trade_wto_e.htm.

54. Ikenberry, *Liberal Leviathan*, 224.

55. Amitav Acharya, *The End of American World Order* (Cambridge: Polity, 2014), 37.

56. Joseph S. Nye Jr., review of *The End of American World Order*, by Amitav Acharya, *International Affairs* 90, no. 5 (2014): 1246–1247. Nye repeated this point in a subsequent essay, "The Future of American Power: Dominance and Decline in Perspective," *Foreign Affairs* 89, no. 6 (2010): 2–12, www.foreignaffairs.com/united-states/future-american-power.

57. Cited in Micah Zenko, "The Myth of the Indispensable Nation," *Foreign Policy*, November 6, 2014, https://foreignpolicy.com/2014/11/06/the-myth-of-the -indispensable-nation/. In October 1998, Albright made another contribution, with words said at least halfway in jest at a roast, a comical event where jokes are made about a guest of honor, in this case columnist William Safire: "Some say our foreign policy is hegemonic, that we are arrogant and seek to impose our views and values on others. But let's be honest. Who cares what they think?" From Official State Dept. transcript, cited in Michael Dobbs, *Madeleine Albright: A Twentieth-Century Odyssey* (New York: Henry Holt, 1999), 409.

58. Ikenberry, *Liberal Leviathan*, 224.

59. Evan Luard, *War in International Society* (London: I. B. Tauris, 1986), appendix 5.

60. Mohammed Ayoob, "Regional Security and the Third World," in *Regional Security in the Third World: Case Studies from Southeast Asia and the Middle East*, ed. Mohammed Ayoob (London: Croom Helm, 1986), 3–23.

61. Nye, "Future of American Power," 2–12.

62. White House, "Remarks by the President in State of the Union Address," news release, January 24, 2012, https://obamawhitehouse.archives.gov /the-press-office/2012/01/24/remarks-President-state-union-address.

63. Jim Manzi, "A Post-American World?," *National Review*, May 7, 2008, www .nationalreview.com/corner/post-american-world-jim-manzi/; Christopher Chase-Dunn et al., "The Trajectory of the United States in the World-System: A Quantitative Reflection," *Sociological Perspectives* 48, no. 2 (2005): 233–254, https://doi .org/10.1525/sop.2005.48.2.233; Stephen G. Brooks and William C. Wohlforth, *World Out of Balance: International Relations and the Challenge of American Primacy* (Princeton, NJ: Princeton University Press, 2008), 31.

64. Malcolm Scott and Cedric Sam, "Here's How Fast China's Economy Is Catching Up to the U.S.," *Bloomberg*, May 12, 2016, www.bloomberg.com/graphics /2016-us-vs-china-economy/.

Chapter 13: The Return of the Rest

1. "Speech by President Sukarno of Indonesia at the Opening of the Conference," in *Asia-Africa Speaks from Bandung* (Jakarta, Indonesia: Toko Gunung Agung, 2005), 5. This is a reproduction of the text originally published by Ministry of Foreign Affairs, Republic of Indonesia, 1955.

2. Ibid., 6.

3. F. S. Tomlinson, "Position Regarding Afro-Asian Conference," January 12, 1955, Foreign Office, National Archives, London.

4. Roger Makins, telegram from British Embassy, Washington, to Foreign Office, London, February 26, 1955, National Archives, London.

5. J. E. Cable, "Afro-Asian Conference," March 2, 1955, Foreign Office, Far Eastern Department, National Archives, London.

6. Tomlinson, "Position Regarding Afro-Asian Conference."

7. "Results of the Bandung Conference: A Preliminary Analysis," US Department of State, intelligence report No. 6903, April 27, 1955, contained in telegram from British Embassy, Washington, to Foreign Office, London, April 27, 1955, National Archives, London.

8. O. C. Morland, "Some Impressions of the Bandung Conference by R.W. Parkes," memo from Bandung Conference sent to Mr. Macmillan at British Foreign Office, CO 936-350, TNA, PRO.

9. Cable, "Afro-Asian Conference."

10. Fareed Zakaria, *The Post-American World: And the Rise of the Rest* (New York: Penguin Books, 2011).

11. T. R. Sareen, "Subhas Chandra Bose, Japan and British Imperialism," *European Journal of East Asian Studies* 3, no. 1 (March 2004): 69–97.

12. *Merriam-Webster*, s.v. "nation (n.)," accessed July 13, 2024, www.merriam -webster.com/dictionary/nation#word-history; *Online Etymology Dictionary*, s.v. "nation (n.)," last modified January 29, 2024, www.etymonline.com/word /nation.

13. Göran Therborn, "States, Nations, and Civilizations," *Fudan Journal of the Humanities and Social Sciences* 14, no. 2 (June 2021): 225–242.

14. Ibid.

15. Chin-Hao Huang and David C. Kang, "State Formation in Korea and Japan, 400–800 CE: Emulation and Learning, Not Bellicist Competition," *International Organization* 76, no. 1 (2022): 1–31.

16. Anthony D. Smith, "The Diffusion of Nationalism: Some Historical and Sociological Perspectives," *British Journal of Sociology* 29, no. 2 (June 1978): 236, 238, 240.

17. Daniel Philpott, *Revolutions in Sovereignty: How Ideas Shaped Modern International Relations* (Princeton, NJ: Princeton University Press, 2001), 191.

18. Benedict Anderson, *Imagined Communities: Reflections on the Origin and Spread of Nationalism*, rev. ed. (London: Verso, 2016).

19. Pramoedya Ananta Toer, *This Earth of Mankind*, trans. Max Lane (New York: Penguin Books, 1975) 336.

20. Jawaharlal Nehru, "The Unity of India," *Foreign Affairs* 16, no. 2 (January 1938): 231–243.

21. Arthur L. Basham, *The Wonder That Was India: A Survey of the History and Culture of the Indian Sub-Continent Before the Coming of the Muslims*, 3rd ed. (London: Picador, 2004), 34.

22. Sun Yat-sen, *China and Japan: Natural Friends—Unnatural Enemies: A Guide for China's Foreign Policy* (Shanghai: China United Press, 1941), 15.

23. Francisco J. Yanes, "A Glance at Latin-American Civilization," *Journal of Race Development* 4, no. 4 (1914): 384.

24. Arie Marcelo Kacowicz, *The Impact of Norms in International Society: The Latin American Experience, 1881–2001* (Notre Dame, IN: University of Notre Dame Press, 2005), 50.

25. Ibid.

26. Cited in Eric Helleiner and Antulio Rosales, "Toward Global IPE: The Overlooked Significance of the Haya-Mariátegui Debate," *International Studies Review* 19, no. 4 (December 1, 2017): 670, https://doi.org/10.1093/isr /vix034.

27. Asian Relations Organization, *Asian Relations: Being Report of the Proceedings and Documentation of the First Asian Relations Conference* (New Delhi: Indian Council of World Affairs, 1947).

28. Ibid., 302.

29. Cited in Rebecca E. Karl, "Creating Asia: China in the World at the Beginning of the Twentieth Century," *The American Historical Review* 103, no. 4 (October 1998): 1106.

30. *Encyclopaedia Britannica Online*, s.v. "Jamāl al-Dīn al-Afghānī," by Elie Kedourie, March 15, 2024, www.britannica.com/biography/Jamal-al-Din-al-Afghani.

31. Kenneth Ray Glaudell, "An Afghan of Unknown Views: Sayyid Jamal al-Din al-Afghani and the Role of Shi'ism in Islamic Political Thought" (PhD diss., University of Wisconsin, Madison, 1996), 245, www.proquest.com/docview /304291433/abstract/3283B499955646EEPQ/1.

32. W. E. B. DuBois, *The Wisdom of W. E. B. DuBois*, ed. Aberjhani (New York: Citadel Press, 2003), 8.

33. Ibid., 83.

34. Kwame Nkrumah, *Africa Must Unite* (New York: Praeger, 1963), 136.

35. The discussions at the San Francisco Conference are well documented and can be found in *Documents of the United Nations Conference on International Organization, San Francisco, 1945* (New York: United Nations Information Organizations, 1945), https://digitallibrary.un.org/record/1300969. See also Amitav Acharya, "Race and Racism in the Founding of the Modern World Order," *International Affairs*, 98, no. 1 (January 2022): 23–43.

36. Adom Getachew, *Worldmaking After Empire: The Rise and Fall of Self-Determination* (Princeton, NJ: Princeton University Press, 2019), 71.

37. Johannes Morsink, *The Universal Declaration of Human Rights: Origins, Drafting and Intent* (Philadelphia: University of Pennsylvania Press, 1999).

38. "Final Communique of the Asian-African Conference," in *Asia-Africa Speaks from Bandung*, 156, 158.

39. Declaration on the Granting of Independence to Colonial Countries and Peoples, UN Res. 1514, General Assembly 15th Session, December 14, 1960.

40. Rupert Emerson, *From Empire to Nation: The Rise of Self Assertion of Asian and African Peoples* (Cambridge, MA: Harvard University Press, 1962), 395.

41. "A Review of the Afro-Asian Conference," Research Department, Foreign Office, London, May 5, 1955, National Archives, London.

42. Liliana Obregon, "The Universal Declaration of Human Rights and Latin America," *Maryland Journal of International Law* 24, no. 1 (2009): 95–96.

43. "History of the Declaration," United Nations, accessed July 13, 2024, www.un.org/en/about-us/udhr/history-of-the-declaration.

44. Niraja Gopal Jayal, "Hansa Mehta: An Early Indian Feminist," London School of Economics Blogs, March 6, 2024, https://blogs.lse.ac.uk/lsehistory/2024/03/06/hansa-mehta-an-early-indian-feminist/.

45. Devaki Jain, *Women, Development, and the UN: A Sixty-Year Quest for Equality and Justice* (Bloomington: Indiana University Press, 2005), 20; Rebecca Adami, *Women and the Universal Declaration of Human Rights* (New York: Routledge, 2018), 65–68. As Adami points out, a French draft had proposed, "All men are brothers being endowed with reason, members of one family." This would change to "all members of the human family" in the UDHR preamble, and article 1 would read "all human beings" instead of "all men."

46. Morsink, *Universal Declaration of Human Rights*, 102.

47. Ibid., 103.

48. Acharya, "Race and Racism in the Founding of the Modern World Order"; Morsink, *Universal Declaration of Human Rights*, 103. The Indian amendment that added 'colour' to 'race' passed with a vote of ten to none, with six abstentions.

49. UN, "History of the Declaration."

50. Christian Reus-Smit, "Building the Liberal International Order: Locating American Agency" (paper prepared for the Annual Meeting of the American Political Science Association, Washington, DC, August 28–31, 2014), 12–13.

51. Harry Truman, "Inaugural Address," January 20, 1949, Harry S. Truman Library, www.trumanlibrary.gov/library/public-papers/19/inaugural-address.

52. Wolfgang Sachs, "The Archeology of the Development Idea," *Interculture* 28, no. 4 (1990): 3.

53. Cited in Lamont C. Colucci, *The National Security Doctrines of the American Presidency: How They Shape Our Present and Future* (Santa Barbara, CA: Bloomsbury Publishing USA, 2012), 2:532.

54. Eric Helleiner, "Southern Pioneers of International Development," *Global Governance* 20, no. 3 (2014): 379–380.

55. Sun Yat-sen, *The International Development of China* (New York: G. P. Putnam's Sons, 1922), www.gutenberg.org/files/45188/45188-h/45188-h.htm.

56. Ha-joon Chang, *The East Asian Development Experience: The Miracle, the Crisis and the Future* (Penang, Malaysia: Third World Network, 2006).

57. Cited in Khadija Haq and Richard Ponzio, introduction to *Pioneering the Human Development Revolution: An Intellectual Biography of Mahbub ul Haq* (New Delhi, India: Oxford University Press, 2008), 8.

58. Cited in Amitav Acharya, "'Idea-Shift': How Ideas from the Rest Are Reshaping Global Order," *Third World Quarterly* 37, no. 7 (July 2, 2016): 1156–1170, https://doi.org/10.1080/01436597.2016.1154433.

59. Amartya Sen, "A 20th Anniversary Human Development Discussion with Amartya Sen," Red Bag, n.d., www.scribd.com/doc/88007185/Amartya-Sen-Interview-Transcript-1.

60. Heather Smith and Tari Ajadi, "Canada's Feminist Foreign Policy and Human Security Compared," *International Journal* 75, no. 3 (September 1, 2020): 367–382, https://doi.org/10.1177/0020702020954547.

61. Francis Deng, *Idealism and Realism: Negotiating Sovereignty in Divided Nations* (Uppsala, Sweden: Dag Hammarskjöld Foundation, 2010), 13, www.dagham marskjold.se/wp-content/uploads/2014/08/DH_Lecture_2010.pdf.

62. "Statement by Mr. Francis M. Deng, Representative of the Secretary-General of Internally Displaced Persons—Commission on Human Rights, 57th Session," UN Office of the Human Rights Commissioner, April 12, 2001, www .ohchr.org/en/statements/2009/10/statement-mr-francis-m-deng-representative -secretary-general-internally.

63. Mohamed Sahnoun, "Africa: Uphold Continent's Contribution to Human Rights, Urges Diplomat," *All Africa*, July 21, 2009, https://allafrica.com/stories /200907210549.html.

64. Einar H. Dyvik, "Top Contributors of Troops to UN Peacekeeping Efforts Globally in 2023," Statista, September 11, 2023, www.statista.com/statistics /871432/largest-contributors-of-troops-to-united-nations-peacekeeping/.

65. Bruce Jones and Adrianna Pita, "UN Reform and the Global South at the 2023 General Assembly," September 29, 2023, in *Current*, podcast, Brookings Institution, www.brookings.edu/articles/un-reform-and-the-global-south-at -the-2023-general-assembly/.

66. Dominic Wilson, Alex L. Kelston, and Swarnali Ahmed, "Is This the 'BRICs Decade'?," *BRICs Monthly* 10, no. 3 (May 20, 2010), www.goldmansachs .com/intelligence/archive/archive-pdfs/brics-decade-pdf.pdf.

67. Council of Councils, "The BRICS Summit 2023: Seeking an Alternate World Order?," Council on Foreign Relations, August 31, 2023, www.cfr .org/councilofcouncils/global-memos/brics-summit-2023-seeking-alternate -world-order.

68. Cited in Paul Blustein et al., *Recovery or Relapse: The Role of the G-20 in the Global Economy* (Washington, DC: Global Economy and Development at Brookings, 2010), www.brookings.edu/wp-content/uploads/2016/06/0618_g20 _summit.pdf.

69. Javier Solana, "The Cracks in the G-20," *Project Syndicate*, September 8, 2010, www.project-syndicate.org/commentary/the-cracks-in-the-g-20.

70. David Shorr and Thomas Wright, "The G20 and Global Governance: An Exchange," *Survival* 52, no. 2 (May 2010): 181–198.

71. Barbara Stallings, "Save a Seat for the Global South," *East Asia Forum*, January 19, 2024, https://eastasiaforum.org/2024/01/19/save-a-seat-for-the-global -south/.

72. Joakim Reiter, "UNCTAD and South-South Cooperation" (speech, Conference on South-South Cooperation, New Delhi, India, March 10, 2016), https://unctad.org/osgstatement/conference-south-south-cooperation.

73. World Bank, "GDP, PPP (Current International $)," accessed July 13, 2024, https://data.worldbank.org/indicator/NY.GDP.MKTP.PP.CD.

74. National Intelligence Council, *Global Trends 2040: A More Contested World*, March 2021, www.dni.gov/files/ODNI/documents/assessments/Global Trends_2040.pdf.

75. PwC, *The World in 2050: Will the Shift in Global Economic Power Continue?*, February 2015, www.pwc.com/gx/en/issues/the-economy/assets/world-in-2050 -february-2015.pdf.

76. "GDP Based on PPP, Share of World," IMF, accessed 2023, www.imf.org /external/datamapper/PPPSH@WEO/OEMDC/ADVEC/WEOWORLD.

77. Nada Hamadeh, Catherine Van Rompaey, and Eric Metreau, "World Bank Group Country Classifications by Income Level for FY24," *Data Blog*, World Bank,

June 1, 2023, https://blogs.worldbank.org/opendata/new-world-bank-group
-country-classifications-income-level-fy24.

78. Andrew Mold, "Why South-South Trade Is Already Greater than North-North Trade—and What It Means for Africa," Brookings Institution, December 11, 2023, brookings.edu/articles/why-south-south-trade-is-already-greater-than
-north-north-trade-and-what-it-means-for-africa/.

79. Xiaojun Grace Wang, "South-South Cooperation Brings Strong Partnerships to the New Development Agenda," *South-South Global Thinkers* (blog), UN, January 23, 2017, www.ssc-globalthinkers.org/news/blog/South-South-Cooperation
-brings-strong-partnerships-to-the-new-development-agenda.

80. Diego Lopes da Silva et al., *Trends in World Military Expenditure, 2021* (Solna, Sweden: Stockholm International Peace Research Institute, 2022), www.sipri
.org/publications/2022/sipri-fact-sheets/trends-world-military-expenditure
-2021.

81. US Department of Defense, *Military and Security Developments Involving the People's Republic of China 2023: Annual Report to Congress*, 2023, https://media
.defense.gov/2023/Oct/19/2003323409/-1/-1/1/2023-military-and-security
-developments-involving-the-peoples-republic-of-china.pdf.

82. Ibid.

83. Eric Heginbotham et al., *The U.S.-China Military Scorecard: Forces, Geography, and the Evolving Balance of Power, 1996–2017* (Santa Monica, CA: RAND Corporation, 2015), 343, www.rand.org/pubs/research_reports/RR392.html.

84. "An Interactive Look at the U.S.-China Military Scorecard," RAND Corporation, September 14, 2015, www.rand.org/paf/projects/us-china-scorecard
.html. The assessment of the overall military superiority of US in South China Sea still holds.

85. Press Trust of India, "US Worried Over China's Military Goals," *Deccan Herald*, March 27, 2010, www.deccanherald.com/sports/us-worried-over-chinas
-military-2481105.

86. Peter Apps, "For First Time in Centuries, Asia's Military Spending Overtakes Europe," Atlantic Council, March 7, 2012, www.atlanticcouncil.org/blogs
/natosource/for-first-time-in-centuries-asias-military-spending-overtakes
-europe/.

87. Eric Schmidt, "Innovation Power: Why Technology Will Define the Future of Geopolitics," *Foreign Affairs*, February 28, 2023, www.foreignaffairs.com
/united-states/eric-schmidt-innovation-power-technology-geopolitics.

88. Personal conversation, November 3, 2023, Washington, DC.

Chapter 14: The Once and Future World Order

1. Wang Gungwu, *The Universal and the Historical: My Faith in History* (Singapore: Soka Association, 2006), 27.

2. Louis Dalrymple, *School Begins*, January 25, 1899, chromolithograph, Library of Congress Prints and Photographs Division, Washington, DC, www.loc.gov/pictures/item/2012647459/.

3. Olúfẹ́mi Táíwò, "Out of Africa," *Foreign Affairs*, April 19, 2022, www.foreignaffairs.com/reviews/review-essay/2022-04-19/out-africa.

4. Stanley Hoffmann, "An American Social Science: International Relations," *Daedalus* 106, no. 3 (1977): 41–60.

5. Sarah Cleeland Knight, "Even Today, a Western and Gendered Social Science: Persistent Geographic and Gender Biases in Undergraduate IR Teaching," *International Studies Perspectives* 20, no. 2 (2019): 203–225.

6. Qin Yaqing, "Why Is There No Chinese International Relations Theory?," *International Relations of the Asia-Pacific* 7, no. 3 (September 1, 2007): 313–340, https://doi.org/10.1093/irap/lcm013.

7. Sanjay Subrahmanyam, *Connected History: Essays and Arguments* (London: Verso, 2022).

8. Niall Ferguson, *Civilization: The Six Killer Apps of Western Power* (London: Penguin Books, 2012), 306.

9. Gideon Rachman, "China, India and the Rise of the 'Civilisation State,'" *Financial Times*, March 4, 2019, www.ft.com/content/b6bc9ac2-3e5b-11e9-9bee-efab61506f44.

10. Ibid.

11. Christopher Coker, *The Rise of the Civilizational State* (Cambridge: Polity, 2019), Kindle edition.

12. Adrian Pabst, "China, Russia and the Return of the Civilisational State," *New Statesman*, May 8, 2019, www.newstatesman.com/world/2019/05/china-russia-and-the-return-of-the-civilisational-state.

13. Glenn Thrush and Julie Hirschfeld Davis, "Trump, in Poland, Asks if West Has the 'Will to Survive,'" *New York Times*, July 6, 2017, www.nytimes.com/2017/07/06/world/europe/donald-trump-poland-speech.html.

14. Joel Gehrke, "State Department Preparing for Clash of Civilizations with China," *Washington Examiner*, April 30, 2019, www.washingtonexaminer.com/policy/defense-national-security/state-department-preparing-for-clash-of-civilizations-with-china.

15. Somdeep Sen, "NATO and the Global Colour Line," *International Affairs* 100, no. 2 (2024): 491–507; Marwan Bishara, "Josep Borrell as Europe's Racist 'Gardener,'" Al Jazeera, October 17, 2022, www.aljazeera.com/opinions/2022 /10/17/josep-borrell-eu-racist-gardener.

16. "Xi Says 'No Clash' of Civilizations amid US Trade War," Tasnim News Agency, May 15, 2019, www.tasnimnews.com/en/news/2019/05/15/2011893/xi -says-no-clash-of-civilizations-amid-us-trade-war.

17. Narendra Modi, "Prime Minister's Keynote Address at Shangri La Dialogue," June 1, 2018, Indian Ministry of External Affairs, https://mea.gov.in /Speeches-Statements.htm?dtl/29943/Prime_Ministers_Keynote_Address_at _Shangri_La_Dialogue_June_01_2018; Rupam Jain and Tom Lasseter, "By Rewriting History, Hindu Nationalists Aim to Assert Their Dominance over India," Reuters, March 6, 2018, www.reuters.com/investigates/special-report /india-modi-culture/.

18. Alejandro Beutel, "The New Zealand Terrorist's Manifesto: A Look at Some of the Key Narratives, Beliefs and Tropes," National Consortium for the Study of Terrorism and Responses to Terrorism, April 30, 2019, www.start.umd.edu/news /new-zealand-terrorists-manifesto-look-some-key-narratives-beliefs-and-tropes.

19. Borzou Daragahi, "How the New Zealand Terror Attack Has Become a Key Factor in Turkey's Upcoming Elections," *Independent*, March 19, 2019, www .independent.co.uk/news/world/middle-east/new-zealand-terror-attack-turkey -elections-erdogan-christchurch-mosques-islam-crusades-a8828396.html.

20. On this debate, see Fouad Ajami, "The Summoning: 'But They Said, We Will Not Hearken,'" *Foreign Affairs* 72, no. 4 (October 1993): 2–9; Liu Binyan, "Civilization Grafting: No Culture Is an Island," *Foreign Affairs* 72, no. 4 (October 1993): 19–21; Mark Beeson, "Play It Again, Sam," *Conversation*, August 15, 2014, https://theconversation.com/play-it-again-sam-30588; Joshua R. Fattal, "Israel vs. Hamas: A Clash of Civilizations?," *Huffington Post*, August 22, 2014, www.huffing tonpost.com/joshua-r-fattal/israel-vs-hamas-a-clash-o_b_5699216.html.

21. Antony J. Blinken, "The Administration's Approach to the People's Republic of China" (speech, George Washington University, Washington, DC, May 26, 2022), www.state.gov/the-administrations-approach-to-the-peoples-republic -of-china/.

22. S. Cendrowski, "Inside China's Global Spending Spree," *Fortune*, December 12, 2016, http://fortune.com/china-belt-road-investment/; "China Wants to Put Itself Back at the Centre of the World," *Economist*, February 6, 2020, www .economist.com/special-report/2020/02/06/china-wants-to-put-itself-back-at-the -centre-of-the-world.

23. Madiha Afzal, *"At All Costs": How Pakistan and China Control the Narrative on the China-Pakistan Economic Corridor* (Washington, DC: Brookings Institution, 2020), www.brookings.edu/wp-content/uploads/2020/06/FP_20200615_china _pakistan_afzal_v2.pdf.

24. *Economist,* "China Wants."

25. On the BRI's extent and limits, see Charles Clover and Lucy Hornby, "China's Great Game: Road to a New Empire," *Financial Times,* October 13, 2015, www .ft.com/content/6e098274-587a-11e5-a28b-50226830d644; Brook Larmer, "Is China the World's New Colonial Power?," *New York Times,* February 2, 2017, www.ny times.com/2017/05/02/magazine/is-china-the-worlds-new-colonial-power.html.

26. Amitav Acharya, *The End of American World Order* (Cambridge: Polity, 2014).

27. Amitav Acharya, "Hierarchies of Weakness: The Social Divisions That Hold Countries Back," *Foreign Affairs* 101, no. 4 (2022): 74–82.

28. Craig Charney, *Global Governance Survey 2023* (Washington, DC: Stimson Center, 2023), 13, www.stimson.org/2023/global-governance-survey-2023/.

29. Ibid., 17–18.

30. White House, "Remarks by the President at the United States Military Academy Commencement Ceremony," news release, May 28, 2014, https:// obamawhitehouse.archives.gov/the-press-office/2014/05/28/remarks-president -united-states-military-academy-commencement-ceremony.

31. Thomas L. Friedman, interview with Ian Bremmer, "How the Israel-Gaza War Could End—if Netanyahu Wants It To," April 7, 2024, in *GZERO World,* podcast, www.gzeromedia.com/gzero-world-with-ian-bremmer/how-the-israel-gaza -war-could-end-if-netanyahu-wants-it-to.

32. UN Secretary-General, "Launching Three Our Common Agenda Policy Briefs, Secretary-General Urges Member States to Tackle New Challenges That Restore Trust in International Cooperation," news release, June 5, 2023, https:// press.un.org/en/2023/sgsm21824.doc.htm.

33. Andrew Mold, "Why South-South Trade Is Already Greater than North-North Trade—and What It Means for Africa," Brookings Institution, December 11, 2023, brookings.edu/articles/why-south-south-trade-is-already-greater-than -north-north-trade-and-what-it-means-for-africa/.

34. Claire Fu, Brooks Barnes, and Daisuke Wakabayashi, "Why China Has Lost Interest in Hollywood Movies," *New York Times,* January 23, 2024, www .nytimes.com/2024/01/23/business/china-box-office-hollywood.html.

35. Tanushree Basuroy, "Box Office Distribution in India 2022 by Language," Statista, March 22, 2023, www.statista.com/statistics/948615/india-box -office-share-by-language/.

36. Daya Kishan Thussu, *International Communication: Continuity and Change*, 3rd ed. (London: Bloomsbury Academic, 2018), 185.

37. "Taste the World: New Study Reveals the Most Popular Cuisines of 2023," *Oklahoma Farm Report*, April 11, 2024, www.oklahomafarmreport.com /okfr/2023/04/11/%F0%9F%8D%95-taste-the-world-new-study-reveals-the -most-popular-cuisines-of-2023/.

38. Amartya Sen, "Our Global Civilization," *Procedia Social and Behavioral Sciences* 2, no. 5 (2010): 6996–6999, https://doi.org/10.1016/j.sbspro.2010.05.052.

39. Jan Nederveen Pieterse, *Globalization and Culture: Global Mélange*, 4th ed. (Lanham, MD: Rowman & Littlefield, 2019); Thussu, *International Communication*.

40. Amitav Acharya, "How the Two Big Ideas of the Post–Cold War Era Failed," *Washington Post*, June 24, 2015, www.washingtonpost.com/news/monkey-cage /wp/2015/06/24/how-the-two-big-ideas-of-the-post-cold-war-era-failed/.

41. Ibn Khaldun, *The Muqaddimah: An Introduction to History*, abr. and ed. N. J. Dawood, trans. Franz Rosenthal (Princeton, NJ: Princeton University Press, 2015), 30.

Index